Classic Texts in Mission and World Christianity

The *American Society of Missiology Series,* in collaboration with Orbis Books, seeks to publish scholarly works of high merit and wide interest on numerous aspects of Missiology—the study of mission. Able presentations on new and creative approaches to the practice and understanding of mission will receive close attention.

Previously published in The American Society of Missiology Series

No. 1 *Protestant Pioneers in Korea*
by Everett Nichols Hunt, Jr.

No. 2 *Catholic Politics in China and Korea*
by Eric O. Hanson

No. 3 *From the Rising of the Sun*
by James M. Phillips

No. 4 *Meaning Across Cultures*
by Eugene A. Nida and William D. Reyburn

No. 5 *The Island Churches of the Pacific*
by Charles W. Forman

No. 6 *Henry Venn*
by Wilbert Shenk

No. 7 *No Other Name?*
by Paul F. Knitter

No. 8 *Toward a New Age in Christian Theology*
by Richard Henry Drummond

No. 9 *The Expectation of the Poor*
by Guillermo Cook

No. 10 *Eastern Orthodox Mission Theology Today*
by James J. Stamoolis

No. 11 *Confucius, the Buddha, and the Christ*
by Ralph Covell

No. 12 *The Church and Cultures*
by Louis J. Luzbetak

No. 13 *Translating the Message*
by Lamin Sanneh

No. 14 *An African Tree of Life*
by Thomas G. Christensen

No. 15 *Missions and Money*
by Jonathan J. Bonk

No. 16 *Transforming Mission*
by David J. Bosch

No. 17 *Bread for the Journey*
by Anthony J. Gittins

No. 18 *New Face of the Church in Latin America*
by Guillermo Cook

No. 19 *Mission Legacies*
edited by Gerald Anderson, et al.

American Society of Missiology Series, No. 20

Classic Texts in Mission and World Christianity

Edited, with Introductions by
Norman E. Thomas

Maryknoll, New York 10545

The Catholic Foreign Mission Society of America (Maryknoll) recruits and trains people for overseas missionary service. Through Orbis Books, Maryknoll aims to foster the international dialogue that is essential to mission. The books published, however, reflect the opinions of their authors and are not meant to represent the official position of the society.

Published by Orbis Books, Maryknoll, New York 10545, U.S.A.

Manufactured in the United States of America.

Library of Congress Cataloging-in-Publication Data

Classic texts in mission and world Christianity / edited, with
introductions by Norman E. Thomas.
p. cm. — (American Society of Missiology series ; no. 20)
Includes bibliographical references and indexes.
ISBN 1-57075-006-8 (pbk.)
1. Missions. 2. Missions and Christian union. I. Thomas, Norman
E. II. Series.
BV2061.C58 1995
266—dc20 94-44033
CIP

In Memoriam
DAVID JACOBUS BOSCH (1929-1992)
creative missiologist
witness to the ecumenical vision
generous friend

Contents

Preface to the Series

The purpose of the ASM Series is to publish—without regard for disciplinary, national, or denominational boundaries—scholarly works of high quality and wide interest on missiological themes from the entire spectrum of scholarly pursuits relevant to Christian Mission, which is always the focus of books in the Series.

By "mission" is meant the effort to effect passage over the boundary between faith in Jesus Christ and its absence. In this understanding of mission, the basic functions of Christian proclamation, dialogue, witness, service, worship, liberation, and nurture are of special concern. And in that context questions arise, including, How does the transition from one cultural context to another influence the shape and interaction between these dynamic functions, especially in regard to the cultural and religious plurality that comprise the global context of Christian mission?

The promotion of scholarly dialogue among missiologists and among missiologists and scholars in other fields of inquiry may involve the publication of views that some missiologists cannot accept, and with which members of the Editorial Committee do not agree. Manuscripts published in the Series reflect the opinions of their authors and are not understood to represent the position of the American Society of Missiology or of the Editorial Committee. Selection is guided by such criteria as intrinsic worth, readability, and accessibility to a range of interested persons and not merely to experts or specialists.

The ASM Series Editorial Committee
James A. Scherer, Chair
Mary Motte, FMM
Charles Taber

Foreword

In 1989, Professor David Bosch and I renewed our long friendship while attending the World Conference on Mission and Evangelism in San Antonio, Texas. There he shared with me the draft of *Transforming Mission*. Immediately I sensed that this book would become an indispensable classic in the theology of mission. In 1991, while visiting at the University of South Africa, he shared with me a progress report, including news that the original two-volume manuscript would be condensed into a single volume, omitting much of the historical material. Eagerly I awaited its publication in 1991, with hopes to use it as the text for a new course at United Theological Seminary on the Theology of Mission.

The news of David Bosch's untimely death grieved all who attended the American Society of Missiology's annual meeting in June, 1992. There I shared with colleagues my hope to produce a companion volume to *Transforming Mission* which would contain longer source documents than Professor Bosch was able to include. Many encouraged me to press on in this undertaking. Unfortunately, I was unable to recover the longer Bosch manuscript.

Since majoring in European History, Art, and Literature at Yale College in the 1950s, I have encouraged my students to read primary source documents and come to their own historical interpretations. My seminary course on Third World Christianity could have been entitled "Rewriting History," as I challenged participants to rewrite the history of the church in Africa, Asia, Latin America, and Oceania from the perspective not of First World missionaries but of indigenous Christians. My first selection of source documents, however, came from the notes and bibliography of the Bosch volume, with initial evaluation by my students as to their usefulness.

A new concern arose in 1993. Analysis of sources used by Bosch disclosed that his dialogue was primarily with scholars in Europe and North America. While he provided some coverage of emerging thought in Africa, Asia, and Latin America, it is contained mostly in his chapters on contemporary paradigms of mission as justice, liberation, and witness to people of other living faiths. As for women scholars, one looks in vain for their contributions.

Would it be possible to include voices of women and men and women from Africa, Asia, Latin America, and Oceania in chapters related to Bosch's thirteen contemporary paradigms of mission? A search produced what I believe are quality contributions in each subject area. In addition, I have made a beginning in locating sources by women and from the Two-thirds World for the historical paradigms.

Some gold has been discovered. I hope that other scholars may be encouraged to prospect for other nuggets in the future.

Classic Texts in Mission and World Christianity is offered as a sourcebook for courses in a variety of theological disciplines: church history, theology, as well as missiology.

I am indebted to David Bosch for the schema of historical and contemporary paradigms of mission contained in this volume. Citations are provided with each selection, together with the relevant pages in *Transforming Mission,* to encourage further reading. Selections have been placed in chronological order within each chapter. The decision to include excerpts from 180 documents necessitated abbreviation of many of them; readers are encouraged to seek out the full texts as cited.

Many persons assisted in research for this volume. I am indebted to the staff of the United Theological Seminary Library: Elmer J. O'Brien (librarian), Betty O'Brien, Paul Schrodt, Suzanne Smailes, Janet McDermott, and Shelomith D. Eichenauer. Dominico Nigrelli, Daniel Hofmann, and Paul Schrodt assisted with translations. Daniel Auman typed the manuscript, and Marti Anderson prepared it for publication.

It is an honor to have this book appear in the *American Society of Missiology Series.* I am grateful to the ASM's Board of Publication, to James A. Scherer, Mary Motte, FMM, and Charles R. Taber as editors of the ASM series, and to William Burrows of Orbis for their support and encouragement.

Special appreciation goes also to my wife, Winnie, for her encouragement during the long nights and weekends of research and writing.

Norman E. Thomas
Dayton, Ohio

Abbreviations

AAS	*Acta Apostolicae Sedis* (the Vatican gazette of official statements)
ANC	*Ante-Nicean Fathers*
CDCWM	*Concise Dictionary of the Christian World Mission*
CELAM	Latin American Bishops' Conference
DEM	*Dictionary of the Ecumenical Movement*
EATWOT	Ecumenical Association of Third World Theologians
FOC	*The Fathers of the Church*
IBMR	*International Bulletin of Missionary Research*
IMC	International Missionary Council
IRM	*International Review of Mission*
LCC	*Library of Christian Classics*
NCCUSA	National Council of Churches in the United States of America
TM	*Transforming Mission* (1991) by David Bosch (Orbis)
VC2	*Vatican Council II: The Conciliar and Post Conciliar Documents*
WCC	World Council of Churches

Classic Texts in Mission and World Christianity

Part I

HISTORICAL PARADIGMS OF MISSION

1

The Early and Eastern Church

Why mission? This was an open question for the eleven disciples before Pentecost. Matthew records that they went to Galilee. Even when the risen Christ appeared to them, some doubted (28:17). Followers on the road to Emmaus told Him how they "had hoped that [Jesus] was the one to redeem Israel" (Luke 24:21). Only when filled with the Holy Spirit at Pentecost did they recall Christ's commission to go and make disciples of all nations and obey (Acts 2:4; Mt. 28:19). As Peter, Paul, and other apostles gave their witness—both through sermons and public defense—the reason for being apostles, persons sent on a mission, took shape.

This sourcebook is a compendium of rationales and understandings of Christian mission from Pentecost to the present. In organization, it follows Transforming Mission*—David Bosch's historical survey of "paradigm shifts in theology of mission." A* paradigm *is a constellation of beliefs and values of a given community. It is the model of interpretation by which a people give meaning to their lives. Christians, forming a distinct community of faith, need in every place and time to explain who they are and will be, in relation to God and God's purpose for their lives and to those outside the faith. It is their theology of mission.*

Following Hans Küng, Bosch divides the entire history of Christianity into six major "paradigms": the apocalyptic of primitive Christianity, the Hellenistic of the patristic period, the medieval Roman Catholic, the Protestant (Reformation), the modern Enlightenment, and the emerging ecumenical paradigm. To Küng's argument that each period reveals a peculiar understanding of the Christian faith, Bosch adds that each offers a distinctive understanding of Christian mission.[1]

The first period of primitive Christianity included an urgency of mission in expectation of an imminent end. Peter, in his Pentecost sermon, included Joel's prophecy concerning the last days (Acts 2:17). Paul rejoiced that the Thessalonians had "turned to God from idols, to serve a living and true God" and "to wait for his Son... Jesus, who rescues us from the wrath that is coming" (1 Thess. 1:9-10). For Paul, apocalyptic fervor and missionary strategy went hand in hand: the mission to the Gentiles had highest priority as part of God's plan. Roger Aus contends that Paul earnestly desired to reach Spain, understanding it as the Tarshish of Isaiah's apocalyptic prophecy (Is. 66:19) and literally "the ends of the earth."[2] *Paul's apocalyptic, rather than resulting in a passive waiting, led to active participation in God's plan of redemption. He and the Christian community had confidence that God had a plan that they shine "like stars in the world" (Phil. 2:12-15; 3:7-14).*

The church of the second to fourth centuries faced different challenges and opportunities in mission. The motivation for living as an interim eschatological community faded. The destruction of Jerusalem in 70 C.E. closed the book on the Jewish mission. The new challenge was to redefine mission both in a Greek cultural milieu and for a growing church increasingly accepted as a bearer of culture and a civilizing presence in society (TM 192-93).

The "Letter to Diognetus," written by an apologist about 129 C.E., illustrates the early church's conviction that every believer is so to live in obedience to Christ that others, seeing their exemplary lives, will want to follow Christ also. Mission measured by being rather than doing would later become a recurring theme of Orthodox mission theology. The selection from Eusebius, the early church historian, tells of the important work of itinerant charismatic evangelists in the spread of the gospel throughout the Roman Empire.

Christian witness in a culture dominated by Greek language and thought required new conceptual bridges for Christian mission. The prologue to John's Gospel, "in the beginning was the logos,*" is an early "dynamic-equivalent" translation of the message into Greek thought. As early as 202, Clement of Alexandria embraced Greek philosophy as the handmaiden of theology. He accepted it as more than a preparation for the gospel, since he wrote, "those among the Greeks who have philosophized accurately, see God."*

During the age of persecution, the Christian martyr provided the most compelling witness. When Christianity became the official religion of the Roman Empire, that role passed to the monk. St. Athanasius, in his life of St. Antony written about 360, presented a model of Christian spirituality that served as an inspiration for others in an age of much nominal Christianity.

The conversion of Emperor Constantine provided a model for winning whole peoples in the centuries that followed. Gregory of Tours, in recounting the 496 baptism of Clovis, king of the Franks, and the subsequent mass conversions of his people, notes the comparison with Constantine. Almost four centuries later, Cyril and Methodius went as pioneer missionaries to the Slavic peoples of Moravia and Bohemia. The account of their work reveals three elements that became ongoing themes in the Orthodox missionary paradigm: use of the vernacular, alliance with rulers, and the centrality of the liturgy.

Missions in non-Roman Asia required the faith to be expressed in a variety of cultures: Coptic, Syriac, Maronite, Armenian, Ethiopian, Indian, and even Chinese. The Nestorian Monument, erected in 781, tells the remarkable story of 156 years of ministry by Nestorian monks in China. Not until its discovery in 1623 did the outside world know of this earliest Christian mission to China. Other early Nestorian documents help scholars understand better this serious effort to contextualize Christianity in Chinese thought patterns.

EXEMPLARY CHRISTIANS

"What the soul is in the body, that Christians are in the world."

■ *How was Christianity to gain a following in a world of many faiths? During the second century, the apologists wrote to persuade nonbelievers that Christianity was the preeminent faith. The "Letter to Diognetus," written about 129 C.E., is of that genre. The argument is set in the context of a theology of history—that Christianity is of divine initiative, in contrast to the Jewish and Gentile faiths of human creation. In the following irenic passage, however, the writer presents Christianity as that which brings vitality and grace and love to a hateful world.*

*The Church in the World**

For Christians cannot be distinguished from the rest of the human race by country or language or customs. They do not live in cities of their own; they do not use a peculiar form of speech; they do not follow an eccentric manner of life. This doctrine of theirs has not been discovered by the ingenuity or deep thought of inquisitive men, nor do they put forward a merely human teaching, as some people do. Yet, although they live in Greek and barbarian cities alike, as each [one's] lot has been cast, and follow the customs of the country in clothing and food and other matters of daily living, at the same time they give proof of the remarkable and admittedly extraordinary constitution of their own commonwealth. They live in their own countries, but only as aliens. They have a share in everything as citizens, and endure everything as foreigners. Every foreign land is their fatherland, and yet for them every fatherland is a foreign land. They marry, like everyone else, and they beget children, but they do not cast out their offspring. They share their board with each other, but not their marriage bed. It is true that they are "in the flesh," but they do not live "according to the flesh" (Cf. 2 Cor. 10:3; 5:16; Rom. 8:4; Jn. 17:13-19; 18:36, 37). They busy themselves on earth, but their citizenship is in heaven (Cf. Phil. 3:20; Eph. 2:19-22; 1 Pet. 2:9-17).

DIVINE TRUTH THROUGH PHILOSOPHY

"Those among the Greeks who have philosophized accurately, see God."

■ *Christianity must have taken root early in Alexandria, Egypt, the second city of the Roman Empire. Many Jews lived there. The learned Jew Philo, an elder contemporary of Paul, says that the Jewish population of Alexandria and all Egypt totalled a million. Alexandria was a center of philosophy and, in the early*

---

*Excerpts from "Letter to Diognetus," in *Early Christian Fathers,* ed. Cyril C. Richardson, *The Library of Christian Classics* (Philadelphia: Westminster Press, 1953), 1:216-18; cf. Bosch, TM, 191-92.

Christian era, a hotbed of gnosticism. To this city came a young Christian named Clement (ca. 160-215), who traveled the Mediterranean Sea looking for knowledge of God from Italy to Palestine, but then settled in Alexandria. He sought connections between Christianity and Greek culture. The excerpts below are from the third work of his great trilogy entitled "The Miscellanies" (Stromateis).

*Philosophy the Handmaid of Theology**

Accordingly, before the advent of the Lord, philosophy was necessary to the Greeks for righteousness.[3] And now it becomes conducive to piety; being a kind of preparatory training to those who attain to faith through demonstration. "For thy foot," it is said, "will not stumble, if thou refer what is good, whether belonging to Greeks or to us, to Providence" (Prov. 3:23). For God is the cause of all good things; but of some primarily, as of the Old and New Testament; and of others by consequence, as philosophy. Perchance, too, philosophy was given to the Greeks directly and primarily, till the Lord should call the Greeks. For this was a schoolmaster to bring "the Hellenic mind," as the law, the Hebrews, "to Christ" (Gal. 3:24). Philosophy, therefore, was a preparation, paving the way for him who is perfected in Christ.

"Jerusalem, Jerusalem, how often would I have gathered thy children, as a hen her chickens!" (Mt. 23:37; Lk. 13:34). And Jerusalem is, when interpreted, "a vision of peace." He therefore shows prophetically, that those who peacefully contemplate sacred things are in manifold ways trained to their calling. What then? He "would," and could not. How often, and where? Twice; by the prophets, and by the advent. The expression, then, "How often," shows wisdom to be manifold; and in every mode of quantity and quality, it by all means saves some, both in time and in eternity. "For the Spirit of the Lord fills the earth."[4]

That the Philosophers Have Attained to Some Portion of Truth

Since, then, the Greeks are testified to have laid down some true opinions, we may from this point take a glance at the testimonies. Paul, in the Acts of the Apostles, is recorded to have said to the Areopagites, "I perceive that ye are more than ordinarily religious. For as I passed by, and beheld your devotions, I found an altar with the inscription, To The Unknown God. Whom therefore ye ignorantly worship, Him declare I unto you..." (Acts 17:22-28). Whence it is evident that the apostle, by availing himself of poetical examples from the *Phenomena* of Aratus, approves of what had been well spoken by the Greeks; and intimates that, by the unknown God, God the Creator was in a roundabout way worshipped by the Greeks; but it was necessary by positive knowledge to apprehend and learn Him by the Son.

---

*Excerpts from Clement of Alexandria, *The Stromata,* I: 5, 19, in *The Ante-Nicene Fathers* (reprint ed., Grand Rapids, MI: Eerdmans, 1971), 2: 305-06, 321-22; cf. Bosch, TM, 195.

Whether, then, they say that the Greeks gave forth some utterances of the true philosophy by accident, it is the accident of a divine administration (for no one will, for the sake of the present argument with us, deify chance); or by good fortune, good fortune is not unforeseen. Or were one, on the other hand, to say that the Greeks possessed a natural conception of these things, we know the one Creator in nature; just as we also call righteousness natural; or that they had a common intellect, let us reflect who is its father, and what righteousness is in the mental economy.

The divine apostle writes accordingly respecting us: "For now we see as through a glass" (1 Cor. 13:12); knowing ourselves in it by reflection, and simultaneously contemplating, as we can, the efficient cause, from that, which, in us, is divine. For it is said, "Having seen thy brother, thou hast seen thy God": methinks that now the Saviour God is declared to us. But after the laying aside of the flesh, "face to face,"—then definitely and comprehensively, when the heart becomes pure. And by reflection and direct vision, those among the Greeks who have philosophized accurately, see God.

ITINERANT EVANGELISTS

"Pious disciples...spreading the Gospel...far and wide."

■ *How did the Gospel spread to every corner of the Roman Empire within two centuries? Possessed by a burning faith conviction, Christians witnessed to the power of the risen Christ. Many, like the apostles, became itinerant charismatic evangelists. Threats of persecution did not dissuade them from their passion to spread the Gospel. The first great church historian, Eusebius of Caesarea (ca. 260-340), conveys the dynamic of their mission effort in the following passage.*

*How the Gospel Spread**

Among those who were celebrated in these times was also Quadratus,[5] who, report holds, was distinguished along with the daughters of Phillip by a gift of prophecy, and many more others besides were known at this time, who take first rank in the apostolic succession. And these, being pious disciples of such great men, built in every place upon the foundations of the churches already established everywhere by the Apostles (1 Cor. 3:10), spreading the Gospel more and more, and scattering the saving seeds of the kingdom of heaven far and wide throughout the whole world. Indeed, most of the disciples of that time, struck in soul by the divine Logos with an ardent love of philosophy,[6] first fulfilled the Saviour's command (Mt. 10:9; Mk. 6.8; Lk. 9:3) and distributed their goods among the needy (Mt. 19:21), and then, entering upon long journeys, performed the work of evan-

---

*Excerpts from Eusebius of Caesarea, *Ecclesiastical History* 3:37, *The Fathers of the Church* (New York: FOC, 1953), 19:200-201; cf. Bosch, TM, 191.

gelists (Rom. 15:20, 21), being eager to preach everywhere to those who had not yet the word of faith and to pass on the writing of the divine Gospels (Eph. 9:19, 20). As soon as they had only laid the foundations of the faith in some foreign lands, they appointed others as pastors and entrusted to them the nurture of those who had recently been brought in, but they themselves went on to other lands and peoples with the grace and co-operation of God, for a great many marvelous miracles of the divine spirit were still being worked by them at that time, so that whole multitudes...at the first hearing eagerly received within their souls the religion of the Creator of the universe.

Since it is impossible for us to enumerate all by name who at some time in the early succession of the Apostles became pastors or evangelists in the churches throughout the world, we have naturally made mention by name of those only through whose writings the tradition of the teachings of the Apostles has been brought down to us in our time.

MONASTICISM—THE MISSIONARY IDEAL

"Virtue...lies in us...if only we shall will it."

■ *Jesus said, "the kingdom of God is among you" (Lk. 17:21). The first Christians, filled with the Holy Spirit, sought to live in holiness rather than transform society. However, after Emperor Constantine embraced Christianity in 313 C.E., large numbers entered the church whose lives tended to conform more to the society's norms than to the Christian ideal. It was Antony of Egypt (ca. 251-356) who inspired countless monks to return to the Christian ideal as monastics in the desert. A young Copt of inherited wealth, Antony heard Jesus' command to the rich young ruler to sell all that he had and give to the poor as the Savior's call to himself. While he lived in the desert as a hermit, Antony was able to move in and out of contact with people. In certain periods, he served almost as a spiritual director for others. Upon his death, Athanasius (ca. 300-373), Bishop of Alexandria, the dynamic leader of Christianity in Egypt, used monastic records to write the "Life of St. Antony," a prototype work of Christian spirituality and hagiography.*

*The Life of St. Antony**

Through regular conversation [Antony] strengthened the resolve of those who were already monks, and stirred most of the others to a desire for the discipline, and before long, by the attraction of his speech, a great many monasteries came into being, and like a father he guided them all.

One day when he had gone out, all the monks came to him, asking to hear a

---

*Excerpts from St. Athanasius, "The Life of Antony," in *Athanasius: The Life of Antony and the Letter to Marcellinus,* trans. Robert C. Gregg, *The Classics of Western Spirituality* (New York: Paulist Press, 1980), 16:43-45, 46-47; cf. Bosch, TM, 201-02.

discourse. In the Egyptian tongue he told them these things: "The Scriptures are sufficient for instruction, but it is good for us to encourage each other in the faith....

"Let none among us have even the yearning to possess. For what benefit is there in possessing these things that we do not take with us? Why not rather own those things that we are able to take away with us—such things as prudence, justice, temperance, courage, understanding, love, concern for the poor, faith in Christ, freedom from anger, hospitality? If we possess these, we shall discover them running before, preparing hospitality for us there in the land of the meek....

"Having therefore made a beginning, and set out already on the way of virtue, let us press forward to what lies ahead (Cf. Phil. 3:13). And let none turn back as Lot's wife did, especially since the Lord said, *No one who puts his hand to the plow and* turns back *is fit for the Kingdom of heaven* (Lk. 9:62). Now 'turning back' is nothing except feeling regret and once more thinking about things of the world."

"The Kingdom of God Is within You"

Do not be afraid to hear about virtue, and do not be a stranger to the term. For it is not distant from us, nor does it stand external to us, but its realization lies in us, and the task is easy if only we shall will it. Now the Greeks leave home and traverse the sea in order to gain an education, but there is no need for us to go abroad on account of the Kingdom of heaven, nor to cross the sea for virtue. For the Lord has told us before, *the Kingdom of God is within you* (Lk. 17:21). All virtue needs, then, is our willing, since it is in us, and arises from us....John's urging was: *Make your paths straight* (Mt. 3:3). As far as the soul is concerned, being straight consists in its intellectual part's being according to nature, as it was created. But when it turns from its course and is twisted away from what it naturally is, then we speak of the vice of the soul. So the task is not difficult, for if we remain as we were made, we are in virtue, but if we turn our thoughts toward contemptible things, we are condemned as evil. If the task depended on something external that must be procured, it would be truly difficult, but since the matter centers in us, let us protect ourselves from sordid ideas, and, since we have received it as a trust, let us preserve the soul for the Lord, so that he may recognize his work as being just the same as he made it.

MASS CONVERSIONS

"Pious king, we reject the mortal gods."

■ *The end of the fifth century saw an event recognized as one of the turning points of Christian history, the baptism of Clovis, king of the Franks, in 496 C.E. Three years earlier he had married a Christian princess, Clotilde of Burgundy, who tried to convert him without success. Praying to the Christian God on the eve of battle, he swore that he would be baptized if victorious. The victory was his. Gregory of Tours recounts King Clovis's baptism with three thousand of his warriors. This was the pattern of mass conversions by which Christianity was to spread to northern Europe in subsequent centuries. Clovis's embrace of Christian orthodoxy, rather than the Arianism of neighboring states, enhanced the influence of Roman Christianity, with Gaul as the highroad by which missionaries would pass first from Rome to the British Isles, and later from Ireland to other parts of northern Europe.*

*The Conversion of Clovis**

The queen never ceased to entreat the king to recognize the true God and give up idols, but nothing could move him to believe these things until he was engaged in a war with the Alemanni in which he was compelled by constraint to confess what he had refused to do voluntarily. It came to pass that his army was in danger of being wiped out. Thereupon, lifting his eyes to heaven, with compunction of heart and moved to tears, he cried, "Jesus Christ, who art according to Clotilde the Son of the living God, who art said to give aid to those in trouble and victory to those who hope in Thee...I beseech Thee...if Thou wilt give me victory over mine enemies I will believe in Thee and be baptized in Thy name. I have called upon my gods and they are far removed from helping me. Hence I believe they are powerless, since they do not succour their followers. I now call upon Thee. Only save me from mine enemies." When he had thus spoken the Alemanni turned their backs and took to flight...Clovis returning related to the queen how he had won the victory by calling upon the name of Christ. Then the queen with haste secretly summoned Remigius, the bishop of Rheims, that he should instruct the king in the word of salvation. He began privately to tell his majesty that he should believe in the true God, the maker of heaven and earth and should give up idols. The king said, "Willingly, holy father, but there is one difficulty. My people will not give up their gods. But I will go and speak to them according to your word." But before he had opened his mouth all the people cried, "Pious king, we reject the mortal gods and are ready to follow the immortal God, whom Remigius preaches." Then the bishop with great joy gave orders to prepare the fount. The church was resplendent with banners, flickering candles and the scent of wax and incense, so that those present believed that they partook of the savor of heaven. The king asked that he be baptized by the pontiff. Like a new Constantine Clovis ascended to the laver, putting off his former leprosy. As he went down into the water the bishop said, "Bow thy neck. Adore what you have burned. Burn what you have adored." Now the holy bishop Remigius, a man of consummate learning and of great sanctity, may fitly be compared to the holy Sylvester [who baptized Constantine].

---

*Excerpts from "The Conversion of Clovis; Translated from Gregory of Tours," *Historia Francorum*, in *Patrologia Latina* 71: 225, section xxx; translation by Roland Bainton in Roland Bainton, *The Medieval Church* (Huntington, NY: Robert E. Krieger, 1979), 99-100; cf. Bosch, TM, 193-94.

FIRST MISSION TO CHINA

"Try to unite those that are beyond the pale."

■ *When the Jesuits reached China in the sixteenth century, they found a colony of Jews in Kaifeng, but no Christians. Were the reports of ancient missions to China (the legend of St. Thomas, the reports of Marco Polo, and so forth) mere wishful thinking? Then came a dramatic discovery. In 1623, workmen digging near the present city of Xian at the site of the ancient T'ang dynasty capital of Chang'an uncovered a great limestone more than nine feet high. Beneath a design of the cross rising from a lotus blossom was the account of the first Christian mission to China. Erected in 781, it told the story of the Nestorian mission from the arrival of the monk Alopen in the Chinese capital in 635. Of particular interest are those passages conveying the theology and perspective on mission of the Nestorians after 156 years of ministry in China. The writings are theologically orthodox concerning both Christology and evangelization, but with serious efforts to contextualize the faith in a Chinese religious milieu.*

*Salvation**[7]

Fulfilling the old Law as it was declared by the twenty-four Sages,[8] He (the Messiah) taught *how to rule both families and kingdoms*[9] according to His own great Plan. *Establishing His New Teaching of Nonassertion*[10] which operates silently through the Holy Spirit, another Person of the Trinity, He formed in [humanity] the capacity for well-doing through the Right Faith. Setting up the standard of the *eight cardinal virtues,*[11] He purged away the dust from human nature and perfected a true character. Widely opening the Three Constant Gates,[12] He brought Life to light and abolished Death. *Hanging up the bright Sun*[13] He swept away the abodes of darkness. All the evil devices of the devil were thereupon defeated and destroyed. He then took an oar in the *Vessel of Mercy*[14] and ascended to the Palace of Light. *Thereby all rational beings were conveyed across the Gulf.*[15] His mighty work being thus completed, He returned at noon to His original position (in Heaven)....

The Means of Conversion

The Great Means of Conversion (or leavening, i.e., transformation) were widely extended, and the sealed Gate of the Blessed Life was unlocked.

His law is to bathe with water and the Spirit, and thus to cleanse from all vain

---

*Excerpts from the Nestorian Monument (781), text in Samuel Hugh Moffett, *A History of Christianity in Asia* (San Francisco: Harper San Francisco, 1991), 1: 514-15.

delusions and to purify men [and women] until they regain the whiteness of their nature.

(His ministers) carry the Cross with them as a Sign. They travel about wherever the sun shines and try to reunite those that are beyond the pale (i.e., those that are lost).

MISSION TO THE SLAVS

"Enduring exile for the sake of propagating the true faith."

■ *The Balkans, home of the western Slavs, have been fought over by armies and sought after by missionaries for centuries. Felicitously, the first Christian mission to Moravia was led by Constantine (better known as Cyril) and Methodius in 863 C.E. Born in Thessalonica of Byzantine Greek parents, they clearly were bilingual (Greek and Slavic). After they served a missionary apprenticeship among the Muslim Khazars, the Byzantine emperor, Michael III, sent them at the request of the Moravian prince Rostislav to give religious instruction. The Orthodox missionary paradigm is evident in the account of their pioneer mission: use of the vernacular (initially opposed by Rome), alliance with rulers, and the centrality of the liturgy.*

*A Brief Account of Saints Cyril and Methodius . . .**

During the time of the renowned teacher, Blessed Augustine, after the sun of justice had diffused the holy Christian faith throughout the earth with rays, Saint Cyril came to Moravia, where he won a number of people for Almighty God with His help. Being highly educated in Greek and Latin letters, he previously converted Bulgaria to the faith of Jesus Christ in the name of the Holy Trinity and Indivisible Unity. And having invented new signs or letters, he translated the Old and New Testaments from Greek and Latin into Slavic speech, determining that the mass and the other canonical hours be celebrated in church in the Slavic language, which to this day is observed in Bulgaria and in many Slavic regions. And in this way many souls were won for Christ the Lord.

Then, after this Cyril had gathered many sheaves into the Lord's barn, he left his brother, named Methodius—a zealous man, adorned with all manner of sanctity—in Moravia, and went to Rome for devotional purposes. There he was accused of introducing the custom of singing divine services in the Slavic language by the pope and other authorities.

Taking hold of the Psalter and finding the verse which says, "Let every thing that hath breath praise the Lord" (Ps. 150:6), he vindicated himself humbly. Now

---

*Excerpts from "A Brief Account of Saints Cyril and Methodius and the Baptism of the Moravian and Bohemian Lands" in Marvin Kantor, *The Origins of Christianity in Bohemia: Sources and Commentary* (Evanston, IL: Northwestern University Press, 1990), 247-51; cf. Bosch, TM, 205.

he said: "If every thing that breathes is to praise the Lord, why, O chosen fathers, do you forbid me to celebrate divine services in Slavic when God created this speech as well as the others? And when I was unable to help those people with the salvation of their souls in another way, God inspired me through this means, by which I have won a great many of them for Him. Therefore, pardon me, O holy fathers and lords. For the Blessed Apostle Paul, the best teacher of the pagans, also says in his epistle to the Corinthians, "Forbid not to speak with tongues" (1 Cor. 14:39). Hearing this and marveling at the faith of this great man, they now decreed in an apostolic decision and confirmed in writing that the mass and other canonical hours be sung in those regions in the language mentioned above....

Methodius Converts Bohemia's Rulers

But the Bohemian Slavs, who were settled under Arcturus in the climes of the Rhipaen Mountains and given to idol worship, long remained without law or a prince....And in the course of time a most gracious prince, Boivoj, was born of this famous family. Shining with the bloom of outstanding beauty and youthful strength, he took a wife by the name of Ludmila—the daughter of a prince named Slavibor from the land of the Milane—who as a young girl made offerings to the idols.

Thus, this Boivoj once visited the Moravian king, Svatopluk the First, and was kindly invited by him and his magnates to a banquet. However, he was not allowed to sit among Christians, but was seated before the table on the floor in the pagan manner. And here, they say, Bishop Methodius regretted his humiliation and said to him: "What a pity, you are such an outstanding man but not ashamed to be excluded from sitting with princes although yourself of princely rank! You would rather sit on the ground for the sake of shameful idol worship!"

Then he said: "To what danger would I expose myself for this matter? What good will the Christian religion bring me?" Bishop Methodius said, "If you renounce idols and the evil spirits residing in them, you will be the lord of your lords, and all your enemies will be subordinate to your power, and your progeny will increase like a great river into which pours the flow of various streams."

And, verily, this prophecy was fulfilled in the Bohemian princes.

And Boivoj said, "If that is so, what prevents me from being baptized?" Bishop Methodius said, "Nothing, but be prepared to believe with all your heart in God the Father Almighty and in His only begotten Son, Our Lord Jesus Christ, and in the Consoler, the Spirit, the Enlightener of all faithful souls, not only for the sake of worldly bliss, but also to attain salvation of body and soul, and to win the glorious palm of eternity and become a partaker of ineffable joy in the community of saints."

The youth's mind was roused by means of this and similar encouragement which flowed like honey, and he longed to receive the grace of baptism. Casting himself, together with all those accompanying him, to the ground at the bishop's feet, he besought him most earnestly that this take place without delay.

What need was there for more words! On the following day he instructed the prince and the thirty men accompanying him in the fundamentals of faith and regenerated them in the sacred fountain of baptism after they had observed the customary ritual of the fast. And when he had educated them thoroughly in Christ's faith, he allowed him to return home, having enriched him with many gifts....

After a short time Methodius, mentioned above, came to Bohemia and baptized Saint Ludmila, along with many others. And thus did the Christian faith spread in a land of roughness and uncultivated wilderness....

Saintly Queen Ludmila

This first founder of holy places, assembler of priests, and supporter of the Christian religion had three sons and as many daughters with his wife, the aforementioned Ludmila. And as Blessed Methodius had predicted to him, not only did he gain worldly power day by day, but he also flourished in all virtues, blossoming like a lily.

And Blessed Ludmila became a true handmaid of Christ, emulating him not only in the religion of Jesus Christ, but even rising above him.

After him Vratislav, the father of Saint Wenceslas, ascended the princely throne. Having strengthened his realm, he built the basilica of Saint George the Martyr. Radiant with all manner of sanctity and with his noble way of life, he exchanged this fleeting world for life eternal.

NOTES

1. Hans Küng, *Theologie im Aufbruch: Eine ökumenische Grundlegung* (Munich: Piper Verlag, 1987), p. 157; TM, 181-85.

2. Roger D. Aus, "Paul's Travel Plans to Spain and the 'Full Number of the Gentiles' of Rom. XI 25," *Novum Testamentum* 21 (1979): 232-62; TM, 146.

3. See Elucidation 7.

4. A favorite expression of the Fathers, expressing hope for the heathen. See Elucidation 8.

5. All that is known of this Quadratus is contained here and below, 5.16. The identification of this Quadratus with Quadratus the apologist (cf. 4.3) is by no means certain.

6. I.e., the ascetic way of living; cf. below, 6.3.

7. Translation by P. Y Saeki from *The Nestorian Documents and Relics in China,* 2d. rev. and enlarged (Tokyo: Maruzen, 1951), pp. 54-56. Moffett has used italics to draw attention to possible borrowing from Chinese religious concepts, as explained in the notes accompanying the text.

8. The writers of the Old Testament, according to some rabbinical traditions.

9. A core Confucian phrase, as in the "Great Learning" of the *Book of Rites.*

10. A Taoist principle, but it has its Christian parallels.

11. A Buddhist formula, but one that might by some counts refer as well to the Beatitudes.

12. Faith, hope, and love?

13. A phrase occasionally found in Buddhism, but more probably referring to the crucifixion. See A. C. Moule, *Christians in China Before the Year 1550* (London: S.P.C.K., 1930), p. 37 n. 20.

14. Cf. the amitabha Buddha's boat to paradise, or Kuan-yin, who is called the goddess or "boat" of mercy.

15. J. Legge, *The Nestorian Monument of Hsi-an Fu in Shen-hsi* (London: Trubner, 1881), p. 7 detects a reference here to the 63rd hexagram of the Confucian (and Taoist) *Book of Changes* (the *I Ching*).

2

The Middle Ages and Roman Catholic Missions

As a historical period, the Middle Ages generally refers to Europe between 600 and 1500. It begins with the papacy of Gregory the Great and ends with the Muslim seizure of Constantinople (1453) and the Portuguese and Spanish voyages of discovery. Our coverage will extend back to include Augustine of Hippo (354-430), whose thought inaugurated the medieval paradigm of mission, and forward to include the Roman Catholic missions of the sixteenth century.

Augustine of Hippo knew that he lived at a hinge of history as Rome was sacked by Alaric and his Goths in 410. Responding to a Dalmatian bishop, Hesychius, who saw in these events signs of the world's imminent end, Augustine argued that Christ's Great Commission had not yet been fulfilled, as there were nations that had not yet received the Gospel. This was the same motive for mission that William Carey would rediscover in 1792! Augustine is better known for his influential theory of history presented in De Civitate Dei (The City of God). *In it he describes two "cities" that live side by side. The first, the city of God, endures forever with God but manifests itself (in part) on earth as the* communio sanctorum *(communion of saints) of God's pilgrim people. The second, the city of earth, includes both those who worship false gods and persons striving for justice and peace. For Augustine, the intermingling of those two cities provides the vibrant contexts in which Christians are called to faithful witness and service.*

How was the Christian ideal to be upheld amid the social disruptions of Europe's Dark Ages? Bosch joins others in the judgment that monasticism preserved much of authentic Christianity (TM, 230). While the eastern form developed traditions of individuals living saintly lives, western monasticism was essentially communal. Its careful structure began with St. Benedict's (ca. 540) rule for monasteries. "By patience share in the sufferings of Christ," Benedict advised. That sounds like an admonition to withdraw from concern for the world's needs. That the life of piety should include concern for salvation of souls and the care of travelers and the poor can be seen in the life of St. Bertilla, a remarkable woman monastic leader of the early eighth century.

How should pagan peoples be won to Christ? Irenic and atypical was the instruction of Pope Gregory the Great to pioneer missionaries to England in 601. He urged Augustine to adapt heathen temples for the worship of the true God. More common, in an age of constant warfare between peoples, was the practice of indirect and direct "missionary wars." The words of Jesus, "go out into the highways and hedges and compel them to come in" (Lk. 14:23) were interpreted as a biblical mandate for the crusades. St. Thomas Aquinas's answer to the question, "should infidels be compelled to believe?" influenced many. In dissent against the crusading spirit, Raymond Lull devoted his life as a missionary to Muslims. He believed that interreligious dialogue, rather than crusades, was the better way to reach Muslims and Jews.

The crusading spirit dominated western approaches to mission from the eleventh century attempt to recapture Jerusalem from the Muslims, through the fifteenth century expulsion of the Moors from Spain, to the Spanish conquests in the "New World" in the sixteenth century. Incensed by the exploitation and murder of native peoples, Bartolomé de Las Casas, chaplain for the Spanish conquest in Hispanola, experienced a spiritual conversion in 1514. He devoted the rest of his life to the defense of native peoples against Spanish tyranny. He sought conversions, but only "by gently attracting or exhorting the will." For a brief time—represented by the papal bull Sublimis Deus *of Pope Paul III in 1537—the Las Casas position was sanctioned by the pope.*

Where missionaries worked independently of colonial power, however, the mission approach radically changed. Francis Xavier, for example, introduced Christianity to poor fisher folk on the south coast of India in the 1540s. Despite his minimal knowledge of Tamil, he taught the rudiments of Christian beliefs and encouraged worship in the vernacular language. Early Christian models were repeated as the blood of martyrs became the seed of a growing community of faith.

GREAT COMMISSION NOT FULFILLED

> "In nations where the Church does not yet exist, she must come into existence."

■ *Predictions of the imminent end of the world have been a recurrent source of debate throughout Christian history. In 418, Augustine of Hippo received a letter from a Dalmatian bishop, Hesychius, who saw in the spread of the faith throughout the Roman empire a sign of the world's imminent end. In his reply, excerpted below, Augustine predates by more than fifteen centuries William Carey's analysis that the apostles did not complete the Lord's Great Commission to "go into all the world." Augustine's rationale for missions will be taken up again in premillennial thought in the nineteenth century.*

*Who Will Fill the World with the Gospel?**

I do not know whether one can discover anything more definite on this question (supposing one had the knowledge or ability to do so) than what I wrote in my previous letter—that the Lord's coming will take place when the whole world is filled with the gospel. Your Reverence's opinion that this was already achieved by the apostles themselves is, I am sure on the basis of definite evidence, not true. Here in Africa there are innumerable barbarian tribes to whom the gospel has not yet been preached, as can be learned from the daily evidence of those who have been taken prisoner and are now in slavery to the Romans. Admittedly, over the last few years it has happened in the case of some, but only very few and very occasionally; some of those who live on the Roman frontier and have been pacified have as a result had governors appointed by the Roman empire instead of having kings of their own—and these governors have begun to be Christians. But those in the interior who are untouched by Roman authority are totally unaffected by the Christian religion. At the same time one cannot possibly say that the promises of God have nothing to do with them.

What the Lord promised to the seed of Abraham was not the Romans but all nations; and he promised it with an oath. In accordance with this promise it has already happened that several nations who do not fall under Roman jurisdiction have accepted the gospel and joined the Church as she bears fruit and grows throughout the world (see Col. 1:6). She still has room for growth before the prophecy is fulfilled which was made about Christ as prefigured by Solomon: "He shall rule from sea to sea and from the river to the ends of the world" (Ps. 72:8)....

Since true prophecy cannot lie, it must be the case that all the nations that God has made will worship him. But how will they worship him unless they call on him? And, "how will they call on him in whom they have not believed? And how will they believe in him of whom they have not heard? And how will they hear without a preacher? And how will they preach unless they are sent?" (Rom. 10:14-15). He sends his messengers and gathers his elect from the four winds, that is, from the whole world. Accordingly, in nations where the Church does not yet exist, she must come into existence; but this does not mean that all who live in them must come to believe. The promise refers to "all nations," not to all members of all nations; "for not all have faith" (2 Thess. 3:2). Each nation believes in the persons of all who were chosen "before the foundation of the world" (Eph. 1:4); in the persons of the rest it does not believe, and, indeed, hates those who do believe. How else will the saying be fulfilled: "You will be hated by all nations for my name's sake" (Matt. 24:9)? It can only be fulfilled if in all nations there are those who hate and those who are hated.

So how can this prophecy have been fulfilled by the apostles when, as we know for a fact, there are still nations in which its fulfillment is just beginning, as well as

---

*Excerpts from Augustine of Hippo, "Letter 199" (ca. 419), in *Documents in Early Christian Thought*, ed. Maurice Wiles and Mark Santer (Cambridge, UK: Cambridge University Press, 1975), 259-60; cf. Bosch, TM, 218.

nations in which it has not yet begun? Consequently, when the Lord said: "You shall be my witnesses in Jerusalem and in all Judaea and Samaria and to the end of the earth" (Acts 1:8), he did not mean that those to whom he was then speaking were to fulfil such a task by themselves. It was like those other words, apparently addressed to them alone: "Behold, I am with you always, to the close of the age" (Matt. 28:20). Everyone understands these words as a promise to the universal Church which is to last through succeeding generations, each born and dying in its turn, from now until the close of the age.

MISSION IN TWO CITIES

> "The heavenly and the earthly...and intermingled from beginning to end."

■ *Augustine began to write* De Civitate Dei (The City of God), *his monumental theology of history, three years after Rome first collapsed and opened its gates to a barbarian invader. Alaric and his Goths sacked the city in 410. Pagans responded with the argument that the neglect of the old gods brought about by the Christians was the cause of the calamity. Augustine's magnum opus was the major work of refutation. In it he argued that God's salvation history has a place not only for faithful witnesses, but for the dissensions of the heretics. The intermingling of two cities, the heavenly and the earthly, provides the vibrant context in which Christians are called to faithful witness and service.*

*All Nations Believing in Christ**

First the church spread from Jerusalem, and when a great many in Judea and Samaria had believed, other peoples also were visited, as those proclaimed the gospel whom he himself had prepared by his word, like torches, and had kindled by the Holy Spirit. For he had said to them: "Fear not those who slay the body but cannot slay the soul" (Mt. 10:28). And that they might not be frozen with fear, they burned with the fire of love. Finally, the gospel was preached throughout the whole world, not only by those who had seen and heard him both before and after his passion and resurrection but also after their death by their successors amid dreadful persecutions and all manner of tortures and deaths of martyrs. So God himself bore witness by signs and portents and varied examples of his power as well as of the working of the Holy Spirit, in order that the people of the nations, believing in him who was crucified for their redemption, might venerate with Christian love the blood of the martyrs that they had shed with devilish fury, and in order that the very kings by whose laws the church was devastated might for their own healing be subjected to that name which they had cruelly tried to banish from the earth, and

---

*Excerpts from Augustine of Hippo, *The City of God,* Book 18, Chaps. 50, 51, 54 (Cambridge, MA: Harvard University Press, 1966), 6:65-67; cf. Bosch, TM, 220.

might begin to persecute the false gods for whose sake the worshippers of the true God had hitherto been persecuted.

Faith Confirmed through Dissension

But the devil,...stirred up heretics to resist the Christian doctrine under the guise of Christianity, as if they could be kept indifferently in the city of God without any reproof, even as the city of confusion kept indifferently the philosophers who held diverse and conflicting beliefs....even so their wickedness benefits those true catholic members of Christ, since God makes a good use even of the wicked, and "all things work together for good for those who love him" (Rom. 8:28). For all the enemies of the church, however blinded by error or depraved by wickedness, are useful. If given the power of inflicting bodily harm, they exercise her patience. If they oppose her only by their wrong opinions, they exercise her wisdom. Moreover, to bring it about that even enemies shall be loved, they exercise her benevolence or even her beneficence, whether she deals with them by winsome doctrine or by fearsome discipline.

False and True Gods

But let us now at last bring to a close this book, in which we have discoursed thus far and shown sufficiently, as it seemed, what is the mortal course of the two cities, the heavenly and the earthly, which are intermingled from beginning to end. One of them, the earthly, has created for herself from any source she pleased, even out of [humanity], false gods to worship with sacrifice; the other, a heavenly pilgrim on earth, does not create false gods, but is herself created by the true God, whose true sacrifice she is herself. But both alike in this life either enjoy good things or suffer evils, until they are separated by the last judgement, and each receives her own end, of which there is not end. Our next topic must be the said ends of the two.

THE MISSION OF MONASTICISM

"By patience share in the sufferings of Christ."

■ *The social disruptions that resulted from the collapse of the Roman empire, the invasions from the north, and the Islamic conquests led later historians to characterize the fifth to twelfth centuries in Europe as the Dark Ages. It was the monastery, however, which developed during this era not only as the center of culture and civilization, but also of mission. In the western monastic tradition, Saint Benedict (480?-547?) stands as the most influential leader. Upon choosing the monastic life, Benedict first lived a life of monastic solitude. Responding to the call of others for monastic community, he began a new monastic model at Monte Cassino, near Rome. Liturgical prayer, reading, and work were to be the three instruments by which the monks lived a life in the presence of God.*

Benedict's "Rule," adopted by hundreds of monasteries, led men and women to a life of both religious devotion and Christian service in the world.

*Christian Life as Service**

Listen, my son, to your master's precepts, and incline the ear of your heart (Proverbs 4:20). Receive willingly and carry out effectively your loving father's advice, that by the labor of obedience you may return to Him from whom you had departed by the sloth of disobedience.

To you, therefore, my words are now addressed, whoever you may be, who are renouncing your own will to do battle under the Lord Christ, the true King, and are taking up the strong, bright weapons of obedience.

...first of all, whatever good work you begin to do, beg of Him with most earnest prayer to perfect it, that He who has now deigned to count us among His [children] may not at any time be grieved by our evil deeds. For we must always so serve Him with the good things He has given us, that He will never as an angry Father disinherit His children, nor ever as a dread Lord, provoked by our evil actions, deliver us to everlasting punishment as wicked servants who would not follow Him to glory.

Let us arise, then, at last, for the Scripture stirs us up, saying, "Now is the hour for us to rise from sleep" (Rom. 13:11). Let us open our eyes to the deifying light, let us hear with attentive ears the warning which the divine voice cries daily to us...

Having our loins girded, therefore, with faith and the performance of good works (Eph. 6:14), let us walk in His paths by the guidance of the Gospel, that we may deserve to see Him who has called us to His kingdom (1 Thess. 2:12).

For if we wish to dwell in the tent of that kingdom, we must run to it by good deeds or we shall never reach it.

St. Benedict's Monastic Rule

And so we are going to establish a school for the service of the Lord. In founding it we hope to introduce nothing harsh or burdensome. But if a certain strictness results from the dictates of equity for the amendment of vices or the preservation of charity, do not be at once dismayed and fly from the way of salvation, whose entrance cannot but be narrow (Mt. 7:14). For as we advance in the religious life and in faith, our hearts expand and we run the way of God's commandments with unspeakable sweetness of love (Ps. 118:32). Thus, never departing from His school, but persevering in the monastery according to His teaching until death, we may by patience share in the sufferings of Christ (1 Pet. 4:13) and deserve to have a share also in His kingdom.

---

*Excerpts from *St. Benedict's Rule for Monasteries* (Collegeville, MN: St. John Abbey Press, 1948), 6; cf. Bosch, TM, 233.

ADAPT PAGAN TEMPLES

"Adapt them [heathen temples] for the worship of the true God."

■ *Pope Gregory the Great initiated the first Christian mission to England. In 596, he personally dispatched Augustine and his party of monks to Canterbury, the capital of King Ethelbert of Kent. The monks were well received, since the king had wedded Bertha, a Christian princess from Gaul [France]. The monks' virtuous life and preaching made such a deep impression on the king that within a year he became a Christian and Augustine was able to baptize 10,000 Saxons. Mass movements to Christianity can be broad but shallow. How much of traditional Saxon culture could be infused with Christian meaning? Augustine wondered. The 601 letter from the Pope to the pioneer missionary, conveyed by Abbot Mellitus, is a classic document on contextualization.*

Contextualization in Frontier Missions to Britain*

The heathen temples of these people need not be destroyed, only the idols which are to be found in them....If the temples are well built, it is a good idea to detach them from the service of the devil, and to adapt them for the worship of the true God....And since the people are accustomed, when they assemble for sacrifice, to kill many oxen in sacrifice to the devils, it seems reasonable to appoint a festival for the people by way of exchange. The people must learn to slay their cattle not in honour of the devil, but in honour of God and for their own food; when they have eaten and are full, then they must render thanks to the giver of all good things. If we allow them these outward joys, they are more likely to find their way to the true inner joy....It is doubtless impossible to cut off all abuses at once from rough hearts, just as the man who sets out to climb a high mountain does not advance by leaps and bounds, but goes upward step by step and pace by pace.

THE MISSION OF WOMEN MONASTICS

"Speed the salvation of souls."

■ *The monastery of Chelles near Paris in the seventh century was a training ground for monastics as missionaries. Founded about 650 by the queen of the Franks of Neustria, St. Balthild, it became a popular training center for Anglo-Saxon nuns and a link with developing Christianity in the British Isles. Bertilla is said to have lived at Chelles for forty-six years after its foundation*

---

*Pope Gregory the Great, "Letter to Augustine," in Bede, *Ecclesiastical History of the English Nation* (601), 1:30; quoted in Stephen Neill, *A History of Christian Missions,* 2nd ed. (Harmondsworth, United Kingdom, and New York: Penguin Books, 1986), 59; cf. Bosch, TM, 226.

and to have served as its fourth abbess. The "Life of Bertilla" was probably first put together at Chelles about six or seven years after her death.[1] Among works of that literary genre, it is remarkable in the absence of miracles or the extolling of the heroine for heroic qualities. Instead, the author presents Bertilla as the exemplary monastic whose faithful observance of monastic rules enabled Chelles to be a center of spirituality and mission.

*An Example and Model of Piety**

Through her continence and fullest love, blessed Bertilla was an example and model of piety to all. She carefully taught religious customs to her subjects not only through holy speech but even more through her own sanctity, so that they might love one another in charitable affection and behave purely, soberly and chastely in all things and be ever ready for offices and prayers and to take care of guests and the poor with fond concern and to love their neighbors. Through holy communion, she drew the monastic household and its near neighbors to do the penance given for their sins in confession.[2] Thus she gained the improvement of many and gained much profit for their souls and rewards for herself.

Christ's servant Bertilla had the highest devotion for the adornment of churches and altars for Christ. She ordered her priests daily to offer their sacred hosts to God for the salvation of the souls of the faithful and the right state of God's Holy Church. She was always assiduous in vigils and prayers and abstinence from food and above all it was wonderful how little she drank. And in constancy of faith, she kept her unswerving mind always on the Lord Jesus Christ. And when she carried out these and other most honest customs, her holy example was edifying to the Christianity of her brothers and sisters; meanwhile paupers and pilgrims were comforted by her munificent largesse.

Mission to England

Through her, the Lord collected such great fruits for the salvation of souls that even from over the seas, the faithful kings of the Saxons, through trusted messengers, asked her to send some of her disciples for the learning and holy instruction they heard were wonderful in her, that they might build convents of men and nuns in their land.[3] She did not deny these religious requests which would speed the salvation of souls. In a thankful spirit, taking counsel with her elders and heeding her brothers' exhortations, with great diligence and the protection of the saints, she sent many volumes of books to them. That the harvest of souls in that nation might increase through her and be multiplied by God's grace, she sent chosen women and devout men. And we trust that this has been fulfilled to the praise of God and Lady Bertilla.

---

*Excerpts from *Sainted Women of the Dark Ages,* edited and translated by Jo Ann McNamara and John E. Halborg with E. Gordon Whatley (Durham, NC, and London: Duke University Press, 1992), 285-86.

COMPULSION OR PERSUASION OF UNBELIEVERS?

"Should infidels be compelled to believe?"

■ *"Compel them to come in" (Lk. 14:23) may be the most used missionary text of the medieval period. Much of the conversion of northern Europe took place when rulers decided that Christianity should be the religion in their realms. Militancy increased as many of these rulers joined the crusades that were aimed ostensibly at wresting Jerusalem from the control of the "infidels." Among theologians, Thomas Aquinas's views were most influential. He wrote* Summa *at the time of the seventh and eighth crusades, in which his friend St. Louis IX of France played a leading part.*

*Ought Infidels to Be Compelled to Believe?**

THE EIGHTH POINT[4]: 1. It would seem that by no means should they be compelled. For in the Parable of the Wheat and the Tares, the servants of the householder in whose field weeds had been sown, asked him, *Do you want us to go and gather them?* But he replied, *No, lest in gathering the weeds you root up the wheat along with them* (Mt. 13:28). Chrysostom's interpretation is that *our Lord says this in order to forbid the slaying of men. For it is not right to slay heretics, since in doing so you must needs destroy many innocent persons at the same time.*[5] For a parallel reason neither should infidels be compelled to believe.

2. Besides, canon law states, *The Holy Synod prescribes that in respect of the Jews none are henceforth to be forced to believe.*[6] In like manner, therefore, other unbelievers are not to be coerced into the faith.

3. Again, Augustine writes that *a man can do other things unwillingly, but he cannot believe unless he be willing.*[7] Therefore it seems that unbelievers are not to be forced to believe.

4. Finally, it is said in God's person, *I desire not the death of a sinner* (Ez. 18:23). Now we should conform our will to God's, as we have agreed.[8] So we should not even wish unbelievers to be killed.

ON THE OTHER HAND WE are told, *go out into the highways and hedges, and compel them to come in* (Lk. 14:23). Now men [and women] enter the house of God, that is the Church, through faith. Therefore some should be compelled to the faith.

REPLY: Among unbelievers there are some who have never received the faith, such as heathens and Jews. These are by no means to be compelled, for belief is voluntary. Nevertheless the faithful, if they are able, should compel them not to

---

*Excerpts from Thomas Aquinas, *Summa Theologica*, II:2, Q.10, Art.8 (New York: McGraw-Hill; London: Eyre & Spottiswoode, 1964), 32:61, 63, 65; cf. Bosch, TM, p. 237.

hinder the faith whether by their blasphemies or evil persuasions or even open persecutions. It is for this reason that Christ's faithful often wage war on infidels, not indeed for the purpose of forcing them to believe, because even were they to conquer them and take them captive, they should still leave them free to believe or not, but for the purpose of stopping them obstructing the faith of Christ.

However there are other unbelievers who at one time accepted and professed the faith, such as heretics and apostates of all sorts, and these are to be submitted to physical compulsion that they should hold to what they once received and fulfil what they promised.

Hence: 1. Some have understood this authoritative text to forbid, not the excommunication, but the slaying of heretics, as appears from the words of Chrysostom....

2. Jews who have not accepted the faith should in no way be coerced into it. Those however who have accepted it should be compelled to keep it, as the same chapter states.

3. Even as taking a vow is a matter of freewill yet keeping it is a matter of obligation, so the acceptance of faith is a matter of freewill yet keeping it when once it has been received is a matter of obligation. And so heretics should be compelled to hold to the faith. Augustine writes, *What do these people mean by their cry, We may believe or not believe just as we choose. Whom does Christ force? Let them recognize that Christ compelled Paul and afterwards taught him.*[9]

4. In the same letter Augustine writes, *No one wishes a heretic to perish. But the house of David did not deserve to have peace unless his son Absolom had been killed in the war he raised against his father. Thus too the Catholic Church, if she gather some by the loss of others, comforts the pain of her maternal heart by the delivery of so many.*[10]

INTERFAITH DIALOGUE

> "Finding a new method...by which those in error might be shown the path to glory."

■ *Raymond Lull (ca. 1235-1316) was one of the most notable missionaries of the thirteenth and fourteenth centuries. He lived at a time when missionaries of both the Franciscan and Dominican orders had a passion to convert Muslims through missions, yet joined neither order. Born on the island of Majorca near Spain shortly after it had been retaken from the Muslims, it was natural that he should think of missions to the Islamic world. From the large Muslim population in Majorca he learned Arabic, and devoted his life as a scholar, teacher, poet, and mystic to missions. As the passages below illustrate, Lull believed that interreligious discourse, rather than military crusades, was the high road to evangelization of persons of other faiths.*

*A New Method**

Since for a long time we have had dealings with unbelievers and have heard their false opinions and errors; and in order that they may give praise to our Lord God and enter the path of eternal salvation, I, who am blameworthy, despicable, poor, sinful, scorned by others, unworthy of having my name affixed to this book or any other, following the manner of the Arabic *Book of the Gentile,* wish to exert myself to the utmost—trusting in the help of the Most High—in finding a new method and new reasons by which those in error might be shown the path to glory without end and the means of avoiding infinite suffering.

This work is divided into four books. In the first book we prove that God exists, that in Him are contained the flowers of the first tree, and that the Resurrection exists. In the second book the Jew tries to prove that his belief is better than those of the Christian and the Saracen. In the third book the Christian tries to prove that his belief is worthier than those of the Jew and the Saracen. In the fourth book the Saracen tries to prove that his belief is worthier than those of the Jew and the Christian.

By divine dispensation it came to pass that in a certain land there lived a Gentile very learned in philosophy, who began to worry about old age, death, and the joys of this world.

While in the midst of these thoughts and tribulations, the Gentile conceived in his heart the idea of leaving his land and going to a foreign land, to see if he could find a remedy for his sadness.

Mission by Reasoning—Not War

One of the three wise men said: "If the Gentile, who was so long in error, has conceived such great devotion and such great fervor in praising God, that he now states that in order to do so he would not hesitate to suffer any hardship or death, no matter how harsh it were, then how much greater should be our devotion and fervor in praising the name of God, considering how long we have known about Him, and all the more so since He has placed us under such obligation by the many blessings and honors He has given us and gives us every day. We should debate and see which of us is in truth and which in error. For just as we have one God, one Creator, one Lord, we should also have one faith, one religion, one sect, one manner of loving and honoring God, and we should love and help one another, and make it so that between us there be no difference or contrariety of faith or customs, which difference and contrariety cause us to be enemies with one another and to be at war, killing one another and falling captive to one another. And this war, death, and servitude prevent us from giving the praise, reverence, and honor we owe God every day of our life.

---

*Excerpts from Raymond Lull, *The Book of the Gentile and the Three Wise Men* (1275?), in *Selected Works of Ramon Lull,* edited and translated by Anthony Bonner (Princeton, NJ: Princeton University Press, 1985), I:110-11, 301-2; cf. Bosch, TM, 236.

DEFENSE OF THE INDIANS

"Persuading the understanding…attracting…the will."

■ *Arriving in the New World in 1502, Bartolomé de Las Casas (1474-1566), a friend of Columbus, began as both a colonialist and a slaveholder. Ordained a priest in 1507 in Rome, he reached Cuba as chaplain for the Spanish conquest in 1512-13. Incensed in 1514 by the exploitation and often murder of the Indians, Las Casas resolved to devote his life to challenging injustices in the system. Las Casas argued that the conversion of all persons should be by peaceful means. Following the example and precepts of Christ, preachers should convert nonbelievers "by persuading the understanding…and by attracting the will"[11] as Las Casas did in his mission to Tuzulutlán. Las Casas refutes the theory of conquistadors and worldly ecclesiastics like Bishop Fonseca that the Indians should first be forcibly subjugated and then later converted.*

*The Only Method of Teaching the True Religion**

The one and only method of teaching [persons] the true religion was established by Divine Providence for the whole world, and for all times, that is, by persuading the understanding through reason, and by gently attracting or exhorting the will. This method should be common to all [persons] throughout the world, without any distinction made for sects, errors or corrupt customs.

This conclusion will be proved in many ways by arguments drawn from reason; by examples of the ancient Fathers; by the rule and manner of preaching which Christ instituted for all times; by the practices of the Apostles; by quotations from holy teachers; by the most ancient tradition of the Church and by her numerous ecclesiastical decrees.

Conquest: The Wrong Method of Conversion

A method contrary to the one we have been defending would be the following: that…the pagans should first be subjected, whether they wished to be or not, to the rule of the Christian people, and that once they were subjected, organized preaching would follow. In this case, the preachers would not compel them to believe but would convince them by arguments and also draw them gently, once the many impediments which preaching could encounter had been removed by the said subjection.

---

*Excerpts from Bartolomé de Las Casas, "The Only Method of Attracting All People to the True Faith" (1530s) in *Witness: Writings of Bartolomé de Las Casas,* edited and translated by George Sanderlin (Maryknoll, NY: Orbis Books, 1992), 137-42; cf. Bosch, TM, 236.

But since no pagan, above all no pagan kings, would wish voluntarily to submit to the rule of a Christian people, or of any prince, it would certainly be necessary to come to a war.

However, war brings with it these evils: the crash of arms; sudden attacks and invasions, impetuous and furious; violence and deadly confusion; licentiousness, deaths and massacres; rapine, pillage and plunder; parents deprived of their sons, and sons of their parents; captivities; kings and natural lords deprived of their estates and dominions; the devastation and desolation of innumerable towns and cities. And all these evils fill kingdoms...with sad laments.

Laws are silent, humane feelings are mocked, nowhere is there rectitude, religion is an object of scorn, and there is absolutely no distinction made between the sacred and the profane. War also fills every place with highwaymen, thieves, ravishers, fires, and murders. Indeed, what is war but general murder and robbery among many? And the more widespread it is, the more criminal it is. Through war extreme misfortune is brought upon thousands of innocents who do not deserve the injury that is done them. To sum up, in war [persons] lose their riches, their bodies, and their souls....

For if things which are gentle, mild, and pleasing cause a man [or woman] to listen to new matters willingly...and to lend faith to what he [or she] hears, contrary things must produce a contrary effect. Therefore, this method of subjecting pagans by war to the rule of the Christian people so that the Gospel may be preached to them is contrary to the natural and gentle method described earlier.

CONVERT BY PREACHING AND EXAMPLE

> "Convert...by preaching...and by the example of good and holy living."

■ *Bartolomé de Las Casas was only one of many participants in a lengthy controversy among the Spanish and Portuguese over the intellectual capacities of Native Americans. Some conquistadors classed them as animals* (bruta animalia) *and in doing so justified appropriating the property and brutalizing the lives of defenseless natives. Meanwhile Dominicans led by Las Casas, Bernardino de Minaya, and Julian Garcés, Bishop of Tlaxcala in New Spain, made representations to the Pope concerning the spiritual equality and basic humanity of all, including Native Americans. Paul III (1534-1549) reflected their position in the Bull* Sublimis Deus *issued June 2, 1537. Emperor Charles V, upon reading it, became so concerned over its effects in his New World dominions that he brought pressure on the Pope to revoke it. A second bull on June 19, 1538, removed censures and penalties against* conquistadors, *but retained the stance concerning the Indians' capacity for conversion.*

*Capable to Receive the Faith**

The sublime God so loved the human race that He created man [and woman] in such wise that he [or she] might participate, not only in the good that other creatures enjoy, but endowed him [and her] with capacity to attain to the inaccessible and invisible Supreme Good and behold it face to face; and since man [and woman], according to the testimony of the sacred scriptures, has been created to enjoy eternal life and happiness, which none may obtain save through faith in our Lord Jesus Christ, it is necessary that he [and she] should possess the nature and faculties enabling him to receive that faith; and that whoever is thus endowed should be capable of receiving that same faith. Nor is it credible that any one should possess so little understanding as to desire the faith and yet be destitute of the most necessary faculty to enable him [or her] to receive it. Hence Christ, who is the Truth itself, that has never failed and can never fail, said to the preachers of the faith whom He chose for that office "Go ye and teach all nations." He said all, without exception, for all are capable of receiving the doctrines of the faith.

The enemy of the human race, who opposes all good deeds in order to bring [humankind] to destruction, beholding and envying this, invented a means never before heard of, by which he might hinder the preaching of God's word of Salvation to the people: he inspired his satellites who, to please him, have not hesitated to publish abroad that the Indians of the West and the South, and other people of whom we have recent knowledge should be treated as dumb brutes created for our service, pretending that they are incapable of receiving the Catholic Faith.

We, who, though unworthy, exercise on earth the power of our Lord and seek with all our might to bring those sheep of His flock who are outside into the fold committed to our charge, consider, however, that the Indians are truly [human] and that they are not only capable of understanding the Catholic Faith but, according to our information, they desire exceedingly to receive it.... the said Indians and all other people who may later be discovered by Christians, are by no means to be deprived of their liberty or the possession of their property, even though they be outside the faith of Jesus Christ;...the said Indians and other peoples should be converted to the faith of Jesus Christ by preaching the word of God and by the example of good and holy living.

CATHOLICISM TO INDIA

"Bringing the natives into the fold of Jesus Christ."

■ *Francis Xavier (1506-1552), one of the greatest missionaries of all time, was born in the Basque country and died on a small island off the China coast while hoping to bring the Gospel to that country. In 1533, Xavier attached himself to*

---

*Excerpts from Pope Paul III, *Sublimis Deus* (1537), in *Documents of American Catholic History,* edited by John Tracy Ellis (Wilmington, DE: Michael Glazier, 1987), I: 7-8; cf. Bosch, TM, 227.

Ignatius Loyola, becoming one of the first six members of the Society of Jesus. Sent to India as papal legate and representative of the King of Portugal in 1541, he began his ministry in the Portuguese enclave of Goa. Soon he was attracted to the poor Parava fisher folk of the Coromandel Coast at the southern tip of India. They had responded in a mass baptism in 1534 when the Portuguese promised military help against their northern neighbors. With limited knowledge of the Tamil language, Xavier devised the plan of missionary catechetics described below. Although he departed in 1542 to introduce Christianity in Malacca and Japan, a succession of able Jesuits continued his mission plan, and the Paravas became a stable Christian community.

*Catechetics**

...Now I speak of what I know you are most anxious to hear about—the state of religion in India. In this region of Travancore, where I now am, God has drawn very many to the faith of His Son Jesus Christ. In the space of one month I made Christians of more than ten thousand. This is the method I have followed. As soon as I arrived in my heathen village where they had sent for me to give baptism, I gave orders for all, men, women and children, to be collected in one place. Then, beginning with the first elements of the Christian faith, I taught them there is one God—Father, Son, and Holy Ghost; and at the same time, calling on the three divine Persons and one God, I made them each make three times the sign of the cross; then, putting on a surplice, I began to recite in a loud voice and in their own language the form of general Confession, the Apostles' Creed, the Ten Commandments, the Lord's Prayer, the *Ave Maria,* and the *Salve Regina.* Two years ago I translated all these prayers into the language of the country, and learned them by heart. I recited them so that all of every age and condition followed me in them.

Martyrs

The island of Manaar is about 150 miles from this place. Its inhabitants sent me some of their people to beg me to go there to baptize them, as they had determined to become Christians. I was occupied on affairs of the greatest importance, relating to the interests of religion, and so could not go myself; but I persuaded a certain priest to go instead of me and baptize as many as possible. He had already baptized a great number, when the Raja of Jafanapatam, under whose dominion the island lies, most cruelly put to death a large number of the converts, simply because they had become Christians. Let us give thanks to our Lord Jesus Christ that even in our time He does not let us lack martyrs and that while He sees so few souls avail themselves of all His divine mercy and indulgence to work out their salvation, He

---

*Excerpts from Francis Xavier, "Letter of January 1545," in *History of Christianity in India: Source Materials,* compiled by M. K. Kuriakose (Madras, India: Senate of Serampore College, 1982), 32-34.

permits, in the mystery of His providence, that human barbarity should fill up the destined ranks and number of the blessed.

NOTES

1. "Vita Bertilae abbatissae Calensis," 4:534-46, in *Scriptores rerum merowingicarum* (*Momumenta Germaniae Historica*), edited by Societas Aperiedis Fontibus Rerum Germanicarum Medii Aevi, vols. 3-5 by B. Krusch (Hannover: Impensis Bibliopolii Hahniani, ca. 1937-).

2. Confessional practices were particularly associated with Irish discipline. Rule 23 of Bishop Donatus of Besançon, written expressly for women monastics, recommends at every hour of every day, "nothing to be hidden from the spiritual mother."

3. Queen Bathild, Bertilla's patron and predecessor as abbess, was English and interested in the fate of her countrywomen. See Bede, *History of the English Church and People* (Baltimore: Penguin Books, 1968), 3:8 and 4:23, for confirmation of the training of young women at Chelles to rule new English houses.

4. Cf. *In Matt.* 13.

5. *In Matt.* XLVI. PG 58, 477.

6. Gratian, *decretum* 1, 45, 5. RF 1, 161.

7. *In Joan* XXV. ON *John* 7, 44. PL 35, 1607.

8. 1a2a/e?. 19, 9 & 10.

9. *Ad Bonifacium Comitem. Ep.* CLXXXV, 6. PL 33, 803.

10. Op cit. 8. PL 33, 807.

11. Bartolomé de Las Casas, *Del Único Modo de Atraer a Todos los Pueblos a la Verdadera Religión,* ed. Agustín Millares Carlo (México City: Fondo de Cultura Económica, 1942), p. 6.

3

The Protestant Reformation

In 1514, Copernicus, the Polish astronomer, privately circulated his manuscript claiming that the earth revolves around the sun—a challenge to ancient authority that would require a new cosmology. Two years later, Erasmus produced the first printed Greek New Testament, making the original text available to any educated person of the day. In 1517, Martin Luther nailed his ninety-five theses to the church door in Wittenberg, thereby launching the Protestant Reformation. A paradigm shift was underway in northern Europe.

As Augustine of Hippo had rediscovered Paul in the fifth century, Luther recovered his theology in the sixteenth. The central thrust of Paul's theology in Romans 1:16 was that the Gospel "is the power of God for salvation to everyone who has faith." This, together with the conviction that "the just shall live by faith" (Rom. 1:17, KJV), became the missionary text for the new Protestant paradigm.

David Bosch identifies five features of the Protestant theology of mission shared in common by the Reformers, whether Lutheran, Calvinist, Zwinglian, or Anabaptist. He contrasts each with the earlier Roman Catholic theology. First is justification by faith, starting not from what people could and ought to do for their salvation, but with what God has already done in Christ. Second is the Fall, starting not with a record of sins committed, but rather with the essential sinfulness of humanity. Third is the subjective dimension of salvation, starting not with "reasoned science" but with personal religious experience. Fourth is the priesthood of all believers, rather than the sacredotal prerogatives of the clergy. Fifth is the centrality of the Scriptures in the life of the church, rather than church tradition and the sacraments (TM, 241-42).

However, no great missionary impulse resulted from this new theology. Having dispensed with monasticism, the major method of Catholic missions from the sixth to sixteenth centuries, no alternative strategy developed for the next 275 years. For Martin Luther, the kingdom would come through God's action through the Word, faith, and "the final revelation." The next selection contains Luther's interpretation that the Great Commission was given only to the apostles and already fulfilled by them. John Calvin concurred, arguing that whereas God appoints pastors and teachers in every age, he raised up the "extraordinary offices" of apostles, prophets, and evangelists only in the apostolic age. In his Sermons on 2 Samuel, *Calvin argued that King David won Jerusalem from the Jebusites only by God's election. As for this world, Calvin urged the believers to "pray God that his reign might increase…since the power to do so is not in us." By 1597, Philipp Nicolai, a noted theologian and hymn writer, developed a "geography of missions" in his widely published apocalyptic work,* De Regno Christi. *On every continent he found peoples with beliefs similar in some way to those of Christians. Therefore, he concluded that the Good News must have been proclaimed there also by the apostles.*

Two exceptions to Reformation orthodoxy on this issue should be noted. Anabaptists felt convicted by the mandate of the Great Commission. They provoked both Lutheran and Reformed church leaders by their insistence on freedom to wander in ministry wherever they felt called to serve. Balthasar Hubmaier, their most noted early theologian, argued that the Lord's apostolic commission to go, preach, and baptize was as compelling now as when first spoken. Adrian Saravia, a Dutch Reformed theologian and younger contemporary of Calvin, concurred that the Great Commission continues to obligate the church to preach the Gospel to all nations.

The breakthrough from mandate to missionary action began, for Protestants influenced by Pietism, in the seventeenth century (Bosch, TM, 252-55). The movement combined joy in personal experiences of salvation with an eagerness to share that joy abroad. Where established parishes felt no urgency, small revived communities inside the church (ecclesiola in ecclesiae) *voluntarily picked up the challenge. Bartholomäus Ziegenbalg, the first Pietist missionary, belied the common stereotype of Pietism by his holistic concern to serve both body and soul in mission. Count Zinzendorf, the benefactor of early Moravian missions, found in the parable of the marriage feast (Mt. 22:2; Lk. 14:17) the basis for passionate concern for those living apart from Christ.*

THE MISSIONARY MESSAGE OF THE CHURCH

> "Only Christ could have brought the world everywhere to believe."

■ *In his sermon on the Marcan account of the Ascension and Great Commission (Mk. 16:14-20), Martin Luther interpreted the command to "go into all the world" as that given to the apostles and fulfilled by them. He contrasted God's power and authority with that of all temporal rulers. Luther emphasized the action of the apostles as participants in God's saving work, but said little about how other Christians participate in the history of salvation.*

*Preach Christ**[1]

We should so preach Christ as one who will reject nobody, however weak he [or she] may be, but will gladly receive and comfort and strengthen everybody; that we may always picture him to ourselves as a good shepherd. Then hearts will turn to him of their own accord, and need not be forced and driven. The Gospel graciously invites and makes men [and women] willing, so that they desire to go, and do go, to him with all confidence. And it begets a love for Christ in their hearts, so that they willingly do what they should, whereas formerly they had to be driven and forced. When we are driven, we do a thing with displeasure and against our will. That is not what God desires; therefore it is done in vain. But when I see that God deals with me graciously, he wins my heart, so that I am constrained to fly to him; consequently, my heart is filled with happiness and joy.

Do Not Confine the Gospel[2]

We have often said heretofore that the Gospel, properly speaking, is not something written in books, but an oral proclamation, which shall be heard in all the world and shall be cried out freely before all creatures, so that all would have to hear it if they had ears; that is to say, it shall be preached so publicly that to preach it more publicly would be impossible. For the Law, which was of old, and what the prophets preached, was not cried out in all the world before all creatures, but it was preached by the Jews in their synagogues. But the Gospel shall not be thus confined; it shall be preached freely unto all the world.

The Great Commission[3]

The command of a temporal ruler goes no farther than to the confines of his own kingdom; likewise that of a father to his own household: but this commission of Christ (Mk. 16:14-20) concerns all kings, princes, countries and people, great and small, young and old, simple and wise, sinners and saints. With this one message he claims all dominion and power, all wisdom, holiness, majesty and the right to rule on earth with unlimited authority. What else can the world think and say about this: What! this one man and his eleven poor beggars dare to assume authority over Moses and all the prophets, yes, even over all people? Even Moses was sent only to Pharaoh and his people in Egypt. Is this man, then, to have the whole world for his? He is in relation to it no more than a common laborer!

It must be a master of no mean authority who dares to exercise the right to send forth messengers not only to one or several crowned heads, but to all rulers throughout the world. Christ does all this as though he possessed full power and authority over them as his subjects, charging his disciples that they should fear no one, no matter how great and powerful he might be, but should cheerfully go forth,

*Excerpts from Martin Luther, "Gospel Sermon, Second Sunday after Easter," and "Gospel Sermon, Ascension Day," in *Luther's Works*, ed. J. N. Lenker (Minneapolis: Lutherans in All Lands Co., 1907), vol. 12, pp. 25-26, 183-84, 214-16; cf. Bosch, TM, 244-45.

continuing to the remotest parts of the world, and preach the Gospel, with the assurance that they could not fail to be heard and that no one was able to hinder them.

Thus was it fulfilled. "Beginning at Jerusalem," the kingdom touched the whole world. No other kingdom ever had such power. There never yet lived a ruler who achieved supremacy over even one-half of the world. How is it then, that from Jerusalem to the remotest corners of the earth all men know of this king who is called Christ? And all this was accomplished without a single sword-thrust and without military power; simply through these poor beggars, whom Christ sent forth into so many kingdoms and principalities that resisted them with the sword, with fire and water and with their whole might. If the apostles had been dependent upon their own power, they would have miserably failed before crossing their own thresholds. They had been afraid of their own people, the Jews, and had hidden themselves behind bolted doors. But later on, upon the strength of this commission, they boldly went forth, not only among their own people, but in all kingdoms, through all principalities, and in the face of all powers and resistance of the world and the devil.

Whence did they obtain such courage and strength? Surely not from any king of Persia nor emperor of Rome, Turkey or Tartary. No, it was from the Lord alone, who ascended into heaven and commanded them to go and preach to the whole creation. And as Christ began to set up his kingdom, so it will continue till the end of the world.

REPRESENT CHRIST

"One preaches that people should believe and trust in God."

■ *The Anabaptists have been called "the Party of the Restitution" to distinguish them from the Reformers. Seeking to restore the vitality of the early church, they found their scriptural mandate in the words of Jesus and the Book of Acts. In contrast to Luther and Calvin, they believed that the Lord's commission to preach and baptize (Mt. 28:16-20; Mk. 16:15-18) was as compelling today as when first spoken. Balthasar Hubmaier (1480?-1528), although a participant in the Anabaptist wing of the Reformation for less than three years from his baptism to his martyrdom in 1528, gained a well-earned reputation as the most able theologian among the early Anabaptists. His essay "On the Office of the Apostles" is representative of the Anabaptist motive for mission of the period.*

*On the Office of the Apostles**

"Jesus said to his disciples once again: 'Peace be with you. As the Father sent me, so I send you.' And when he said this, he breathed on them and said to them:

---

*Excerpts from Balthasar Hubmaier, "On the Christian Baptism of Believers" (1525) in *Balthasar Hubmaier: Theologian of Anabaptism,* ed. H. Wayne Pipkin and John H. Yoder (Scottdale, PA: Herald Press, 1989), 114-16, 118, 122; cf. Bosch, TM, 246.

'Receive the Holy Spirit. To whomsoever you remit their sins, to them they are remitted, and to whomsoever you retain them, to them they are retained' " (Jn. 20:20 f.). "Therefore, go forth into all the world, preach the gospel to all creatures, teach all peoples, and baptize them in the name of the Father, son, and Holy Spirit. Whoever believes and is baptized will be saved; whoever does not believe will be damned" (Mk. 16:15; Mt. 28:19 f.).

From these words one understands clearly and certainly that this sending of the apostles consists of three points or commands: first, preaching; second, faith; and third, outward baptism.

Preaching

The preaching of the apostles was: as God promised to send the world his Word because of sin, as the prophets and Moses proclaimed this promise everywhere, God has now done that and the Word has become flesh, Jesus Christ, our Savior....

Christ sent out his disciples as God his father had sent him: that as he, Christ himself, said on earth to the believers, "Take heart, rise, go forth, your sins are forgiven you." Likewise his disciples should now represent him henceforth during the time of his bodily absence and guarantee to all believers a sure and certain remission of their sin through him, Jesus Christ (Rom. 5:1.)....

Faith

The second article is faith. Therefore one preaches that people should believe and trust in God (Joel 2)....So faith comes through preaching, preaching, however, through the Word of God. Therefore one preaches so that people believe, trust God, expect all good things from God our heavenly Father and believe that he is our gracious, good, gentle, benevolent, and merciful Father in heaven, who carries, protects, and shields us as a human being [shields] his child, or like a hen her chicks under her wings....

Baptism

The water baptism follows. Not that the same cleanses the souls but rather the "yes" of a good conscience toward God which preceded inwardly in faith....

It is written in Mark 16:15 f.: "Go forth into all the world and preach the gospel to all creatures. He who believes and is baptized will be saved but he who does not believe will be damned." Well, it is stated very clearly: (1) go, (2) preach, (3) he who believes, (4) and is baptized, (5) will be saved. Here you see a well-structured speech of which no single letter will fall. It must be kept as it is.

"THY KINGDOM COME"

"God's kingdom comes to us...in time, through the Word and faith, and...through the final revelation."

■ *Luther's* Larger Catechism *of 1529 has been an essential part of the agreed bases for Lutheran doctrine since the Concord of 1580. In the following passage on "Thy kingdom come," the second petition of the Lord's Prayer, Luther expected the kingdom to come to two groups. To the faithful believers, it could come now, as they respond to God's word. To others, however, Luther believed that it would come only upon Christ's return at the end of time. Did this emphasis on divine sovereignty undercut the missionary motivation, as some scholars believe?*

*God's Kingdom**

What is the kingdom of God? Answer: Simply what we learned in the Creed, namely, that God sent his Son, Christ our Lord, into the world to redeem and deliver us from the power of the devil and to bring us to himself and rule us as a king of righteousness, life, and salvation against sin, death, and an evil conscience. To this end he also gave his Holy Spirit to teach us this through his holy Word and to enlighten and strengthen us in faith by his power.

We pray here at the outset that all this may be realized in us and that God's name may be praised through his holy Word and our Christian lives. This we ask, both in order that we who have accepted it may remain faithful and grow daily in it and in order that it may gain recognition and followers among other people and advance with power throughout the world. So we pray that, led by the Holy Spirit, many may come into the kingdom of grace and become partakers of salvation, so that we may all remain together eternally in this kingdom which has now made its appearance among us.

Mission and the Kingdom

God's kingdom comes to us in two ways: first, it comes here, in time, through the Word and faith, and secondly, in eternity, it comes through the final revelation.[4] Now, we pray for both of these, that it may come to those who are not yet in it, and that it may come by daily growth here and in eternal life hereafter to us who have attained it. All this is simply to say: "Dear Father, we pray Thee, give us thy Word, that the Gospel may be sincerely preached throughout the world and that it may be

---

*Excerpts from Martin Luther, "Large Catechism: Third Part, The Lord's Prayer," Par. 41-54, in *The Book of Concord,* ed. Theodore G. Tappert (1959), 426-27; cf. Bosch, TM, 244-45.

received by faith and may work and live in us. So we pray that thy kingdom may prevail among us through the Word and the power of the Holy Spirit, that the devil's kingdom may be overthrown and he may have no right or power over us, until finally the devil's kingdom shall be utterly destroyed and sin, death, and hell exterminated, and that we may live forever in perfect righteousness and blessedness."

THE APOSTLES AS MISSIONARIES

> "Apostles or evangelists...[have] no place in well-constituted churches."

■ *The Great Commission (Mt. 28:16-20) received a quite different interpretation by John Calvin than that common today. In his magnum opus,* The Institutes of the Christian Religion, *the reformer calls the apostles "the first architects of the Church, appointed to lay its foundations all over the world." Was the Great Commission that was mandated fulfilled by the first apostles? Calvin's reply is equivocal. On the one hand, he admits that God later raised up other apostles, prophets, and evangelists. On the other hand, he finds no place for such "extraordinary" offices in "well-constituted churches."*

*Apostles, Prophets, and Evangelists**

Those who preside over the government of the Church, according to the institution of Christ, are named by Paul, first, "apostles;" secondly, "prophets;" thirdly, "evangelists;" fourthly, "pastors;" lastly, "teachers" (Eph. 4:11). Of these, only the two last sustain an ordinary office in the Church: the others were such as the Lord raised up at the commencement of his kingdom, and such as he still raises up on particular occasions, when required by the necessity of the times. The nature of the apostolic office is manifest from this command: "Go preach the gospel to every creature" (Mk. 16:15). No certain limits are prescribed, but the whole world is assigned to them, to be reduced to obedience to Christ; that by disseminating the gospel wherever they could, they might erect his kingdom in all nations. Therefore Paul, when he wished to prove his apostleship, declares, not merely that he had gained some one city for Christ, but that he had propagated the gospel far and wide, and that he had not built upon the foundation of others, but had planted Churches where the name of the Lord had never been heard before. The "apostles," therefore, were missionaries, who were to reduce the world from their revolt to true obedience to God, and to establish his kingdom universally by the preaching of the gospel. Or, if you please, they were the first architects of the Church, appointed to lay its

---

*Excerpts from John Calvin, *Institutes of the Christian Religion* (1559), IV, 3, 4, ed. Warfield (Grand Rapids, MI: Eerdmans, 1949), II: 320-21; cf. Bosch, TM, 245.

foundations all over the world. Paul gives the appellation of "prophets," not to all interpreters of the Divine will, but only to those who were honoured with some special revelation. Of these, either there are none in our day, or they are less conspicuous. By "evangelists," I understand those who were inferior to the apostles in dignity, but next to them in office, and who performed similar functions. Such were Luke, Timothy, Titus, and others of that description; and perhaps also the seventy disciples, whom Christ ordained to occupy the second station from the apostles (Lk. 10:1). According to this interpretation, which appears to me perfectly consistent with the language and meaning of the apostle, those three offices were not instituted to be of perpetual continuance in the Church, but only for that age when Churches were to be raised where none had existed before, or were at least to be conducted from Moses to Christ. Though I do not deny, that, even since that period, God has sometimes raised up apostles or evangelists in their stead, as he has done in our own time. For there was a necessity for such persons to recover the Church from the defection of Antichrist. Nevertheless, I call this an extraordinary office, because it has no place in well-constituted Churches.

CHURCH GROWTH ONLY BY GOD'S POWER

> "Pray God that his reign might increase...since the power to do so is not in us."

■ *John Calvin (1509-1564), like his contemporary Martin Luther, emphasized the sovereignty of God in his theology. In the following excerpt from a 1562 sermon on 2 Samuel 5:6-12, Calvin compared the fortunes of the contemporary church to that of King David seeking to win Jerusalem, which was occupied by the Jebusites, the enemies of God. God's reign shall increase, but not by human work or church effort. It will come only by God's electing love.*

*God Must Build His Church**

Inasmuch as the kingdom of David was a type of our Lord Jesus Christ, which is the state of the Church, it was not enough that God, in one swoop, should establish the kingdom of his Son. Rather, he had to cause it to grow and multiply day by day, which is quite necessary. For when God had given some sign of advancing his Church and making it fruitful, it seems that all has been won, and that only laughter awaits us—and we, like foolish people, despise this grace which is so necessary. It is the same as if we no longer had the least need of God, and were carrying in our pocket everything that we could wish. It says that God must build his Church, give it foundations and direct it (cf. Eph. 2:20). On the other hand, he must maintain it,

---

*Excerpts from John Calvin, Sermon on "David's Dealings with the Jebusites and Hiram" (1562), in *Sermons on 2 Samuel, Chapters 1-13* (Edinburgh: Banner of Truth Trust, 1992), 193-95; cf. Bosch, TM, 245.

and not only that, but he must make it grow and increase. For the reign of our Lord Jesus Christ will never be perfect in this world. Far from it.…Even the faithful will be full of many weaknesses and imperfections. Hence, it means nothing for the reign of Jesus Christ to be set up once in our midst unless it is maintained. For, because we are so fragile without his help, all will fall down like water if not fortified from on high.

The Kingdom Must Keep Growing

Then in the second place, we must increase and this kingdom must keep growing, that is, in numbers. Hence, those who have disposed the doctrine of the Gospel, and have been open enemies of God, must be held in check, in order to give place to it. And the hypocrites must be known, or at least held back in such a way that they cannot do harm. Also, he must augment the gracious influence of his Spirit in those whom he has already renewed. In brief, he must bless us in such a way that the kingdom of Jesus Christ will increase. From whence will it come? We must always remind ourselves of this word: "God must do it." For if it were a question of conforming ourselves to him by our own action, far from doing so, we would discover ourselves to be utterly weak; it would only take a blow to knock us down. Well, the devil strikes a hundred thousand times a day. We would thus be thrown back every minute if God did not sustain us with his hand.

Pray That God's Reign Might Increase

It should incite us to prayer and intercession when it says that God was with David. And why? Because that is where growth and increase come from. Let us notice, in the first place, how much the Church in general needs to be increased, for the number of believers is very small. Indeed, there are many who are being butchered in the mouths of wolves. We see our poor brothers killed and slashed. We see raving wolves who spare them not, and it ought to make our hair stand on end. We see so many countries which are still peacefully in the possession of the devil and of antichrist. When, therefore, we see that the reign of our Lord Jesus Christ is only over a small handful of people here and there—one could even say that the state of the Church is in disarray and that it would take practically nothing to reduce it to destruction and ruin—we have good reason to pray God that he will be pleased to increase and advance us. Moreover, even when we see that some are preaching and publishing the Word of God in several places without contradiction, and that great and small want to obey it, let us realize that we are still very far from seeing it advance as it should. Our very life misleads us, for we have so many vices that turn us aside from following our leader that it almost seems that we are turning our back on him, rather than approaching him. All the more, therefore, should we pray God that his reign might increase, that he will watch over it and keep his hand upon it, since the power to do so is not in us.

A CONTINUING APOSTOLIC AUTHORITY

"The Church...must continue to care for the preaching of the gospel to the unbelieving nations."

■ *Only one theologian of the Reformation period was able to emancipate himself completely from the dominant Lutheran and Calvinist view that the Great Commission was fulfilled by the apostles. The Dutch theologian Adrian Saravia (1531-1613) was a younger contemporary of Calvin. He was a Reformed pastor first in Antwerp, next in Brussels, and later preacher and professor in Leyden (1582-87). Fleeing persecution in 1587, he crossed over to England, where he attained high esteem and died as Dean of Westminster in 1613. In his tract,* De diversis ministrorum, *Saravia argued that the apostles themselves could only in limited measure have carried out the Great Commission. Two centuries later, William Carey would popularize Saravia's contention that the Great Commission applies to the whole Church in all subsequent times.*

*Apostolic Guidance Does Not Cease**

The form of apostolic guidance does not cease with the death of the apostles and evangelists.

It is a fact that the form of apostolic guidance, believed to have come to an end at the death of the apostles, can in no way be demonstrated as such from the authority of scripture, nor by reason, nor even by the example of the fathers. It matters not at all that the apostles are said to have had extraordinary power; for indeed by the same reason it would be possible to deny anyone the power of baptizing and of preaching the gospel. For if there were extraordinary things with the apostles, they were not able to leave them to posterity; and the same reasoning demands that neither were they able to leave the authority for preaching the gospel or for baptizing after their own time. I should therefore wish to establish the cause why rather the form of ruling the church which was under the apostles should today cease, as the preaching of the gospel, as well as the administration of baptism and of the Lord's supper. For the power of all these things was equally extraordinary, as indeed the guidance of the church....

The Great Commission Our Mandate

The command to preach the gospel to all nations, once received by the apostles who are now departed, continues to obligate the church, and for which there is necessary a continuing apostolic authority.

---

*Adrian Saravia, *De Diversis Ministrorum Evangelii Gradibus, sicut a Domino fuerunt instituti* (London: 1590), Chaps. 16, 17, pp. 64-67; excerpts translated from the Latin by Paul Schrodt; cf. Bosch, TM, 247.

The command of preaching the gospel and the sending to every nation are precepts to be understood of the apostles, but are also understood to obligate the church. For the command of announcing the gospel to unbelieving nations referred not only to the age of the apostles, but to all peoples which might exist until the end of the world. Indeed, Matthew in his last chapter where the Lord says there is given to him all power in heaven and on earth, and here orders that, going they should teach all nations, etc., says: "I am with you, even to the end of the world." And this phrase manifestly cannot refer to the apostles alone, but to all those whom he commands in a confident spirit, and to whom he promises to accompany himself.

This promise may not be separated from a higher precept. Whence it is apparent that the church is so mandated by Christ that, once the apostles have passed away, it must continue to care for the preaching of the gospel to the unbelieving nations according to a plan with due respects for times, places, and persons for which a certain suitability may be discovered for the affair.

If the apostolic authority had been temporary, a purely personal and peculiar gift, and not intended for their associates and helpers, they would be present for the Lord's work for which they were destined. Yet since they knew their ministry and those things for which they enjoyed authority rather to have been given to the church than to persons, they understood the making of companions in their apostolic power, whom they also understood as their successors.

Such a work could not be accomplished with only a few men. In the same way that the command of the Lord obligated the apostles so far as they were able to stretch themselves in their own mortality, that is, for a very short time in which they were to be victorious after the reception of the Holy Spirit—even in that time there did not cease the promise of help nor the deputation to the nations by the Lord of the gospel.

It is necessary, therefore, to have many helpers and colleagues for the Lord's work. And if they are not able to perfect it themselves, what is begun is left to those following to complete.

And if indeed with the apostles there were to have migrated to heaven the apostolic deputation, and especially the care of the several churches, the bishops whom the apostles left as their successors would have judged the further propagation of the gospel in no way as referring to them, and the kingdom of Christ would never have grown to such an extent.

Has the Gospel Come to Every Nation?

Is it necessary to parade examples of the fathers from the primitive church? With what application, with what labor, and with what blood of martyrs have not the churches been planted and irrigated? The story is so well known that simply to rehearse it would not be profitable.

There are nevertheless too many today (in my judgment) who reject this opinion as an Anabaptist fable, when the church is still said to have apostolic men [and women], if not apostles. Yet they themselves should understand. Has indeed the gospel after these fifteen hundred years come to every nation? In the intervening time how many nations (to whom the apostles did not come) can one list who have received Christ the Lord through the preaching of pious [Christians] (who have succeeded the apostles)? From such reasoning do I then conclude that the mandate of this deputation for preaching the gospel retains its force and obligation in the church for so long as there are peoples who do not know the Lord.

That today no one is sent by the churches of Christ to the nations which are ignorant of Christ does not argue about the power of sending, but of the poverty of those sending those who are suitable, or indeed of the lack of zeal for propagating the kingdom of Christ.

Apostolic Authority

No one should tempt the Lord. For he even turned the feet of his apostles towards Jerusalem to discharge the duty for which they were chosen, in anticipation of their receiving the Holy Spirit. It is necessary for a [person] first to be equipped in the necessary gifts of the Holy Spirit for such a task before [they] might initiate it. But since the judgment of one person can be rash or even erroneous, it is necessary for the authority of the church to intercede. For the apostolic authority is necessary which, if the church did not exercise it, no matter how many suitable [persons] it might acquire, it would have no power for sending them.

No one is able to confer on another what [one] does not have. And to [one] who is sent (whether apostle, evangelist, or bishop if you so call him), there is not needed less power than Timothy or Titus exercised in a former time when taking on a province.

The church therefore possesses this designated authority through the keys, which the Lord gave not so much to Peter and his colleagues as to the church. It can then do today what formerly in the right circumstances it was capable of, namely of committing to [those] suitable for the purpose the office of preaching the gospel with apostolic authority.

A COMMISSION ALREADY FULFILLED

> "The voice of the apostles...penetrated even the most remote corners of the world."

■ *The seventeenth century, the age of Lutheran orthodoxy in Germany, was not a time of systematic mission activity to other lands. The arguments used were: 1) that the original apostles preached the Good News in all the world, thereby fulfilling the Great Commission; 2) that the church, therefore, has no commission left for a "mission to the world"* (vocatio universalis); *3) this mission is binding today only for the ruler of a specific country; and 4) they will act only as God provides a more appropriate time and opportunity. Philipp Nicolai (1556-1608), the famous hymn writer, was a principal exponent of this argu-*

ment. In De Regno Christi *in 1597, he developed a "geography of missions," attempting to prove that the Gospel had been proclaimed throughout the whole world in the apostolic age as well as in later times.*

*Prophets and Apostles Reached All Nations**

It is certain that the kingdom of our Lord and Savior Jesus Christ, by its external characteristics of service of the word, exists in the exercise of the sacraments bound with the Gospel. This is as the Lord ordered that every one is to preach to every creature and to all peoples.... The starting point of this Kingdom should be, as the prophets have witnessed to, in Jerusalem, and from there at the time of the fourth world monarchy (Daniel 2:40 ff.), extend and expand from Zion across all peoples and nations....

I want in this chapter [to] move on to the kingdoms farther on in the North, East, South, and West and talk about the present expansion there of the Kingdom of Christ.... I will begin with the peoples of the North... Directly beneath the North Pole is Iceland.... The majority of its people were once convinced that the entrance to hell was located on this island underneath Mount Heckel. Out of the depths of this terrible abyss one was supposed to hear the lament and forlorn wailing of the damned, so that their voices could be heard a mile away.... Lasting honor is due the most pious kings of Denmark and Norway, who... were especially concerned that even the most remote islands of their kingdoms, including Iceland, would be freed from the dross of popish superstition, and won over by the bright light of the Gospel.... Thus the Christian faith is practiced even in the nations close to the Pole... and covered by the soothing aroma of Christ.

Asia

Let us now travel to the East. The Persians are even further East and rule over a vast empire... they are even quite humane... and they permit the Christian religion in the Ethiopian rites amongst their provinces.... Thus the Christian faith grows amidst the Persians, gains on importance and leads those peoples dependent upon Islam to largely abandon the superstition of their barbaric religion....

Due East of Persia is India.... Even though that people is ravaged by the vain belief in false gods (i.e. Hinduism), they still retain in their sacred rites some rather clear indications of Christian religion who were once introduced by the apostles.... That is because their priests, whom they call Brahmans... believe that God in human form (Shiva and Vishnu) walked on earth in order to redeem humankind from eternal damnation. The educated among them revere very faithfully Sun-

---

*Philipp Nicolai, *Commentariorum de Regno Christi, Vaticaniis Propheticis et Apostolicis Accomodatorum*, I:1-95 *passim* (Frankfurt, 1597); translated by Daniel Hofmann from the excerpts in German in *Mission in Quellentexten,* ed. Werner Raupp (Erlangen: Verlag der Evang.-Luth. Mission, 1990), 64-66; cf. Bosch, TM, 249-51.

day....Furthermore, India is, apart from the indigenous people, who have fallen prey to the superstitions of the Brahmans, inhabited by a large number of those who have accepted the teachings of the Gospel of the apostle Thomas and who have...themselves always demonstrated by an invincible faith and steadfastness....

The Jesuits...when they try to convince the superstitious Indians of the merits of Christianity, they begin not with the authority of the Roman Church, nor with human statutes, or the mass, purgatory, good works, or the deal with indulgences, but, during their first encounter, they talk about Fall of the first parents, about Damnation...and the undeserved salvation through Christ alone, whom one must have faith in and in whose name one must be baptized....Thus these Jesuits, no matter how popish they may be otherwise, have begun a work amongst oriental heathens of which one cannot be too critical.

Since the East has by far the most Christians, and since in Armenia, Persia, Chaldea, Asia Minor, and the remaining provinces of the eastern world many admirers of our faith may be found, so much so that for every one Muslim thirty Christians will confront him...Islam could easily be done away with, so that, while the *Qu'ran* is slowly fading away, Christendom alone will be victorious.

Africa

To the South lies Africa....On the other side of Egypt and Syria...stretches the enormous empire of that Christian monarch, Ethiopia....There is no doubt that Ethiopians have come to Jerusalem to pray...as one can see in the example of the court official of queen Candace...[Acts 8:27-39]. Upon his return to Ethiopia, he supposedly baptized the queen and a majority of the royal family as well as the people.

Other African coastal nations are subject to the rule of Spain, and are rumored to have accepted the entire Christian faith, albeit only the popish rites....In this city [Fes, the most important center of Islam in Morocco]...more than 80,000 people have rejected the Muslim heresy and have accepted the Christian faith....

The Americas

Prior to the arrival of the Spanish, the peasant-like, simple, peaceful and barbaric native peoples possessed only a horrible and loathsome crudeness, this with the exception of the Peruvians and Mexicans who are more human than the rest....Their religion is pagan,...but not without some indication that they once had been exposed to Christianity...Johannes Lerius tells about Brazilians [sixteenth-century Geneva Mission to Brazil]...that many years ago a man came and tried...to lead them to obedience to God....Because it would be almost impossible, that such a huge part of the world and such a big community of the human race would have remained untouched by the voice of the apostles for such a long time, since, according to Psalm 19, their witness came to all the peoples and in accordance with God's will penetrated even the most remote corners of the world....However, the truth of the Gospel came to a standstill due to the thanklessness of the people and their apathy toward that Gospel, and it disappeared altogether due to the ignorance of the human heart.

The Depths of God's Kingdom

What I have written thus far...will certainly be welcomed by pious readers, so that they can imagine the depths of God's Kingdom...[and see that] there is now no place on earth, no island, no empire, no people, where the call of the Christian religion has not entered....Someone could ask now whether I consider the seeds of the roman doctrine and papal hierarchy...as a way of growth of Christendom, and whether I consider the teachings of the Ethiopians [i.e., the Coptic Church] and the Moskovites [i.e., the Russian Orthodox Church], which has not just a few faults in itself, as the Kingdom of the Gospel. To this I respond:...The text of Holy Scripture, the Decalogue, the Lord's Prayer, the Sacraments, Baptism and Lord's Supper, are ways in which the church is planted and multiplied. These do not cease to be what they are, even when they are managed by impure men, who are spoiled and covered by the scum of diverse heresies. They remain, despite the apostasy of the teachers, tools of grace, by whose help the hearts of many people are attracted...and converted....It is precisely in this way in which Jesuits and papal priest achieve with the sowing of the Christian articles of faith, the Decalogue, and the Lord's Prayer...as well as the performing of baptism the Church of Jesus Christ...in the name of God among Indians and Americans....

As I close this first chapter, the pious readers will be able to be assured with no small certainty of faith, as they ponder upon it, that even though the origins of the Kingdom and Christ's Church were insignificant, how marvelously since then the expansion of it occurred, and how it now reaches beyond all nations and borders...[and] that all the kingdoms of the world are now subject to it.

SERVING BOTH SOUL AND BODY

> "The service of the body [is] connected with the service of the soul."

■ *Bartholomäus Ziegenbalg (1682-1719), in his theology of mission, is representative of the finest Pietist thought of the early eighteenth century. It reflects the teaching of the noted theologian A. H. Francke, under whom he studied at the University of Halle. Although German by nationality, he and H. Plüschau were ordained in Copenhagen and sponsored by the Danish crown as the first Protestant missionaries to India. Arriving in the Danish colony of Tranquebar in 1706, Ziegenbalg, by thorough study of the Tamil language, culture, and of Hinduism, as well as wise catechesis, laid foundations for creative mission that have proven efficacious even to this day.*

*Devoted Service**

As the body is bound to the soul, so precisely is the service of the body connected with the service of the soul, and these cannot be separated from each other. This work demands the service of the whole [person]. If I deny such service, I deny that in which the Scripture places the proper manner of faith and love.... The more one devotes [oneself] to the service of [neighbors], and gladly helps [them] in bodily and spiritual needs, the stronger one must be in Christianity.

THE PROPER PURPOSE OF PREACHING

"Millions...called through the preaching of the Gospel."

■ *Nikolaus Ludwig, Count of Zinzendorf (1700-1760), is noted as the promoter of Moravianism. He was reared in a strongly Pietist atmosphere and educated at Halle under the tutelage of August Hermann Francke. His Pietism took the form of an ardent devotion to Jesus and a passion to spread the Christian faith throughout the world. From the village of Herrnhut on his estate, Bishop Zinzendorf sent out Moravian missionaries to various parts of the world, including those who profoundly influenced John Wesley. In 1746, the bishop traveled to London to clarify the relationship of the Moravians to the Church of England and, on September 4, 1746, at the Fetters Lane Chapel, preached sermons containing his missionary motivation.*

*The Blessed Calling***

Preached on the same day, September 4, 1746

TEXT: Matthew 22:2 and Luke 14:17. "The kingdom of heaven may be compared to a king who gave a marriage feast for his son"; "and at supper-time he sent his servants to say to those who had been invited, 'Come; everything is ready.'"[5]

My friends! We must establish this principle, that the blessed, fruitful, and almost irresistible[6] "calling in" of many thousands of souls presupposes a little flock in the house which cleaves to the Saviour, with body and soul, souls which are already there, united with the Saviour, so that one may point to these very people with the finger when one wants to invite others. It is an advantage, a blessing, a

---

*Excerpt from Bartolomäus Ziegenbalg, "Letter to Christopher Wendt, 15th August 1718," in E. Arno Lehmann, *It Began at Tranquebar* (Madras: Christian Literature Society, 1956), 87; cf. Bosch, TM, 254.

**Excerpts from Nikolaus Ludwig Count von Zinzendorf, *Nine Public Lectures on Important Subjects in Religion . . . 1746*, translated and edited by George W. Forell (Iowa City: University of Iowa Press, 1973), 25, 32; cf. Bosch, TM, 253-54.

sound preaching of the Gospel, when one can say, "Come, everything is ready. I can show you the people who are already there; just come and see." This is the suppertime, when bride and bridegroom are already prepared, have already spoken with each other, have already completed their blessed engagement, and now, in order to solemnize it still more, make their appearance at a place. One perceives a people of God with whom the bridegroom concerns himself, people who glory in him, as he does in them.

Millions Awaiting Salvation

But there are still millions of souls who come to participation in this salvation who are at the marriage and are also joyful, who draw a conclusion about the future from the present blessedness, and who join the supper as invited guests; and they are always called through the preaching of the Gospel.

Therefore there is no ground to debate whether God performs the work of conversion in a soul Himself or whether He makes use of men [and women] to this end. Certainly He is in need of no one, for He Himself can draw, can beget, can bring forth, through His Spirit all the souls whom He wants to give to His Son, whom He will marry to Him at the time when He will be the consecrator, when the creature shall marry the Creator. And this He actually does. But these are not enough; they do not make a *numerus clausus,* a number which may not be exceeded. Rather, the number is innumerable; the multitudes who through the Gospel of merits and death of Jesus receive the invitation to go to the marriage will exceed all thought. "Compel people to come in, that my house may be filled" (Lk. 14:23), that innumerable more may share my salvation; "Come, O blessed of my Father, inherit the kingdom prepared for you," etc. (Mt. 25:34).

This is an admirable thing, to know that our Lord, as rich and great and generous as He is, nevertheless is not satisfied that He has His assured reward, the souls of whom He is sure; but, having already been crucified and dead, he wants to be looked at and to manifest Himself as the Saviour of all...."Go into all the world and preach the gospel to the whole creation: (Mk. 16:15); whoever will now believe you, whoever will hold to me, whomever I will please, whoever will come to love me,...shall be saved; [and] shall be delivered from this present evil world and from the wrath to come and shall enter into my rest."

This then is the ground and purpose of the preaching of the Gospel plain and clear.

NOTES

1. "Gospel Sermon, Second Sunday after Easter" (Lenker Edition, vol. 12, no. 20).
2. "Gospel Sermon, Ascension Day" (Lenker Edition, vol. 12, no. 3).
3. Ibid., vol. 12, nos. 11-15.
4. I.e., the return of Christ.
5. Zinzendorf gives Matthew 22:1 ff. as the text. But the verse from Luke, which is cited

later in the lecture, matches the German exactly. Matthew 22:1 has relevance only as an introduction, and Matthew 22:2 takes care of only the first half of the cited text.

6. Zinzendorf uses the English word.

4

Mission in the Wake of the Enlightenment

Let others creep by timid steps, and slow,
On plain experience lay foundations low,
By common sense to common knowledge bred,
And last, to Nature's cause thro' nature led,
All-seeing in thy mists, we want no guide,
Mother of arrogance, and source of pride!
We nobly take the high priori road,
And reason downward, till we doubt of God.[1]

In 1743, Alexander Pope wrote this critique of the Enlightenment thought of his day. He catches its dominant characteristic—radical anthropocentrism.

Bosch delineates seven "contours of the Enlightenment worldview":

1) the undisputed primacy of reason:
2) the separation between subject and object;
3) the substitution of the cause-effect scheme for belief in purpose;
4) the infatuation with progress;
5) the unsolved tension between "fact" and "value";
6) the confidence that every problem and puzzle could be solved; and
7) the idea of the emancipated, autonomous individual (TM, 342).

Emerging in the seventeenth century, the paradigm received full development in the eighteenth, and then was applied in efforts to transform society in the nineteenth and early twentieth centuries.

During the same period, immense social and political changes also influenced mission thinking and practice. Among them, Bosch identifies modified relationships between church and state, migrations of peoples, and western colonialism and imperial expansion (TM, 274-84).

Like the plurality of political systems in which they operated, the churches during this period developed a variety of mission motifs—often in tension and conflict with one another. The selections below are chosen to represent the following motifs identified by Bosch.

1. The Glory of God. *Classic Calvinism emphasized God's sovereignty and initiative in saving people. In the Enlightenment era, this became modified to include an increasing place for human response to God's providence. Jonathan Edwards, theologian of the First Great Awakening in North America and missionary to Native Americans in western Massachusetts, believed in the importance of the faithfuls' fervent prayers for the extension of God's kingdom. The diary of David Brainerd, a pioneer missionary to Native Americans (1743-47), discloses his consuming passion to witness for the glory of God and to work for the salvation of others. A missionary sermon of 1805 in the Maine* Piscatagua Evangelical Magazine *includes the conviction that the glory of God "ought to be the governing motive in all missionary exertions."*

2. The Biblical Motif. *Although Saravia and Hubmaier on the continent argued for the abiding validity of the Great Commission, it was the English Baptist William Carey who popularized Matthew 28:18-20 as* the *major biblical mandate for missions. One of the missionaries inspired by Carey's argument, Adoniram Judson, became the pioneer Baptist missionary to Burma.*

3. Mission and the Millennium. *Apocalyptic expectations waxed and waned during this period. Samuel Hopkins wrote (1793) during the Napoleonic Wars and Europe's general upheaval. His urgency for mission was related to his premillennial conviction that conversion of sinners, faithfulness of true Christians, and promotion of benevolence must take place before Christ's second coming. Eighty-two years later, in 1875, James Hudson Taylor, father of "faith missions" and founder of the China Inland Mission, related his conviction that "the coming of the Lord" was "the strongest motivation for consecration and service" in the New Testament.*

4. The Gospel and Culture. *In the wake of the scientific revolution that gave technological superiority to the West, bringing the benefits of "Christian civilization" to native peoples was heard increasingly as a motive for mission. Samuel Worcester, clerk of the American Board of Commissioners for Foreign Missions (ABCFM) in 1816, articulated this position in the board's objectives for Native American missions.*

5. Mission and Manifest Destiny. *Others went further. Heman Humphrey, delivering the ordination sermon for pioneer missionaries to the Sandwich (Hawaiian) Islands in 1819, expressed his belief that God in his providence had given the land as the "American Israel," as Yahweh had given the Israelites the promised land to be possessed.*

6. Mission and Colonialism. *Where European powers expanded their colonies in the eighteenth and nineteenth centuries, missionaries of those nations were not far behind. Almost always these missionaries became advocates for colonial expansion. Returning to England in 1860 after his cross-Africa exploration to open up the "dark continent," David Livingstone advocated an alliance for "commerce, civilization and Christianity." This became a common motive for mission among British Protestants in the colonial era.*

7. Voluntarism. *The Enlightenment ideal of the emancipated, autonomous individual found its corollary in the autonomous voluntary missionary society, as well as in the goal of forming autonomous self-reliant churches. Rufus Anderson, secretary of the ABCFM from 1826 to 1866, championed the latter, arguing that it was consistent with Paul's missionary spirit. The selection by L. H. Daggett on the Women's Missionary Movement in 1894 captures the spirit of voluntarism in mission societies organized and directed by women to support women in mission.*

8. Missionary Fervor, Optimism, and Pragmatism. *Enlightenment belief in progress and confidence that every problem can be solved found its missionary spokesperson in John R. Mott who, amid the general euphoria in 1900, wrote that "there is no insuperable obstacle to world-wide evangelization."*

EARNESTLY PRAY FOR REVIVAL

> "This is the chief season for the bestowment of ...the benefits of Christ's redemption."

■ *Jonathan Edwards (1703-1758) is best known as the first great North American theologian. In addition, he was both a prominent leader in the First Great Awakening and a missionary to Native Americans in western Massachusetts. Receiving from friends in Scotland a proposal for a "Concert of Prayer" to unite Christians concerned with church revival on both sides of the Atlantic, Edwards published a pamphlet that became an influential tract promoting mission spirituality and Christian unity.* The Humble Attempt... *was read as widely in the American colonies and Great Britain as David Brainerd's* Diary. *In 1792, Edwards inspired William Carey and leaders of the first mission society in the United States to include in their missionary endeavors fervent prayers for the extension of God's kingdom.*

*A Proposed Concert of Prayer**

Let us go speedily to pray before the Lord, *and to seek the* Lord *of hosts. I will go also. Yea, many people and strong nations shall come to seek the* Lord *of hosts* (Zech. 8:21).

In October, A.D. 1744, a number of ministers in Scotland, taking into consideration the state of God's church, and of the world...judged that the providence of God, at such a day, did loudly call upon such as were concerned for the welfare of Zion, to *united extraordinary* applications to the God of all grace, suitably acknowledging him as the fountain of all spiritual benefits and blessings of his church, and earnestly praying to him, that he would *appear in his glory*, and favour Zion, and

---

*Excerpts from Jonathan Edwards, "An Humble Attempt to Promote Explicit Agreement and Visible Union of God's People in Extraordinary Prayer" (1748), in *The Works of President Edwards* (New York: S. Conserve, 1829; facsimile reprint ed., New York: Burt Franklin, 1968), 2: 431, 440, 447-48, 461; cf. Bosch, TM, 277-78, 280.

manifest his compassion to the world...by an abundant effusion of his *Holy Spirit* on all the churches, and the whole habitable earth, to revive true religion in all parts of *Christendom*, and to deliver *all nations* from their great and manifold spiritual calamities and miseries, and bless them with the unspeakable benefits of the kingdom of our glorious Redeemer, and *fill the whole earth with his glory.* Consulting one another on the subject, they looked upon *themselves,* for their own part, obliged to engage in this duty; and, as far as in them lay, to persuade *others* to the same: and to endeavour to find out and fix on some *method*, that should most effectually tend to promote and uphold such extraordinary application to heaven among God's people....

The Coming Global Church Growth

It is evident from scripture, that there is *yet remaining* a great *advancement* of the interest of *religion* and the *kingdom of Christ* in this world, by an *abundant outpouring of the Spirit of God,* far greater and more extensive than ever yet has been. It is certain, that many things, which are spoken concerning a *glorious* time of the church's *enlargement* and *prosperity* in the *latter days*, have never been fulfilled. There has never yet been any propagation and prevalence of religion, in any wise, of that *extent* and *universality* which the prophecies represent. It is often foretold and signified, in a great variety of strong expressions, that there should a time come, when *all nations,* through the whole habitable world, should embrace the true religion, and be brought into the church of God. It was often promised to the patriarchs, that *in their seed all the nations,* or (as it is sometimes expressed) *all the families of the earth shall be blessed* (Gen. 12:3, 18:13, 22:18, 26:4, 28:14). Agreeably to this, it is said of the Messiah that *all nations shall serve him* (Ps. 72:11); and in verse 17, *[All] shall be blessed in him, and all nations shall call him blessed.* And in Isaiah 2:2 it is said, that *all nations shall flow unto the mountain of the house of the Lord.* And Jeremiah 3:17 that *all nations shall be gathered unto the name of the Lord of Jerusalem, and shall walk no more after the imagination of their evil heart. That all flesh shall come and worship before the Lord* (Isa. 66:23). *And that all flesh should see the glory of God together* (Isa. 60:5). *And that all flesh should come to him that hears prayer* (Ps. 65:2). Christ compares the *kingdom of heaven* in this world *to leaven, which a woman took and hid in three measures of meal, till the whole was leavened* (Mt. 13:33)....

God has appointed Christ to be the heir of the world in his kingdom of grace, and to possess and reign over all nations, through the propagation of his gospel, and the power of his Spirit communicating the blessing of it....

But of all the time we have been speaking of this is the *chief season,* for the bestowment of this blessing; the *main season* of success to all that Christ did and suffered in the work of our redemption. Before this, the Spirit of God is given but very sparingly, and but few are saved; but *then* it will be far otherwise; wickedness shall be rare then, as virtue and piety had been before: and undoubtedly, by far the greatest number of them that ever receive the benefits of Christ's redemption, from the beginning of the world to the end of it, will receive it in that time.*

CONVERSION OF THE INDIANS

"God is powerfully at work...true and genuine convictions of sin."

■ *David Brainerd (1718-1747) was born in Haddam, Connecticut. Touched by the Great Awakening, he entered Yale College in 1739 only to be expelled shortly thereafter for attending a separatist meeting and making disparaging remarks about the college rector. In 1743, he decided to give himself to work among the Indians and was appointed by agents of the Scottish Society for the Promotion of Christian Knowledge (SPCK) for work in western Massachusetts. Tuberculosis, which he contracted at an early age, led to his death five years later in the home of Jonathan Edwards, his protégé and prospective father-in-law. Fortunately Edwards gained possession of Brainerd's diary and published this account of Brainerd's travels, work, and meditations in 1749. In it Brainerd reveals the spirit of the Great Awakening in his consuming passion for the glory of God and the salvation of all persons. For more than a century, the* Diary *was a classic among North Atlantic Protestants, profoundly influencing John Wesley, William Carey, Henry Martyn, and others in their motivations for missions.*

*The Rise and Progress of a Remarkable Work of Grace***

August 2. In the evening I retired, and my soul was drawn out in prayer to God; especially for my poor people, to whom I had sent word that they might gather together that I might preach to 'em the next day. I was much enlarged in praying for their saving conversion; and scarce ever found my desires of anything of this nature so sensibly and clearly (to my own satisfaction) disinterested, and free from selfish views. It seemed to me I had no care, or hardly any desire to be the instrument of so glorious a work as I wished and prayed for among the Indians: If the blessed work might be accomplished to the honor of God and the enlargement of the dear

---

*The number of the inhabitants of the earth will doubtless then be vastly multiplied; and the number of redeemed ones much more. . . . instead of the *few* true and thorough christians now in some few countries, every *nation* on the face of the whole earth shall be converted to christianity, and every country shall be full of true christians; so that the successive multiplication of true saints through the *thousand years,* will begin with that vast advantage, beyond the multiplication of [humankind]; . . . it is probable that there will be an *hundred thousand* times more, that will actually be redeemed to God by Christ's blood, during that period of the church's prosperity, than ever had been before, from the beginning of the world to that time.

**Excerpts from Jonathan Edwards, *The Life of David Brainerd* (1749), ed. Norman Pettit, vol. 7 in *The Works of Jonathan Edwards* (New Haven, CT, and London: Yale University Press, 1985), 304-05, 314-15; cf. Bosch, TM, 278.

Redeemer's kingdom, this was my desire and care; and for this mercy I hoped, but with trembling; for I felt what Job expresses, chapter 9:16. My rising hopes respecting the conversion of the Indians have been so often dashed, that my spirit is as it were broken, and courage wasted, and I hardly dare hope.

August 3. Having visited the Indians in these parts in June last, and tarried with them some considerable time, preaching almost daily: at which season God was pleased to pour upon them a spirit of awakening and concern for their souls, and surprisingly to engage their attention to divine truths, I now found them serious, and a number of them under deep concern for an interest in Christ....

August 16. Spent considerable time in conversing privately with sundry of the Indians. Found one that had got relief and comfort after pressing concern, and could not but hope, when I came to discourse particularly with her, that her comfort was of the right kind.

In the afternoon, preached to them from John 6:26-34. Toward the close of my discourse, divine truths were attended with considerable power upon the audience, and more especially after public service was over, when I particularly addressed sundry distressed persons.

There was a great concern for their souls spread pretty generally among them: But especially there were two persons newly awakened to a sense of their sin and misery, one of whom was lately come, and the other had all along been very attentive, and desirous of being awakened, but could never before have any lively view of her perishing state. But now her concern and spiritual distress was such, that I thought I had never seen *any* more pressing. Sundry old men were also in distress for their souls; so that they could not refrain from weeping and crying aloud, and their bitter groans were the most convincing as well as affecting evidence of the reality and depth of their inward anguish. God is powerfully at work among them! True and genuine convictions of sin are daily promoted in many instances, and some are newly awakened from time to time; although some few, who felt a commotion in their passions in days past, seem now to discover that their hearts were never duly affected. I never saw the work of God appear so independent of means as at this time. I discoursed to the people, and spoke what (I suppose) had a proper tendency to promote convictions, and God's manner of working upon them appeared so entirely supernatural, and above means, that I could scarce believe he used me as an instrument, or what I spake as means of carrying on his work: for it seemed, as I thought, to have no connection with, nor dependence upon means in any respect. And although I could not but continue to use the means I thought proper for the promotion of the work, yet God seemed (as I apprehended) to work entirely without them: so that I seemed to do nothing and indeed to have nothing to do but to "stand still and see the salvation of God" (Ex. 14:13), and found myself obliged and delighted to say, "Not unto us," not unto instruments and means, "but to thy name be glory" (Ps. 115:1). God appeared to work entirely alone, and I saw no room to attribute any part of this work to any created arm.

THE GREAT COMMISSION A PRESENT OBLIGATION

"Pity...humanity...[who] call loudly for every possible exertion to introduce the gospel amongst them."

■ *In the late eighteenth century, the prevailing view was that the Great Commission of Jesus, "Go therefore and make disciples of all nations" (Mt. 28:19), had been fulfilled by the apostles and no longer applied to Christians. It was William Carey (1761-1834) who challenged this interpretation. In 1792, he was an impoverished and youthful Baptist pastor, part-time teacher, and shoemaker in England. Initially his 87-page pamphlet,* An Enquiry . . . *had a small sale. It was a brief, compact mission survey of the world, with an introduction refuting the traditional interpretation of the Great Commission. Shortly after its publication, Carey preached his famous sermon, "Expect great things from God; attempt great things for God." Less than five months later, the Baptist Missionary Society was formed, followed in quick succession by the London Missionary Society, the Church Missionary Society, the Religious Tract Society, the British and Foreign Bible Society, and others. Carey sailed for India, and his exhortation and example inspired so many that he became known as the father of Protestant missions.*

*The Lord's Still-binding Commission**

Our Lord Jesus Christ, a little before his departure, commissioned his apostles to *Go, and teach all nations*; or, as another evangelist expresses it, *Go into all the world, and preach the gospel to every creature.* This commission was as extensive as possible, and laid them under obligation to disperse themselves into every country of the habitable globe, and preach to all the inhabitants, without exception, or limitation. They accordingly went forth in obedience to the command, and the power of God evidently wrought with them. Many attempts of the same kind have been made since their day and which have been attended with various success, but the work has not been taken up or prosecuted of late years (except by a few individuals) with that zeal and perseverance with which the primitive Christians went about it. It seems as if many thought the commission was sufficiently put in execution by what the apostles and others have done; that we have enough to do to attend to the salvation of our own [citizens]; and that, if God intends the salvation of the heathen, he will some way or other bring them to the gospel, or the gospel to them. It is thus that multitudes sit at ease, and give themselves no concern about the far greater part of their fellow-sinners, who to this day, are lost in ignorance and idolatry. There seems also to be an opinion existing in the minds of some, that

---

*Excerpts from William Carey, *An Enquiry into the Obligations of Christians to Use Means for the Conversion of the Heathens* (Leicester: Ann Ireland, 1792; facsimile ed., London: Carey Kingsgate, 1961), 3-9, 13; cf. Bosch, TM, 279-81.

because the apostles were extraordinary officers and have no proper successors, and because many things which were right for them to do would be utterly unwarrantable for us, therefore it may not be immediately binding on us to execute the commission, though it was so upon them. To the consideration of such persons I would offer the following observations.

FIRST, If the command of Christ to teach all nations be restricted to the apostles, or those under the immediate inspiration of the Holy Ghost, then that of baptizing should be so too; and every denomination of Christians, except the Quakers, do wrong in baptizing with water at all.

SECONDLY, If the command of Christ to teach all nations be confined to the apostles, then all such ordinary ministers who have endeavoured to carry the gospel to the heathens, have acted without a warrant, and run before they were sent. Yea, and though God has promised the most glorious things to the heathen world by sending his gospel to them, yet whoever goes first, or indeed at all, with that message, unless [they] have a new and special commission from heaven, must go without any authority for so doing.

THIRDLY, If the command of Christ to teach all nations extend only to the apostles, then, doubtless, the promise of the divine presence in this work must be so limited; but this is worded in such a manner as expressly precludes such an idea. *Lo, I am with you always, to the end of the world....*

Home Versus Foreign Missions

It has been objected that there are multitudes in our own nation, and within our immediate spheres of action, who are as ignorant as the South-Sea savages, and that therefore we have work enough at home, without going into other countries. That there are thousands in our own land as far from God as possible, I readily grant, and that this ought to excite us to ten-fold diligence to our work, and in attempts to spread divine knowledge amongst them is a certain fact; but that it ought to supersede all attempts to spread the gospel in foreign parts seems to want proof. Our own country[folk] have the means of grace, and may attend on the word preached if they choose it. They have the means of knowing the truth, and faithful ministers are placed in almost every part of the land, whose spheres of action might be much extended if their congregations were but more hearty and active in the cause; but with them the case is widely different, who have no Bible, no written language (which many of them have not), no ministers, no good civil government, nor any of those advantages which we have. Pity therefore, humanity, and much more Christianity, call loudly for every possible exertion to introduce the gospel amongst them.

DISINTERESTED BENEVOLENCE

"Before the millennium...thousands must be converted."

■ *Although Calvinists placed a strong emphasis on God's sovereignty, they also encouraged men and women to "work out your own salvation with fear and trembling; for it is God who is at work in you" (Phil. 2:12). A generation after Jonathan Edwards, Samuel Hopkins (1721-1803), pastor of the First Congregational Church in Newport, Rhode Island, was the principal exponent of Edwards's revivalistic Calvinism. Hopkins stressed the doctrine of "disinterested benevolence"—the idea that holiness consists in disinterested love for "being in general." Since blacks, Indians, and underprivileged people, wherever they may be, are part of "being in general," they must receive the true Christian's concern. Hopkins believed in the theory of general atonement: that Christ died to save all sinners, both Indians and New England Congregationalists. In his* Treatise on the Millennium, *he argued that the conversion of sinners, the faithfulness of true Christians, and the promotion of benevolence must take place before Christ's second coming.*

*Before the Millennium**

As to the distance of that happy day of salvation from this time; two hundred years, or near so many, will pass off before it will arrive, according to the calculation which has been made from scripture; so that none, now on the stage of life, will live to see and enjoy it on earth. But much may be done by christians who live in this age, to promote its coming on in the proper time, by prayer, and promoting the interest of religion, and the conversion of sinners: For that good day would not come, unless the cause of Christ be maintained to that time, and sinners be converted to keep up the church, and prevent the total extinction of it. In order to this, thousands must be converted, and there must be a succession of professing and real christians down to that day. The doctrines, institutions, and duties of christianity, must be maintained; and there will doubtless be remarkable revivals of religion in many places, and knowledge will increase among true christians, and there will be advances made in the purity of doctrines and worship, and all holy practice, by bringing all these nearer to the standard of the holy scriptures: And the churches will be formed into a greater union with each other; being more and more conformed to the divine pattern, contained in the Bible. Here then is work enough to do, by those who desire and are looking for such a day, to prepare the way for it, and it may be introduced in the proper time; and there is no want of encouragement to do it, even in this view, to be stedfast and unmoveable, always abounding in the work of the Lord, for as much as they may know, that their labour will not be in vain in the Lord (1 Cor. 15:58).

Disinterested and Benevolent

And christians may now have a great degree of enjoyment of that day, and joy

*Excerpts from Samuel Hopkins, *A Treatise on the Millennium* (Boston: Isaiah Thomas and Ebenezer T. Andrews, 1793; reprint ed., New York: Arno Press, 1972), 152-54; cf. Bosch, TM, 290.

in it, though they do not expect to live on earth till it shall come. True christians are disinterested and benevolent to such a degree, that they can enjoy and rejoice in the good of others, even those who may live many ages hence, and in the good and prosperity of the church, and the advancement of the cause and kingdom of Christ in this world, though they should not live to see it. The stronger their faith is, that this good day is coming, and the clearer and more constant view they have of it, and the more desirable it appears to them, that there should be such a time; the higher enjoyment, and greater joy they will have in it, and in the prospect of it. Thus Abraham looked forward by his faith, and saw this day of Christ, when all nations of the earth should be blessed in him, and derived great comfort and joy in this prospect. "Your father Abraham rejoiced to see my day; and he saw it, and was glad" (Jn. 8:57)....

The Christian Dispensation

On the whole, it is hoped that it does appear from what has been said in this dissertation, that there will be a thousand years of prosperity of the church of Christ, in this world; that this is abundantly foretold and held up to view in the Bible; that this will be about the seventh millenary of the world; that it will be a most happy and glorious day, in which the christian dispensation shall have its proper and full effect on earth, in the salvation of men [and women]; to which all the preceding times and events are preparatory: That the degeneracy and increasing prevalence of ignorance, error and wickedness now in the world, especially in Christendom, is preparing for, and hastening on the battle of that great day of God Almighty, in which [hu]mankind will be punished, and the greatest part then on earth destroyed; and then the Millennium will be introduced:—That this is an important and pleasing subject, suited to support and comfort christians in all the dark and evil days which precede it, and to excite them to earnest, constant, united prayer for this coming of Christ, and patient waiting for him, and to constant exertions in all proper ways, to promote his interest and kingdom in the world.

TO THE GLORY OF GOD

> "The glory of God...ought to be the governing motive, in all missionary exertions."

■ *During the first years of the United States, service to the glory of God was the primary missionary motivation. The missionary movement was viewed as God's own action. God's grand design was for the redemption of the whole universe. This work began in creation, continues in acts of divine providence, and will be consummated in God's future time. Jonathan Edwards and the earliest missionary preachers had stressed this belief. The following excerpts from a sermon preached before the Piscataqua Missionary Society in New England in 1805 is representative of thought of the period.*

*The Governing Motive**

"Because for His name sake they went forth taking nothing of the Gentiles. We therefore ought to receive such, that we might be fellow-helpers to the truth" (3 Jn. 7-8).

After having briefly illustrated this passage and shewn that the glory of God, a regard to his honor and praise in the spread of the gospel, ought to be the governing motive in all missionary exertions and the animating principle in the breast of missionaries, the preacher proceeds to shew that it is the duty of all who love Zion, or wish its prosperity, who feel a compassion for their fellow sinners destitute of the means of religious knowledge, of those ordinances and institutions, by which God ordinarily bestows faith, and saves them that believe, to minister to the support and encouragement of such as go forth in this service,...proceeding in his address in the following manner:...

Where shall we find an object that has more numerous or higher claims upon the charity and compassion of the pious and humane of those that love God, or [humanity], than that which is the object of religious missionary societies? While the present reputation, comforts and usefulness of [others] are not totally disregarded, the great object of missionary societies is, to secure these and all their other interests, by affording the means of that knowledge without which the heart cannot be good, in the dispersing of books and pamphlets upon religious and moral subjects, and preaching of that gospel which was designed to open blind eyes, to turn sinners from darkness to light, and from the power of sin and satan unto God....

God in his providence and grace, has awakened in his people an uncommon spirit of pious charity, of missionary enterprize and exertion to carry the joyful sound of the gospel to those who have not heard it, to nations that have as yet sat in the region of the shadow of death....

The Missionary Society

Suffer me then, christian friends, to solicit your patronage to the infantine institution in this state, which has assumed the name of the PISCATAQUA MISSIONARY SOCIETY, and which this day holds out its feeble hands soliciting that you would uphold and strengthen them by your cheerful charity....

Our object is to promote the glory of God, in the spread of the gospel of Jesus Christ, to extend the beneficial influence of that divine system of truth and duty, by furnishing our destitute fellow sinners with the instituted means of religion, that they may be wise to salvation, and with us be prepared for the riches of the inheritance of the saints in light.

---

*Excerpts from *The Piscataqua Evangelical Magazine,* 2 (1805): 206-09; cf. Bosch, TM, 285-86.

CIVILIZING AND CHRISTIANIZING

> "To make the whole tribe English in their language, civilized in their habits, and Christian in their religion; this is the present plan."

■ *The American Board of Commissioners for Foreign Missions (ABCFM), from its founding in 1810, was for its first half-century the largest agency in North America to sponsor missionaries. After beginning its work in India and the Sandwich Islands [Hawaii], it turned its attention in 1816 to missions to Native Americans. In doing so, it renewed a mission engagement pioneered by Congregationalists John Eliot in the 1630s and David Brainerd in the 1740s. Samuel Worcester, clerk of the ABCFM, described the board's objectives as "civilizing and christianizing," in that order. Although missionaries were to learn the native languages, English was to be the medium of instruction in schools to be established, so that the Indians would "more readily become assimilated in habits and manners to their white neighbors." The results of such policies can only be described as depressing failures.*

*The Objects of Native American Missions**

Although the object of civilizing and christianizing the small and scattered tribes of American Indians bears no comparison in magnitude with that of evangelizing the vastly numerous and crowded population of the eastern world; yet it is an object of too great importance to be overlooked, deeply interesting in itself, and presenting very peculiar claims upon the consciences, the feelings, and the liberalities of American Christians. Nor should it be regarded as a hopeless enterprise. The history of missions records few instances since the apostolic age, perhaps, indeed none in proportion to the expense and exertion of greater success in the conversion of the heathens, than that which attended the labors of Eliot, the Mayhews, and Brainerd, among the Indians. It is no wonder that since their day little has been achieved; for little, very little, has been attempted. The spirit of Eliot, of the Mayhews, and of Brainerd, has for a long time slept. Never indeed has the work of civilizing and christianizing our Indian tribes been taken up on a well concerted and extended plan, and conducted with vigor and perseverance; never has such an experiment been made as is now contemplated. To establish schools in the different parts of the tribe under missionary direction and superintendence, for the instruction of the rising generation in common school learning, in the useful arts of life, and in Christianity, so as gradually, with the divine blessing to make the whole tribe English in their language, civilized in their habits, and Christian in their religion;

---

*Excerpts from Samuel Worcester, "1816 Report," in *First Ten Annual Reports of the American Board of Commissioners for Foreign Missions with Other Documents of the Board* (Boston: ABCFM, 1834), 135-36; cf. Bosch, TM, 292, 296.

this is the present plan: and the more it has been contemplated, the more it has presented itself to the minds of the Committee, as being decidedly preferable to any other which has been adopted or proposed. Were the Bible now translated into all the languages of the Indian tribes, it would be of no more use to them than our English Bible; for they could read it no better. They might be taught to read the Bible in the English language with as much ease, as they could be taught to read it in their own; and having learned to read the English language, the sources of knowledge and means of general improvement then opened to them will be incomparably greater and more various than their own language could ever procure for them. Assimilated in language, they will more readily become assimilated in habits and manners to their white neighbors; intercourse will be easy and the advantages to them incalculable. The missionaries, mean while, will make themselves acquainted with the language of the tribe and preach to the aged as well as to the young; and they will avail themselves of the various and precious advantages, which the education of the children will afford, to gain the most favorable access to the parents; and to communicate the knowledge of salvation, and the blessings of civilized life to the people of every age.

LAND TO BE POSSESSED

> "Christendom...is solemnly bound...to set up her banners in every heathen land."

■ *Ordination and commissioning services for missionaries are excellent sources on missionary motivations during the Enlightenment era. In 1819, the Reverend Heman Humphrey, pastor of the Congregational Church in Pittsfield, Massachusetts, delivered the ordination sermon for Hiram Bingham (1789-1869) and Asa Thurston (1787-1868), the pioneer American Board missionaries to the Sandwich Islands [Hawaii]. Humphrey preached on "The Promised Land," using a text from the thirteenth chapter of Joshua. He contended that for the modern church, as for the Israelites, "there remaineth yet very much land to be possessed." He believed that in the divine plan of salvation the United States, like Israel, had been given a special place. He called the land the "American Israel" and believed that if the people supported missionaries with but a fraction of what the nation spent on armaments, God's plan for the conversion of the world would be forwarded.*

*Israel's Mission of Conquest**

"And there remaineth yet very much land to be possessed" (Josh. 13:1).

---

*Excerpts from Heman Humphrey, *The Promised Land: A Sermon delivered at Goshen, (Conn.) at the Ordination of the Rev. Messrs. Hiram Bingham & Asa Thurston as Missionaries to the Sandwich Islands, Sept. 29, 1819* (Boston: Samuel T. Armstrong, 1819), 3-6, 11-14, 16-17; cf. Bosch, TM, 300.

God, as the supreme Ruler and absolute Proprietor of the world, thought fit to give all the land of Canaan to Abraham and his posterity for an everlasting inheritance. This grant was again and again renewed and confirmed to Isaac and Jacob, as heirs of the promise. But they were not to take immediate possession....

Joshua proved himself, in all respects, worthy of the high trust reposed in him. He was pre-eminent both in counsel and in valor. Putting himself at the head of the chosen tribes, he passed the river, and led them at once into the heart of the enemies' country. Every where the idolatrous inhabitants trembled at his approach and nothing could surpass the celerity of his marches, or the impetuousity of his attacks. Nothing could *arrest,* and scarcely could any thing *retard,* his progress. Of the fortifications which had been trusted in as impregnable, one after another submitted to his arms, and, in a word, victory crowned every enterprize. Now, had the Israelites in this state of things, vigorously pushed their advantages with a humble trust in God, they might soon have completed the conquest of Canaan. But their courage seems to have failed them in the midst of the most brilliant success. They wanted faith.... *There remaineth yet very much land to be possessed,* was a cutting reproof of their inactivity and unbelief. And that no more time might be lost, the aged Joshua was commanded to divide this remainder by lot among the tribes, and require them immediately to drive out the heathen, and take possession for themselves and their children.

Our Mission of Conquest

The text admits of an easy, and I think a legitimate application to the present comparative state of the church and the world. As the nation of Israel was then *militant,* so is the church now. As the land of Canaan belonged to Israel, in virtue of a divine grant, so does the world belong to the church; and as God's chosen people still had much to do, before they could come into full and quiet possession of the land, so has the church a great work to accomplish, in subduing the world "to the obedience of Christ." In this spiritual and most interesting sense, *there remaineth yet very much land to be possessed.* The plan of my discourse, therefore, will naturally embrace the following topics: viz.

That immense regions of the earth, which belong to the church, are still unsubdued.

That the ultimate conquest and possession of all these is certain.

That, although the excellency of the power is of God, this great work is to be accomplished by human instrumentality.

That but for the lamentable and criminal apathy of the church, it might have been accomplished ages ago.

That as Christendom now possesses ample resources and ability, she is solemnly bound in the name of God, and with the least possible delay to set up her banners in every heathen land. And,

That the aspects of Divine Providence are peculiarly auspicious to the missionary enterprizes of the day.

Our Work to Accomplish

Although the excellency of the power is of God, this great work is to be accomplished by human instrumentality....

How was the Gospel first propagated, even in an age of miracles? By toil, by perseverance, by encountering a thousand dangers:—by assailing the strong holds of Jewish infidelity and Pagan idolatry. Had the Apostles shut themselves up in Jerusalem, what would have been the consequence? In vain would they have *waited* for the conversion of the heathen. Their commission was, "Go and teach all nations"; and with what zeal did they engage in the perilous undertaking! How great was their self-denial! What inhospitable regions did they visit: how diligently did they plant and water; how skillfully did they wield "the weapons of their warfare, and how mighty were they through God, to the pulling down of strong holds!" It was thus that the spiritual conquest of extensive and populous regions was achieved by the first missionaries; and it was by human instrumentality, in a subsequent age, that the immense fabric of Paganism was demolished in the greatest empire of the world, and that the standard of the cross was planted on the battlements of Rome....

...In the same manner, by the use of means and instruments, is the whole world to be subdued and rendered fruitful. The missionaries now in service must be supported and must receive strong reinforcements. Every foot of ground that has been gained must be kept. Every new advantage must be zealously followed up. The Bible must be translated into all languages, and the means of sending it to every human habitation must be provided. The Gospel must be carried to the heathen, before we can expect them to embrace it. "How shall they call on him in whom they have not believed? And how shall they believe on him of whom they have not heard? And how shall they hear without a preacher? And how shall they preach except they be sent?" Missionaries then must be *sent.* The conversion of the world is to be effected, by the blessing of God upon the prayers and labors of the church.

OBEY!

"God never commands an impossibility."

■ *After the publication of William Carey's* Obligation *in 1792, the last command of Christ from Matthew 28:16, "Go ye into all the world," became the major biblical motive for Protestant missions for more than a century. Adoniram Judson (1788-1850), the pioneer Baptist missionary to Burma, affirmed it clearly throughout his life. The following extended quotes from his official biography cover both ends of his missionary career. In his December 18, 1837, letter to the Rev. Dr. Chapin, president of Columbian College, he recounts his initial call to missions, and that of others, at Andover Theological Seminary in 1809. The second passage is from his final public appearance in the United States, a monthly "concert of prayer for missions" in 1846 prior to his embarkation and return to Burma.*

The Missionary Call*

My dear Brother Rice: You ask me to give you some account of my first missionary impressions, and those of my earliest associates. Mine were occasioned by reading Buchanan's "Star in the East," in the year 1809, at Andover Theological Seminary. Though I do not now consider that sermon as peculiarly excellent, it produced a very powerful effect on my mind. For some days I was unable to attend to the studies of my class, and spent my time in wondering at my past stupidity, depicting the most romantic scenes in missionary life, and roving about the college rooms, declaiming on the subject of missions. My views were very incorrect, and my feelings extravagant; but yet I have always felt thankful to God for bringing me into that state of excitement, which was perhaps necessary, in the first instance, to enable me to break the strong attachment I felt to home and country, and to endure the thought of abandoning all my wonted pursuits and animating prospects. That excitement soon passed away; but it left a strong desire to prosecute my inquiries, and ascertain the path of duty. It was during a solitary walk in the woods behind the college, while meditating and praying on the subject, and feeling half inclined to give it up, that the command of Christ, "Go into all the world, and preach the gospel to every creature," was presented to my mind with such clearness and power, that I came to a full decision, and though great difficulties appeared in my way, resolved to obey the command at all events. But, at that period, no provision had been made in America for a foreign mission, and for several months, after reading Buchanan, I found none among the students who viewed the subject as I did, and no minister in the place or neighborhood who gave me any encouragement; and I thought that I should be under the necessity of going to England and placing myself under foreign patronage.

My earliest missionary associate was Nott; who, though he had recently entered the seminary (in the early part of 1810), was a member of the same class with myself. He had considered the subject for several months, but had not fully made up his mind. About the same time, Mills, Richards, and others joined the seminary from Williams College, where they had, for some time, been in the habit of meeting for prayer and conversation on the subject of missions....

I have ever thought that the providence of God was conspicuously manifested in bringing us all together, from different and distant parts. Some of us had been considering the subject of missions for a long time, and some but recently. Some, and indeed the greater part, had thought chiefly of domestic missions, and efforts among the neighboring tribes of Indians, without contemplating abandonment of country, and devotement for life. The reading and reflection of others had led them in a different way; and when we all met at the same seminary, and came to a mutual understanding on the ground of *foreign* missions and *missions for life,* the subject assumed in our minds such an overwhelming importance and awful solemnity, as

---

*Excerpts from Francis Wayland, *A Memoir of the Life and Labors of the Rev. Adoniram Judson, D.D.* (Boston: Phillips, Sampson, & Co., 1853), 1:51-53; 2:519-21; cf. Bosch, TM, 339-41.

bound us to one another, and to our purpose, more firmly than ever. How evident it is that the Spirit of God had been operating in different places, and upon different individuals, preparing the way for those movements which have since pervaded the American churches, and will continue to increase until the kingdoms of this world become the kingdoms of our Lord and his Anointed!

Obedience to Christ's Last Command [2]

What is the object on which the heart of the Saviour is set? For what purpose did he leave the bosom of the Father, the throne of eternal glory, to come down to sojourn, and suffer, and die in this fallen, rebellious world? For what purpose does he now sit on the mediatorial throne, and exert the power with which he is invested? To restore the ruins of paradise—to redeem his chosen people from death and hell—to extend and establish his kingdom throughout the habitable globe. This is evident from his whole course on earth, from his promises to the church, and especially from his parting command, "Go ye into all the world, and preach the gospel to every creature." . . .

All Must Obey

Let me now submit, that the command can be obeyed by every believer—that it is of universal obligation—and that no profession ought to be regarded as sincere, no love to the Saviour genuine, unless it be attended with a sincere endeavor to obey. But you will reply, How can I, unqualified and encumbered as I am, arise and go forth into the wide world and proclaim the gospel? Please to remember that all great public undertakings are accomplished by a combination of various agencies. In commerce and in war, for instance, some agents are necessarily employed at home, and some abroad; some at the head quarters, and some on distant expeditions; but however differently employed, and in whatever places, they are all interested, and all share the glory and the gain. So, in the missionary enterprise, the work to be accomplished is the universal preaching of the gospel, and the conversion of the whole world to the Christian faith; and in order to this, some must go, and some must send and sustain them that go. "How can they hear without a preacher, and how can they preach except they be sent?" Those who remain at home and labor to send and sustain those that go, are really employed in the work, and do as really obey the Saviour's command as those who go in their own persons. See you not, then, that the great command can be obeyed, and is actually binding on every soul? Feel you not that you are under obligation to do your utmost to secure that object at which the Saviour aimed, when he gave that command? It is possible there is some one in this assembly to whom it may be said, You will find, on examination, that you have not done your utmost—that indeed you have never laid this command to heart, or made any very serious effort to obey it; if so, how can you hope that your love to the Saviour is any thing more than an empty profession? How is it possible that you love the Saviour, and yet feel no interest in that object on which his heart is set? What, love the Saviour, who bled and died for this cause and yet spend your whole existence on earth in toiling for your personal sustenance, and gratification, and vain glory! O, that dread tribunal to which we are hastening! Souls stripped of all disguise there! The final Judge, a consuming fire! "Search me, O God, and know my heart; try me, and know my thoughts; and see if there be any wicked way in me, and lead me in the way everlasting."

MISSION AND COLONIALISM

> "Those two pioneers of civilization—Christianity and commerce—should ever be inseparable."

■ *In the 1820s, the British cartographers of Africa sought to be scientific. At a time when maps of India were as detailed as those of English counties, the center of Africa was left blank for the first time, where formerly it had been filled with speculations from legends. All that changed in 1856, as the great missionary-explorer David Livingstone completed his cross-Africa exploration. His feat electrified the British nation. Botanists and bishops, professors and politicians, attended his lectures at Oxford and Cambridge universities and at the British Association for the Advancement of Science.[3] Through them and his best-selling accounts of his travels, Livingstone launched that alliance for "commerce, civilization, and Christianity" which was to characterize British Protestant missions in the colonial era.*

*The Two Pioneers of Civilization**

My object in going into the country south of the desert was to instruct the natives in a knowledge of Christianity, but many circumstances prevented my living amongst them more than seven years, amongst which were considerations arising out of the slave system carried on by the Dutch Boers.

I resolved to go into the country beyond, and soon found that, for the purposes of commerce, it was necessary to have a path to the sea. I might have gone on instructing the natives in religion, but as civilization and Christianity must go on together, I was obliged to find a path to the sea, in order that I should not sink to the level of the natives....

My object is to open up traffic along the banks of the Zambesi, and also to preach the Gospel. The natives of Central Africa are very desirous of trading, but their only traffic is at present in slaves, of which the poorer people have an unmitigated horror: it is therefore most desirable to encourage the former principle, and thus open a way for the consumption of free productions, and the introduction of Christianity and commerce. By encouraging the native propensity for trade, the advantages that might be derived in a commercial point of view are incalculable; nor should we

---

*Excerpts from David Livingstone, *Dr. Livingstone's Cambridge Lectures,* ed. William Monk (London: Deighton, Bell & Co., 1860), 151, 165, 168; cf. Bosch, TM, 306-07.

lose sight of the inestimable blessings it is in our power to bestow upon the unenlightened African, by giving him the light of Christianity. Those two pioneers of civilization—Christianity and commerce—should ever be inseparable....

I beg to direct your attention to Africa;—I know that in a few years I shall be cut off in that country, which is now open; do not let it be shut again! I go back to Africa to try to make an open path for commerce and Christianity; do carry out the work which I have begun. I LEAVE IT WITH YOU!

PLANT CHURCHES

"Plant and multiply self-reliant, efficient churches."

■ *Two "giants" among missionary strategists, Henry Venn of the British Church Missionary Society (CMS) and Rufus Anderson of the American Board of Commissioners for Foreign Missions (ABCFM), promoted the goal in the mid-nineteenth century of planting autonomous and self-supporting native churches. Anderson has been called "the outstanding American organizer and theorist of foreign missions in the nineteenth century."[4] Born in Yarmouth, Maine, in 1796, educated at Bowdoin College and Andover Seminary, he had been strongly affected by the ordination service in 1812 for the first ABCFM missionaries. While a student at Andover, he began to work for the American Board and, although he volunteered for service in India, instead served the board as assistant secretary from 1826 and as foreign secretary from 1832 to his retirement in 1866. In 1866, he returned to his beloved Andover Seminary to deliver a series of Lectures on Foreign Missions, subsequently published as* Foreign Missions. *In presenting his principles and methods of foreign missions, Anderson promoted "the value of local native churches as a prominent instrumentality for renovating the heathen world" (viii).*

*An Opening World**

It is proper that I enter upon my subject by showing, in the first place, how the unevangelized world has of late been providentially opened to Christian missions; secondly, how Christendom meanwhile has been in a process of unconscious preparation of evangelizing it; and, thirdly, the consequent development, in the Evangelical Church, of a missionary spirit, and of missionary organizations, with the avowed expectation and purpose—for the first time since the apostolic age—of laboring for the conversion of the whole heathen world.

Paul's Principles and Methods

I am now prepared to state, in concise but positive form, what I believe to be the

*Excerpts from Rufus Anderson, *Foreign Missions* (New York: Charles Scribner, 1870), 1, 109-10, 115, 117-19; cf. Bosch, TM, 331-2.

true and proper nature of a mission among the heathen. The mission of the Apostle Paul, as described in the fourth chapter, embraced the following things:

1. The aim of the apostle was to save…souls.

2. The means he employed for this purpose were spiritual; namely, the gospel of Christ.

3. The power on which he relied to give efficacy to these means was divine; namely, the promised aid of the Holy Spirit.

4. His success was chiefly in the middle and poorer classes—the Christian influence ascending from thence.

5. When he formed local churches, he did not hesitate to ordain presbyters over them, the best he could find; and then to throw upon the churches, thus officered, the responsibilities of self-government, self-support, and self-propagation. His "presbyters in every church," whatever their number and other duties, had doubtless the pastoral care of the churches.

Our Strategic Plan

Wherein, then, do our modern missions differ from those of the apostolic age?…

Such is the simple structure of our foreign missions, as the combined result of experience, and of the apostolic example; in all which the grand object is to plant and multiply self-reliant, efficient churches, composed wholly of native converts, each church complete, with its pastors of the same race with the people. And when the unevangelized nations are so filled with such churches, that all…have it within their power to learn what they must do to be saved, then may we expect the promised advent of the Spirit, and the conversion of the world.…

Salvation Only in Christ

The proper test of success in missions is not the progress of civilization, but the evidence of a religious life.

The gospel is applicable equally to all false religions. Generically considered, there can be but two religions: the one looking for salvation by *grace*; the other, by *works*. The principle of evil in all unbeliev[ers], is the same. The refuges of lies in Popery, in Judaism, in Mohammedanism, in Brahminism, Buddhism and every form of paganism, are wonderfully alike. There is one disease, and one remedy. Before the gospel, the unbelieving world stands an undistinguished mass of rebellious sinners; unwilling that God should reign over them, unwilling to be saved except by their own works, and averse to all real holiness of heart and life. There is power in the doctrine of the cross, through grace, to overcome this. The doctrine of the cross—as will more clearly appear when we come to the evidences of success in missions—is the grand instrument of conquest. Not one of the great superstitions of the world could hold a governing place in the human soul, after the conviction has once been thoroughly produced, that there is salvation only in Christ. Be [their] system what it may, [persons] thus convinced, would flee from it, as [they] would from a falling house in the rockings of an earthquake.

MISSION AND THE MILLENNIUM

> "The coming of the Lord...the strongest motivation for consecration and service."

■ *James Hudson Taylor (1832-1905) was born at Barnsley, in Yorkshire, England, the son of a chemist. At age seventeen he underwent a deep conversion experience, followed by a vivid call to China, which was closed to missionaries except for five treaty ports. To prepare for such service, he evangelized the poor in the English cities of Hull and London and studied medicine, meanwhile disciplining himself to rely on God alone for his needs. Sent to China by the short-lived Chinese Evangelization Society in 1854, he soon reacted against the prevailing mission compound approach, identifying himself with the Chinese people and seeking to reach the interior of China. The opening came in 1865, and Taylor began a model "faith mission" that was to become the China Inland Mission. His missionary motivation, with its strong premillennial focus, is found in the following excepts from his retrospection on his life's calling and work.*

*The Call to Service**

About this time a friend drew my attention to the question of the personal and pre-millennial coming of our Lord Jesus Christ, and gave me a list of passages bearing upon it, without note or comment, advising me to ponder the subject. For a while I gave much time to studying the Scriptures about it, with the result that I was led to see that this same Jesus who left our earth in His resurrection body was so to come again, that His feet were to stand on the Mount of Olives, and that He was to take possession of the temporal throne of His father David which was promised before His birth. I saw, further, that all through the New Testament the coming of the Lord was the great hope of His people, and was always appealed to as the strongest motive for consecration and service, and was the greatest comfort in trial and affliction. I learned, too, that the period of His return for His people was not revealed, and that it was their privilege, from day to day and from hour to hour, to live as [persons] who wait for the Lord; that thus living it was immaterial, so to speak, whether He should or should not come at any particular hour, the important thing being to be so ready for Him as to be able, whenever He might appear, to give an account of one's stewardship with joy, and not with grief.

---

*Excerpts from J. Hudson Taylor, *A Retrospect* (London: China Inland Mission, 1875, 1954), 18-19, 112, 114; cf. Bosch, TM, 316.

Beginning the Faith Mission

In the study of that Divine Word I learned that, to obtain successful labourers, not elaborate appeals for help, but, *first* earnest *prayer to God to thrust forth labourers,* and *second,* the deepening of the spiritual life of the Church, so that *men [and women] should be unable to stay at home,* were what was needed. I saw that the Apostolic plan was not to raise ways and means, but *to go and do the work,* trusting in His sure Word who has said, "Seek ye *first* the Kingdom of God and His righteousness, and all these things shall be added unto you." . . .

On Sunday, June 25th, 1865, unable to bear the sight of a congregation of a thousand or more Christian people rejoicing in their own security, while millions were perishing for lack of knowledge, I wandered out on the sands alone, in great spiritual agony; and there the Lord conquered my unbelief, and I surrendered myself to God for this service. I told Him that all the responsibility as to issues and consequences must rest with Him; that as His servant it was mine to obey and to follow Him—His, to direct, to care for, and to guide me and those who might labour with me. Need I say that peace at once flowed into my burdened heart? There and then I asked him for twenty-four fellow-workers, two for each of eleven inland provinces which were without a missionary, and two for Mongolia; and writing the petition on the margin of the Bible I had with me, I returned home with a heart enjoying rest such as it had been a stranger to for months, and with an assurance that the Lord would bless His own work and that I should share in the blessing. I had previously prayed, and asked prayer, that workers might be raised up for the eleven then unoccupied provinces, and thrust forth and provided for, but had not surrendered myself to be their leader.

THE WOMEN'S MISSIONARY MOVEMENT

"How may a woman help Christ's kingdom come?"

■ *Before 1800, Protestant mission societies were composed exclusively of men. Then, on October 9 of that year, Mary Webb gathered together fourteen Baptist and Congregational women and organized the Boston Female Society of Missionary Purposes. So began "the first feminist movement in North America."*[5] *The women's missionary movement grew rapidly following the Civil War. The societies were organized and directed by women for the purpose of sending women to the foreign field to evangelize women. By 1894, there were thirty-three such societies that had sponsored some 1,000 women teachers, doctors, evangelists, and relief workers. The following excerpt from an 1883 survey of women's missionary societies in North America and England captures both the rationale and passion for women in mission.*

*Women in Mission**

Manifestly, the chief purpose and work of the Christian church is to be about its Father's business in recovering to him the lost allegiance of the race. Only as we have some comprehension of the magnitude and some conviction of the importance of this work—only as we gauge it from the height of God's love to the depth of man's need—through all its manifold relations, out, on, into the illimitable, unspeakable future, do we realize that for its completion there must be the effectual working in its measure of every part, the development and exercise of every force. Manhood and womanhood must each bring its distinctive offerings as of old, in the typical tabernacle and temple, before throughout the whole earth shall arise an holy temple unto the Lord. The paeon of praise is to be universal, but the harmony will not be complete until there be added to the deep bass and strong tenor, the trill of the treble and the softness of the alto.

Two-thirds of the Christian church, having this work in hand, are women, and few questions are better worth considering, how all that is on her, all that is distinctively, peculiarly feminine, may be wrought into this grand consummation, to accomplish which Christ came, and for which he waits, expecting until his enemies be made his footstool.

The interest of this problem is only equalled by its importance. How may a woman help Christ's kingdom come? Is there any spring in the machinery which only her fingers can touch and move? Are there any crooked or narrow places where only her feet can travel—any rough spots that only her touch may smooth—any low levels which only her hands can raise—any recesses of sin or sorrow where only her voice can be heard? Then, from her Master she hears her call, and from him receives her commission. The full answer to these queries, and the clear solution of this problem, comes to us only in the light of the nineteenth century.

The Spirit's Work

This has well been called the Missionary epoch of the Church. In it she has heard the voice of her Lord crying, "Awake, awake, put on thy strength, O Zion, put on thy beautiful garments, O Jerusalem." In it almost all the great organized aggressive agencies of the church have had birth—the Missionary, the Bible, the Tract, the Sabbath-School cause, have assumed their magnificent proportions and are wielding their tremendous powers. The century had about attained its meridian when a new want is felt among these agencies, and in response thereto a new voice is heard—a still small voice—yet none the less its whispers may reach where thunder tones might fail—the woman's missionary movement appears. Like its Lord, "it doth not strive nor cry, neither shall its voice be heard in the street." Like the

---

*Excerpts from L. H. Daggett, ed., *Historical Sketches of Woman's Missionary Societies in America and England* (Boston: L. H. Daggett, ca. 1883), 7-11; cf. Bosch, TM, 328.

kingdom of heaven, it cometh without observation. Like all movements born from above, it came in the fulness of time. The Spirit prompted, and Providence prepared the way for it. The fields were just right for this sowing; the harvest was just ripe for these reapers; the world was just ready and reaching out for this agency. The missionary work had come to a point where it must have this help. The march of civilization had broken up the fallow ground, and gospel seed as dropped from pulpit and press had fallen into receptive and responsive soil. Yet the women sit in darkness and silence and chains. No man's presence may peer into that darkness—no man's voice break that silence—no man's hand loose those chains. So, while point after point was gained, and battlement after battlement was won, the citadel—the home where life is generated and character formed, and destiny shaped—was intact and unapproachable. Evidently, some new factors are to be employed, some new forces exerted. Some key must be found which shall fit in the lock that is barring out Christ from the homes of heathendom. It avails not much to purify the streams if we may not touch the fountain. And womanhood is everywhere, under all conditions, in all civilizations, the fountain of life and influence. Who will, who can, teach, rescue, renew, raise, the women of heathendom? Then *down* goes heathendom and *up* the family, the community, the civilization, the country, the race! *That* the momentous question to be answered, and *these* the tremendous issues at stake. These various women's missionary movements the practical response, the agencies God is employing in answering these questions....

Eminently Fitting

The philosophy of them is in the very nature of things; the argument for them in their necessity; the justification of them in their fruits. Here a woman may find a fitting field for the exercise of all her energies and powers—here, in a way most womanly and most Christly, may she expand all her gifts of head and heart and life. And it is eminently fitting that she who came the nearest to Christ in his birth and in his death, at his manger and at his tomb—she who ever found in him when on earth fullest comprehension and deepest sympathy—she who now finds in him, in him alone, the Divine Human, combining infinite tenderness with infinite strength, the full supply of every want of her nature—she who owes him most, having received from him most—she who wears as her crowning glory what is hurled at her as her supremest taunt, that the religion of Christ is good for the women and children and the weak—it is eminently fitting that the fulness of her gratitude and love should expend itself in seeking to raise other women from the depths to the same heights of renewing, redeeming grace. It is eminently fitting, it is blessed compensation, it is Divine retribution, that she who brought sin into the world, should also bring the Saviour—and that she, also, who brought the Saviour, should in these last days further on the finished work of human salvation, should bring the top-stone to the temple, with shoutings of "Grace! grace unto it!"

EVANGELIZE THE WORLD

"There is no insuperable obstacle to world-wide evangelization."

■ *The mantle of spokesperson for global missions among Protestants at the turn of the nineteenth century fell upon a Methodist layman, John Raleigh Mott (1865-1955). While a student at Cornell University, he fell under the influence of the popular evangelist Dwight L. Moody. In 1886, Mott was among the first 100 college youths to sign the declaration that "God willing, I propose to become a missionary." In the next decade, Mott excelled in organizing young people for united Christian witness through the Student Volunteer Movement for Foreign Missions (SVM), the Young Men's Christian Association (YMCA), and the World Student Christian Federation (WSCF). In 1910, he chaired the Edinburgh World Missionary Conference and later its Continuation Committee and the International Missionary Council (IMC). As a founder of the ecumenical movement, he became Honorary President of the World Council of Churches in 1948. Missions remained his life passion. More than any other leader, Mott lifted up the vision of "the evangelization of the world in this generation." The following excerpts are from his 1900 book by that title.*

The Great Commission *

It is important that we clearly understand at the outset what is meant by the evangelization of the world in this generation. It means to give all...an adequate opportunity to know Jesus Christ as their Saviour and to become His real disciples. This involves such a distribution of missionary agencies as will make the knowledge of the Gospel accessible to all.... It would seem that Christ logically implied this when He commanded His followers, "Go ye into all the world and preach the gospel to the whole creation" (Mk. 16:15)....

Our Commission in This Generation

If the Gospel is to be preached to all...it obviously must be done while they are living. The evangelization of the world in this generation, therefore, means the preaching of the Gospel to those who are now living. To us who are responsible for preaching the Gospel it means in our life-time; to those to whom it is to be preached it means in their life-time. The unevangelized for whom we as Christians are responsible live in this generation; and the Christians whose duty it is to present Christ to them live in this generation. The phrase "in this generation," therefore, strictly speaking has a different meaning for each person. In the last analysis, if the

---

*Excerpts from John R. Mott, *The Evangelization of the World in This Generation* (New York: Student Volunteer Movement for Foreign Mission, 1900), 3, 6-7, 15-16, 105, 109, 115, 116-17, 120, 128-31; cf. Bosch, TM, 337-38.

world is to be evangelized in this or any generation it will be because a sufficient number of individual Christians recognize and assume their personal obligation to the undertaking.

To consider negatively the meaning of the evangelization of the world in this generation may serve to prevent some misconceptions. It does not mean the conversion of the world within the generation. Our part consists in bringing the Gospel to bear on unsaved men [and women]. The results are with [those] whom we would reach and with the Spirit of God. We have no warrant for believing that all who have the Gospel preached unto them will accept it. On the other hand, however, we have a right to expect that the faithful preaching of the Gospel will be attended with conversions. We should not present Christ in an aimless and unexpectant manner, but with the definite purpose of influencing those who hear us to believe on Him and become His disciples. Like St. Paul at Thessalonica, we should preach the Gospel "in much assurance" (1 Thess. 1:5). We are not responsible for the results of our work, however, but for our fidelity and thoroughness....

The evangelization of the world in this generation should not be regarded as an end in itself. The Church will not have fulfilled her task when the Gospel has been preached to all men [and women]. Such evangelization must be followed by the baptism of converts, by their organization into churches, by building them up in knowledge, faith and character and by enlisting and training them for service. While the missionary enterprise should not be diverted from the immediate and controlling aim of preaching the Gospel where Christ has not been named, and while this work should have the right of way as the most urgent part of our task, it must ever be looked upon as but a means to the mighty and inspiring object of enthroning Christ in individual life, in family life, in social life, in national life, in international relations . . . and, to this end, of planting and developing in all non-Christian lands self-supporting, self-directing and self-propagating churches which shall become so thoroughly rooted in the convictions and hearts of the people that if Christianity were to die out in Europe and America, it would abide in purity and as a missionary power in its new homes and would live on through the centuries....

Opportunities and Resources

A survey of the opportunities and resources of the Church and the facilities at her disposal will make it plain that she is more favorably situated in this than she has been in any preceding generation for the evangelization of the world.

For the first time in the history of the Church practically the whole world is open....

The greatly enlarged and improved means of communication constitutes one of the chief facilities of which the Church of this generation can avail herself....

The influence and protection of Christian governments is an immense help to the work of missions. In no age in the past could the ambassadors for Christ carry on their work with such safety. Over one-third of the inhabitants of the unevangelized world are under the direct sway of Christian rulers. Moreover, the Protestant powers are in a position to exert an influence that will make possible the free preaching of the Gospel to the remaining two-thirds of the people of the earth who have not heard of Christ....

The Church not only has an unexampled opportunity to evangelize the world, as well as great facilities at her disposal, but she also possesses remarkable resources: ...her membership...millions of spiritually-minded and consecrated men and women...[and] the money power of the Church is enormous....

Among the greatest resources of the Church are the missionary societies, together with their workers and agencies on the foreign field. At the beginning of the nineteenth century there were six Protestant missionary organizations. Dr. Dennis gives 537 as the present number of foreign missionary societies and auxiliaries.[6] . . .

The native Church is the human resource which affords largest promise for the evangelization of the world. It is not only an impressive monument to the power of Christian missions, but an earnest of the vast fruitage which may be expected within our generation. It constitutes both the end of evangelization and its principal means....

The Divine resources of the Church are immeasurably more powerful and more important than all others. The evangelization of the world is not [our] enterprise but God's. Christ at the right hand of God is the leader of the missionary movement, and with Him resides all power in heaven and on earth. The Spirit of God is as able to shake communities now as in the days of St. Peter and St. John. The Word of God possesses dynamic and transforming power. Prayer can still remove mountains....

It Seems Entirely Possible

If the Church instead of theorizing and speculating will improve her opportunities, facilities and resources, it seems entirely possible to fill the earth with the knowledge of Christ before the present generation passes away. With literal truth it may be said that ours is an age of unparalleled opportunity. "Providence and revelation combine to call the Church afresh to go in and take possession of the world for Christ."[7] Everything seems to be ready for a general and determined engagement for the forces of Christendom for the world-wide proclamation of the Gospel. "Once the world seemed boundless and the Church was poor and persecuted. No wonder the work of evangelizing the world within a reasonable time seemed hopeless. Now steam and electricity have brought the world together. The Church of God is in the ascendant. She has well within her control the power, the wealth, and the learning of the world. She is like a strong and well appointed army in the presence of the foe. The only thing she needs is the Spirit of her Leader and a willingness to obey His summons to go forward. The victory may not be easy but it is sure."[8]

NOTES

1. Alexander Pope, *Dunciad,* Book iv (London: 1743; 1965 ed.), pp. 386-87.

2. Address by Dr. Adoniram Judson, July 5, 1846, at the monthly Baptist concert of prayer for missions in Boston, Massachusetts, his last public appearance before his embarkation.

3. The first public lecture quoted here was delivered December 4, 1857, in the Senate House at the University of Cambridge.

4. William R. Hutchison, *Errand to the World: American Protestant Thought and Foreign Missions* (Chicago: University of Chicago Press, 1987), p. 78.

5. R. Pierce Beaver, *American Protestant Women in World Mission,* rev. ed. (Grand Rapids, MI: Wm. B. Eerdmans, 1980), p. 3.

6. James S. Dennis, "Centennial Statistics," a paper prepared for the Ecumenical Conference on Foreign Missions (New York, 1900), pp. 17, 18.

7. "Memorial of the Student Volunteer Missionary Union," *The Student Volunteer* (of Great Britain), New Series, No. 15, p. 77.

8. Dr. Clavin W. Mateer, letter in the archives of the Student Volunteer Movement.

Part II

CONTEMPORARY PARADIGMS OF MISSION

5

Mission as the Church-with-Others

In 1981, the Catholic Church in South Korea organized a "Year for the Evangelization of the Neighbor." It was characterized by "sensitivity to neighbor's needs, apostolic witness and missionary action." The whole approach was direct person-to-person, family-to-family contact in a small community.[1] *Such mission is an example of Bosch's first contemporary paradigm—mission as the church-with-others.*

In the earlier period, most Christians of Europe and North America viewed mission as activity "out there" carried on by mission specialists. The local parish was most often "in mission" through support of others rather than through direct action.

Shifts in Protestant thought regarding the relationship between church and mission began early in the twentieth century. Roland Allen, an Anglican missionary to China, was an early voice calling for recovery of the apostolic church model. He contrasted mission methods of his day, which resulted in more-or-less permanent dependency of the mission church upon foreign leadership and support, with St. Paul's method of establishing fully organized indigenous churches. Out of the IMC Tambaram Conference of 1938 came the clear statement that "the essential task of the Church is to be an ambassador of Christ." To the traditional marks of the true church (where the word of God is preached faithfully and the sacraments duly administered) were added devoted service to society and a missionary spirit. Dietrich Bonhoeffer's statement that "the church is the church only when it exists for others," written in 1944 from a Nazi prison, is the most quoted statement of this motif. The IMC Ghana Assembly of 1958 added the conviction that the mission "is Christ's, not ours." In a time when human "management by objectives" was coming into vogue, Ghana chose to judge mission motives and programs by the standard of Christ's servant ministry. Out of the WCC's 1961-66 study of "The Missionary Structure of the Congregation" came the image of "the church for others." Believing that the living Christ is at work outside the walls of the church, Christians in mission were encouraged to join Christ where the world provides the agenda for mission.

Roman Catholics were also rethinking the relation between church and mission during this period. Yves Congar of France, like Allen, recovered models of mission from the apostolic church. The "apostolic function," for Congar, includes a new mobility "of going everywhere, of intervening everywhere" with the authority of Christ. Vatican II gave a firm mandate for the entire church to be in mission. "The Church on earth is by its very nature missionary," declared the bishops in Ad Gentes, *the Decree on the Missionary Activity of the church. From* Lumen Gentium *(Light of All Nations) came a restatement of images of the church as "messianic people" and "pilgrim church."*

To Bosch's analysis of this paradigm as developed in Europe and North America can be added other images from Third World and feminist perspectives.

Harry Sawyerr of Sierra Leone, out of African culture, provides the powerful image of the church as the extended family. Within it, responsibility for the other is not based on wealth, proximity, or close family ties. Instead, it is based on oneness in the "great family." The church as the "great family" should be a caring community transcending clan and tribe. Letty Russell of Yale University judges many existing church structures "heretical" because they thwart the church's mission. She proposes an "open ecclesiology" in which churches move outside parish walls in new and creative ministries. Mathai Zachariah of India shares that vision. The church is but the nucleus of a "people's movement" which bears a liberating gospel in the process of becoming a new humanity. Mercy Oduyoye of Nigeria finds new images for the church in mission in "the sacrificial life of the woman." Self-emptying, living for the other, Christ-bearing—images from the life of women—are needed if the church in mission is to be emptied of pride, power, and privilege. Finally, Pablo Richard of Chile writes of the "church of the poor" as a new model in contrast to the dominant Christendom model. He believes that the church must arise out of "the liberating potential of the poor."

ESTABLISHING APOSTOLIC PLAN CHURCHES

"St. Paul's...principles are assuredly applicable."

■ *One of the twentieth century's radical criticisms of missionary policy and practice came from a most unlikely source. Roland Allen (1868-1947) served only briefly as an Anglican missionary in China at the turn of the century, and even more briefly as a parish priest in England. He never held important offices in church, mission, or academic institutions. Nevertheless, few persons had such broad and lasting influence on movements for renewal and reform in Christian mission. Furthermore, his principal writings,* Missionary Methods: St. Paul's or Ours? *(1912) and* Spontaneous Expansion of the Church and the Causes Which Hinder It *(1927), were largely ignored in his own day. But the validity of his central argument was indisputable and a challenge that mission leaders increasingly took to heart after his death. Allen advocated, as Henry Venn and Rufus Anderson had nearly a century earlier, the selfhood of local churches around the world (self-supporting, self-governing, and self-propagating). Let us return to the Pauline model of mission, he pleaded, with the full authority of local churches empowered by the Holy Spirit and shared leadership among clergy and laity.*

The Teaching of Converts*

If there is a striking difference between St. Paul's preaching and ours there is still greater difference between his method of dealing with his converts and that common among us today. . . .

The first and most striking difference between his action and ours is that he founded "Churches" whilst we found "Missions." The establishment of Missions is a peculiarity of our modern methods...The theory is that the Mission stands at first in a sort of paternal relationship to the native Christians: then it holds a co-ordinate position side by side with the native organization; finally it ought to disappear and leave the native Christians as a fully organized Church. But the Mission is not the Church. It consists of a missionary, or a number of missionaries, and their paid helpers, supported by a foreign Society. There is thus created a sort of dual organization. On the one hand there is the Mission with its organization; on the other is the body of native Christians, often with an organization of its own. The one is not indeed separate from the other, but in practice they are not identified. The natives always speak of "the Mission" as something which is not their own. The Mission represents a foreign power, and natives who work under it are servants of a foreign Government. It is an evangelistic society, and the natives tend to leave it to do the evangelistic work which properly belongs to them. It is a model, and the natives learn simply to imitate it. It is a wealthy body, and the natives tend to live upon it, and expect it to supply all their needs. Finally, it becomes a rival, and the native Christians feel its presence as an annoyance, and they envy its powers....

St. Paul...set up no organization intermediate between his preaching and the establishment of a fully organized indigenous Church. It is interesting to speculate what would have happened, if, at the end of his first missionary journey, St. Paul had hastened back to Antioch to entreat for assistance of two or three presbyters to supervise the growth of the Churches in South Galatia, pleading that unless he could secure this help he would be unable to enter the open door which he saw before him; or if instead of ordaining elders he had appointed catechists, keeping the administration of the sacraments in his own hands....

The facts are these: St. Paul preached in a place for five or six months and then left behind him a Church, not indeed free from the need of guidance, but capable of growth and expansion....In the space of time which amongst us is generally passed in the class of hearers, men were prepared by St. Paul for the ministry. How could he prepare men for Holy Orders in so brief a time? How could he even prepare them for Holy Baptism? What could he have taught them in five or six months? If

---

*Excerpts from Roland Allen, *Missionary Methods: St. Paul's or Ours?* 3rd. ed. (London: World Dominion Press, 1956), ix, 107-10, 181-82; cf. Bosch, TM, 379.

any one today were to propose to ordain men within six months of their conversion from idolatry, he would be deemed rash to the verge of madness. Yet no one denies that St. Paul did it. The sense of stupefaction and amazement that comes over us when we think of it, is the measure of the distance which we have travelled from the Apostolic method.

Principles and Spirit

If we look out over the mission field today we see that we have made most amazing progress....Nevertheless, there are everywhere three very disquieting symptoms:

(1) Everywhere Christianity is still an exotic. We have not yet succeeded in so planting it in any heathen land that it has become indigenous. If there is one doubtful exception to that rule, it is a country where from the very beginning Pauline methods were followed more closely than elsewhere. But generally speaking it still remains true that Christianity in the lands of our missions is still a foreign religion. It has not yet really taken root in the country.

(2) Everywhere our missions are dependent. They look to us for leaders, for instructors, for rulers. They have as yet shown little sign of being able to supply their own needs. Day by day and year by year there comes to us an unceasing appeal for men and money for the same missions to which we have been supplying [personnel] and money for the last fifty or sixty years, and there seems at present little hope that that demand will change its character. If we do not send [persons] and money the missions will fail, the converts will fall away, ground painfully won will be lost: that is what we are told. When the day comes in which the demand is for [personnel] and money to establish new missions in new country, because the old are capable of standing alone, the end of our work will be in sight. But at present that day still seems far distant.

GOD'S PILGRIM PEOPLE

"As the visible Body of Christ, the Church shapes a people."

■ *Yves Congar (b. 1904) is one of this century's most influential and consistently pioneering Roman Catholic ecumenists. Ordained in 1930 after entering the Dominican order, he taught at Le Saulchoir near Paris.* Chrétiens Déunis, *Congar's influential work on the nature of the church, was published in 1937. In it he pointed out the importance and value of the concept of the people of God. His thought influenced both the growing liturgical movement and the new lay enthusiasm expressed through Christian Action and the priest-worker movement after World War II. At Vatican II he helped draft documents on the church in the modern world, revelation, religious freedom, missionary activity, and ecumenism.*

*Christ Shapes a People**

The embodiments of Christ must shape a people who are always concerned with how to shape a people—a people who are themselves the members of Jesus Christ, a people of "brothers" [and sisters], of "saints." The [spiritual] unity of [persons] before Christ, therefore, must be visible, evident and social; it must become visible. The Church is like a theophany or a christophany in a collective and societal form, continuing therefore the mission of praise and witness by which the royal and priestly people are being carried (cf. 1 Pet. 2: 5, 9-10, referring to Ex. 19:6). The Church is the Body of Christ, her glory, her human and collective humanity. The Christ, it is said,[2] is in need of the Church as a *pneuma* (spirit) is in need of a *soma* (body).

As the visible Body of Christ, the Church shapes a people, all united in God, and the ensuing unity of every one with another becomes human reality and human development of a united life between persons, that is to say, a developed community partnership. From one end to the other, the ancient documents present to us the Church as *one* and *unique*; there are "churches," but they themselves are not to a degree the Church to give account to it.[3]

A Concern to Spread Unity

Nowhere is one able to understand that which will permit division...within the existence of the church as such....This Church *is* the same visibility of the Lord, the human form of his Body; she is right, she is one and unique, as the Lord is one and unique, as are unique the baptism which he introduced, the faith and the spirit which are given to us for living, the hope that here calls us (Eph. 4:4-6). To maintain this visible and societal unity of the New Israel is the great concern of the Twelve, [and] of that exceptional Apostle, Paul. The ancient documents are filled with the concern for the spreading *of unity* (and perhaps more for that unity than for that spreading)....This is the great apostolic concern;[4] this is also the benefit that assures to the Church the apostolic function as such: this possibility of going everywhere, of intervening everywhere, of recapturing, of exhorting, of teaching universally with the same authority of Christ.

Finally, the Christian life is very strongly presented as a help, and this life in the Church, this collective life as the helping life, is affirmed as the same life which edifies Christ; it represents and realizes between Christians the same spiritual unity which exists between God and all those gathered in Christ. That again is one of the...most striking acts of the primitive Church (Rom. 15:25, 16:2, 1 Cor. 12:4-30, etc.). Therefore, in every way, the embodiments of Christ shape a societal unity of a human type, where the life of the group as such is Christian and set to grow through Christ.

---

*Excerpts from Yves Congar, *Chrétiens Déunis: Principes d'un "Oecuménisme" Catholique* (Paris: Les Éditions du Cerf, 1937), 86-92; cf. Bosch, TM, 373.

THE ESSENTIAL TASK OF THE CHURCH

"The essential task...to be the ambassador of Christ."

■ *The International Missionary Council's meeting at Tambaram, Madras, India, in December 1938 was in its time the most widely representative assembly of Christians ever held—471 people from 69 countries. "The World Mission of the Church" was its central theme. Gathered at a time of unprecedented international tensions, with China and Japan already at war, the delegates were concerned about the witness-bearing character of the church.*

*To Be the Ambassador of Christ**

The task of the Church is described in Matthew 28: 19-20: "Go ye therefore and teach all nations, baptizing them in the name of the Father and of the Son and of the Holy Ghost, teaching them to observe all things, whatsoever I have commanded you, and lo, I am with you always, even unto the end of the world." The place where this task is centered is the local church or congregation. As dead or disunited congregations are the greatest hindrance to the fulfillment of the Church's task, living congregations are the foremost agencies used by God for the accomplishment of it. The life of a living congregation is its life lived with God in worship, in the hearing of the Word and the use of the Sacraments, in prayer and intercession. The marks of its being alive are the regularity of common worship by its members, the sacrificial and transforming love among them, their [human] discipline, devoted service to society, study of the Scriptures, and missionary spirit. In the congregation the cell of life is the consecrated family and household.

The essential task of the Church is to be the ambassador of Christ, proclaiming His Kingdom. While the Church has no universally valid political or economic program, through its very existence within state and society it should serve as a waking and active conscience to emphasize Christian principles in social life...all the Church's activities, whether social service, education, the spreading of Christian literature, the healing of body and mind, or any other work undertaken...follow from the essential task committed to it. They are signposts pointing to Christ as the Savior of [all] and of human society. They are manifestations of His love in the hearts of His servants. They are the inevitable outcome of true and living faith in Him.

In its worship and witness the Church is sustained by the assured hope of its final fulfillment in the eternal Kingdom of God.

---

*Excerpts from International Missionary Council (Tambaram, Madras, India, 12-29 December 1938), *The World Mission of the Church: Findings and Recommendations ..(London: IMC, 1939), 26-27; cf. Bosch, TM, 369-70.*

THE CHURCH FOR OTHERS

"The church is the church only when it exists for others."

■ *Dietrich Bonhoeffer (1906-1945), executed by the Nazis in the final days of 1945, was already recognized as a gifted Protestant theologian. His* Letters and Papers from Prison *contains the seeds of a creative post-modern theology. For Bonhoeffer, "the world that has come of age is more godless, and perhaps for that very reason nearer to God, than the world before its coming of age." (LPP, 200). To live "in Christ," Bonhoeffer believed, meant to be a church which exists not for the pious faithful but for others.*

*The Future Church in the World**

The church is the church only when it exists for others. To make a start, it should give away all its property to those in need. The clergy must live solely on the free-will offerings of their congregations, or possibly engage in some secular calling. The church must share in the secular problems of ordinary human life, not dominating, but helping and serving. It must tell [persons] of every calling what it means to live in Christ, to exist for others. In particular, our own church will have to take the field against the vices of *hubris,* power-worship, envy, and humbug, as the roots of all evil. It will have to speak of moderation, purity, trust, loyalty, constancy, patience, discipline, humility, contentment, and modesty....I hope it may be of some help for the church's future.

THE ONLY TRUE MOTIVE OF MISSION

"Mission is Christ's not ours"

■ *"What does it mean in theological terms and in practice in this ecumenical era, for the Church to discharge its mission to the world?" This was a major concern of some 200 persons who gathered at Accra for the Ghana Assembly of the International Missionary Council held from December, 28, 1957, to January, 7, 1958. The theme of the meeting was "The Christian Mission at This Hour." The conference statement, although not formally adopted by the assembly, is an interpretation of "certain convictions which came home to those who shared in it with great insistence or in a new form."*

---

*Excerpts from Dietrich Bonhoeffer, *Letters and Papers from Prison: The Enlarged Edition,* ed. Eberhard Bethge (New York: Macmillan, 1971), 382-83; cf. Bosch, TM, 375.

The Christian Mission at This Hour*

The Christian world mission is Christ's, not ours. Prior to all our efforts and activities, prior to all our gifts of service and devotion, God sent His Son into the world. And He came in the form of a servant—a servant who suffered even to the death of the Cross.

This conviction...[is] the only true motive of Christian mission and the only standard by which the spirit, method and modes of Christian missionary organization must be judged. We believe it is urgent that this word of judgment and mercy should be given full freedom to cleanse and redeem our present activities, lest our human pride in our activities hinder the free course of God's mission in the world.

THE PILGRIM CHURCH

"Messianic people...the pilgrim Church."

■ *The church—its nature and mission—was "the principal object of attention of the Second Vatican Ecumenical Council" of 1962-1965, according to Pope Paul VI, who presided there. "Lumen Gentium" ("Light of All Nations") are the first two words of the authoritative "Dogmatic Constitution of the Church" from the council. The church's leaders saw the need for a radically different vision of the church, one which would be more biblical, grounded in the historical, dynamic, and inspiring the church to renewal.*

The Church and the Kingdom**

(From Chapter 1, "The Mystery of the Church")

5.... When Jesus, having died on the cross for [humanity], rose again from the dead, he was seen to be constituted as Lord, the Christ, and as Priest for ever (cf. Acts 2:36; Heb. 5:6; 7:17-21), and he poured out on his disciples the Spirit promised by the Father (cf. Acts 2:23). Henceforward the Church, endowed with the gifts of her founder and faithfully observing his precepts of charity, humility and self-denial, receives the mission of proclaiming and establishing among all peoples the kingdom of Christ and of God, and she is, on earth, the seed and the beginning of that kingdom. While she slowly grows to maturity, the Church longs for the

---

*Excerpts from International Missionary Council (Ghana, December 28, 1957, to January 7, 1958), *Minutes of the Assembly...(London and New York: IMC, 1958), 89; cf. Bosch, TM, 370.*

**Excerpts from "Lumen Gentium" (1964), in *Vatican Council II: The Conciliar and Post Conciliar Documents, New Revised Edition,* ed. Austin Flannery, O.P. (Northport, NY: Costello Publishing Company, 1992), hereafter cited as *VC2,* 353, 360, 408; cf. Bosch, TM, 374, 377.

completed kingdom and, with all her strength, hopes and desires to be united in glory with her king.

The New Israel

(From Chapter 2, "The People of God")

9.…As Israel according to the flesh which wandered in the desert was already called the Church of God (2 Esd. 13:1; cf. Num. 20:4; Deut. 23:1ff), so too, the new Israel, which advances in this present era in search of a future and permanent city (cf. Heb. 13:14), is called also the Church of Christ (cf. Mt. 16:18). It is Christ indeed who has purchased it with his own blood (cf. Acts 20:28); he has filled it with his Spirit; he has provided means adapted to its visible and social union. All those, who in faith look towards Jesus, the author of salvation and the principle of unity and peace, God has gathered together and established as the Church, that it may be for each and everyone the visible sacrament of this saving unity.(1) Destined to extend to all regions of the earth, it enters into human history, though it transcends at once all times and all racial boundaries. Advancing through trials and tribulations, the Church is strengthened by God's grace, promised to her by the Lord so that she may not waver from perfect fidelity, but remain the worthy bride of the Lord, until through the cross, she may attain to that light which knows no setting.

The Pilgrim Church

(From Chapter 7, "The Pilgrim Church")

48.…Already the final age of the world is with us (cf. 1 Cor. 10:11) and the renewal of the world is irrevocably under way; it is even now anticipated in a certain real way, for the Church on earth is endowed already with a sanctity that is real though imperfect. However, until there be realized new heavens and a new earth in which justice dwells (cf. 2 Pet. 3:13) the pilgrim Church, in its sacraments and institutions, which belong to this present age, carries the mark of this world which will pass, and she herself takes her place among the creatures which groan and travail yet and await the revelation of the sons of God (cf. Rom. 8:19-22).

THE MISSIONARY CHURCH

"The Church on earth is by its very nature missionary."

■ *Both the "Decree on the Missionary Activity of the Church"* (Ad Gentes) *and Vatican II's "Constitution on the Church"* (Lumen Gentium) *begin with a reference to Isaiah 61:1, which presents the People of God as being sent into the world to be the light and salvation of the unbelieving nations—the* gentes. *This is a reaffirmation of the true biblical nature of the church and its mission to unbelievers.*

By Its Very Nature Missionary*

(From Chapter 1, "Doctrinal Principles")

2. The Church on earth is by its very nature missionary since, according to the plan of the Father, it has its origin in the mission of the Son and the Holy Spirit.[5] This plan flows from "fountain-like love," the love of God the Father. As the principle without principle from whom the Son is generated and from whom the Holy Spirit proceeds through the Son, God in his great and merciful kindness freely creates us and moreover, graciously calls us to share in his life and glory. He generously pours out, and never ceases to pour out, his divine goodness, so that he who is creator of all things might at last become "all in all" (1 Cor. 15:28), thus simultaneously assuring his own glory and our happiness. It pleased God to call [persons] to share in his life and not merely singly, without any bond between them, but he formed them into a people, in which his children who had been scattered were gathered together (cf. Jn. 11:52).

THE MISSIONARY TASK OF THE CHURCH

> "The missionary Church is not concerned with itself—it is a Church for others."

■ *In 1961, the World Council of Churches, at its Third Assembly in New Delhi, India, authorized a study of "The Missionary Structure of the Congregation." It grew out of a concern to define what forms or patterns of life would best serve the missionary task of the church. A number of regional groups worked on the theme from 1961 to 1966. The excerpts below are from the final report of the project,* The Church for Others, *summarizing findings of the European and North American working groups. Both groups began with the premise that the main task of mission is to discern God's presence in the world. The aim and goal of mission was described as "shalom" by the European group and as "humanization" by the North Americans. Existing forms of parish life were severely criticized as "come structures." Favored were "go structures," through which the church could help victims of injustice, racial hatred, loneliness, and other personal crises. The understanding of* congregation *was radically different from prevailing Roman Catholic usage referring to celibate orders and from that of Protestants referring to local parishes. Instead, the congregation in mission was to be a flexible structure evolving around specific needs of people in the world. Laity were encouraged to be bearers of that mission through their secular occupations and community involvements.*

---

*Excerpts from "Ad Gentes" (1965), in *VC2,* 814; cf. Bosch, TM, 371-74.

*The Christ Outside**

To speak of God's action in the contemporary world is to raise the problem of *Christus extra muros ecclesiae*—of Christ outside the walls of the Church. We cannot confine the divine activity to ecclesiastical activity, we also have to recognize that the event of Christ has irreversibly changed the world, and we have therefore to seek traces of this among [persons] who may have little or no connexion with the churches as they are today. But how do we recognize Christ? Our faith is in the one Christ who is present both within and outside the Church; the signs of his presence are the same, but they can only be discerned and understood in faith...

There follow from this certain important consequences:

1. The Church must not think it can separate itself from the world nor must it segregate itself within a position of spiritual pride. The Church can only be the true Church when it knows that it is a part of the world which God loves and to which he reveals his love.

2. The Church loves in order that the world may recognize its true nature. Hence the Church's most important duty is to be present in the world in the knowledge that any loss of contact with it is disobedience to God's will for the world and leads to the destruction of the Church itself.

3. When the Church is aware that the presence and activity of God are not only manifest in itself, it will be constantly vigilant to discern any signs whereby God makes himself known to the world. There is no true Church without a humble dialogue with non-Christians or without fellowship with them. In this dialogue the role of the Church is that of a partner ready to listen and receive.[6]

The World Provides the Agenda[7]

...The missionary character of the congregation depends much more on its faith in that God, who loves the world, has sent his people to love the world, to share in its life, to serve all men in all their needs. It is thus the *missionary* character of the congregation that demands a variety of shapes. Orientation towards the world and openness to it are essential before any new patterns may be evolved to replace traditional structures which have become obsolete or even obstacles to mission. In a fragmented society, filled with stress and tension, the churches must at all times be available to all men and must therefore maintain the necessary flexibility of structures to meet a constantly changing variety of situations. In the present circumstances the growth of vocational groups, factory or student congregations, professional associations, movements for social service or political action, are all indicative of the flexibility and variety required. This flexibility implies that any new patterns emerging must be under constant review to avoid their becoming

---

*Excerpts from World Council of Churches, *The Church for Others and the Church for the World: A Quest for Structures for Missionary Congregations* (Geneva: WCC, 1967), 7, 11-12, 23; cf. Bosch, TM, 379.

standard types and so encouraging a revision into a fresh morphological fundamentalism.

THE CHURCH AS THE GREAT FAMILY

> "The Church as 'the Great Family'...[is] that unifying influence which transcends tribe and clan."

■ *Harry Sawyerr (b. 1909) was one of the first Africans of modern times to achieve a high academic standing in theology. Faithful to the message of the universality of the gospel centered on Jesus Christ, he has constantly explored how African traditional beliefs may be rediscovered in a Christian setting. His educational service in his native Sierra Leone included twenty years (1948-68) at Fourah Bay College as tutor, chaplain, first professor of theology, principal, and vice-chancellor of the University of Sierra Leone, to which it became affiliated. His book,* Creative Evangelism *(1968), is a pioneer work in African theology relating biblical images to African cultural themes.*

*Presenting Jesus Christ in Africa**

African Christians should be helped to realize that Jesus Christ was born as *I* was, grew up as *I* did, perhaps with all the innocent mischief found in a growing boy or girl, and was later persecuted by His contemporaries because He was fully dedicated to the service of God; He therefore suffered death because of His unflinching loyalty to God. But God raised Him from the dead because He was "that Man in whom God lived, and acted (and still does act) humanwise."[8] In this way, we could affirm our Lord's affinity to [humanity] as a basis for presenting the Church as "the Great Family," of which Jesus Christ is the Head.

Christian Africans will thus be able to find in the Church that unifying influence which transcends tribe and clan, and particularly the many divisive influences which national independence tends to engender. The Church as the Body of Christ represents the *primum ens* from which all Christians take their origin, and so tribal affiliations of Christians give way to the totality of the community of the Church, with Jesus Christ as its first member.

Jesus, Founder of the Great Family

The Church as the whole Christ, members of the Body integrated into the Head (*membra cum capite*), is therefore, in our opinion, more likely to appeal to the true feelings of the African because the idea of Jesus Christ as the first-born among many...can readily be introduced in this context. Such an approach would be most

---

*Excerpts from Harry Sawyerr, *Creative Evangelism: Towards a New Christian Encounter with Africa* (London: Lutterworth Press, 1968), 72, 83; cf. Bosch, TM, 389.

effective in presenting the contrast between the ancestors to whom *primacy in time* is attributed, on the one hand, and Jesus Christ to whom we must unreservedly attribute a *primacy in essence,* on the other. This presentation is more germane to the earlier statement that in Jesus Christ we have the fundamental factor of perfect [humanness] associated with perfect godhead—two fundamentals without which the doctrine of the Incarnation is empty of all substance.

OPEN ECCLESIOLOGY

> "The church is called to become open to the world, to others, and to the future."

■ *"What are fitting missionary structures for local congregations?" This was the focus question for a North American working group from 1961 to 1966. Sponsored by the WCC, the twelve theological educators included one woman, Letty Russell of Yale University. In her 1974 pioneer work on liberation theology, Russell drew on the group's work of the preceding decade. This included the judgment that existing church structures are often "heretical" because they thwart the church's mission. Recommended is an "open ecclesiology" which would include "accreditation" of non-parish-based groups as "real" churches.*[9]

*Communion in Dialogue**

The vision of new humankind where there is true partnership is hard to actualize in a world in which hierarchical structures dominate our lives. Such structures are painfully present, not only in politics, economics, and family but also in the church—the very community that is called to be a sign of partnership and humanization. The church oppresses the lives of Third World people by legitimatizing the status quo and helping to support white, Western imperialism. It oppresses the lives of the laity by perpetuating a clerical caste system that dominates the affairs of most confessional bodies and inhibits participation of all believers. It oppresses the lives of women by excluding them from decision-making and equality, and endorsing the cultural myths of their ontological inferiority. Small wonder, then, that liberation theologies have a tendency to number the church among the oppressors, and to speak of it mainly as an institution *from* which we must be liberated!

Liberation theologians, however, need to work together with others to set the church free *for* its true calling to participate in God's Mission in the world. Regardless of its particular ecclesiastical organization, the center of a Christian community is the person and presence of Christ, who promises to be with his people wherever they gather to call upon his name (Mt. 18:20). Where Christ is, there is the church, and there also is freedom. This freedom has to be actualized in helping

---

*Excerpts from Letty Russell, *Human Liberation in a Feminist Perspective—A Theology* (Philadelphia: Westminster Press, 1974), 155-56, 157-59; cf. Bosch, TM, 382.

people hear the word of the gospel and begin to live it out among themselves and with and for others.

The structures of the church are often *heretical structures* that prevent the word from being heard and shared so that it becomes a blessing for others. Those forms of organization which stand in the way of God's Mission have to be subjected to a searching analysis so that they can be replaced or supplemented in order to help the church become a sign of God's intended future.[10]

Open Ecclesiology

There are many perspectives on ecclesiology, but when the missionary nature of the church as God's representative in the world is the chosen perspective, this leads to what is sometimes called *open ecclesiology.*[11] This is an open-ended view of ecclesiology which investigates the variety of possible shapes the church might take in order to participate in God's traditioning activity. It is a marked change in the method of doing ecclesiology. Previously theologians tended to begin with the nature of the church and argued from its nature to its function. Open ecclesiology begins with the function of participation and moves from there to understanding the form and nature of the church....

Open to the World

The church has no walls, nor does it draw a circle around itself that separates it from the world. The community of faith forms an "open circle" around its center: the presence of Jesus Christ. The circle should be open enough for other people to see and join in the central Christ event (1 Cor. 14:13-19). It should also be open enough for the congregation to move out from the center to see and join in the Christ event with others wherever it happens in the world. Those who have been called by Christ are only separate from the world in order to be prepared for this engagement with the world....Thus the church is seen, not as a religious assembly, temple, synagogue, or sect which is closed or sacred, but as a part of the world where it joins God's action in becoming a pressure group for change.

THE CHURCH: A PEOPLES' MOVEMENT

> "The saving work is not co-terminus with the boundaries of the Church."

■ *The radical reevaluation of the church in mission in the 1970s was taking place not just in North America and Western Europe, but also in the Two-thirds World of Africa, Asia, Latin America, and Oceania. The National Christian Council of India, for example, faced the reality that "the classical methods of proclaiming Christ are no longer open or relevant."[12] The reports of their five-year study, all edited by the council's general secretary, Mathai Zachariah, reflect in their titles the key themes:* The Indian Church: Identity and Fulfilment *(1971),* Beyond

Identity, On to Participation *(1973), and* The Church: A Peoples' Movement *(1975).*

New Frontiers of Witness*

The Church in India has reached a nodal point because of both practical and theological reasons. A nodal point is a point of saturation, a point of no growth, and often a point of stagnation. If we are to survive, we have to take new shoots at this point, and new shoots are always a sign of life.

Let us look at the practical reasons first. Today, the classical methods of proclaiming Christ are no longer open or relevant and so we have to seek new methods and new frontiers of witness.

The Church in past has played the role of a *diakonia,* benefactor and compassionate guide. This diakonia role is being increasingly diminished in a welfare state and the state is moving into areas—educational, medical, community service—in which it was the privilege of the Church to serve. Our earlier studies have shown that on the whole we live in India today in the context of the rejection of Christianity and that this rejection is partly due to socio-cultural and political reasons....

The liberating Gospel came to India as a cutting edge and as an emancipator and there were large scale conversions. Then the sleeping giant—Hinduism—slowly awakened and reacted. Aided by the surge of nationalistic feelings the Hindu society awakened to its selfhood, to its own identity. They began to ask whether conversion to Christianity was really a conversion to a higher spiritual life and to a real and personal experience of Christ or whether it is a simple change of rites, myths, concepts and social customs, bearing too often the mark of "made in the West."...

God Saving the Church and the World

In early days we thought of Corpus Christanum, the Church Triumphant, the Church becoming co-terminus with society. But slowly we were compelled—and let us thank God for that—to give more attention to what is happening outside the boundaries of the Church. We have tried to interpret what God is doing in the secular world and in the world of other religions and slowly have come to the realisation of God's presence in the other religions.

In earlier days we saw the picture of the Church going forth, to gather all the nations unto her fold. Today the picture which captures the vision of many devoted Christians is different. It is the glorious picture of Christ leading his whole creation and his whole human family towards the goal of unity in him. In this saving work he is using all human movements of progress, liberation and humanisation. The Church is not his only instrument. It remains central to his purpose, for it is the

---

*Excerpts from Mathai Zachariah, "Introduction," in *The Church: A Peoples' Movement* (Nagpur, India: National Christian Council of India, 1975), 4-5, 6, 8-9; cf. Bosch, TM, 388-89.

place where he is explicitly known and confessed and adored. But the saving work is not co-terminus with the boundaries of the Church; it concerns the whole cosmos....

The New Humanity

While God's saving purpose is not limited to the Church we believe that the Church is the nucleus, the first fruits, *pars pro toto,* the sign and instrument of God's purpose to unite all things in Christ. But the Church is not itself the new humanity. The new humanity transcends the Church. But where do we find this new humanity?...

It is exactly at the point of the humanising process in India that the new humanity is found, because that exactly is the point at which India needs redemption. That is our this-worldly *telos.* The Christian gospel has always met people at the point of their elemental needs and struggles. In earlier days it met the needs of our people through schools, colleges and hospitals. Today our institutions have been dwarfed by the massive government institutions of a welfare state. Also these institutions are serving mostly the elite. Today we are called to enter into the area of the disinherited, of unorganised labour, of the share croppers, of all who are exploited. We are called to be in solidarity with the helpless masses of our country. This is our area of needs and struggles. This is our new frontier....The Church should no longer be just a "gathered community," a "chosen people," or not even a "scattered community"; it should be a peoples' movement, helping the community by being its pathfinder. This is a difficult task we are taking upon ourselves. But if we are the bearers of the liberating Gospel, nothing less than this is asked of us.

SACRIFICE AND SELF EMPTYING

> "If the church can begin to function more effectively as an instrument of Christ it must follow the sacrificial life of the woman."

■ *If the church exists for mission, her primary locus of mission is not the sanctuary but the "secular" world. If every Christian is to be in mission and ministry, then the majority in mission are women. This is the reality brought to light by Oduyoye in the following selection. A Ghanaian, Mercy Amba Oduyoye was educated in the University of Ghana and Cambridge University. Deputy General Secretary of the World Council of Churches, she was one of the first African women to participate in the Ecumenical Association of Third World Theologians. Her concern goes far deeper than recognition of women's leadership in the church—women can provide a Christlike model of servant leadership that has radical implications for the church in ministry in the world.*

*Churchwomen and the Church's Mission**

Jesus called people to become involved in the announcement of the rule of God in the world....The church is in the world to announce, proclaim, and live the kingdom and to do so with all forthrightness. This prophetic function is exercised not only with words that hang in the air or simply become a part of the reasoning and conversation of people, but words that become incarnate in deeds. The church is called to be the bearer of the New Humanity like the mother of our Lord.

The manner of executing the mission cannot be separated from the mission itself. It is in this respect that I wish to situate the Christian's call to self-denial, forgoing privilege and embracing a simplicity of life whose wealth is not only in being poor-in-spirit but in being a church of the poor for the sake of the kingdom. The style of mission is to be the style of the Christian bride who intends to live in mutual obedience with a loving husband in a household whose head is Christ....The church, like a bride, has signed on to be integrally part of a costly enterprise which demands forsaking all and denying self for the sake of the glorious life of the kingdom. Christians are those who have opted to be involved in God's work of transforming the human community into a people ruled by God. Unlike women in their role as wives, the church is totally assured of the love of God and may therefore confidently proceed in this enterprise in the spirit of total dependence upon God. Unlike a woman the church is assured that losing itself in the life of Christ (being in Christ) is the only way of being truly the church. There are therefore no ifs and buts around its call to live the "truly human" life—which in the human ordering of community is demanded only of women. It is the whole church that is called upon to sing with Charles Wesley "Behold the Servant of the Lord."[13] Hence the woman becomes the model of the church, and the discipleship of Mary the mother of Jesus and "the other women" become examples not only for churchwomen but for all Christians.

On earth the church is on a mission, and Christians see themselves as a people who have been sent by Christ. Being sent always means forgoing one thing in order to undertake another, and therefore involves dedicating, consecrating, and setting apart or aside, indeed giving up much so that the new mandate may be fulfilled. Thus Christians individually and corporately as the church are called to a life of sacrifice.

Emptying the Church

The church can begin to function more effectively as an instrument of Christ if it models itself on the sacrificial life of the woman, indeed of Christ himself. Socialized to love, the woman holds together the fabric of society by her costly

---

*Excerpts from Mercy Oduyoye, "Churchwomen and the Church's Mission," in *New Eyes for Reading: Biblical and Theological Reflections by Women from the Third World,* ed. John S. Pobee and Barbel von Wartenberg-Potter (Geneva: World Council of Churches, 1986), 69-70, 76-77, 79-80; cf. Bosch, TM, 374-75.

giving of herself. This living for the other, yes, dying for "friends" is the ultimate evidence of "greater love" which in the final analysis is the only agent of history that struggles to conform to God's project of a new humanity in a new society and to the culminating purpose of making all things new.

Jesus, who is the foundation of the church's mission, leaves us with no illusions about the difficulties inherent in the demands of God whose kingdom the church's mission seeks to foster. His own salvific mission was undertaken in the context of constant submission to the will of God, voluntarily adhered to as in the original "laying aside" of his divinity enshrined for us in the hymn found in the letter to the Philippians cited above.

What will such a self-emptying mean for the church? My observation tends to indicate that whereas the church affirms the death and resurrection of Christ as an indication of the power of powerlessness, in Africa at any rate, it tries to hold on to power; and that in spite of the dominical dictum that to gain true life we must be prepared to lose our life for his sake, the church and its institutions in Africa are trying desperately to hold on to power as a means of holding on to life....A Christ-bearing church will have to empty itself of all pride, self-seeking and, above all, of the fear of death, not to talk of pomp and circumstances surrounding its participation on state occasions. The churches must be like the young girl who braved the ignominy of bearing an "illegitimate child" and, I imagine, the loss of a "society wedding" she had been dreaming of during all her maiden days, assured only by the words of an angel that she was in the employ of God.

THE CHURCH OF THE POOR

> "The church must arise out of the 'liberating potential of the poor.' "

■ *Pablo Richard was born in Chile in 1939. From early childhood, he was exposed to the reality of Latin America's extensive poverty. He studied philosophy in Chile and Austria, theology in Chile and Rome, and sociology in Paris, earning a Ph.D. at the Sorbonne in 1978. He has taught New Testament (Chile, 1970-73), and theology (Costa Rica, 1978-). His identification with the poor in Santiago, where he served as a parish priest, led to his political exile in 1973. Out of the trauma of torture and death of those years, Richard forged a new vision of the church reformed. Rejecting the "Christendom" paradigm with its alliance of church and state, Richard articulates a new model of the church of the poor emerging from the Christian base communities (CBCs).*[14]

*The Popular Church**

The term "popular church" reflects a political or sociological analysis, whereas

---

*Excerpts from Pablo Richard, *Death of Christendoms: Birth of the Church* (Maryknoll, NY: Orbis Books, 1987), 172, 184-85; cf. Bosch, TM, 386.

the thinking behind the expression "church of the poor" is more theological. Both expressions are legitimate and point to a new model of church, one that stands in opposition to Christendom. This is not "another" church but a renewal movement that remains within the unity of the church. . . .

The "Historical Project"

By "historical project" I do not mean a group of tasks or an action program. It is rather a concrete theoretical framework for organizing and guiding the activity of the church within society. Here I shall simply make an outline sketch of this historical project for the church of the poor in Latin America.

First, the church should concentrate its prophetic, priestly and pastoral work where its greatest force and strength lie—in the exploited and believing mass of the people. The power of the popular church is in the spiritual experience of the people; that is the soil in which the church must sink its roots. The church must arise out of the "liberating potential of the poor"—that is, out of the power of the faith of the poor—to discover and announce the true God, who is the liberating God of the Bible, and also out of the power of the faith of the poor to destroy the idolatry and the fetishism of the system of domination. Hence the challenge to the church of the poor is to develop a "popular" kind of pastoral work, a pastoral activity that will reflect the "logic of the majority" and likewise to be a church that is built up as the people of God through its ability to provide pastoral leadership for the people, those who are the majority. Through CBCs the church must grow throughout the whole body of the people, not in order to dominate it as a "people of the church" but to serve it as the "people of God."

Secondly, the church of the poor is not a political project and should never use political power as a means for expanding or defending itself. . . .The church of the poor must not make use of political power in order to deal with the other model of church—namely, Christendom. The popular church must take its support only from the power of the gospel, the power of its faith, hope, and love. This might seem like a weakness of the popular church, but its strength is to be found precisely in that weakness.

Thirdly, the final element of this project in history is ecumenism. This ecumenism is not something accidental to the popular church but basic and intrinsic to it. Nothing is more damaging to the mission of the church than religious sectarianism and proselytism. Ecumenism asserts that human beings are not the private property of any church but that they belong *to God.* Ecumenism is a basic requirement if the church is to be discovered and affirmed as people of God.

NOTES

1. Karl Müller, *Mission Theology: An Introduction* (Nettetal, Germany: Steyler Verlag—Wort und Werk, 1987), p. 101.

2. M. Goguel, "Quelques remarques sur l'unité de l'Église dans le Christianisme primitif," in *Bull. Fac. libre de Théol. protest. de Paris,* May 1936, pp. 1-9.

3. This idea is perhaps that which remains the most firm and most lively among the famous studies of Sohm. Among the most recent, cf. K. L. Schmidt, "Ecclesia," in Kittel, *Worterbuch,* 3: 508.

4. Cf. Rom. 16:17, 1 Cor. 1:10, Col. 2:7, 1 Tim. 6:3 and 6:20-21, 2 Tim. 1:13-14, 2:2, 3:14, Acts 20:28. On the role of the community of Jerusalem, see L. Cerfaux, "Les Saints de Jérusalem," in *Eph. theol. lovan* 2 (1925): 510-29, and "S. Paul et l'unité de l'Église," in *Nouv Rev. théol.* 55 (1926): 657-73; B. Allo, O.P., "La portée de la collecte pour Jérusalem dan les plans de Paul," in *Rev. bibl.* (1936): 529-37.

5. Cf. Dogm. Const. *Lumen Gentium,* 1.

6. W. J. Hollenweger, "Christus intra et extra muros ecclesia," in *Planning for Mission,* ed. Thomas Wieser (New York: U.S. Conference for the World Council of Churches, 1966), pp. 56-61.

7. W. J. Hollenweger, "The World is the Agenda," *Concept* 9 (Sept. 1966): 19-20.

8. Cf. Norman Pittenger, *The Word Incarnate* (New York: Harper, 1959), p. 17.

9. *The Church for Others and The Church for the World* (Geneva: WCC, 1967), p. 92.

10. Ibid., p. 19; Jürgen Moltmann, *The Gospel of Liberation* (Waco, TX: Word Books, 1973), pp. 78-94.

11. *The Church for Others,* p. 92; Joseph Ratzinger, *The Open Circle* (New York: Sheed and Ward, 1966); Michael Novak, *The Open Church* (New York: Macmillan, 1963). In this chapter and elsewhere, I am following current usage in ecclesiology between *ecclesial* (theological perspective on the church) and *ecclesiastical* (church organization).

12. Mathai Zachariah, *The Church: A Peoples' Movement* (Nagpur, India: National Christian Council of India, 1975), p. 1.

13. British Conference, *The Methodist Hymn Book,* 1933, No. 520.

14. Cf. Deane William Ferm, *Profiles in Liberation: 36 Portraits of Third World Theologians* (Mystic, CT: Twenty-Third Publications, 1988), pp. 174-77.

6

Mission as Missio Dei

"Christ has no hands but our hands
To do His work today;
He has no feet but our feet
To lead men in his way;
He has no tongue but our tongues
To tell men how He died;
He has no help but our help
To bring them to His side."[1]

In 1910, John R. Mott, Secretary of the Student Volunteer Movement for Foreign Missions, concluded his call to action:

> *It is indeed the decisive hour of Christian mission....Let each Christian so resolve and so act that if a sufficient number of others will do likewise, all men before this generation passes away may have an adequate opportunity to know of Christ.*[2]

These words are representative of the prevailing understanding of the importance of human agency in Christian mission in the nineteenth and early twentieth centuries. Mission was interpreted in a variety of ways. Sometimes it had a soteriological focus on saving individuals from eternal damnation. Others understood mission primarily in cultural terms, as introducing persons to the blessings and privileges of the Christian West. Still others understood mission as involvement in a historic process of transformation of the world into the kingdom of God (Bosch, TM, 389).

Recovery of the understanding that mission is primarily a divine initiative began slowly in Europe in the 1930s. In 1932, Karl Barth was one of the first to write of mission as an activity of God.

The shift from a church-centered to a theocentric focus accelerated after World War II. The rape of Nanking by the Japanese and the Holocaust stunned persons of conscience. What of the "missions" that obliterated Dresden, Hiroshima, and Nagasaki—attacks designed not to destroy military targets but to break the will of peoples by annihilating whole populations? Was this not also genocide and demonic? As for Christian missions following the war, the hopes for winning the world for Christ in this generation suffered a crushing blow as China, the jewel of Christian missions, was closed to all missionaries in 1950 following the Communist victory.

The idea of the missio Dei, *according to Bosch (TM, 390), first emerged at the Willingen Conference of the IMC in 1952. Delegates affirmed that mission is derived from the very nature of God.*

A similar shift from a church-centered to a God-centered theology was taking place among Roman Catholics. Key documents from Vatican II carried the understandings that mission is God's epiphany (Ad Gentes) *and that God is at work through the Spirit, giving men and women "an unquenchable thirst for human dignity"* (Gaudium et Spes).

But the theocentric mission was soon to acquire new images. James Cone, in a black theology of liberation, understood God as one who identifies with the oppressed like a black Moses hearing the cries of his enslaved brothers and sisters. Cone urged his readers to focus exclusively "in terms of what God does for man and not what man does for himself." In South Africa, Sabelo Ntwasa and Basil Moore also sought new images. Rather than the frequently heard appeals for a disembodied love, they began with the belief that God chooses freedom and wholeness for God's children.

Continuing the shift from church-centered to theocentric mission, Jürgen Moltmann of Germany focused on Christ's messianic mission and the creative mission of the Spirit, in which the church participates. Participation *is Moltmann's key word (rather than human initiation)—participation in creation's liberation, in uniting men and women, in the history of God's suffering, and in God's dealings with the world.*

Speaking out of a Latin American cultural context, Julia Esquivel recalled the power of masks worn in religious processions both to mirror and to hide reality. For her, the religious establishment's images of God as linked to power and privilege are but masks of death for the masses. She calls for Christians to be freed from this charade so they may proclaim the God of Jesus the liberator, who is accessible to the poorest of the poor.

Philip Potter speaks out of the Latin American reality but also as general secretary of the WCC. Emphasizing that mission is God's, not ours, he affirms that the God of the Bible is a sending missionary God, that God has chosen to act in history, and that God seeks a renewed humanity. Out of Asia, C. S. Song of Taiwan emphasizes the compassion of God. From Latin America, Orlando Costas of Puerto Rico affirms that God's mission is not confined to the church but involves God's redemptive activity in the secular affairs of life.

The final selection in this chapter comes from Bishop Anastasios of Androussa, Greece. The recovery of mission for Orthodox Christians, he believes, will involve deeper participation in the life of the Holy Trinity, in which participation in worship and service are inextricably tied together. In that perspective indifference to mission is a denial of Orthodoxy.

THE CHURCH'S MISSIONARY OBLIGATION

"There is no participation in Christ without participation in His mission to the world."

■ *In 1952, the International Missionary Council convened a major meeting at Willingen, Germany, to rethink the nature of the missionary obligation of the church. Revolutionary world changes (the Cold War, newly independent Third World nations, the expulsion of missionaries from China, etc.) raised the question as to whether missions—in the traditional sense—were not already a thing of the past. A new "theology of missions" was called for. The Willingen document on "The Theological Basis of the Missionary Obligation" was a pioneering effort. A theocentric focus on mission as the* Missio Dei *replaced the former church-centric focus.*

*Mission—The Church's Royal Charter**

The missionary obligation of the Church comes from the love of God in His active relationship with [humanity].

For God sent forth His Son, Jesus Christ, to seek out, and gather together, and transform, all [persons] who are alienated by sin from God and their fellows. This is and always has been the will of God. It was embodied in Christ and will be completed in Christ. For God also sends forth the Holy Spirit. By the Holy Spirit the Church, experiencing God's active love, is assured that God will complete what He has set His hand to in the sending of His Son. This is the hope with which the Church looks forward to the goal of its existence, which in fact sets the Church marching onwards. In this sense "mission" belongs to the purpose of the Church.

The work of the Holy Spirit in the Church and through the Church ensures that "mission" should also belong to the continuing life of the Church. By the Holy Spirit the Church only continues to live as the Church when it is the place at which God's love, active in the death of Christ, is both sent forth into the world by witness and re-presented to God by worship. In this sense "mission" belongs to the life of the Church.

Those who are sought out, gathered together, and transformed by Christ are the Church. Their very existence, therefore, springs from God's sending forth of His Son. In this sense "mission" belongs to the basic structure of the Church.

Whatever else ought to be said about the structure, life, and purpose of the Church, this one thing must be said: that "mission" is woven into all three and cannot be separated out from any one without destroying it. When God says to the Church: "Go forth and be my witnesses," He is not giving the Church a commission

---

*Excerpts from International Missionary Council (Willingen, 1952), *Missions Under the Cross*, ed. N. Goodall (London: Edinburgh House Press for the IMC, 1953), 241; cf. Bosch, TM, 390.

that is added to its other duties; but a commission that belongs to its royal charter (covenant) to be the Church.

A MATTER OF DIVINE PURPOSE

> "Mission [is]...not a matter of human goodwill and reparations, but a matter of divine purpose."

■ *Karl Barth (1886-1968) has been called "the chief initiator of a postmodern paradigm in theology."[3] In the general upheaval following World War I and the Great Depression, he was the first to recover the biblical emphasis on God's initiative in salvation. In 1932, at the Brandenburg Missionary Conference, Barth rejected the liberal agenda in which mission was understood as a "civilizing" human activity of witness and service. Mission, for Barth, began with the Divine sending of God's self in the Holy Trinity. The church can be in mission authentically only in obedience to God as* missio.

*"Theology and Mission in the Present"**

As is generally known, mission could also be an instrument of religious or civilizing propaganda, or even an economic-political powerplay, and theology a sport—maybe even an especially dangerous sport of arbitrary speculation and intellectual self-assuredness and self-importance. What mission and what theology could make the claim, by the nature of their conduct, not to be a part of this kind of twilight? What mission and what theology could risk to display even a hint of such conduct that would save them to some degree from the suspicion of wrongdoing? Where their intentions are visible, and where they can be recognized as the works of faith also, there it cannot be their merit, for this takes place not due to pretence, imparted and bestowed upon themselves, but because there is something other than the self, something much greater than their human sanctimoniousness, that has spoken for them and through them. This human sanctimoniousness as such would certainly not be more than an attempt of, and a claim to, ecclesiastical obedience.

Mission by God's Free Omnipotence and Mercy

Such a claim speaks also an affirming internal reason: When mission and theology want to be the works of faith according to their own assessment and declaration, then they try to say with it that they do not carry the justification of their existence within themselves, but that they hope to receive the free grace of God, and without prejudice. Whereas the church in general cannot and does not

---

*Karl Barth, *Theologische Fragen und Antworten* (Zollikon: Evangelischer Verlag, 1957), 104-05, 114-15; excerpts translated from the German by Domenico Nigrelli; cf. Bosch, TM, 389.

exist as the true Church, whereby pious, honest, and eager human beings have a church and want to be the Church, but that always and everywhere God in his own free omnipotence and mercy wants to have a Church, so is this not a matter of human goodwill and reparations, but a matter of divine purpose and confirmation when mission and theology are what they intend to be. If they are what they intend to be, namely the works of faith, then they are built upon the solid rock of God's election, who speaks his word in his time, and whose Spirit blows, wherever he wills. What they are in by themselves cannot keep the best mission, the best theology, from the possibility that they, in reality forsaken by God, could be this altogether other, which they do not want to be. They are justified works of faith if they are kept away from this abyss by God's free and non-prejudiced grace, but not if they attempt to keep or want to keep themselves away on their own. The honor of their success is not their own, but always God's. Concerning their own honor, namely the honor of that which human beings are capable of accomplishing in mission and theology can, after a thorough self-examination, always be no more than a modest attempt. In light of this verdict, mission and theology will have to be inseparable at all cost.

Mission as Obedience

Mission has, in the past as well as today, made it as its primary focus to explain for itself and for the whole Church what its *Missionsmotiv,* its purpose for mission is. What that means is to justify itself as a necessary function of the Church and as an indispensable part of Christendom. . . .

Mission is in need of being justified—like everything else which the church does. That means that one of the most daring things which the church does is the presentation of her motives. This will appear as a transcending of herself, indeed a very special type of justification. But does the Church understand that in the end she cannot justify herself, but that she can only hope to be justified as an act of obedience, without being able to claim that security as one might claim those motives for mission which one would like to appear to have? Are not all motivations of mission, as they have been stated in the past and as they are presented today, mere representations of a motive which one can neither describe nor assume, because it is identical with the current will and order of one person, namely the divine person, the Lord of the Church—a will and an order that does not conform to any system made up of human understanding, points of view, or reasons, even if these were made by the most enlightened Christians. Is not this free will and order something ever new, and always with the courage to begin anew, as read in Holy Scripture, as heard, and as understood? Its content may be an imperative to "go forward," or "stop," or "go back!" Yet, no matter what, it indicates that we cannot will to be self-sufficient, but must always be open and prepared to find it.

Missio—The Divine Sending

Must not even the most faithful missionary, the most convinced friend of missions, have reason to reflect that the term *missio* was in the ancient Church an expression of the doctrine of the Trinity—namely the expression of the divine sending forth of the self, the sending of the Son and the Holy Spirit to the world? Can we indeed claim that we can do it any other way?

THE EPIPHANY OF GOD'S WILL

> "Missionary activity is...a manifestation of God's plan, its epiphany."

■ *The Vatican II "Decree on the Missionary Activity of the Church"* (Ad Gentes) *illustrates the church's rediscovery of the biblical nature of its mission as a manifestation of God's reaching out in saving love to a needy world. The church is to be in mission because God wishes all persons to be saved and to come to a knowledge of the truth (Art. 7).*

*Mission as God's Epiphany**

(From Chapter I, "Doctrinal Principles")

9. The period, therefore, between the first and second coming of the Lord is the time of missionary activity, when, like the harvest, the Church will be gathered from the four winds into the kingdom of God.[4] For the Gospel must be preached to all peoples before the Lord comes (cf. Mk. 13:10).

Missionary activity is nothing else, and nothing less, than the manifestation of God's plan, its epiphany and realization in the world and in history; that by which God, through mission, clearly brings to its conclusion the history of salvation. Through preaching and the celebration of the sacraments, of which the holy Eucharist is the center and summit, missionary activity makes Christ present, he who is the author of salvation. It purges of evil associations those elements of truth and grace which are found among peoples, and which are, as it were, a secret presence of God; and it restores them to Christ their source who overthrows the rule of the devil and limits the manifold malice of evil. So whatever goodness is found in the minds and hearts of men [and women], customs and cultures of peoples, far from being lost is purified, raised to a higher level and reaches its perfection, for the glory of God, the confusion of the demon, and [for human] happiness.[5] Thus missionary activity tends towards eschatological fullness;[6] by it the people of God is expanded to the degree and until the time that the Father has fixed by his own authority (cf. Acts 1:7); of it was said in prophecy: "Enlarge the space for your tent and spread out your tent clothes unsparingly" (Isa. 54:2).[7] By missionary activity the mystical Body is enlarged until it reaches the mature fullness of Christ (cf. Eph. 4:13); the spiritual temple where God is adored in spirit and truth

---

*Excerpts from the "Decree on the Church's Missionary Activity" (*Ad Gentes*), Art. 9 (1965), in *VC2,* 823-24; cf. Bosch, TM, 391.

(cf. Jn. 4:23) grows and is built up on the foundation of the apostles and prophets, Jesus Christ himself being the chief cornerstone (Eph. 2:20).[8]

GOD'S SPIRIT WORKS FOR THE COMMON GOOD

"The Spirit of God...renews the face of the earth."

■ *"What is the relation of the Church to the world?" From the floor during the first session of Vatican II, Cardinal Léon-Joseph Suenens of Belgium proposed that the council provide an answer to this oft-asked question. The result was "The Pastoral Constitution on the Church in the Modern World"* (Gaudium et Spes). *In it the Church's leaders affirmed that God is at work through the Spirit to promote the common good.*

*God's Intention for Human Community**

(From Chapter II, "The Community of Mankind")

The social order and its development must constantly yield to the good of the person, since the order of things must be subordinate to the order of persons and not the other way around, as the Lord suggested when he said that the Sabbath was made for [humankind] and not [humankind] for the Sabbath.[9] The social order requires constant improvement: it must be founded in truth, built on justice, and enlivened by love; it should grow in freedom towards a more humane equilibrium.[10] If these objectives are to be attained there will first have to be a renewal of attitudes and far-reaching social changes.

The Spirit of God, who, with wondrous providence, directs the course of time and renews the face of the earth, assists at this development. The ferment of the Gospel has aroused and continues to arouse in the hearts of men [and women] an unquenchable thirst for human dignity.

GOD'S LOVE AND RIGHTEOUSNESS

"God has made the oppressed condition his own condition."

■ *James H. Cone (b. 1938) has taught theology at Union Theological Seminary in New York since 1966. His work* A Black Theology of Liberation, *published in 1970, was the pioneer work in that field. Covering all the major Christian doctrines, he set forth a systematic treatment of the Gospel in the light of black experience in America. For Cone, the function of theology is to define the meaning of liberation for the oppressed and to make them aware that their struggle for justice is consistent with the Gospel of Jesus Christ. In addition to*

---

*Excerpts from the "Pastoral Constitution on the Church in the Modern World" (*Gaudium et Spes*), Art. 26 (1965), in *VC2,* 927-28; cf. Bosch, TM, 391-92.

his frequent public lectures and scholarly writings, Cone was a founding member of the Ecumenical Association of Third World Theologians.

*God Is Black**

The blackness of God means that God has made the oppressed condition God's own condition. This is the essence of the biblical revelation, By electing Israelite slaves as the people of God and by becoming the Oppressed One in Jesus Christ, the human race is made to understand that God is known where human beings experience humiliation and suffering. It is not that God feels sorry and takes pity on them (the condescending attitude of those racists who need their guilt assuaged for getting fat on the starvation of others); quite the contrary, God's election of Israel and incarnation in Christ reveal that the *liberation* of the oppressed is a part of the innermost nature of God. Liberation is not an afterthought, but the essence of divine activity.

The blackness of God means that the essence of the nature of God is to be found in the concept of liberation. Taking seriously the Trinitarian view of the Godhead, black theology says that as Creator, God identified with oppressed Israel, participating in the bringing into being of this people; as Redeemer, God became the Oppressed One in order that all may be free from oppression; as Holy Spirit, God continues the work of liberation. The Holy Spirit is the Spirit of the Creator and the Redeemer at work in the forces of human liberation in out society today....

The Love and Righteousness of God

The theological statement "God is love" is the most widely accepted assertion regarding the nature of God. All theologians would agree that it is impossible to speak of the Christian understanding of God without affirming the idea of love as essential to the divine nature....

Black theology agrees that the idea of love is indispensable to the Christian view of God. The exodus, the call of Israel into being as the people of the covenant, the gift of the promised land, the rise of prophecy, the second exodus, and above all the incarnation reveal God's self-giving love to oppressed humanity.

We do not read far in the biblical tradition without recognizing that the divine-human fellowship is to be understood exclusively in terms of what God does for humankind and not what humankind does for itself or for God.

GOD IS FREEDOM

> "If God is about true humanness and thus freedom and wholeness, we need new images of God."

---

*Excerpts from James H. Cone, *A Black Theology of Liberation*, Twentieth Anniversay Edition (Maryknoll, NY: Orbis Books, 1990), 63-64, 66, 68-69; cf. Bosch, TM, 392.

■ *Black theology, as developed by James Cone and others, found a responsive chord in South Africa. Moses, M. L. King, Jr., and Steven Biko—out of oppression—experienced God as a liberator who would lead God's children out of bondage. A series of 1971 conferences on black theology, sponsored by the Black Theology Project of the University Christian Movement, was the catalyst that launched black theology into prominence in that country. Although its leaders were persecuted and its thought banned in South Africa, the new black theology of liberation flourished. The following excerpt by the editors captures some of the key concepts concerning liberation as God's mission.*[11]

*Relational Symbols of God**

Traditional Christianity has always asserted God's transcendence and his immanence, the images of which have been of a great Father-figure "out there" and a loving Son "amongst us." For the reasons already given, these symbols must be rejected.

If true humanness—and hence freedom and wholeness—lies in the spaces between people, and if God is about true humanness and thus freedom and wholeness, we need new images of God which give content and direction to the "spaces between people," i.e., we need relational images of God.

If, for example, we say with St. John that "God is love" and take this literally rather than figuratively (i.e., God is a "Person" who "loves me"), then it is possible to conceive transcendence and immanence in new ways. We know something of immanent love in our own experience, and learn its meaning more deeply as we explore our history. At every point where love is known and felt and shown, there God is experienced and revealed to us, in us, and through us. Some men [and women] know and show love fleetingly and imperfectly. Others, like Christ, are burning, glowing incarnations of it. But despite all we know, have learned and have experienced of love, we know that we have not yet experienced it in all its fullness. We know nothing of how a totally loving and life-affirming society would be. There is, we believe and hope, always a "beyond"' to love. This "beyond" (call it transcendence if it helps) calls us forward to bold new ventures.

Thus there is the known, the experienced, the immanent in the personal relationships of love, but there is also the unknown, the not-yet-experienced, the transcendent. And if anyone tells us that love is nothing but an abstract construct without power, we can only reply that [that person] has not yet begun to live.

But in exploring a new relational image of God we need something more total and more vital than the much-abused "love." Perhaps such an image would be "God is Freedom." God is the freedom made known in our history. God is the freedom fleetingly and incompletely known in our own experience. But God is also the

---

*Excerpts from Sabelo Ntwasa and Basil Moore, "The Concept of God in Black Theology," in *Black Theology: The South African Voice,* ed. Basil Moore (London: C. Hurst, & Co., 1973), 26-28; cf. Bosch, TM, 392.

freedom beyond anything we have yet known, the freedom that calls us out of our chains of oppression into a wholeness of life. God is this wholeness which exists in the spaces between the people when their dignity and worth is mutually affirmed in love, truth, honesty, justice and caring warmth.

If we were attempting to depict God understood in this new symbol of Freedom that means wholeness, we would take seriously the old Hebrew dictum that God cannot be represented in any created object. But we would depict people in love, or people throwing off their shackles of slavery, or people raising their fists aloft in a call and salute to freedom.The old Negro spiritual sings our new hymn well:

> Oh Freedom, oh Freedom,
> Oh Freedom over me.
> And before I'll be a slave
> I'll be buried in my grave,
> and go home to my Lord and be free.

MESSIANIC MISSION—THE WHOLE CHURCH'S CALLING

> "The church participates in Christ's messianic mission and in the creative mission of the Spirit."

■ *Jürgen Moltmann has been a creative catalyst in the contemporary church's rediscovery of mission as the* missio Dei. *Since 1967, he has been professor of systematic theology at the University of Tübingen in Germany. He is known through his writings primarily as a theologian of hope. In the first two volumes of his systematic theology, Moltmann arrives at Pentecost and the sending of the Holy Spirit by way of Easter* (Theology of Hope) *and Good Friday* (The Crucified God). *In the third,* The Church in the Power of the Spirit, *he developed his theology of the church as a fellowship in total, radical reliance on the presence and power of the Holy Spirit as it renews itself in fellowship with Christ. Concerning its mission, he writes: "What we have to learn is not that the church 'has' a mission, but the very reverse: that the mission of Christ creates its own church. Mission does not come from the church; it is from mission and in the light of mission that the church has to be understood."*[12]

*The "Experience" of God**

God experiences history in order to effect history. He goes out of himself in order to gather into himself. He is vulnerable, takes suffering and death on himself in order to heal, to liberate and to confer new life. The history of God's suffering in the passion of the Son and the sighings of the Spirit serves the history of God's

---

*Excerpts from Jürgen Moltmann, *The Church in the Power of the Spirit* (New York: Harper & Row, 1977), 64-65; cf. Bosch, TM, 390.

joy in the Spirit and his completed felicity at the end. That is the ultimate goal of God's history of suffering in the world. But once the joy of union is complete the history of suffering does not become obsolete and a thing of the past. As suffering that has been endured, and which has brought about liberation, eternal life and union, it remains the ground of eternal joy in the salvation of God and his new creation.

The Participation of the Church in the History of God

In the movements of the trinitarian history of God's dealings with the world the church finds and discovers itself, in all the relationships which comprehend its life. It finds itself on the path traced by this history of God's dealings with the world, and it discovers itself as one element in the movements of the divine sending, gathering together and experience. It is not the church that has a mission of salvation to fulfil to the world; it is the mission of the Son and the Spirit through the Father that includes the church, creating a church as it goes on its way. It is not the church that administers the Spirit as the Spirit of preaching, the Spirit of the sacraments, the Spirit of the ministry or the Spirit of tradition. The Spirit "administers" the church with the events of word and faith, sacrament and grace, offices and traditions. If the church understands itself, with all its tasks and powers, in the Spirit and against the horizon of the Spirit's history, then it also understands its particularity as one element in the power of the Spirit and has no need to maintain its special power and its special charges with absolute and self-destructive claims. It then has no need to look sideways in suspicion or jealousy at the saving efficacies of the Spirit outside the church; instead it can recognize them thankfully as signs that the Spirit is greater than the church and that God's purpose of salvation reaches beyond the church.

The church participates in Christ's messianic mission and in the creative mission of the Spirit. We cannot therefore say *what* the church is in all circumstances and what it comprises in itself. But we can tell *where* the church happens. The phrase "The church is present where..." used in article VII of the Augsburg Confession and in article III of the Barmen Declaration, is a correct one, but it cannot be restricted merely to "true proclamation" and "a right administration of the sacraments." Both are included, yet we shall have to say more comprehensively: the church is present wherever "the manifestation of the Spirit" (1 Cor. 12.7) takes place.

The church participates in the glorifying of God in creation's liberation. Wherever this takes place through the workings of the Spirit, there is the church. The true church is the song of thanksgiving of those who have been liberated.

The church participates in the uniting of men [and women] with one another, in the uniting of society with nature and in the uniting of creation with God. Wherever unions like this take place, however fragmentary and fragile they may be, there is the church. The true church is the fellowship of love.

Love participates in the history of God's suffering. Wherever men [women] take up their cross and in their self-giving are made like the one who was crucified, wherever the sighings of the Spirit are heard in the cry for freedom, there is the church. The true church is "the church under the cross."

But in suffering and under the cross the church also participates in the history of the divine joy. It rejoices over every conversion and every liberation, because it is itself the fellowship of the converted and the liberated. Wherever the joy of God can be heard, there is the church. The true church is joy in the Spirit.

Thus the whole being of the church is marked by participation in the history of God's dealings with the world.[13] The Apostles' Creed expresses this truth by integrating the *credo ecclesiam* in the *credo in deum triunum.* And no ecclesiology should sink below this level.

FORGER OF OUR HISTORY

"The God that sweats in the streets."

■ *"Your Kingdom Come" was the theme of the WCC's World Conference on Mission and Evangelism held in Melbourne, Australia, in 1980. It was widely representative, with over 600 participants—Orthodox, Roman Catholic, and Protestant—from 100 countries. Two-thirds came from their local involvements in mission, this being their first ecumenical conference outside their own countries. Among them was Julia Esquivel, a lay leader and Bible study organizer in Guatemala, who presented a plenary address. Speaking on "The Crucified Lord: A Latin American Perspective," she described God's pain in the suffering and struggle of the peasants of Guatemala.*

*The God of Jesus, Forger of Our History**

To the extent that the people of faith in Central America have unmasked the god of death, the real God, the God of Jesus, the God of Abraham, Isaac and Jacob, has begun to be accessible to the poorest. He has revealed himself in events and in the communal reading of the Bible. That God has been described in the People's Mass of the Nicaraguans:

> You are the God of the poor,
> The human and humble God,
> The God that sweats in the street
> The God of the worn and leathery face.
> That is why I speak to you,
> In the way my people speak,

---

*Excerpts from Julia Esquivel, "The Crucified Lord: A Latin American Perspective," in World Council of Churches, *Your Kingdom Come: Report on the World Conference on Mission and Evangelism, Melbourne, Australia, 12-25 May 1980* (Geneva: WCC, 1980), 54-55; cf. Bosch, TM, 392.

Because you are God the worker,
Christ the labourer.

Brothers, sisters, that God who perspires in the streets, who shouts through the people asking for freedom, that God who suffers with the people (the suffering servant of today—Isa. 53), that God whom we find in sumptuous and cold temples is the God of the sweaty and pallid face of the tortured peasant of Latin America. He can only reign through a people, in a people that transforms itself, its paths, its life, its history and its future. That is the Justice-God, the Fraternal-God, the Liberation-God who appears also to us in the Exodus of the people of Israel and in each exodus of the people of the earth that march full of faith towards the kingdom of Life.

God Who Brings Changes

This God, unknown in the temples of development, consumerism and capital, whose glory has been usurped by the economic powers, substituted for by technology at the service of wealth, is the God who changes the laws of the transnational free enterprise (the creation of abundance for some and death for many) for laws that safeguard and defend life. It is the God who shall inexorably change the laws of the mighty in order to plant in the hearts of the people the law of love, the law of life (Ezek. 37:24; Isa. 33:22). It is the God who changes hearts of stone into hearts of flesh. It is the God who changes individualism for fraternal communion. Such communion emerges from suffering, from the struggle, and can be seen in the organization of the people who collectively and in solidarity are breaking through the frontiers of geography, sex, race and classes in Central America. It is the God who creates a human family in all the countries of the earth. It is the God who reminds us since the time of his friend Abraham that each nation is a chosen one, that each one has its Easter in Jesus (Eph. 2) and that Easter is the starting point so that bread, that is, all the resources of the earth, may be shared and distributed for the benefit of all [humankind]. That God, our Father, offers to us a fatherhood which of necessity manifests itself in society as a real fraternity which means co-participation in work and in production for the subsistence and maintenance of the life of the people.

MISSION IS GOD'S, NOT OURS

"The church must adapt its forms and structures to God's mission today."

■ *"The Christian world mission is Christ's not ours."*[14] *Philip Potter, the WCC's general secretary, chose this statement of the International Missionary Council in 1958 as a theme for his theology of mission, drawing out its consequences for mission. Born in 1921 in Dominica, West Indies, Potter devoted a long career in church service to mission, ecumenism, and work with youth and students.*

Besides twenty-four years on the WCC staff, including director of its Division of World Mission and Evangelism (1967-72) and general secretary (1972-84), he served as a Methodist missionary to the poor of Haiti, as president of the World Student Christian Federation, and as overseas secretary of the Methodist Missionary Society based in London, England.

*The Mission of God**

The Latin phrase *missio Dei* has become current in the last several years as a means of redefining what is meant by mission today. Quite simply—and quite profoundly—what this phrase means to assert is that *mission is God's, not ours.*

A Missionary God

In the first place, the God of the Bible is a missionary God, a God who *sends.* Through his word and Spirit, he creates man and woman in his own image and sends them out to master creation under his just and merciful will. . . .

Furthermore, this missionary God has chosen to act in history. "God so loved the world that he sent his only Son. . . ." says John, though he goes on to say how hostile this world is to God and his will. But God's love for this world is revealed in his purpose to transform the world—a transformation shown in the life, death, and resurrection of Jesus Christ. This purpose embraces God's action in creation and redemption—with a fully responsible human partner sharing his lordship over creation in justice and peace. In Christ this new humanity has come into being, and the objective of this mission is that all should share in it. . . .

In the third place, the idea that the mission is God's sharpens our focus on the gospel as the good news of renewed humanity in Christ. . . .

The Bible expresses the same reality of the new humanity in the word *shalom,* peace. The goal towards which God is working, the ultimate end of his mission, is the establishment of *shalom.* This involves the realization of the full potentialities of all creation and its ultimate reconciliation and unity in Christ.

Four Consequences

Let me enumerate four consequences of these central insights. In the first place, the church as the people of God is not the centre and goal of mission, but the means and instrument. The church participates in God's mission, in what God is doing in his world, but the church cannot be above Christ, its head, who came as a servant and surrendered his life for the salvation of the world. As Christ took the form or structure proper to God's purpose, so the church must adapt its forms and structures to God's mission today as during every period in history.

---

*Excerpts from Philip Potter, *Life in all its Fullness* (Geneva: WCC, 1981), 70-74; cf. Bosch, TM, 392.

Such an understanding of mission obliges us to reconsider three attitudes very common in all our churches: (a) the tendency to equate the church with the kingdom of God, rather than to see it as a sign of the kingdom; (b) the tendency, by speaking of "our mission," to force those whom we seek to evangelize into *our* patterns of thinking and living; and (c) the tendency to regard our historically conditioned structures as fixed and sacred and indispensable for the fulfillment of God's mission.

Second, if the drama of mission is God's engagement with the world, the church must take with radical seriousness what is happening in that world. Mission may not mean giving the church's answers to its own questions. It is of course true that the church is the messenger of God's questions to humanity and of his answer in Christ. But Christ himself showed deep concern for listening to people's questions before he deepened those questions and gave his answer in word and deed. We express this fundamental reality by saying that we must listen to the world's agenda.... When this takes place, a movement from communication to communion has been initiated.

A third consequence of the conception of mission we have outlined is that the whole world is the mission field, not just what have traditionally been called non-Christian countries. The new humanity which is God's missionary purpose is the quest of every continent and country. All societies and communities, including those where Christians are dominant, are challenged and judged by God's word. Rebellion against God's will runs right across all cultures and societies.

Fourth, the church which participates in God's mission as the servant Body of Christ and takes the world's agenda seriously is itself being renewed to be the sign of the new humanity. The church as the people of God never remains static in the process of mission. Mission is not only concerned with the conversion of others but with the conversion of God's people. As they engage in God's mission to the world, they discover with ever greater depth their involvement in the tragedy of the world's disobedience and rebellion and their need for turning to God and receiving afresh his renewing grace.

GOD AS COMPASSION

> "The compassion of God for all humanity did not come to Asia as if to a foreign land."

■ *Choan-Seng Song has been a leading exponent of Asian theology done by those who have their roots in the lives of Asia's poor and oppressed. He expresses the love of God found in Jesus Christ creatively, in images and themes out of Asian life and spirituality. C. S. Song was born in Taiwan in 1929. After university studies in Taiwan, Scotland, and the United States, Song taught Old Testament and systematic theology at Tainan Theological College, where he also served as principal from 1965 to 1970. After service as associate director of the Faith and Order Commission of the WCC (1973-82) and director of studies for the World Alliance of Reformed Churches (1983-86), he returned to Asia as profes-*

sor of theology and dean of the program for theology and culture at the South East Asia Graduate School of Theology.

*Love with No Strings Attached**

Compassion is not an abstract notion in a theological textbook, but a living force working in us. Compassion is the power to love others and suffer with them. And compassion is ours because it is first God's. We are told by the author of the fourth Gospel that "God loved the world so much that he gave his only son" (Jn. 3:16) to it. . . .

God's Compassion in Asia

That compassion of God for all humanity did not come to Asia as if to a foreign land. Jesus praised the good Samaritan. He commended the faith of the Samaritan cured of leprosy. And he was deeply moved by the Roman soldier who had faith such as he had not found even in Israel.

God's compassion in Jesus must have always been attuned to the rhythms of love vibrating in the heart of this vast area of God's creation. It must have heard its own *hibiki* (echo) in the souls of those selfless followers of the Buddha who dedicated themselves to struggling and suffering humanity. These rhythms Christian missions did not hear. These *hibikis* Christian theology did not feel. Even when these rhythms and *hibikis* have grown much, much louder in recent years, we are still very uncomfortable with them. They still sound strange to our ears. We have not developed the spiritual capacity and theological sensitivity to listen to them intently, understand them deeply, and let them tell us the stories of God's mercy and compassion working in the heart of Asia and its peoples since the beginning of God's creation.

Theology of compassion is the theology of love with no strings attached to it. It does not predetermine how and where God should do God's saving work. It does not assume that God left Asia in the hands of pagan powers and did not come to it until missionaries from the West reached it. That would have left Asia without the God of Jesus for millions of years. Jesus' God could not have been such an irresponsible God. If that was Jesus' God, Jesus would not have commended the faith of the Gentiles who crossed his path. . . .

Divine Sparks in the Darkness

Theology of compassion, however, ought to be able to see something besides the sin of idolization. It must be able to perceive some divine sparks in the midst of human darkness. It should be able to catch sight of God's compassion in a temple

---

*Excerpts from C. S. Song, *Theology from the Womb of Asia* (Maryknoll, NY: Orbis Books, 1985), 165, 167-68; cf. Bosch, TM, 392.

dimmed with the smoke of incense offered by religious devotees. And it must be able to hear some divine words of comfort and assurance out of many wrong and misleading things said and done in the name of gods and lords. There is a lot for the theology of compassion to hear, see, and feel in Asia. It must be attentive to the voice of the compassionate God arising out of the heart of Asian humanity. It may find that voice strangely familiar, resembling the voice of Jesus who said: "The Son of Man did not come to be served, but to serve, and to give up his life as a ransom for many" (Mt. 20:28).

HOLY LOVE AND LOVING OBEDIENCE

> "Contextual evangelization implies witnessing everywhere and at all times in the presence of the total activity of the triune God."

■ *While* missio Dei *became a central missiological theme for Roman Catholics and conciliar Protestants in the 1960s and 1970s, some evangelical Protestants picked up the same theme in the 1980s. For those who have interacted closely at world and regional conferences on mission, news of this inter-stimulation comes as no surprise. Orlando Costas (1942-1987), the late dean of Andover Newton Seminary, was esteemed as a creative thinker by evangelical and conciliar Protestant, Roman Catholic, and Orthodox missiologists alike. Born in Puerto Rico, converted at a Billy Graham crusade in New York, graduate of Bob Jones University and Trinity Evangelical Divinity School, he was a spokesman for the new evangelicals who engaged seriously with those from other traditions concerning a relevant theology of mission. Felled by cancer in 1987 when at the height of his creativity,* Liberating News: A Theology of Contextual Evangelization *(1989), became his final voice. In it Costas expounds a trinitarian foundation of the Gospel—of the dynamic of the divine initiative and of human response in evangelization and mission.*

*The God of the Evangel**

The gospel presupposes a twofold movement: from God to the world and from the world back to God.[15] The first of these movements discloses God as the holy and loving Father of Jesus, and as the loving and obedient Son of the Father. The second reveals God as uniting Spirit. This double movement refers us to God's inner life, where we discover God as holy love sending and seeking, or as a community of mission and unity.

---

*Excerpts from Orlando E. Costas, *Liberating News: A Theology of Contextual Evangelization* (Grand Rapids, MI: Eerdmans, 1989), 73, 74-75, 75-76, 83-84; cf. Bosch, TM, 391.

Holy Love and Loving Obedience

The gospel is the story of the sending of the only begotten Son of the Father to redeem the world. In this action we see reflected the foundation of God's existence: holy love. God is both "light" and "love" (1 Jn. 1:5; 4:8, 16). In other words, God exists in love—that is, in communion—and this love is holy, transparent, without variation self-determined for communion....

Jesus was the faithful covenant partner who heeded God's holy word and followed through on God's will to communion. He was at one with the Father. Like Isaac, he gave himself fully to the will of his Father even at the price of death.[16] He humbled himself and followed through on the Father's holy determination to be honored and glorified in the faithful obedience of the human race. He took the place of the entire human race and willingly gave himself out of love to the Father for the world....

The cross shows a correspondence of wills between Father and Son: both act out love and for love. Thus the cross discloses God's identity as the holy and loving Father and as the loving and obedient Son. There we see the Father passionately delivering the Son out of holy love for the world and the Son suffering death for the world in loving obedience to the Father.

From the World to God: The Uniting Spirit

The Gospel is not only the story of the sending of the Son by the Father to redeem the world, but also of the Holy Spirit bringing the world to God through the Son for the glory of the Father....

The Spirit is also the one who unites the mission of the crucified and risen Son with his future with the Father in glory. Moreover, the Spirit unites the community of faith with the Son and has made possible the unity of the world with God. Indeed, the Spirit keeps alive the redemptive hope of the entire creation (cf Rom. 8:18ff.).

Contextual Evangelization

What, then, is the meaning of contextual evangelization in light of its Trinitarian foundation and dynamic? What does it imply for our evangelistic witness in our respective situations? I offer the following response.

Witness in the Presence of the Triune God

First, *contextual evangelization implies witnessing everywhere and at all times in the presence of the total activity of the triune God.* The Christian church bears witness not to a static God but rather to a dynamic divine community that makes itself known in history as Father, Son, and Spirit, sending and seeking in love, redeeming and uniting the unloved. God is, therefore, present in every situation of life.

This implies that we cannot separate God's redemptive activities in the evangelistic process from what Father, Son, and Spirit are doing in the secular affairs of life. The same God who created the world redeemed it. The same God who provides for the well-being of the earth judges those who exploit and destroy its resources. God is one, but one in community, a Tri-unity. Communicating the good news of salvation with integrity in our respective life situations means relating that message to God's involvement in all the spheres of human life and to the totality of God's concern for the well-being of our planet and the universe.

PARTICIPATING IN THE TRINITY

"Mission...is participation in the life of the Holy Trinity."

■ *With intentionality, beginning in 1974, the World Council of Churches facilitated Orthodox consultations and seminars on missiological issues that are part of the ecumenical agenda. One of the most influential took place at Neapolis, Greece, from April 16 to 24, 1988, attended by sixty representatives of eastern and oriental Orthodox churches. The following excerpts are from the keynote address by Bishop Anastasios (Yannoulatos) of Androussa, Greece. One of the earliest Orthodox participants in ecumenical consultations on mission, Bishop Anastasios was at that time professor of the history of religions at the University of Athens, acting archbishop of the Orthodox Church in East Africa, and moderator of the WCC's Commission on World Mission and Evangelism. From his affirmation of the centrality of the Trinity flows the understanding of Orthodox mission as "participation in the life of the Holy Trinity."*

*Toward the Development of Orthodox Mission**

A firm basis of every missionary effort is taking into consideration and moving in the light of the Revelation and especially of *the mystery of the Trinity.* The starting point of any apostolic activity on our behalf is the promise and order of the Risen Lord in its Trinitarian perspective: "As the Father has sent me, even so I send you....Receive the Holy Spirit" (Jn. 20:21-22). The love of the Father has been expressed through the *sending* of the Son. "For God so loved the world that he gave his only Son...For God sent the Son into the world" (Jn. 3:16-17).

The Son then sends his disciples, with the power of the Holy Spirit, to call all the children of God, who were dispersed, in his kingdom. All, men and women, created in the likeness of God, must return to the freedom of love, share in the life of love of the three persons of the Holy Trinity. God's glory, which radiates upon all creatures, has to transform all things, and to be raised upon the earth and upon the heavens....

---

*Excerpts from Anastasios of Androussa, "Orthodox Mission—Past, Present, Future," in *Your Will Be Done: Orthodoxy in Mission,* ed. George Lemopoulos (Geneva: WCC Publications, 1988), 79-81, 88; cf. Bosch, TM, 390.

The Sending of the Son

The sending of the Son forms the beginning, and defines more especially Christian mission. The work of the Son is not simply an announcement, it is an event. The Incarnation, which is the "assuming" of human nature, is the most predominant event in the history of the universe, the recreation for its regeneration within the life of the Holy Trinity. It opens the way for the *eschaton,* the fulfillment of the world's evolution.

This "assuming" in love, the continuous transfer of life in love, the transfiguration of all things in the light of God's glory is being continued in space and time through the mission of the church, the body of Christ.

The conjunction "as," which is found in John 20:21, remains very decisive for Orthodox mission. It is I who always remains your model, Christ stresses. You must walk in my footsteps and follow my example. Christological dogma defines the way of the mission of the Trinitarian God, which the faithful continue. The most crucial point in mission is not what one announces, but what one lives, what one *is.* Humankind is "becoming" as much as they remain in Christ. "Being in Christ" forms the heart of mission. "He who abides in me, and I in him, he it is that bears much fruit, for apart from me you can do nothing" (Jn. 15:5).

The Sending of the Spirit

From the very beginning, the Holy Spirit shares in the sending of the Son. The Incarnation is realized "by the Holy Spirit and the Virgin Mary." The Spirit cooperates with the one who is the best of humankind: the all Holy Virgin Mary, who without reservation and with much joy submits herself to the will of God, for the realization of the mission of the Son. It is the Spirit in the form of a dove, who at the Jordan river seals the beginning of the public ministry of the Son. In the form of tongues of fire and "like the rush of a mighty wind," the Spirit creates the church, transforming the scared disciples into brave apostles, full of divine light, knowledge and power. It is the Spirit that unceasingly gives life to the church and all members within, transforming them into a living temple of the mystical body of Christ, enabling them to share in the safeguarding of Christ's mission for the salvation of the whole world. The energies of the Trinitarian God are always personal, "from the Father through the Son in the Spirit." This trinitarian faith is to be found in the depth of our thoughts and actions....

Trinitarian Mission

Mission, as everything in Orthodox life, is not only realized "in the name of the Father, and of the Son, and of the Holy Spirit," but mainly, it is a participation in the life of the Holy Trinity, an expression of this love with all the power of existence, "with all (our) hearts, and with all (our) souls, and with all (our) minds." Mission is an essential expression of Orthodox self-conscience, a cry in action for the fulfillment of God's will "on earth as it is in heaven." I would like to stress here what we have been stressing for the past twenty-five years; that indifference to mission is a denial of Orthodoxy.

NOTES

1. Annie Johnson Flint, "Christ and We," in *Masterpieces of Religious Verse,* ed. James Dalton Morrison (New York: Harper & Brothers, 1948), p. 360.

2. John R. Mott, *The Decisive Hour of Christian Missions* (New York: Young People's Missionary Movement of the United States and Canada, 1910), p. 239.

3. Hans Küng, *Theology for the Third Millennium: An Ecumenical View* (New York: Doubleday, 1988), p. 273.

4. Cf. Mt. 24:31; *Didache* 10, 5 (Funk I, p. 32).

5. Dogm. Const. *Lumen Gentium,* 17. St. Augustine, *De Civitate Dei* 19, 17 (*Patrologia Latina* 41: 646.) Instr. S.C.P.F. (*Collectanea* I, n. 135, p. 42).

6. According to Origen, the Gospel ought to be preached before the consummation of this world: *Hom. in Lc.* XXI (G.C.S., *Orig.* IX, 136, 21 ff.); *In Matth. comm.* ser. 39 (XI, 75, 25, FF; 76, 4 ff); St. Thomas Aquinas, *Summa Theol.* Ia IIae, q. 106, a.4 ad 4.

7. Hilary of Poitiers, *In Ps.* 14 (*Patrologia Latina* 9:301); Eusebius of Caes., *In Isaiam* 54, 2-3 (*Patrologia Graeca* 24, 462-63); Cyril of Alex., *In Isaiam* V, ch. 54, 1-3 (*Patrologia Graeca* 70: 1193).

8. See D.62, i, "Norms for Implementing the Decree on the Church's Missionary Activity" (1966), in *Documents of Vatican II* (1975), p. 857.

9. Mk. 2:27.

10. Cf. John XXIII, Litt. Encycl. *Pacem in Terris: Acta Apostolicae Sedis* 55 (1963): 266.

11. The essay on "The Concept of God in Black Theology" was not included in the original edition, *Essays in Black Theology* (Johannesburg: The Black Theology Project of the University Christian Movement, 1972), because Sabelo Ntwasa, the original editor, was placed under house arrest and his writings banned. The essay was restored in *The Challenge of Black Theology in South Africa,* as well as in the U.K. edition entitled *Black Theology* (London: C. Hurst, 1973).

12. Jürgen Moltmann, *The Church in the Power of the Spirit,* p. 10.

13. Cf. also H. Gollwitzer, *Die kapitalistische Revolution* (Munich: Kaiser, 1974), p. 105: "Old and New Testaments see humanity as the object and addressee of a great historical undertaking of cosmic scope, in which God finally defines himself, makes himself known and brings himself to full divinity, that is, to his *doxa.* This continually forward-moving process includes the conversion of the individual brought about by the message, and the coming into being of groups of disciples; and from this process these things take on their wider meaning."

14. IMC Assembly (Ghana, 1957/58), quoted in Philip Potter, *Life in all its Fullness* (Geneva: WCC, 1981), p. 71.

15. I am indebted to Jürgen Moltmann for this insight and perspective on the Trinity; see *The Crucified God,* trans. R. A. Wilson and John Bowden (London: S.C.M. Press, 1974), pp. 235ff.; *The Church in the Power of the Spirit,* pp. 50ff.; and *The Trinity and the Kingdom: The Doctrine of God,* trans. Margaret Kohn (New York: Harper & Row, 1980), *passim.*

16. The allusion to the story of Isaac's sacrifice is a constituent part of early Christian understanding of the atonement.

7

Mission as Mediating Salvation

"Is eternal separation from God more disastrous than going to bed hungry?" For Donald McGavran, this is the crux of "the titanic struggle between theologies of mission going on today."[1]

Bosch judged New Testament and early church understandings of salvation to be holistic and comprehensive. Luke, for example, used "salvation language" referring to a wide range of life-transforming experiences—overcoming poverty, discrimination, illness, demon possession, sin, and so forth. Paul emphasized salvation as reconciliation with God, but as a process that had both social and political consequences (TM, 393-94).

With the institutionalization of the faith came a narrowing of the understanding of salvation. The person and work of Christ were increasingly separated from each other. God's salvific activities were understood as being apart from caring concern for the well-being of individuals and society. Being saved became an individual process of being in right relationship to God or to the church.

The documents below represent efforts, both Catholic and Protestant, to recover a holistic or integral understanding of salvation. Vatican II, in Gaudium et Spes, *analyzed the present human condition and called the church to carry out its God-given task to affirm human dignity, proclaim human rights, and serve the common good. Johannes Hoekendijk led the WCC to replace the traditional God-Church-World understanding with that of God-World-Church. The world (John 3:16) is the primary locus of God's salvific activity. Therefore the church, when faithful in mission, is "the church for others."*

From 1968 to 1973, the WCC carried out a major study project on "Salvation Today." Findings were presented on that theme at the Bangkok Conference of 1972-1973. Salvation was understood in four dimensions (in struggles for economic justice, human dignity, solidarity, and hope) and as a process in both community and personal life. Donald McGavran represented conservative evangelical reactions when he rejected this WCC interpretation as unbiblical and this-worldly.

Can new contributions break through the polarization in the North on this issue? M. M. Thomas of the Mar Thoma Syrian Church of Malabar (India) proposed a deepened spirituality as the means by which Christians can participate in both a sacramental foretaste of ultimate salvation and movements of human liberation.

Letty Russell offers a definition of salvation as shalom—*God's gift of total wholeness and well-being in community. Emilio Castro finds no biblical dichotomy between the word spoken and that made visible in the lives of God's people. For Castro, the church's mission must be in relation to God's purpose to save the human race and the whole creation for its intended fullness. John Mbiti finds affinities between traditional African and Christian understandings of salvation—each holistic and cosmic in their dimensions.*

INTEGRAL SALVATION

"The Church desires...ardently...the common good."

■ Gaudium et Spes *(The Pastoral Constitution on the Church in the Modern World) was addressed by Vatican II "to the whole of humanity...to set forth the way it understands the presence and function of the Church in the world of today" (Art. 2). In a world characterized by anguish and hope, the church affirms its God-given task to affirm human dignity, proclaim human rights, and serve the common good.*

*Hope and Anguish**

(From Introduction, "The Situation of [Humanity] in the World Today")

4. At all times the Church carries the responsibility of reading the signs of the time and of interpreting them in the light of the Gospel....

Ours is a new age of history with critical and swift upheavals spreading gradually to all corners of the earth....Increase in power is not always accompanied by control of that power for the benefit of [humanity]....

In no other age has [humanity] enjoyed such an abundance of wealth, resources and economic well-being; and yet a huge proportion of the people of the world is plagued by hunger and extreme need while countless numbers are totally illiterate. At no time have men [and women] had such a keen sense of freedom, only to be faced by new forms of slavery in living and thinking. There is on the one hand a lively feeling of unity and of compelling solidarity of mutual dependence, and on the other a lamentable cleavage of bitterly opposing camps. We have not yet seen the last of bitter political, social, and economic hostility, and racial and ideological antagonism, nor are we free from the spectre of a war of total destruction. If there is a growing exchange of ideas, there is still widespread disagreement about the meaning of the words expressing our key concepts. There is lastly a painstaking search for a better material world, without a parallel spiritual advancement....our contemporaries...hover between hope and anxiety and wonder uneasily about the present course of events....

---

*Excerpts from *Gaudium et Spes* (1965), Art. 4, 41, 42, in *VC2*, 905-06, 940-43; cf. Bosch, TM, 397, 400.

God Alone Satisfies the Heart

(From Chapter 4, "Role of the Church in the Modern World")

41.... The Church knows well that God alone, whom it serves, can satisfy the deepest cravings of the human heart, for the world and what it has to offer can never fully content it. It also realizes that [persons are] continually being aroused by the Spirit of God and that [they] will never be utterly indifferent to religion—a fact confirmed by the experience of ages past and plentiful evidence at the present day....

Relying on this faith the Church can raise the dignity of human nature above all fluctuating opinions which, for example, would unduly despise or idolize the human body. There is no human law so powerful to safeguard the personal dignity and freedom of man as the Gospel which Christ entrusted to the Church; for the Gospel announces and proclaims the freedom of the sons [and daughters] of God, it rejects all bondage resulting from sin (cf. Rom. 8:14-17), it scrupulously respects the dignity of conscience and its freedom of choice, it never ceases to encourage the employment of human talents in the service of God and [humanity], and, finally, it commends everyone to the charity of all (cf. Mt. 22:39)....

What the Church Offers to Society

42. The union of the [human] family is greatly consolidated and perfected by the unity which Christ established among the sons [and daughters] of God.[2]

Christ did not bequeath to the Church a mission in the political, economic, or social order: the purpose he assigned to it was a religious one.[3] But this religious mission can be the source of commitment, direction, and vigor to establish and consolidate [human] community according to the law of God....

By its nature and mission the Church is universal in that it is not committed to any one culture or to any political, economic or social system. Hence it can form a very close unifying effect on the various [human] communities and nations, provided they have trust in the Church and guarantee it true freedom to carry out its mission....

Whatever truth, goodness, and justice is to be found in past or present human institutions is held in high esteem....

GOD-WORLD-CHURCH

> "Where a liberation to a rightful humanization is taking place...the *Missio Dei,* once again, has reached its goal."

■ *Johannes Christian Hoekendijk (1912-1975) began his mission career as a protégé of Hendrik Kraemer, serving as missions consul in the Dutch East Indies (Indonesia, 1945-46) and as a mission secretary (1947-49) in The Netherlands. As secretary for evangelism of the WCC (1949-1952), he shaped the theses on evangelism of the IMC's Willingen Conference of 1952. According to*

Hoekendijk, the world is the horizon of mission. The church does not carry on mission—it is mission. It is the church only insofar as it allows itself to be used by God for the oikoumene, *understood as the whole inhabited world. He continued to develop these themes during his distinguished teaching career as professor of mission and church history at the University of Utrecht (1953-1965) and professor of missions at Union Seminary in New York (1965-1975).*[4]

*God—World—Church**

1. We attempt to look at things once again from the perspective of *God-World-Church* (rather than God-Church-World). This is the correct (theo-) logical mode of thinking. As soon as we speak of God, we also bring into speech the world as God's theater stage for his action. And it is foremost the Church who knows it and who will respect it. As soon as the Church acknowledges God, she also admits her own implicitly "eccentric" position, hoping that at some point in time it may come true that she can serve as an instrument to honor the world's worth and destiny. This eccentric Church cannot insist on protecting its own structures. She does not possess a private sociology; rather she uses—purely functionally—all available worldly structures, insofar as these are usable.

This, of course, is nothing new or surprising.[5] This is the way it has always been: the house-church, founded as *oikos,* seemed usable as a social unit. In similar ways later on the dioceses, parishes, unions, and associations came to be.

God Is on the Move

2. . . . the world—which is our subject here—is in constant change, and that is not merely by chance or as some kind of side symptom. When God directed his plans toward the world, [God] let them loose in history. [God] is indeed no ba'al, who settles down somewhere and lets a high place be set up. Instead [God] breaks a new path, [God] leaves once again behind any high place, when [there is] something to do in the profane. Herewith the world as the living horizon of God's action is put in motion. It is open toward the future. . . .

History—God's Mission Field

3. . . . the world as history is God's "mission field." The Church can be authenticated only as the church of this "sending" God, when she really lets herself be used in the *Missio Dei.* Her apostolicity (in teaching and in church order) must prove

---

*Excerpts from Johannes Christian Hoekendijk, *Kirche und Volk in der deutschen Missionwissenschaft* (Munich: Chr. Kaiser, 1967), 344-48; excerpts translated from the German by Domenico Nigrelli; cf. Bosch, TM, 396.

itself in the apostolate. *Missio Dei* is the compelling summary of the good news, that God...wills to be a God-for-others. The Church, which is agreeable to this God, takes place where she becomes the church-for-others. The "worldly" and "historicalized" structures, which the church takes up, will only be considered useful when they serve as structures-for-others. Paul dared to perceive the ignorant and unbelieving ones as criteria of what rightly belongs in the service of God. With it, in my judgment, is given the canon for the deconstructioning and reconstructioning of the Church's life. Only those structures can be termed authentic which bring the un-initiated and the unbelievers to a disclosure of their human existence and, thus, also to a conviction that the *Missio Dei* has also reached them (1 Cor. 14:24ff).

Mission as Shalom

4. The content of the *Missio Dei* can be described in manifold ways, given its nature. As a reaction to all our past programs of christianization, in the last years the term "humanization" has been emphatically brought to prominence as a keyword.[6] This is what God is concerned about: [God] wants to let the human race be whole again and no longer *homines religionis,* who, after all, are still fettered in their chains. At the cross and at the resurrection, there was made a beginning of this humanizing process, and it is working in culture as fermentation. Where a liberation to a rightful humanization is taking place, one can conclude that the *Missio Dei,* once again, has reached its goal.

Personally, I prefer a different description. And I am happy that this option is being tested out by others. To be as concise as possible: in my opinion, the *Missio Dei* is about what I call "Shalom-ization" of the whole life; that is, about a judging and hope-bringing intervention in the course of things, through which it becomes possible that people may again be people (without "persona," that is, mask; "God does not look on this persona") and things may again be things (and no longer idols or material objects). In the horizon of creation, shalom is the promise of life; in the horizon of history, a new creation of justice is announced (in all the spectrum of variations of Ps. 85:8-13); and where this happens, a messianic horizon is opened around us, which frees to us the view of the kingdom of God.[7] To shalom-atize means then to be busy with life and to be engaged with life in such a manner that, with dirty hands...three horizons of hope (life, justice, and the kingdom of God) will be established. I would like to call it the "messianic way of life," with the characteristics of the interwovenness of impatience ("he cannot delay too much longer") and patience ("but he will come"). When we look for a model, we must heed to the servant of God of Deutero-Isaiah and of Philippians 2:5-11. For years this model of life and also of mission has been summarized in five key words: Chosen (for)—Service—Witness—Self-identification—Suffering.[8] And all of this stands in the hopeful perspective of Shalom.

Seen in this way, *Missio Dei* can now be described, in accordance to its content, as the entirety of God's action which is focused upon the sharing of the messianic way of life with people, so that, in the perspective of Shalom, the horizons of hope are opened up for all.

SALVATION IN A SECULAR WORLD

"A community serving the world in the love of Christ."

■ *"What is the form and content of the salvation which Christ offers [persons] in the secular world?" With this question, in 1968 the WCC's Commission on World Mission and Evangelism initiated a five-year study project on "Salvation Today." It culminated in the 1972-1973 conference on that theme in Bangkok, Thailand, attended by 330 participants from 69 countries. Section meetings followed an "action-reflection" model of personal sharing, rather than a deliberative perfecting of conference documents. No consensus was sought on the main theme of salvation. However, the final report, with its four affirmations on salvation today, became the catalyst for an international and often heated debate on social versus personal dimensions of salvation.*

*Salvation and Social Justice**

...The salvation which Christ brought, and in which we participate, offers a comprehensive wholeness in this divided life. We understand salvation as newness of life—the unfolding of true humanity in the fullness of God (Col. 2:9). It is salvation of the soul and the body, of the individual and society, [humanity] and "the groaning creation" (Rom. 8:19). As evil works both in personal life and in exploitative social structures which humiliate humankind, so God's justice manifests itself both in the justification of the sinner and in social and political justice.

As guilt is both individual and corporate so God's liberating power changes both persons and structures. We have to overcome the dichotomies in our thinking between soul and body, person and society, human kind and creation. Therefore we see the struggles for economic justice, political freedom and cultural renewal as elements in the total liberation of the world through the mission of God. This liberation is finally fulfilled when "death is swallowed up in victory" (1 Cor. 15:55). This comprehensive notion of salvation demands of the whole of the people of God a matching comprehensive approach to their participation in salvation....

Salvation in Four Dimensions

Within the comprehensive notion of salvation, we see the saving work in four social dimensions:

---

*Excerpts from WCC/CWME, *Bangkok Assembly 1973: Minutes and Report of the Assembly* . . . (Geneva: WCC, 1973), 88-90; cf. Bosch, TM, 396-97.

a. Salvation works in the struggle for economic justice against the exploitation of people by people.

b. Salvation works in the struggle for human dignity against political oppression of human beings....

c. Salvation works in the struggle for solidarity against the alienation of person from person.

d. Salvation works in the struggle of hope against despair in personal life.

In the process of salvation, we must relate these four dimensions to each other. There is no economic justice without political freedom, no political freedom without economic justice. There is no social justice without solidarity, no solidarity without social justice. There is no justice, no human dignity, no solidarity without hope, no hope without justice, dignity and solidarity. But there are historical priorities according to which salvation is anticipated in one dimension first, be it the personal, the political or the economic dimension. These points of entry differ from situation to situation in which we work and suffer. We should know that such anticipations are not the whole of salvation, and must keep in mind the other dimensions while we work. Forgetting this denies the wholeness of salvation.

ETERNAL, NOT THIS-WORLDLY, SALVATION

> "The vertical relationship [with God] must not be displaced by the horizontal."

■ *The "crisis in the modern understanding of salvation" (Bosch, TM, 97) reached a flash point in 1968 as evangelicals led by Donald McGavran criticized the World Council's preoccupation with social justice issues at the Uppsala Assembly. In 1972, it became a conflagration as the WCC at Bangkok defined salvation more as a struggle for economic justice, human dignity, and solidarity than as personal salvation. Once again Donald McGavran, dean of the Fuller School of World Mission, was the WCC's most strident critic in North America. He charged that the world body had turned away from the classic aim of mission ("to further the proclamation of the Gospel to all...that they may believe and be saved") and had redefined "being saved" to mean "more this-worldly improvements" of food, clothes, production, freedom, justice, peace, and so on. He drew a sharp distinction between vertical and horizontal dimensions of salvation—a position that also became a focal point in the ongoing debate concerning the meaning of salvation.*

*What Is Salvation Today?**

...Does the word salvation, according to the Bible, mean eternal salvation or

---

*Excerpts from Donald McGavran, "Salvation Today," in *The Evangelical Response to Bangkok*, ed. Ralph Winter (South Pasadena, CA: Wm. Carey Library, 1973), 27, 29-32; cf. Bosch, TM, 398-99.

does it mean this-worldly improvements? Which is the basic meaning? It appears as if the conciliar forces are set to maintain, on the basis of the Old Testament, that salvation means primarily if not exclusively this-worldly improvements. Evangelicals will maintain, on the basis of the total biblical record (the New Testament as well as the Old) that "salvation" means a change in status of the soul, the essential person, is achieved through faith in Jesus Christ alone, and results in abundant life in this world.... If "salvation today" means political liberation, land distribution, better pay for factory workers, the downfall of oppressive systems of government, and the like, then the whole apparatus of missions is rightfully used to achieve these ends. Evangelism will be downgraded. Churching the unchurched will be neglected and ridiculed. The airplane of missions will be diverted away from the propagation of the Gospel to the establishment of utopias....

The Evangelical Response

Evangelicals should work and pray that this deliberate debasing of Christian currency cease and that the reformation of the social order (rightly emphasized) *should not be substituted for salvation.* Salvation is something which the true and living God confers on His creatures in accordance with His once-for-all revelation in Jesus Christ, God and Saviour according to the Bible. Salvation is a vertical relationship...(with God) which issues in horizontal [human] relationships. The vertical must not be displaced by the horizontal.

Desirable as social ameliorations are, working for them must not be substituted for the biblical requirements of/for "salvation."...

SALVATION—A LIBERATION SPIRITUALITY

"Turn 'from idols to serve a living God.'"

■ *At the time of the WCC's debate on the meaning of "Salvation Today," M. M. Thomas was moderator of the world body's Central Committee. Born in 1916 in Kerala, India, Madathilparampil Mammen Thomas was already acclaimed as a pioneering Asian ecumenical thinker and layman. Since Oslo 1947, he had been an organizer and frequent speaker at world Christian youth and ecumenical conferences. His experiences as director of the Christian Institute for the Study of Religion and Society in Bangalore, India (1962-1975) led him to advocate a broadening of ecumenical discussions on theology, ecclesiology, and ethics to include dialogue with persons of other faiths and ideologies. The following passage illustrates that concern, as well as his advocacy for a deepened spirituality representative of his own church, the Mar Thoma Syrian Church of Malabar.*

*True and False Spirituality**

Human spirituality undergirds all human strivings for health and sex, for development and justice. The only question is whether it is a true or false spirituality, that is whether the structure of ultimate meaning and sacredness to which it is committed is the meaning and sacredness which is truly ultimate, i.e., of God, or simply created by men in their self-centredness and rejection of God, and therefore idolatrous.

True and False Sacredness

...The primary concern of the Christian mission is...with the salvation of human spirituality, with...right choices in the realm of self-transcendence, and with structures of ultimate meaning and sacredness—not in any pietistic or individualist isolation, but related to and expressed within the material, social and cultural revolution of our time. The secular strivings for fuller human life should be placed and interpreted in their real relation to the ultimate meaning and fulfilment of human life revealed in the divine humanity of the crucified and risen Jesus Christ. They should be seen as the means to acknowledge and witness to the God and Father of our Lord Jesus Christ as the only God worthy of [a person's] ultimate worship and obedience. It is then that men [and women] and their strivings are truly saved and made human, and become sacrament and foretaste of the ultimate Salvation freely offered by God in Christ to all [humankind]. Herein lies the mission of the Church: to participate in the movements of human liberation in our time in such a way as to witness to Jesus Christ as the Source, the Judge and the Redeemer of the human spirituality and its orientation which are at work in these movements, and therefore as the Saviour of [humankind] today.

Law, Sin, and Death

...Alienated from God in the structure of our spirit and in the resultant fear of ultimate disintegration, we make frantic efforts to achieve self-redemption by creating new religions and salvationist ideologies, only to see our idealism crumbling to the ground, leaving in its wake frustration and disintegration....This is the same old vicious circle of law, sin and death (Rom. 7) and we are today more conscious of its reality and its power than during any previous period....

Our message of Christ's Salvation is ever the same; it is the call to [persons] and nations to turn "from idols to serve a living God" who has "translated us from the domain of darkness into the Kingdom of his dear Son" Jesus Christ. In him we have divine forgiveness and are delivered from the ultimate spiritual insecurities of the

---

*Excerpts from M. M. Thomas, "The Meaning of Salvation Today—A Personal Statement," *IRM* 62 (1973): 162-65; cf. Bosch, TM, 399-400.

self that seeks justification through its own efforts, and are "made free to love." Today "idols" and "darkness" have a new character; and "love" too must have new implications.

SALVATION AS HUMANIZATION

"Shalom: liberation and blessing."

■ *It is significant that 1973 was the year not only of the redefinition of "salvation" at the WCC conference in Bangkok, but also the year of the publication in English of* A Theology of Liberation *by Gustavo Gutiérrez. In 1974, Letty Russell published* Human Liberation in a Feminist Perspective—A Theology. *In it she drew upon the burgeoning literature on "liberation" to discuss related terms in current usage: salvation, shalom, liberation, and humanization.*

*Salvation as Shalom**

...In a world of diversity and change, people feel free to use a variety of definitions of salvation. In the search for meaning every religion and ideology is explored for its offer of liberation, wholeness, and blessing.[9] There is a growing awareness of the wholeness of human beings in their body, mind, and spirit and in their social relationship in today's world. For some this has led to a renewed stress on *shalom* as a gift of total wholeness and well-being in community.[10]...

Nowhere is the stress on salvation as seen in the motifs of *shalom* clearer than among those searching for ways of expressing the good news of God's traditioning action in situations of oppression, hunger, and alienation in our sorry world. Liberation theologies, which seek to reflect on the praxis of God's liberation in the light of particular circumstances of oppression, are returning to the motifs of liberation and blessing as they are found in the biblical tradition. Without denying that salvation includes the message of individual deliverance from sin and death (Rom., chs. 5 to 7) they, nevertheless, place emphasis on the total goal of salvation (Rom., ch. 8) which is the gift of *shalom* (complete social and physical wholeness and harmony)....

Shalom as Liberation

...The first motif of *liberation* is seen as the gift of God's action in history, as well as the agenda of those who join together in community to transform the world. For Third World and Fourth World people the motif of liberation expresses an important aspect of the *shalom* for which they seek....

---

*Excerpts from Letty Russell, *Human Liberation in a Feminist Perspective—A Theology* (Philadelphia: Westminster Press, 1974), 109-10, 111-13; cf. Bosch, TM, p. 396.

Shalom as Blessing

The second motif that overlaps with liberation is the meaning and experience of *shalom* as *blessing.* In the writers concerned with liberation theology this is usually interpreted as *humanization:* the setting free of all humanity to have a future and a hope. The blessings of the Patriarchs are now interpreted in modern contexts as the need for full personal and social well-being, as well as the need for the power to participate in shaping the world.

For those who experience *shalom* as new wholeness and liberation as human beings, *sin* is also viewed as a collective reality. The social as well as the individual responsibility for sin is stressed so that *oppression* is itself viewed as a symbol of the social reality of sin....

In various liberation theologies sin is viewed not only as the opposite of liberation or the oppression of others but also as the opposite of humanization or the *dehumanization* of others by means of excluding their perspectives from the meaning of human reality and wholeness.

In summary we can say that salvation today, as well as the understanding of sin today, has regained its social and communal emphasis in writings on liberation theology. Not denying individual responsibility and accountability, they still drive us also to see the dimension of responsibility and accountability in terms of the liberation and blessing for all oppressed and defuturized persons. For many people today, liberation is understood as a gift of God at once personal and social which is only ours as it is constantly shared with others.

SALVATION—THE PURSUIT OF REAL JUSTICE

"Obedience and militant participation in [humanity's] vital struggles."

■ *Emilio Castro (b. 1927) was present at the WCC's Bangkok Conference on "Salvation Today" as director-designate of the sponsoring WCC Commission on World Mission and Evangelism. A Uruguayan Methodist minister, he was active in a wide range of church and ecumenical activities. From 1965 to 1972, he coordinated the Commission for Evangelical Unity in Latin America (UNELAM). In his essay written following the Bangkok conference, Castro introduced themes that continue to characterize his ecumenical leadership, especially a biblical theology of mission that combines evangelical concerns for personal salvation with ecumenical advocacy of its social justice dimensions.*

*No Biblical Dichotomy**

The communication of the evangel in its fullness to every person is a mandate of the Lord Jesus to his community. There is no biblical dichotomy between the

*Excerpts from Emilio Castro, "Salvation Today—An Evangelistic Approach," in *Beginning in Jerusalem,* ed. Rueben P. Job (Nashville, TN: Tidings, 1974), 35-39; cf. Bosch, TM, 399-400.

word spoken and the word made visible in the lives of God's people. Men and women will look as they listen, and what they see must be at one with what they hear. The Christian community must chatter, discuss, and proclaim the gospel. It must express the gospel in its life as the new society, in its sacrificial service to others as a genuine expression of God's love, and its prophetic exposing and opposing all demonic forces that deny the Lordship of Christ and keep people from being less than fully human. God's people must pursue real justice for all humanity; they must act as caring trustees of God's creation and its resources....

The mission of the church must be seen in relation to this saving purpose of God which incorporates the fullness of the human race, the fullness of the whole of creation. The church is a people aware of the divine purposes, who sees them in action, who accompanies and proclaims them.

God's mission thus seeks to overcome the total alienation of [humanity]—the alienation of [persons] from God, from [their] neighbors, from [themselves], from nature—to overcome all opposition, to bring everything to an ultimate harmony in which his love is recognized as sovereign. Churches and individual Christians are therefore taking part in a battle of the Spirit in which God himself is involved; local mission and transcultural mission are different ways of collaborating with God in the overall process of liberation. In other words, we live in an era of world mission. We cannot and must not distinguish between the service which we give to God and our neighbor in our immediate vicinity, and service given in a remote corner of the planet. The important thing is that the immediate and the distant should be integral parts of a conscious and intelligent participation in the spiritual battle, in which we join with God to struggle towards the goal of the redemption of all things in Jesus Christ....

SALVATION IN AFRICAN EXPERIENCE

> "The African traditional experiences of salvation belong ultimately within the walls of the cosmic work of Christ."

■ *Is the longing for a "comprehensive" view of salvation (Bosch, TM, 399) a chimera amid the pluralism of local theologies? Is it a manifestation of that worldview of the North that aspires for conceptual unity? John Mbiti's essay on African experiences of salvation today is representative of those Two-thirds World advocates of a more pluralistic understanding with sensitivity to cultural diversities. Mbiti (b. 1931), after higher education in Uganda, the United States, and England (Ph.D. Cambridge, 1963) returned to teach both New Testament and African religions at Makerere University (1964-74). His books* African Religion and Philosophy *(1969) and* Concepts of God in Africa *(1970) were pioneer works challenging the long-held prejudice that traditional African beliefs and religious customs were of little value. He wrote the essay below while serving as director and professor at the WCC's Ecumenical Institute in Bossey, Switzerland (1974-1980).*

*African Understandings of Salvation**

The idea of salvation is very much present in African life, even if the abstract concepts related to it may be rare or non-existent as such. This means that Christianity did not introduce the concept of salvation as something uniquely new except in so far as salvation is mediated in and through Christ....

African experience of the Christian concept of salvation has underscored the areas of salvatory needs as found in traditional African life and religion; and only within those needs has the idea of salvation from sin also found a place....The idea of salvation extending to the hereafter is probably the main new element in African experience of Christian salvation since it promises to do something which African Religion never contained or never could do even if it were to see the need, namely the recovery of the intimate proximity between God and man which was in the original state of human existence. At the same time, Christian salvation promises the recovery of the lost gifts of rejuvenation, immortality and resurrection....Christian salvation, sweeps over the physical and spiritual welfare of the believers, and applies as well for this life as for the life to come. This message has found a home in African Christians, and some have died for it, many more will be willing to die for it, and thousands of them are proclaiming it every day, every month and every year.

The Cosmic Dimension of Salvation

There is, finally, the cosmic dimension of salvation which must be given its place in African Christianity. So far, in the day-to-day experiences of salvation, emphasis has been laid on mainly the individual and the community. This dimension is necessary and meaningful when considering the personalization of salvation. True theological perspectives of salvation in the New Testament embrace the cosmic consequences of the Christ event. This cosmicization of salvation does not seem to attract the attention of the majority of African Christians. But to understand or take Christian salvation only on a community or personal level, is ultimately to ignore its cosmic dimension and thereby to distort the Christian message seriously. In its major concern with saving souls, evangelization in Africa has noticeably ignored the cosmic dimension of salvation. Only the Orthodox Church in Ethiopia and Egypt, like other Orthodox Churches, has maintained in its liturgies, the recognition of the cosmic dimension of salvation. It seems necessary to explore the implications of the cosmic work of Christ within the African context and in the light of African cosmology. In that cosmic sweep it may well become clear that in a limited way, the African traditional experiences of salvation belong ultimately within the walls of the cosmic work of Christ.

---

*Excerpts from John Mbiti, "Some Reflections on African Experience of Salvation Today," in *Living Faiths and Ultimate Goals: Salvation and World Religions,* ed. S. J. Samartha (Maryknoll, NY: Orbis Books, 1974), 114, 115-19; cf. Bosch, TM, 399-400.

NOTES

1. "Conclusion," in Arthur F. Glasser and Donald A. McGavran, *Contemporary Theologies of Mission* (Grand Rapids, MI: Baker Book House, 1983), pp. 237, 239.

2. Cf. Dogmatic Constitution *Lumen Gentium,* ch. 2, n. 9: *Acta Apostolicae Sedis* 57 (1965), pp. 12-14.

3. Cf. Pius XII, *Allocution to Historians and Artists,* March 9, 1956; *Acta Apostolicae Sedis* 48 (1956), p. 212.

4. Horst Rzepkowski, *Lexikon der Mission* (1992), pp. 402-03; Libertus A. Hoedemaker, "Hoekendijk's American Years," *Occasional Bulletin of Missionary Research* 1:2 (Apr. 1977): 7-10.

5. Hans Storck, *Die Zeit draengt.* (Berlin: Käthe Vogt, 1957), pp. 15ff.; by the same author, *Kirche im Newland der Industrie* (Berlin: Käthe Vogt, 1959).

6. Paul Louis Lehmann, *Ethics in a Christian Context* (New York: Harper & Row, 1963).

7. I follow here Eugen Biser, "Friede," in H. Freis, *Handbuch theologischer Grundbegriffe* (Munich: Kösel-verlag, 1962), I: 419ff.; and I am aware that in this part I am dependent on Jürgen Moltmann, *Theologie der Hoffnung,* 5th ed. (Munich: Chr. Kaiser Verlag, 1965).

8. Frederich William Dillistone, *Revelation and Evangelism* (London: Lutterworth, 1948).

9. *Salvation Today and Contemporary Experience: A Collection of Texts for Critical Study and Reflection* (Geneva: WCC, 1972).

10. Gabriel Fackre, *Do and Tell: Engagement Evangelism in the '70s* (Grand Rapids, MI: Eerdmans, 1973), p. 34; Letty M. Russell, "Shalom in Postmodern Society," in John A. Westerhoff III, ed., *A Colloquy on Christian Education* (Philadelphia: United Church Press, 1972), pp. 97-105; *Colloquy,* National Shalom Conference Issue, 6:3 (March 1973).

8

Mission as the Quest for Justice

"Keep religion out of politics!" This has been a recurring battle cry, both from those fearing undue sectarian influence upon government and those fearing contamination of the faith by worldly concerns.

Such polarization of religion and politics was not characteristic of the Old Testament. Social justice was at the very heart of the prophetic tradition. The early Christian church, however—at best tolerated and at worst persecuted by the Roman Empire—gave mixed signals as to whether the mission of the church included a quest for justice. Constantine Christianity provided the model of an established church which, of necessity, was brought into a close relationship with the state. Augustine of Hippo, in the aftermath of the sack of Rome by the Visigoths, enunciated a polarity between the divine and human cities in the City of God, *with the human judged to be evil and unredeemed.*

With the advent of the Enlightenment, a new secular typology gained ascendancy. Distinction was made between the public world of facts and the private world of ideas. Religion, considered divorced from reason and dealing primarily with human feelings and experience, was relegated to the private worlds of church and family. That this paradigm was not accepted by many Christians engaged in missions can be demonstrated by their extensive colonial-era involvement in education, health and social welfare at home and abroad. Much of this work was done in countries with "established church" traditions, whether Roman Catholic, Orthodox, Anglican, or Protestant.

The selections below all date from the 1966-1990 period. They represent the centrist movement within both Catholicism and Protestantism that sought to redefine mission as a quest for justice. This movement included Roman Catholics, conciliar Protestants, and the "New Evangelicals."

Those who posit an evangelical-ecumenical polarization on this paradigm need to reread the Wheaton Declaration *of 1966, with its clarion call for evangelical social action. In theology, it is akin to that of Willem Visser 't Hooft, first general secretary of the WCC, who argued that "the vertical, God-given, dimension is essential for any action on the horizontal, inter-human plane." The* Uppsala Report *of the WCC's Fourth Assembly of 1968 gave the strongest urgency to Christian involvement "in this worldwide struggle for meaning, dignity, freedom and love." Pope Paul VI's apostolic exhortation* Evangelii Nuntiandi *(1975), while focusing on the imperative and task of evangelization, included a clear affirmation that evangelization and human advancement (development and liberation) are inextricably linked together.*

The documents that follow by authors from the South attest that neither the body-spirit dualism of the Greeks nor the Enlightenment's public-private dualism had affinity with worldviews in Africa, Asia, and Latin America. Canaan Banana's "Our Father" is a cry for help to God, who is already in the ghetto with suffering humanity. Peruvian Samuel Escobar warned evangelicals at the Lausanne I Congress on Evangelization (1974) to avoid the temptation of reducing the Gospel to a spirituality without discipleship. Emilio Castro of Uruguay believes that liberation, development, humanization, and *evangelization are all "essential, integral parts of the mission entrusted to us." For those accustomed to think in sinner-saved dichotomies, Raymond Fung of Hong Kong adds a new dimension: Those usually characterized as "sinners" are also the "sinned against." He sees a struggle in which all participants need forgiveness and reconciliation—all struggling "against the forces of sin in an evangelizing context."*

The imperative that evangelism and social action be held together in the church's mission is echoed in the final three documents. The Kairos Document *(1985) was not only an affirmation that "evangelism and social action go hand in hand" but also a call for a prophetic theology that would challenge the political and social establishment, sanctioning pressures (including violence) to topple unjust structures. Virginia Fabella of the Philippines finds Jesus as liberator the norm by which both women and men can act to reform lives and renew society. She is active in the Ecumenical Association of Third World Theologians (EATWOT), whose conference reports are rich veins on this theme, as evidenced by the selection from their 1986 tenth anniversary conference at Oaxtepec, Mexico.*

MISSION AND SOCIAL CONCERN

> "We urge all evangelicals to stand openly and firmly for ...social justice."

■ *Following World War II, several organizations became forums through which a distinctively evangelical mission theology could be articulated. Among them in North America were the Interdenominational Foreign Mission Association (IFMA), linking independent "faith" mission groups, and the Evangelical Foreign Missions Association (EFMA), acting as the missionary agency of the National Association of Evangelicals (NAE). These agencies co-sponsored the influential Congress on the Church's Worldwide Mission held April 9-16, 1966, at Wheaton College, Illinois. The 938 delegates, while mostly North Americans, included evangelicals from 71 countries. The conference was hailed as "the largest ecumenical strategy conference of Protestant missionaries ever held in North America."[1] In his paper on "Mission and Social Concern," Horace L. Fenton, Jr., gave a strongly worded warning (based on his Latin American experience) that an evangelism which ignores social concern is incomplete and unscriptural in nature and will be unheeded by many. Recognition of the close relationship between evangelism and social involvement found expression in the following section of the Congress's Declaration.*

The Underlying Issues*

Whereas evangelicals in the Eighteenth and Nineteenth Centuries led in social concern, in the Twentieth Century many have lost the biblical perspective and limited themselves only to preaching a gospel of individual salvation without sufficient involvement in their social and community responsibilities.

When theological liberalism and humanism invaded historic Protestant churches and proclaimed a "social gospel," the conviction grew among evangelicals that an antithesis existed between social involvement and gospel witness.

Today, however, evangelicals are increasingly convinced that they must involve themselves in the great social problems men [and women] are facing. They are concerned for the needs of the whole [person], because of their Lord's example, His constraining love, their identity with the human race, and the challenge of their evangelical heritage.

Evangelicals look to the Scriptures for guidance as to what they should do and how far they should go in expressing this social concern, without minimizing the priority of preaching the gospel of individual salvation.

The Witness of the Scriptures

The Old Testament manifests God's concern for social justice (Mic. 6:8). Our Lord, by precept and example, stressed the importance of ministering to the physical and social, as well as spiritual needs of [persons] (Mt. 5-9). His dealings with the Samaritans involved Him in racial and social issues (Lk. 9:51-56; Jn. 4:1-30; Lk. 10:25-37).

His disciples followed His example (Gal. 2:10; Col. 3:11; Jas. 1:27; 2:9-11). They taught and respected the role of government in promoting civil justice (Rom. 13 and 1 Pet. 2). The two great commandments are: "Love the Lord thy God ...and thy neighbor as thyself" (Mk. 12:29-31).

We Therefore Declare

That, we reaffirm unreservedly the primacy of preaching the gospel to every creature, and we will demonstrate anew God's concern for social justice and human welfare.

That, evangelical social action will include, wherever possible, a verbal witness to Jesus Christ.

---

*Excerpts from "Wheaton Declaration," in *The Church's Worldwide Mission,* ed. Harold Lindsell (Waco, TX: Word Books, 1966), 234-35; cf. Bosch, TM, 404.

That, evangelical social action must avoid wasteful and unnecessary competition.

That, when Christian institutions no longer fulfill their distinctively evangelical functions they should be relinquished.

That, we urge all evangelicals to stand openly and firmly for racial equality, human freedom, and all forms of social justice throughout the world.

INCARNATION AND SOCIAL CONCERN

"No horizontal advance without vertical orientation."

■ *While a polarization of theologies of mission characterized much of the debate between evangelical and ecumenical Protestants in the 1960s, a convergence on a holistic theology of mission was emerging. Willem Visser 't Hooft (1900-1985), the first general secretary of the World Council of Churches, was one such voice. As a YMCA secretary in the 1920s and general secretary of the World Student Christian Federation in the 1930s, he had been deeply involved in the Life and Work stream of the ecumenical movement. As WCC general secretary (1948-1966), he was an architect of that imaginative merging of concerns for common faith, witness, service, and mission by Christians from diverse nations and churches. His 1968 valedictory address to the WCC's Fourth Assembly at Uppsala contained the following clarion call for a holistic theology of mission.*

*No Horizontal Advance Without Vertical Orientation**

I believe that, with regard to the great tension between the vertical interpretation of the Gospel as essentially concerned with God's saving action in the life of individuals, and the horizontal interpretation of it as mainly concerned with human relationships in the world, we must get out of that rather primitive oscillating movement of going from one extreme to the other, which is not worthy of a movement which by its nature seeks to embrace the truth of the Gospel in its fulness. A Christianity which has lost its vertical dimension has lost its salt and is not only insipid in itself, but useless for the world. But a Christianity which would use the vertical preoccupation as a means to escape from its responsibility for and in the common life of [humanity] is a denial of the incarnation, of God's love for the world manifested in Christ.

The whole secret of the Christian faith is that it is [human]-centred because it is God-centred. We cannot speak of Christ as the [person] for others without speaking of him as the [one] who came from God and who lived for God.

This is a very practical truth. For on it depends the relevance of the Christian witness in the world....

---

*Excerpts from Willem A. Visser 't Hooft, "The Mandate of the Ecumenical Movement," in WCC, *The Uppsala Report,* ed. Norman Goodall (Geneva: WCC, 1968), 317-18, 319-20; cf. Bosch, TM, 408.

On God's Side with All Humanity

Christians have more reason than anyone else to be advocates of humanity. They are not humanitarians in the sentimental sense that it is nice to be nice to other people. They are not humanists in the aristocratic sense that learning and culture constitute a bond between the privileged few of all nations. They are on the side of *all* humanity because God is on that side and his Son died for it. So they do not get so easily discouraged when the service of [hu]mankind proves to be a much tougher task than was anticipated. They do not say: We will let you have economic justice if you fulfil my conditions. For it is their very *raison d'être* as followers of Christ to ensure that his suffering brothers [and sisters] receive what they need.

It seems to me that no amount of resolution-making and moralising can help us in our present predicament if we do not first recover in theology, in our teaching, and in our preaching the clear biblical doctrine of the unity of [hu]mankind and so give our churches the strong foundation for a new approach to the whole question of world economic justice and to a better and more convincing motivation for development aid. It must become clear that church members who deny in fact their responsibility for the needy in any part of the world are just as much guilty of heresy as those who deny this or that article of the faith. The unity of [hu]mankind is not a fine ideal in the clouds; it is part and parcel of God's own revelation. Here if anywhere the vertical, God-given, dimension is essential for any action on the horizontal, inter-human plane.

RADICAL RENEWAL INTO FULL HUMANITY

> "The gift of a new creation ...is a radical renewal of the old and the invitation ...to full humanity."

■ *Mission as humanization was the dominant theology of mission at the World Council of Churches' Fourth Assembly (Uppsala 1968). The 704 delegates from 235 member churches, plus more than 2,000 additional participants, met to discuss the theme, "Behold, I make all things new." The section on "Renewal in Mission" was affected by the spirit of the age, with its student revolts, wars, and assassinations, symbolized by the empty pulpit of Uppsala cathedral as the address of the slain civil rights leader, Dr. Martin Luther King, Jr., was read. In a draft document, mission had been envisaged as "the new humanity." This provoked Dr. McGavran's attack that the WCC was proposing a secularized gospel and neglect of the two billion persons who have never heard of Jesus. The final report from the Uppsala study section, as adopted by the assembly, promoted a new humanity in Christ as the goal of mission, linking evangelism to that theme.*

*A Mandate for Mission**

We belong to a humanity that cries passionately and articulately for a fully human life. Yet [our] very humanity ...and ...societies [are] threatened by a greater variety of destructive forces than ever. And the acutest moral problems all hinge upon the question: What is [the human]? We Christians know that we are in this worldwide struggle for meaning, dignity, freedom and love, and we cannot stand aloof. We have been charged with a message and a ministry that have to do with more than material needs, but we can never be content to treat our concern for physical and social needs as merely secondary to our responsibility for the needs of the spirit. There is a burning relevance today in describing the mission of God, in which we participate, as the gift of a new creation which is a radical renewal of the old and the invitation to [persons] to grow up into their full humanity in the new man, Jesus Christ.

Responsible Children of God

Men [and women] can know their true nature only if they see themselves as [children] of God, answerable to their Father for one another and for the world. But because [we refuse] both the obedience and the responsibility of [adoption], his God-given dominion is turned into exploitation, and harmony into alienation in all ...relationships. In this condition [persons] with all [their] amazing power, suffer an inescapable dread of [their] own helplessness and [their] deepest cry, albeit often unrecognized, is for the Triune God.

Jesus Christ, incarnate, crucified and risen, is the new man. In him was revealed the image of God as he glorified his Father in a perfect obedience. In his total availability for others, his absolute involvement and absolute freedom, his penetrating truth and his triumphant acceptance of suffering and death, we see what [persons are] meant to be. Through that death on the Cross, [our] alienation is overcome by the forgiveness of God and the way is opened for the restoration of all.... In the resurrection of Jesus a new creation was born, and the final goal of history was assured, when Christ as head of that new humanity will sum up all things....

Open and Humble Partnership

[Humanity] is one indivisible whole. Science today furnishes us with constantly increasing knowledge about [a person's] inner being and his [or her] interdependence with society. We must see achievements of greater justice, freedom and dignity as a part of the restoration of true [personhood] in Christ. This calls for a more open and humble partnership with all who work for these goals even when they do not

---

*Excerpts from WCC (4th Assembly, Uppsala, 1968), *The Uppsala Report: Official Report of the Fourth Assembly*..., ed. Norman Goodall (Geneva: WCC, 1968), 27-28, 29; cf. Bosch, TM, 408.

share the same assumptions as ourselves. But it also calls for a clearer acceptance of the diversity of gifts of the spirit within the Church. "He gave some to be apostles"—the bearers and strategists of the Gospel in a modern age, "some to be prophets"—to equip the saints for their ministry in the world and to be the protesting conscience of society, "some to be pastors"—to heal spiritual and psychological ills, "some to be evangelists"—the interpreters of the Gospel for the secular [person] or the [person] of another faith, "some to be teachers"—equipped with biblical light on contemporary perplexities. [Persons], knowing [their] need of the gifts of ...others, contribute [their] own in a single, saving outreach to bring [persons] to the measure of the fullness of the stature of Christ.

THE GOSPEL ACCORDING TO THE GHETTO

"Forgive us our docility as we demand our share of justice."

■ *"The Gospel According to the Ghetto" is an attempt to interpret the Christian message within the context of the experience of those who are victims of a hostile society. It is an attempt to affirm the liberating hand of God through the willingness of the oppressed to become co-partners with God in the divine mission of moral, economic, political and social revolution. The Rev. Canaan Banana first published it in 1974, while a student at Wesley Theological Seminary in Washington, D.C. It is the prayer of anguish of the black youth of that city and of those in Zimbabwe who Rev. Banana had inspired as a Methodist minister, urban-industrial mission specialist, and political leader. In 1976, Banana returned to Zimbabwe and was placed in political detention for four years, but later was named the first president of Zimbabwe (1980-1988).*

The Lord's Prayer*

Our Father which art in the Ghetto,
Degraded is your name
Thy servitude abounds,
Thy will is mocked,
As pie in the sky.
Teach us to demand,
Our share of gold,
Forgive us our docility,
As we demand our share of justice.
Lead us not into complicity,
Deliver us from our fears.
For ours is thy sovereignty,

---

*Excerpt from Canaan Banana, *The Gospel According to the Ghetto* (Gwelo, Zimbabwe: Mambo Press, 1980), 1; cf. Bosch, TM, 408.

The power and the liberation,
For ever and ever ... Amen.

EVANGELIZATION AND HUMAN ADVANCEMENT

"Evangelization involves an explicit message ...about peace, justice and development."

■ *At the Second Vatican Council (1961-1965), the Roman Catholic bishops sought to fit the church better for proclaiming the Gospel to twentieth-century peoples. Later synods of the bishops linked evangelization and concerns for peace, justice, and development increasingly understood as human liberation. In 1975, Pope Paul VI, in his apostolic exhortation* Evangelii Nuntiandi, *addressed "to the episcopate, to the clergy and to all the faithful of the entire world," expressed clearly this growing consensus. Although focused on the imperative and task of evangelization, it contained the following clear affirmation linking that task to justice concerns.*

*Message Touching Life as a Whole**

(From Chapter 3, "The Content of Evangelization")

29. But evangelization would not be complete if it did not take account of the unceasing interplay of the Gospel and of [humanity's] concrete life, both personal and social. This is why evangelization involves an explicit message, adapted to the different situations constantly being realized, about the rights and duties of every human being, about family life without which personal growth and development is hardly possible,[2] about life in society, about international life, peace, justice and development—a message especially energetic today about liberation.

Necessarily Linked to Human Advancement

31. Between evangelization and human advancement—development and liberation—there are in fact profound links. These include links of an anthropological order, because the [person] who is to be evangelized is not an abstract being but is subject to social and economic questions. They also include links in the theological order, since one cannot dissociate the plan of creation from the plan of Redemption. The latter plan touches the very concrete situations of injustice to be combatted and of justice to be restored. They include links of the eminently evangelical order, which is that of charity: how in fact can one proclaim the new commandment without promoting in justice and in peace the true, authentic advancement of [humanity]? We ourself have taken care to point this out, by recalling that it is

---

*Excerpts from "Evangelii Nuntiandi" (1975), Art. 29, 31, in *Documents of Vatican II*; cf. Bosch, TM, 403.

impossible to accept "that in evangelization one could or should ignore the importance of the problems so much discussed today, concerning justice, liberation, development and peace in the world. This would be to forget the lesson which comes to us from the Gospel concerning love of our neighbor who is suffering and in need."[3]

EVANGELICALS AND THE WHOLE GOSPEL

> "God is equally interested in our service and in our evangelistic task."

■ *The majority among the 2,430 evangelical participants from 150 countries at Lausanne I (1974) were conservative in theology and western in outlook. However, among the more than 1,000 Third World participants, a new evangelical voice was to be heard. At Lausanne two young Latin American evangelicals argued against the neat separation of evangelism and social concern. Samuel Escobar, a Peruvian, warned evangelicals to avoid the temptation of reducing the Gospel to a spirituality without discipleship. Then secretary of the Intervarsity Christian Fellowship of Canada, he was soon to move to Argentina as president of the Latin American Theological Fraternity. Next, René Padilla, associate general secretary of the International Fellowship of Evangelical Students in Buenos Aires, denounced the "culture Christianity" associated with the American way of life as being as harmful to the Gospel as secular Christianity. Together with others of the evangelical "left," they succeeded in securing in the Lausanne Covenant an affirmation that "evangelism and socio-political involvement are both part of our Christian duty."*[4]

*Transforming Persons and Structures**

Christian service is not optional. It is not something we can do if we want to. It is the mark of the new life. "You will know them by their fruits." "If you love me, you will keep my commandments." If we are in Christ we have the spirit of service of Christ. So to discuss whether we should evangelize or promote social action is worthless. They go together. They are inseparable. One without the other is evidence of a deficient Christian life. So we must not try to justify service for our neighbor by claiming that it will "help us" in our evangelism. God is equally interested in our service and in our evangelistic task. Let us not have a guilty conscience over our schools, hospitals, health centers, student centers, and so on. If they are also used for evangelism, splendid! But let us not use them as a medium

---

*Excerpts from Samuel Escobar, "Evangelism and Man's Search for Freedom, Justice and Fulfilment," in *Is Revolution Change?,* ed. Brian Griffiths (Downers Grove, IL: InterVarsity Press, 1974); reprinted in International Congress on World Evangelization, Lausanne, Switzerland, *Let the Earth Hear His Voice: Official Reference Volume,* ed. J. D. Douglas (Minneapolis, MN: World Wide Publications, 1975), 307, 310; cf. Bosch, TM, 405.

of coercion to force the Gospel on others. It is not necessary. In themselves they are an expression of Christian maturity...it is fundamental to recognize that society is more than just the sum of a number of individuals. It is naive to affirm that all that is needed is new [persons] in order to have a new society. Certainly every [person] should do whatever he [or she] is able to do to get the transforming message of Christ to his fellow citizens. But it is also true that it is precisely these new [persons] who sometimes need to transform the structures of society so that there may be less injustice, less opportunity for [a person] to do evil to [another person], for exploitation.[5]

A Warning to Evangelicals

The temptation for evangelicals today is to reduce the Gospel, to mutilate it, to eliminate any demands for the fruit of repentance and any aspect that would make it unpalatable to a nominally Christian society, even any demands that would make it unpalatable to an idolatrous society. The church must, by all means, keep constantly alert to the needs of the millions who have not heard the Gospel. But with equal zeal it must stress the need for the whole Gospel of Jesus Christ as Savior and Lord whose demands cannot be cheapened. No eagerness for quantitative growth of the church should render us silent about the whole counsel of God.

The danger of evangelicalism is that it will present a saving work of Christ without the consequent ethical demands, that it will present a Savior who delivers from the bondage of spiritual slavery but not a model of the life that the Christian should live in the world. A spirituality without discipleship in the daily social, economic, and political aspects of life is religiosity and not Christianity.

PROCLAMATION AND LIBERATION

"Liberation, development, humanization, or evangelization ...are all essential, integral parts of the mission entrusted to us."

■ *By the late 1970s, calls for a holistic mission theology that combines concerns for evangelization and social justice were heard from Roman Catholic and Orthodox theologians, and conciliar and evangelical Protestants. In 1978, Dr. Emilio Castro, later to become director of the Commission on World Mission and Evangelism (1973-1983) and general secretary (1983-1992) of the World Council of Churches, discussed this growing consensus in his article, "Liberation, Development, and Evangelism: Must We Choose in Mission?" The former president of the Evangelical Methodist Church of Uruguay and coordinator of UNELAM (the Provisional Commission for Latin American Evangelical Unity), Castro represented the consensus of Third World theologians and missiologists that there can be no authentic evangelism without participation in God's mission on behalf of the poor and oppressed.*

*A Growing Consensus**

There is a growing consensus among Christians on the reciprocity between evangelism and Christian service, between proclamation of the gospel of Jesus Christ and participation in human liberation....

There can be no proclamation of the gospel without commitment to God's mission, which includes justice, liberation, and service. Christians [cannot] participate in God's liberating mission or in different forms of service to the community unless [their] life and witness are focused on the hidden reason for [their] participation, as well as on the ultimate secret of the liberation process within [themselves]. There can be no evangelism outside the divine mission in its totality, and no conscious participation in the mission of God without awareness of the revelation involved....

Evangelistic proclamation can—and must—have a point of emphasis, such as the cross, the forgiveness of sins, or the healing of the sick. But it will be "evangel" only to the extent that it points to the wholeness of God's love breaking through in the world, and that it looks forward to the reign of his peace in all human relations. There are a number of things to be said in connection with this dialectical relationship between mission and evangelism.

Mission: The Whole Is Only Equal to its Parts

In carrying out God's mission, we *cannot opt permanently* for one aspect of mission or another, be it liberation, development, humanization, or evangelization. These are all essential, integral parts of the mission entrusted to us and cannot be set against one another without becoming, simply, caricatures of what they really are. Indeed, they exist as parts only, and can only be discovered or recognized separately within the framework of their interrelatedness. For example, as citizens, we may take part, along with others who may or may not be Christians, in the struggle against underdevelopment or against anything that threatens human freedom. Our participation in this process implies a spirit of self-criticism based on eschatological thinking. Since all human effort is ultimately subject to God's judgment, if we participate faithfully in the process of liberation, if we are disciplined participants in the struggles it involves, we bring to it a capacity for critical appraisal which we consider to be constructive and salutary for the whole process, and which questions it in various respects. Our critical approach will be credible only if it is clearly seen to be closely linked to a declaration of our faith in Jesus Christ, if it does not stem from any connection with competing ideologies or rival power groups. As Christians participating in a political liberation struggle, it is absolutely essential that we never lose sight of our commitment to the Christian community as a whole and to the deepest roots of our faith. But, at the same time,

---

*Excerpts from Emilio Castro, "Liberation, Development, and Evangelism: Must We Choose in Mission?" *Occasional Bulletin of Missionary Research* 2 (1978): 88; cf. Bosch, TM, 434.

our evangelism can be credible only when its message is seen to be valid in relation to the often cruel facts of real, everyday situations.

GOSPEL TO THE SINNED-AGAINST

> "A person is not only a sinner, a person is also the sinned against."

■ *A new emphasis at the 1980 WCC World Conference on Mission and Evangelism in Melbourne, Australia, was "a deepened recognition of the fundamentally spiritual nature of the conflict with the powers of exploitation and impoverishment."*[6] *Raymond Fung of Hong Kong made a lasting impression in his understanding of persons not only as sinners but as "sinned-against." Vividly he told of the poor who sat on the ground helplessly watching as their homes were bulldozed away to make room for a summer resort. His ministry with them was as director of the Hong Kong Christian Industrial Committee. Following Melbourne, he joined the staff of the WCC as its Secretary for Evangelism (1981-1991) before returning to his native land as senior secretary for the Hong Kong Christian Institute.*

*Human Sinned-againstness**

We wish to report to the churches that a person is not only a sinner, a person is also the sinned against. That men and women are not only wilful violators of God's laws, they are also the violated. This is not to be understood in a behaviouristic sense, but in a theological sense, in terms of sin, the domination of sin, and of our "struggle against sin ...to the point of shedding our blood" (Heb. 12:4). We would like to report to the churches that [a person] is lost, lost not only in the sins in his [or her] own heart but also in the sinning grasp of principalities and powers of the world, demonic forces which cast a bondage over human lives and human institutions and infiltrate their very textures.

Because of our involvement with the poor, we discover that a person persistently deprived of basic material needs and political rights is also a person deprived of much of his or her soul—self-respect, dignity and will. A fisherman deprived of ...waters, a peasant of ...land, becomes a person deprived physically and spiritually. Dangerous working conditions and lax safety and health protection systems resulting in death and injury not only take away the means of livelihood of thousands of working-class families, but forcibly reduce otherwise proud and independent persons into dependency and self-depreciation. I cannot forget the faces of the poor who sat on the ground helpless seeing their homes bulldozed away

---

*Excerpts from Raymond Fung, "Good News to the Poor—A Case for a Missionary Movement," in World Council of Churches, *Your Kingdom Come: Report on the World Conference on Mission and Evangelism, Melbourne, Australia, 12-25 May 1980* (Geneva: WCC, 1980), 84-85, 88, 89; cf. Bosch, TM, 408.

to make room for a summer resort. There was resentment and hatred on their faces, which turned inward and gnawed at their own soul. I wish to report that hatred is not found in the poor standing up to fight, it is found in the poor crawling into the corner of forced submission. I would like to report to the churches that the destroyer of the body may not be able to kill the soul, but it can, and too often does, rape and maim the soul.

Gospel to the Sinned-against

As it is, I would urge that we do not lose sight of the sinned-againstness of persons in our theological understanding and evangelistic effort. We must rediscover the horror of sin on human lives. There has been too much shallowness in our understanding of sin in the churches' evangelistic enterprises. Could it be that many evangelists of our churches today have no notion of human sinned-againstness? Could it be that in our much-cushioned life we cannot dismiss it as alien or only secondary to theological and evangelistic consideration? Or could it be that having looked into our own Christian experiences and found that our faith has made us prosper, we honestly think we are not the sinned-against, and neither for that matter need anyone else be the sinned-against? If that is the case, then no wonder the poor who experience indignity and injustice every day don't give a hoot about our evangelism.

We would like to report that the Gospel should not only call on the people to repent of their sins, but also must call on them to resist the forces that sin against them. The Church must not only remind the people that God is separated from us on account of our sinfulness. The Church must also proclaim that God loves us and is with us even while we are yet sinners....

Evangelism

...the context of a community of the sinned-against struggling against the forces of sin is an evangelizing context. It is in a community in struggle that evangelism takes place. It is impossible to overemphasize the importance of the community of the sinned-against in the evangelization of the poor. The most dwelt-upon methods of evangelism today—personal evangelism and mass evangelism—are futile among the poor because, among many other reasons, both presuppose a receiving community which is not available to the poor in most of our existing churches today....

Most of those who have left the churches in which they received their baptism simply drifted away. They instinctively understand that the churches want them as spectators and even recipients of Christian services, but not as full members of a caring and sharing community. Let us recognize the fact that there are poor people in our churches. Their presence and their sinned-againstness by economic and political forces make it impossible for the pastoral ministry to be devoid of political dimensions. When the poor are in the churches, to be pro-poor is not a political stand, it is a pastoral stand. Let us also recognize the fact that most of the poor are not in our churches. For them, the evangelizing context is not individual encounter, being confronted with the four spiritual laws for instance; neither is it a mass rally. It is far more personal and far more corporate. Hence this plea for a missionary movement to build communities of the sinned-against among the world's poor.

A RADICAL GOSPEL

"Evangelism and social action go hand in glove."

■ *In 1985, South Africa was like a volcanic cauldron ready to erupt. School and bus boycotts often led to violence. In the towns, black union leaders called 390 strikes involving 240,000 workers. Local government broke down in the black townships. Rural peasants resisted forced removals. In reaction, the white Afrikaner-dominated government declared a state of emergency that extended throughout the country by June 12, 1986. Emergency regulations gave police officers broad powers to ban meetings and arrest and detain persons without trial. In response, liberal church leaders issued the* Kairos Document *in September 1985. Responding to the same "moment of truth" and "crisis of faith," concerned evangelical leaders published the "Evangelical Witness in South Africa in 1986." They condemned those evangelicals who either supported apartheid or preached a pietism divorced from social injustices.*

*Our Theology of Mission and Evangelism**

We believe that God loves this whole world and that God has called us to minister to this whole world. We are called to minister to both the spiritual and social needs of the world. We believe that one cannot meet the spiritual needs of people effectively if this does not touch on or have any bearing on their social needs. Evangelism therefore cannot be separated from social action and social justice. In fact evangelism and social action go hand in glove. If we bear the name of evangelicals we have to be true to our name by preaching good news to the poor, by proclaiming liberty to the captives and recovery of sight to the blind, by setting at liberty those who are oppressed, and by proclaiming the favourable year of the Lord (Lk. 4:18-19).

Repentance: A Radical Demand for Change

It is a maxim that to be an evangelical means to believe in repentance of one's sin(s) and conversion. It means to believe in salvation by faith alone in the Lord Jesus Christ.

It is also equally true that in our proclamation of the gospel, we condemn sin in

---

*Excerpts from *Evangelical Witness in South Africa: A Critique of Evangelical Theology and Practice by South African Evangelicals* (Grand Rapids, MI: Eerdmans, 1986), 42, 43, 45; cf. Bosch, TM, 407.

all its forms: personal, collective and structural. We then also call people to repentance, with the hope of forgiveness of sin, and restoration of relationship with God and with people.

A Radical Gospel at Loggerheads with Apartheid

The Gospel is radical. A call by God to a prophetic ministry is often, if not always, radical. Jeremiah was called by God to minister to nations of his time. God set him "over nations and over kingdoms, to pluck up and to break down, to destroy and to overthrow, to build and to plant" (Jer. 1:10).

This constitutes a call and commission to a radical ministration. We have not done this. We have rather regrettably betrayed the faith. We have cowardly "sold out" the mission of our Lord, we have sold out our birth right. We have mismanaged our responsibility. WE MUST REPENT AND MINISTER ACCORDING TO OUR CALLING.

We call upon all committed evangelicals in South Africa to come out boldly to be witnesses of the gospel of salvation, justice and peace in this country without fear. You have not received the spirit of slavery to fall back into fear (Rom. 8:15) as many of us have done. We have to take a stand now even if it may mean persecution by earthly systems. For if we fail now we shall have no legitimacy in the post-liberation period unless we want to join the hypocrites of this world.

JESUS, THE MODEL OF HOLISTIC MISSION

> "Jesus is the norm for our action in reforming our lives and renewing society."

■ *Virginia Fabella is a Maryknoll sister born in the Philippines. She has worked in Latin America and her homeland, as well as in the United States as director of the Maryknoll Mission Institute in New York. She helped organize the first Ecumenical Dialogue of Third World Theologians in Tanzania in 1976 and since the inaugural has continued as a key leader in EATWOT's ongoing and expanding program. Often an unrecognized group author, in the following selection she articulates her own theology of mission with a Christocentric focus and Jesus as liberator.*

*What It Means to Be Truly Human**

Christology is at the heart of all theology for it is Jesus who has revealed to us the deepest truths about God. In his humanity, Jesus revealed God as a loving God who cares for the weakest and lowliest and wills the full humanity and salvation of

---

*Excerpts from Virginia Fabella, "Christology from an Asian Woman's Perspective," in *We Dare to Dream: Doing Theology as Asian Women,* ed. Virginia Fabella and Sun Ai Lee Park (Maryknoll, NY: Orbis Books, 1990), 4, 10-11, 12-13; cf. Bosch, TM, 408.

all, men and women alike. In his humanity, Jesus has shown us what it means to be truly human, to have life abundantly, to be saved. Thus christology is central and integral to any talk about God, human-God relationship and all right relationships and to any discussion about salvation and liberation.

Jesus as Liberator

In the light of Asian women's reality in general, a liberational, hope-filled, love-inspired, and praxis-oriented christology is what holds meaning for me. In the person and praxis of Jesus are found the grounds of our liberation from all oppression and discrimination: whether political or economic, religious or cultural, or based on gender, race or ethnicity. Therefore the image of Jesus as liberator is consistent with my christology.

In my own culture, however, not many women would be familiar with the figure of a liberating or liberated Jesus. They know him as the suffering or crucified Jesus who understands their own suffering which they passively or resignedly endure. Many remain unaware of their class and gender oppression and simply live on with a "status quo" christology. Nevertheless, an increasing number of women are becoming aware of our subordinate place and exploited state in a patriarchal church and society, and see this as contrary to the will of a just and loving God, who created both men and women in God's own image. As these women strive to change this inequitable situation within the overall struggle against economic, political and social injustices, they, too, see Jesus as their hope and liberator.

In our quest for a world of right human relationships, Jesus has shown us the way, and therefore Jesus is the norm for our action in reforming our lives and renewing society. Jesus never spoke of human rights or the common good or liberation from oppressive structures, yet his whole life, teachings and actions embodied all of them, manifesting what it meant to be human and to act humanly. He showed us that we cannot work toward our true humanity, our true liberation, unless we seek the true humanity, the true liberation, of all. Thus, efforts to transform the existing structures and patterns of domination that prevent the least of our sisters and brothers from living truly human lives and enjoying just, reciprocal relationships, are moral actions.

A More Compelling Witness

Our witness is for the sake of the good news of God's reign; the good news is not just to be preached but lived. Thus our life and work style must conform to the kingdom norms and values. We cannot proclaim a reign of justice, love and peace, while at the same time contradicting its inclusive, non-dominating character in our mission practice and structures. If the kingdom is our focus, then a more collaborative, egalitarian, ecumenical effort in mission will be a more compelling witness.

REAL MODELS OF HOLINESS

"Recognizing and promoting real models of holiness."

■ *To celebrate ten years of its progress and work, the Ecumenical Association of Third World Theologians organized a general assembly of its members in 1986. From December 7-14 in Oaxtepec, Mexico, delegates examined the theme, "Commonalities, Divergences, and Cross-fertilization among Third World Theologies." The final reflection, composed during the conference and later approved by the EATWOT executive, includes the following section on "The Mission of the Church."*

*The Mission of the Church**

From EATWOT's founding at Dar-es-Salaam until the present we have reflected on the meaning of evangelization as the task of the church. In that first dialogue we said: "The church, the body of Christ, needs to become aware of its role in today's reality.... Jesus identified himself with the victims of oppression, thus exposing the reality of sin. Liberating them from the power of sin and reconciling them with God and with one another, he restored them to the fullness of their humanity. Therefore, the church's mission is for the realization of the wholeness of the human person" (from the final statement).

Today, as we continue trying to define the mission of the church, we are more aware that evangelization is linked to human promotion. Evangelization is to share the gift of Jesus, but at the same time it is an opportunity to learn from others. Evangelization cannot be arrogant, as in the past. It has to be considered as a modest and friendly presence on the part of the churches to discover for themselves the wonder of God's grace in every history, culture, and people, and to celebrate that grace and to give thanks; to be open and accept the other's specific gift of truth and God-experience for their own enrichment and growth; to make available to the other their own specific experience of God, love, and hope as these have entered human history in the reality of Jesus of Nazareth; and to join hands with all who stand for human dignity and struggle together for the liberation of all.

Evangelization can no longer be a matter of spiritual conquest or religious colonization. The church can be only a disciple among disciples, and a seeker after fuller and finer participation in God's truth. Everywhere the need is for the church to be local, real, autonomous, responsible. Everywhere the question is about the church's official stand on Third World realities. Everywhere it is a question of recognizing and promoting real models of holiness in the women and men who live

---

*Excerpts from the Second General Assembly of the Ecumenical Association of Third World Theologians, Assembly (Oaxtepec, Mexico, December 1986), *Third World Theologies: Commonalities and Divergences,* ed. K. C. Abraham (Maryknoll, NY: Orbis Books, 1990), 209; cf. Bosch, TM, 408.

out their fidelity to Christ in day-to-day life despite suffering, poverty, temptations, risk, and danger instead of holding up rare models of unreal and artificial sanctity.

NOTES

1. Harold Lindsell, "Precedent-Setting in Missions Strategy," *Christianity Today* 10:15 (April 29, 1966), p. 43.

2. Cf. Second Vatican Ecumenical Council, Pastoral Constitution on the Church in the Modern World *Gaudium et Spes,* 47-52: AAS 58 (1966), pp. 1067-74; Paul VI, Encyclical Letter, *Humanae Vitae*: AAS 60 (1968), pp. 481-503.

3. Paul VI, Address for the opening of the Third General Assembly of Synod of Bishops (September 27, 1974): AAS 66 (1974), p. 562.

4. International Congress on World Evangelization, *Let the Earth Hear His Voice* (Minnealpolis, MN: World Wide Publications, 1975), p. 5; see also Richard Quebedeaux, *The Worldly Evangelicals* (San Francisco: Harper & Row, 1978), pp. 59-61.

5. Samuel Escobar in "The Social Impact of the Gospel," in *Is Revolution Change?* ed. Brian Griffiths (Downer's Grove, IL: InterVarsity Press, 1972), pp. 100 and 98. This chapter is the English text of the message on the subject presented at the Bogota Congress on Evangelism and published with the other papers of the congress under the title *Accion en Cristo para un Continente en Crisis* (ed. Caribe), 1970.

6. Belle Miller McMaster, "Witnessing to the Kingdom," in *Witnessing to the Kingdom: Melbourne and Beyond,* ed. Gerald H. Anderson (Maryknoll, NY: Orbis Books, 1982), p. 37.

9

Mission as Evangelization

"Christians generally do not listen to people," wrote Raymond Fung. He continued:

> *We do not listen to people because we do not hear people crying out to God.... People do not cry out because there is no one there to listen. People came to realize their real needs and exposed them to Jesus because they knew they could depend on his listening to them... not to listen is not just bad evangelism. It is not evangelism.*[1]

These words by the WCC's Secretary for Evangelism relate to key controversies today concerning mission as evangelization. First, what is evangelism (or evangelization)? Is it a broader or narrower concept than mission? Are the two terms interchangeable? Second, what is the scope or range of evangelization? Is it, like mission, an umbrella term for the whole activity of the church sent into the world? Or is it to be defined more narrowly as witness to what God has done, is doing, and will do? Is that witness to be evaluated primarily by results or effectiveness (conversions, discipling, and so on)? Is witness primarily verbal proclamation, or does it include living in obedience to Christ? If the latter, how is evangelism different from mission?

The selections below highlight significant answers to these questions and relate to David Bosch's eighteen understandings of evangelism (TM, 409-20).

Frequently critics of the WCC charge that it has forsaken Christ's commission to go into all the world to proclaim the Gospel and baptize. Examination of the ecumenical body's documents, however, presents a different picture. The note of urgency to proclaim the Gospel to all persons everywhere was sounded at the WCC's inaugural assembly in Amsterdam in 1948. By 1968, however, Donald McGavran challenged the world body, claiming that its preoccupation with issues of humanization had betrayed the two billion persons on earth who did not know of Christ. The selection that follows from the WCC's Uppsala assembly of 1968 uses different language, expressing concern for a renewal of mission "to all who seek full humanity." Eugene Smith presents a critique of McGavran's concept of evangelism, saying that it focuses excessively on individual salvation and is preoccupied with "statistical Christianity," measuring results by numbers rather than by spiritual growth.

From Asia, Latin America, and Africa come creative additional understandings. Much rhetoric by professional evangelists is triumphalistic and separates the "saved" from the "lost." By contrast, D. T. Niles of Sri Lanka would follow Christ's example of empathy with each person. He defined evangelism as "one beggar telling another beggar where to get food." One of the clearest statements of a holistic understanding of evangelism is found in "A Bolivian Manifesto" of 1975. Shared with the world church by Bishop Mortimer Arias in his keynote address to the WCC's Fifth Assembly in Nairobi in 1975, it served as a model for all subsequent WCC statements. J. N. Z. Kurewa of Zimbabwe, the WCC's first evangelism secretary from Africa, contributed two important insights from African culture: that conversion is a lifelong process rather than a single event and that confrontation by Christ and identity with Christ take place within community. Finally, Mother Teresa, out of her ministry to the destitute and dying of Calcutta, witnesses that while retaining the aim of "the salvation of the poor," one waits in expectation that the "poor, seeing you, be drawn to Christ."

A MATTER OF LIFE AND DEATH

> "Evangelism in its ecumenical setting ... [is] burdened by a sense of urgency."

■ *The World Council of Churches, at its inaugural assembly in Amsterdam in 1948, had as its theme "Man's Disorder and God's Design." The purpose of God was understood to include reconciling all persons to God and to one another through Jesus Christ. The Gospel was called "a matter of life and death" and evangelism an urgency for all Christians and an important part of the WCC's new program development.*

*The Purpose of God**

(From Report of Section 2, "The Church's Witness to God's Design")

The purpose of God is to reconcile all [persons] to Himself and to one another in Jesus Christ His Son. That purpose was made manifest in Jesus Christ—His incarnation, His ministry of service, His death on the Cross, His resurrection and ascension. It continues in the gift of the Holy Spirit, in the command to make disciples of all nations, and in the abiding presence of Christ with His Church. It looks forward to its consummation in the gathering together of all things in Christ. Much in that purpose is still hidden from us. Three things are perfectly plain:

---

*Excerpts from World Council of Churches (1st Assembly, 1948), *Man's Disorder and God's Design* (New York: Harper & Brothers, 1949), 5: 69-70; cf. Bosch, TM, 409.

All that we need to know concerning God's purpose is already revealed in Christ. It is God's will that the Gospel should be proclaimed to all [persons] everywhere. God is pleased to use human obedience in the fulfillment of His purpose.

To the Church, then, is given the privilege of so making Christ known to [persons] that each is confronted with the necessity of a personal decision, Yes or No. The Gospel is the expression both of God's love to [humanity], and of His claim to [human] obedience. In this lies the solemnity of the decision. Those who obey are delivered from the power of the world in which sin reigns, and already, in the fellowship of the children of God, have the experience of eternal life. Those who reject the love of God remain under His judgment and are in danger of sharing in the impending doom of the world that is passing away.

"Now Is the Accepted Time"

As we have studied evangelism in its ecumenical setting we have been burdened by a sense of urgency. We have recaptured something of the spirit of the apostolic age, when the believers "went everywhere preaching the word." If the Gospel really is a matter of life and death, it seems intolerable that any human being now in the world should live out his [or her] life without ever having the chance to hear and receive it.

It is not within [human] power alone to create a new evangelistic movement. But the Holy Spirit is at work in [society] with [persons]. In the past He has from time to time quickened the Church with power from on high. It is our earnest hope and prayer that He will do a mighty work in our day, giving the Church again wisdom and power rightly to proclaim the good news of Jesus Christ to [all]. We rejoice that the World Council of Churches has included evangelism in its programme of development. Already we are seeing signs of renewal and fresh life.

EVANGELISM—THE CHURCH'S WAY OF LIFE

> "Evangelism . . . is one beggar telling another beggar where to get food."

■ *Is evangelization an optional extra or an indispensable ministry? Christian church leaders of the Two-thirds World often have led in affirming the imperative of the church's evangelistic task. Among the first was D. T. Niles of Sri Lanka [formerly Ceylon]. He served as secretary of the Department of Evangelism of the World Council of Churches, chairman of the World Student Christian Federation, and executive secretary of the East Asian Christian Conference. In* That There May Be Life, *prepared as a study book for the American Student Volunteer Movement for Christian Missions, he called evangelism a "conversion to discipleship" in holistic witness in the world.*

*The Evangelist**

The recovery of wholeness—that is the purpose of evangelism, the bringing back of the lost to their place in the economy of God. For God so loved the world that He gave His Son, that no one and nothing may perish and become useless, but that everyone and everything may find their true usefulness in the purposes of God (Jn. 3:16). The Gospel must be preached to the whole creation, for that is what the Gospel is. It is God's address to creation as a whole, His action to bring to creation its harmony (Mk. 16:15, Col. 1:23). Every activity, therefore, which seeks to effect this harmony is an activity within the meaning of the term "evangelism." It is part of the working of God. The school, the hospital, the rural center, the laboratory: these are all ways in which God is seeking to bring wholeness into life. No less significant are the ways He adopts through those to whom He has committed power. Through them He effects orderly government that those conditions may prevail in which the Gospel may spread (1 Tim. 2:1-4), and through them also He effects those events which execute His judgment over sin (Lk. 19:41-44)....

The Task

> Woe to me if I do not preach the gospel! For if I do this of my own will, I have a reward; but if not of my own will, I am entrusted with a commission.... I have made myself a slave to all, that I might win the more.... I have become all things to all [people], that I might by all means save some. I do it all for the sake of the gospel, that I may share in its blessings (1 Cor. 9:16-27).

The object of evangelism is conversion, conversion to Christ and personal discipleship to Him. But involved also in this conversion are conversion to the Christian community and conversion to Christian ideas and ideals. All three conversions must take place, even though the order in which they take place may be different. Thus in India with its mass movements the first conversion is largely to the Christian community—proselytism. Then takes place conversion to discipleship—evangelism. And then along with it and because of it follows conversion to Christian ideas and ideals—Christianization. In Christian colleges the order of conversion is usually different. First of all, it is Christianization, then evangelism, and then proselytization. In the case of those driven by spiritual hunger or despair due to the consciousness of sin, the first effect of the Gospel is evangelism, their being won to personal discipleship to Christ, and then follows proselytization and Christianization together.

It is futile and perverse to isolate these three movements of the soul from one another and treat them in opposition to one another. They belong together, each makes the others possible, and they derive meaning from one another.

---

*Excerpts from Daniel T. Niles, *That They May Have Life* (New York: Harper & Brothers, 1951), 57, 82-83, 96; cf. Bosch, TM, 413.

The Non-Christian

Evangelism is witness. It is one beggar telling another beggar where to get food. The Christian[s] do not offer out of [their] bounty. [They have] no bounty. [They are] simply guests at [their] Master's table and, as evangelists, [they] call others too. The evangelistic relation is to be "alongside of" not "over-against." The Christian stands alongside the non-Christian and points to the Gospel, the holy action of God. It is not [one's] knowledge of God that [one] shares, it is to God Himself that [one] points. The Christian Gospel is the Word become flesh. This is more than and other than the Word become speech. The religious quest for self-realization is henceforth pulled up with this demand, that the self is not realized by a flight from the finite and the temporal, but by taking its stand at the point where the finite and the infinite, the temporal and the eternal meet.

DO NOT BETRAY THE TWO BILLION!

> "The Church to be relevant must ...carry ...the water of life ...to 'the two billion' perishing of thirst."

■ *The Conciliar-Evangelical debate over the goal of mission reached its climax in 1968.*[2] *Amid the global upheavals in that year over war and racism, the World Council of Churches' draft document on mission for its Fourth Assembly, to be held in Uppsala, Sweden, made no mention of evangelistic outreach to the two billion who did not know Christ as Savior and Lord. Alarmed, the faculty of the School of Missions at Fuller Theological Seminary, led by Dean Donald McGavran, made the following critique.*

*Will Uppsala Betray the Two Billion?**

By Uppsala I mean, of course, the Fourth Assembly of the World Council of Churches which is to be held at Uppsala, Sweden, in July 1968. By "the two billion" I mean "that great number of [persons] at least two billion, who either have never heard of Jesus Christ or have no real chance to believe on Him as Lord and Savior." These inconceivable multitudes live and die in a famine of the Word of God, more terrible by far than the sporadic physical famines which occur in unfortunate lands.

The Church, to be relevant, to discharge her humane duty to the masses of [humankind], to act with justice, and to manifest compassion, must plan her activity, marshall her forces, carry on her campaign of mercy and liberation, and be faithful to her Lord *with the two billion in mind.* If the sufferings of a few million in Vietnam, South Africa, Jordan, Buchenwald, or the slums of Rio de Janeiro or Detroit rightly excite the indignation and compassion of the Church, how much more should the

---

*Excerpts from Donald McGavran, "Will Uppsala Betray the Two Billion?" in *The Conciliar-Evangelical Debate,* ed. Arthur Glasser and Donald McGavran (Waco, TX: Word Books, 1972), 233-34, 239-40; cf. Bosch, TM, 415.

spiritual sufferings of two thousand million move her to bring multitudes of them out of darkness into God's wonderful light. The Church to be relevant must augment her program to carry the bread of life to starving multitudes and to dig wide, deep channels through which the water of life may flow to "the two billion" perishing of thirst.

By "betray" I mean any course of action which substitutes ashes for bread, fixes the attention of Christians on temporal palliatives instead of eternal remedies, and deceives God's children with the flesh when they long for the spirit. By "betray" I mean planning courses of action whose sure outcome will be that the two billion will remain in their sins and in their darkness, chained by false and inadequate ideas of God and [humanity]. Uppsala will betray the two billion if she, to whom God has given the leadership of such a proportion of the Church, plans a program which leads her affiliated churches away from the precise issues on which Christians need to speak today, away from spreading the knowledge of their Savior to as many of the two billion as it is possible to do....

The Precise Issue

The salvation of the two billion children of God is *the precise issue* on which the Division of World Mission and Evangelism needs to speak. Nothing is more precise or more contemporary.

The committee which drew up this Draft is apparently unaware of the fact that today in many lands of Asia, Africa, and Latin America, an unprecedented receptivity to the gospel exists. Much greater receptivity exists than would have been deemed possible twenty years ago. According to the World Christian Handbooks, the Christian population of Africa south of the Sahara increased from twenty million in 1950 to fifty million in 1968. It is likely to increase to a hundred million by 1990. The precise issue in 1968 when the World Council will meet at Uppsala is this: how can the Christian Church carry the gospel faster and better to the multitudes who want to become Christians? The chief issue is not dialogue with hostile non-Christians. In the days of His flesh, our Lord instructed His disciples to by-pass indifferent and hostile villages and hurry on to the receptive. Such days have again come. This is a time to emphasize discipling, not to turn from it. This is not a time to betray the two billion but to reconcile as many as possible of them to God in the Church of Jesus Christ. For the peace of the world, for justice between [peoples] and nations, for advance in learning, for breaking down hostilities between peoples, for the spiritual health of countless individuals and the corporate welfare of [humankind] *this is a time to disciple the nations, baptizing them in the name of the Father, Son, and Holy Spirit and teaching them whatsoever our Lord has commanded us.*

THE RENEWAL OF MISSION

"New creation which is a radical renewal of the old."

■ *For two years in the 1970s, the WCC's Division of World Mission and Evangelism developed its mandate for mission. Revised at Uppsala, the final draft adopted by the assembly included an affirmation of "an unchanging responsibility to make known the Gospel of the forgiveness of God in Christ to the hundreds of millions who have not heard it." But greater emphasis was given to presenting Christ as the "[person] for others" to those who name the name of Christ yet turn away from Christ's mission. The following is the text as adopted at Uppsala.*

*A Mandate for Mission**

We belong to a humanity that cries passionately and articulately for a fully human life. Yet [our] very humanity and [our] societies [are] threatened by a greater variety of destructive forces than ever. And the acutest moral problems all hinge upon the question: What is [a person]? We Christians know that we are in this worldwide struggle for meaning, dignity, freedom, and love, and we cannot stand aloof. We have been charged with a message and a ministry that have to do with more than material needs, but we can never be content to treat our concern for physical and social needs as merely secondary to our responsibility for the needs of the spirit. There is a burning relevance today in describing the mission of God, in which we participate, as the gift of a new creation which is a radical renewal of the old and the invitation to [persons] to grow up into their full humanity in the new [person], Jesus Christ.

The Church in Mission Is the Church for Others

The Church in mission is for all people everywhere. It has an unchanging responsibility to make known the Gospel of the forgiveness of God in Christ to the hundreds of millions who have not heard it; for those who name his name and yet turn away from his mission; for those who, unknowing, serve the "[person] for others"; and even for those who reject the Church, and yet continue to wait for the new humanity.

Since the Church is for others, its mission must both challenge and include men and women where they are:

—a Reformed banker in Zurich and his Roman Catholic colleague in Buenos Aires
—a Baptist policeman in the Congo, an Orthodox teacher in India
—a Methodist professor at Columbia, a Lutheran art student at the Sorbonne
—a pastor evangelist in New Guinea, a minister in industrial Tokyo
—a Spanish migrant worker in Holland, a West Indian bus conductor in London

---

*Excerpts from WCC (4th Assembly, Uppsala 1968), "Renewal in Mission," in *The Conciliar-Evangelical Debate,* 249, 251-52; cf. Bosch, TM, 415.

—a nurse in Johannesburg, an interpreter in Moscow
—a hungry child in Rio, an unemployed farm worker in Mississippi.

Localities for mission are rich in variety and setting—where there is human need, an expanding population, tension, forces in movement, institutional rigidities, decision-making about the priorities and uses of power, and even open human conflict.

INDIVIDUALISTIC EVANGELISM IS INADEQUATE

> "Most traditional calls to individualistic evangelism are inadequate to our present challenge."

■ *Dr. Eugene L. Smith, executive secretary of the WCC in New York, strongly criticized the McGavran position in his defense of the Uppsala document, "Renewal in Mission." An evangelistic call that focuses on the two billion but forgets the lapsed millions in the West is "tragically inadequate," he argued. To be silent about the myopia of nominal Christians is to support apartheid in South Africa and injustice in Latin America and other continents. It leads to a false emphasis on "statistical Christianity" and focuses excessively on individual and private morality, Smith charged.*

*Do Not Neglect the Lapsed Millions**

The Uppsala document "Renewal in Mission" reflects a deep hesitation about drawing a clear line between the two billion who do not know Christ, and the many millions who bear his name, but whose lives deny his Saviorhood and his Lordship. The great need of these "nominal" or "lapsed" or "unsaved" Christians is to encounter the living Christ, repent and be saved. The service they need from a renewed church is both education and evangelism. An evangelistic call which focuses on the two billion, but forgets these lapsed millions, is tragically inadequate.

Moreover, such a call leads with dangerous ease into assumptions of white superiority. A considerable proportion of the white population is composed of nominal Christians. Most of the colored people are not Christian. Is there no need for true evangelism among the white "Christians" of South Africa who support apartheid; among the white "Christians" in Latin America who maintain corrupt, feudal oligarchies; among the "Christians" who support the neo-nazi movement in Germany? An interpretation of the Christian mission which implies—even indirectly—that the nominal white Christian has no need for repentance and rebirth in Christ, while the great majority of colored persons do need to repent and be saved

---

*Excerpts from Eugene Smith, "Renewal in Mission," in *The Conciliar-Evangelical Debate,* 259-61; cf. Bosch, TM, 415.

arouses hostilities to the Christian mission among those it seeks to reach. It produces mission doomed to failure.

Distrust of "Statistical Christianity"

"Renewal in Mission" reflects an intense concern for the growth of the church spiritually, with a related distrust of "statistical Christianity." It grows in part out of a refusal to measure the results of evangelism by numbers. The evangelization of Africa (or any continent) will have to be done, for the most part, on the human side by the Christians that are there. An essential of the mission of God in Africa is an African church alive in mission, continually renewed in Christ. Without continual renewal in Christ, there is no continuing effectiveness in mission.

Individualistic Evangelism Is Inadequate

It reflects a reaction against the kind of evangelism which focuses excessively on the individual and his [or her] private morality. It performs a needed service to the cause of evangelism by building upon the biblical awareness that personality has both individual and communal dimension, and that the total person must be won for Christ. Thus it uses the biblical phrase of "the new [person]," with its clear implication that this "new creature" lives in Christ and no less in the community which He creates. The "new humanity" is more than a group of converted individuals, held together by loyalty of individuals to Christ. It is a new creation and the source of its existence is Christ himself.

Most traditional calls to individualistic evangelism are inadequate to our present challenge. There is nausea, widespread and justified, about the kind of evangelism which calls [persons] to an altar and tells [them they have] met Christ, but sends [them] out with segregationist racial attitudes unchallenged and unchanged. "By their fruits ye shall know them." By that test it is clear that such [persons have] not met the living Christ, who died for all. It is partly in reaction against such false evangelism, that many who are concerned with the biblical summons to justice become cold to programs labeled "evangelism."

Impelled both by the biblical imperative and by the nature of human need, our task is to be used by Christ in shaping a pattern of witness as broad in vision of justice as the prophets, as deep in power as Pentecost. Development of it will require, on our part, among other things, a deep willingness on the part of those particularly concerned with justice, and those particularly concerned with evangelism, to learn from each other and move out together in joint witness to Him who is both Savior and Lord.

A LIBERATING EVANGELISM

"True evangelism is *holistic*."

■ *When the Evangelical Methodist Church in Bolivia became autonomous as a national church, it published a "Manifesto to the Nation" on Easter 1970. This document, a kind of social creed, announced the commitment of the church to address problems of the society on the basis of its understanding of the Gospel as relevant to the conscientization, humanization, and liberation of humanity. Four years later, the church circulated a second radical manifesto. Entitled "Evangelism in Latin America Today," it had been prepared for the Methodist Consultation on Evangelism (Lima, June-July 1974). Bishop Mortimer Arias produced the first draft, which was later enriched by the church's National Evangelism Team. Quoted extensively in Bishop Arias's keynote address to the WCC's Fifth Assembly (Nairobi 1975),[3] the Bolivian manifesto's holistic approach to evangelism was to have widespread circulation and influence among conciliar Protestants.*

*Evangelism as Witness and Participation**

Evangelism is the proclamation in the Spirit and in its biblical integrity of the good news of God's love manifested in Jesus Christ. This means:

The *announcement* of the total saving message of Jesus Christ;

The *denunciation* of all idols or powers which are opposed to God's purpose for mankind;

The visible *witness*—collective and personal—to the Word which addresses, calls in question, transforms and makes [humankind] conscious;

The engaged *participation* in the struggle for a more just and human society, inspired by the love of Christ;

A *call* to men [and women] to be converted to Jesus Christ and to be incorporated here and now into his people.

True Evangelism

True evangelism is *holistic*: the whole Gospel for the whole man and the whole of [humankind]. Evangelism addresses [persons] in the totality of [their] being: individual and social, physical and spiritual, historical and eternal. We reject, therefore, all dichotomies, ancient and modern, which reduce the Gospel to one dimension or fragment [one] who has been created in the image and likeness of God. We do not accept the idea that evangelism means only "saving souls" and seeking exclusively "a change in the eternal status of the individual"; these concepts are insufficient. We reject also the reduction of the Gospel to a programme for service or social development or to a mere instrument of socio-political programmes (Lk. 4:18-19; Mt. 9:35-38; 1 Tim. 4:6-10; 2 Tim. 1:10; Acts 16:31).

True evangelism is *biblical.* Its message is the apostolic proclamation (*kerygma*) attested in the New Testament and centered in Jesus Christ. Its focus is the call to

---

*Excerpts from "A Bolivian Manifesto on Evangelism in Latin America Today," *A Monthly Letter About Evangelism,* no. 2 (Feb. 1975), 3-4, 4-5; cf. Bosch, TM, 409.

repentance (*metanoia*), conversion and incorporation into the community of faith. Its final goal is the Kingdom of God, the biblical peace (*shalom*), the reconciliation of all [persons] and all things in Jesus Christ. Consequently, evangelism is a permanent process in which we are called in question and converted, once and again, to God and to our neighbour, a call in which there is place for renewal, reconciliation and growth and maturity in Christ (Jn. 5:39; Acts 2:22-42, 10:34-44; 1 Cor. 15:1-4; Eph. 1:9-10; Col. 1:15-23; Gal. 2:11-21; Eph. 4:12-16; Phil. 3:12-15)….

The Priority of Evangelism

Evangelism is *essential* for the Church; it is its *primary* task. Evangelism springs from God's election of "a special people of his own"; it is based on the continued mission of the Son of God among men [and women]; it originates in the Great Commission which Jesus left to his Church and it is sustained by the promise of the Spirit for this salvific community. The fruit of evangelism is the building up of the Body of Christ on earth; the very survival of the Church depends on it (Ex. 19:5; Mt. 10; Jn. 15:16, 17-18; Mt. 28:18-20; Gen. 12:1-2; Mk. 16:15; Acts 1:8-9, 1 Pet. 2:9-10).

Evangelism is also a *normal expression* of the new life in Christ which strives to propagate itself, a fruit of gratitude and love, the discharging of an inexcusable responsibility, the projection of Christ's passion and compassion for all [persons] (1 Cor. 9:16; 2 Cor. 5:14-15).

This right and duty of the Church to evangelize rejoins also the right of every *human being* coming into this world to know Jesus Christ and his liberating Gospel. For "God wants all …to be saved and to come to know the truth." Given the fact that the commandment of Christ enjoins "preaching the Gospel to all creatures" and "making disciples of all nations," every woman or man, every child who is born, becomes our creditor and we are his debtor. The Gospel is not a possession; it is a stewardship. Nobody can deprive us of this privilege or relieve us from this responsibility. Hence the urgency of evangelizing (1 Tim. 2:4; Mk. 16:15; Rom. 1:11-16).

Evangelism is a *permanent task*: "in season and out of season." No situation exempts us from "announcing the great works of he who has called us from darkness into light." Neither secularism, nor the existence of other religions and ideologies, nor the population explosion, nor the demand of other urgent and inexcusable tasks which Christians must fulfil, can relieve the Church of this task that no other human institution can fulfil in its place. Evangelism must be carried on in a capitalist or in a socialist society or in any other which may emerge in history. Only the coming of God's Kingdom in its fulness will relieve us from the task of evangelizing (2 Tim. 4:1-5; 1 Pet. 2:9; 2 Cor. 11:4; Acts 4:12; 1 Tim. 2:5-7).

These vigorous affirmations of the priority of evangelism do not intend to support everything that goes by the name of evangelism in our churches or in other churches. We confess our perplexity, our laziness, our rationalizations, our distortions and reductionisms, our distraction in non-essential tasks, our sterility and the inadequate use of the resources of the Church, our insufficient understanding of the Gospel and of our mission. We are ashamed of having mistaken proselytism for evangelism, of having satisfied ourselves with an intermittent and organized activism which we named "evangelism," of having accepted to be a religious institution closed on itself, dominated by routine, comfort and apathy. And, with God's help, we intend to seek for an authentically biblical, evangelical and relevant evangelism.

CONVERSION AS SACRIFICIAL IDENTITY WITH CHRIST

> "Conversion ...[is] confrontation by Christ, identity with Christ and community solidarity around Christ."

■ *In 1979, Dr. J. N. Zvomunondita Kurewa succeeded Gerhard Hoffman of West Germany as the first WCC Secretary for Evangelism from the Third World. Native of Zimbabwe, United Methodist pastor and theological educator, through his office Dr. Kurewa quickly shared African understandings of evangelization and conversion that emphasized our life in community. The following year he returned to his native Zimbabwe upon its independence to become secretary to Parliament (1980-91) and first president of the Africa Methodist University (1991-).*

*Holistic Conversion**

Conversion experience and the evangelistic efforts of Christian communities are two interrelated aspects of the Christian faith (Mk. 11:22, Col. 2:3). Peter Bohler advised John Wesley, "Preach faith until you have it." This advice may help us understand that just as proclamation of Christ (Jn. 15:26) is an ongoing task of the Christian community, so also the response to Christ's calling, conversion, is an ongoing experience, a growth process to Christian maturity. There can be no growth without, first, the willingness to turn to the living Christ. Neither is there a short cut to Christian maturity. One is constantly being challenged to appropriate "the unsearchable riches of Christ" (Eph. 3:8) to the realities of life in human community and society at large. Therefore we will look at conversion in the African cultural context from the following perspectives: confrontation by Christ, identity with Christ and community solidarity around Christ.

Confrontation by Christ

In reading the Gospels we get the impression that the ministry of Jesus was primarily for the house of Israel (Mt. 10:6, Mk. 7:27, Jn. 12:20-24). After his

---

*Excerpts from J. N. Zvomunondita Kurewa, "Conversion in the African Context," IRM 68 (1979); 161, 162-65; cf. Bosch, TM, 414.

ascension and the descent of the Holy Spirit, however, Christ transcends national and cultural barriers; he becomes God's incarnational reality, no longer to Israel alone but to all peoples of earth.

Thus Christ is enabled to walk along the African paths, from village to village and from city to city. He continues to confront people as individuals and families, in their village setting or chieftainships, depending very much upon the strategy of those who feel sent by him. He has been introduced to urban centres of Africa by involved Christians....

One of the negative things in African Christianity today is the tendency of Christians to continually look back to the time or place of conversion, ignoring what has happened in their lives during the many years since that experience. Conversion is rather an ongoing process where one is constantly challenged to follow Christ and to learn from him at every turn....

Identity with Christ

Conversion also involves identifying oneself with Christ Jesus. It is true that one has to repent, turn away from sin and reorient one's style of life; but it is equally important to see one's own identity in the light of Christ and all that he did for all men and women. No wonder Paul says to the Galatians, "and the life I now live in the flesh I live by faith in the Son of God who loved me and gave himself for me" (2:20)....

If conversion to Christ, however, is going to mean anything at all to those concerned in the life of the Church in Africa today, sacrificial identity with Christ is absolutely essential.

Community Solidarity around Christ

Conversion means turning to Christ and identifying with him; it also means community solidarity around Christ. In other words conversion to Christ means that a new convert takes his or her place with other members of the community around Christ Jesus. As a matter of fact, the most authentic way for anyone to express identity with Christ is to share Christian solidarity with those gathered around Christ....

Probably one of the strongest characteristics of Christianity in Africa has been the ability to function in small group structures. New converts have always found grounds ready to welcome them. These groups have taken different forms depending upon the circumstances.

First, for lack of a better word, there have been what one would call conscientizing groups. The main task of such groups has been evangelism as well as training the new converts in the task of evangelism by apprenticeship. These groups, present in all denominations, have taken the task of evangelism upon themselves.

OUR LIFE OF EVANGELIZATION

"Let the poor, seeing you, be drawn to Christ."

■ *In her sensitive biography of Mother Teresa (b. 1910), Eileen Egan recalls her first memory of the saintly nun.*[4] *It was of a sari-clad woman leaning over the skeletonized remnant of a man, gently stroking his brown, sticklike arm and murmuring consoling words in Bengali. All this took place in the Missionary Sisters of Charity's "House for the Destitute and Dying"—a hall which had been donated for their use by officials of the powerful Hindu temple to the goddess Kali. Can humanitarian mission include evangelization in such a context? Consider as her response the following, extracted from Mother Teresa's instructions to the sisters.*

*Conversion and Sanctification**

The special aim of the society is to labor at the conversion and sanctification of the poor in the slums; that is by nursing the sick and the dying, by gathering and teaching little street children, by visiting and caring for beggars and their children, by giving shelter to the abandoned.

To labor at the conversion and sanctification of the poor in the slums involves hard, ceaseless toiling, without results, without counting the cost....

When we do "our work," visit the families, teach, nurse the sick, help the dying, gather the little children for church, we should do it with one aim in view: "the salvation of the poor." We want to bring them to Jesus and bring Jesus to them....

Give the Whole Christ

If you give to the people a broken Christ, a lame Christ, a crooked Christ—deformed by you, that is all they will have. If you want them to love Him, they must know Him first. Therefore, give the whole Christ—to the Sisters, first, then to the people in the slums. Do I give the Christ who is full of zeal, love, joy, and sunshine? Do I come up to the mark? Or am I a dark light, a false light, a bulb without connection, having no current and therefore shedding no radiance? Put your heart into being a bright light. "Help me to shed thy fragrance everywhere I go."

Let the poor, seeing you, be drawn to Christ. Poverty makes people very bitter, and they speak and act without realizing what they do. But do they remember Christ when they see you—even if they get angry—because you remind them of Christ?

Draw them to God but never, never to yourself. If you are not drawing them to

---

*Excerpts from Mother Teresa, *Total Surrender,* Revised edition (Ann Arbor, MI: Servant Publications, 1995), 121-22, 125-26, 129; cf. Bosch, TM, 420]

God, then you are seeking yourself, and people love you for yourself and not because you remind them of Christ.

NOTES

1. Raymond Fung, *Evangelistically Yours: Ecumenical Letters on Contemporary Evangelism* (Geneva: WCC, 1992), pp. 1, 2.

2. The McGavran essay, "Will Uppsala Betray the Two Million?" first appeared in the *Church Growth Bulletin,* Special Uppsala Issue, May 1968. Later it was reprinted with eight other documents of the debate, including the Uppsala text, "Renewal in Mission," and Eugene Smith's essay by the same title, in *Eye of the Storm* (1972) and *The Conciliar-Evangelical Debate: The Crucial Documents, 1964-1976* (1977).

3. "That the World May Believe," *IRM* 65 (1976): 13-26.

4. Eileen Egan, *Such a Vision of the Street: Mother Teresa, the Spirit and the Work* (Garden City, NY: Doubleday & Co., 1986), p. 2.

10

Mission as Contextualization

Christian mission began at Pentecost as the apostles "began to speak in other languages, as the Spirit gave them ability" (Acts 2:4). Unreached peoples in every age have heard and received the missionary message only as the Christian church has incarnated itself in the life and world of those who have embraced it.

Indigenization *has been the prevalent term among Protestant scholars to describe this dynamic. It is the process of adapting to the conditions or practices of a particular land or environment or people. Roman Catholic scholars, by contrast, have written more often of* inculturation*—a concept to be considered in Chapter 12.*

Those who advocated indigenization, whether of clerical dress or liturgies or moral codes, however, assumed that the Gospel and Christian theology would be the same in all cultures. Deviations from "orthodoxy," whether by Arians or Anabaptists, were judged to be heretical. While Eastern Christians chose creeds as their litmus test of orthodoxy, Roman Catholics added church tradition. Many Protestants, emulating the veneration of science in Enlightenment thought, sought to salvage theology as "science" based on rational knowledge (Bosch, TM, 421-22).

Friedrich Schleiermacher was one of the first to break from this position. He pioneered the view that every theology is influenced, if not determined, by the cultural context in which it has evolved. "Doctrines are only expressions of inward experiences," he argued.

The next two selections are probes from Asia and Latin America concerning indigenization. J. Russell Chandran of India wants Christian revelation to "be reinterpreted and reformulated" so as to call each new generation to repentance and faith. Encounter with persons of other faiths will require a "dynamic dialectical relationship" with their convictions about ultimate concerns. José Míguez Bonino of Argentina, immersed in a social reality involving suffering and struggle, cannot engage in theology as a "purely intellectual exercise." Begin with involvement, engage in social-political analysis, commit yourself to the struggle—that will be the starting point for the theological task, he urges.

In 1973, at a meeting to review the WCC's Theological Education Fund, a new term was coined—contextualization. *It has been defined as "the continual process by which God's truth and justice are applied to and emerge in concrete historical situations."*[1] *Compared with indigenization, the new concept is more holistic (all aspects of the human context and relations between cultures and social groups), more global (applicable to all cultures), and more dynamic (accepting the reality of sociocultural change).*[2] *The WCC consultation judged contextualization of the Gospel to be "a missiological necessity."*

The remaining selections elucidate what Bosch calls "the epistemological break" of contextual theologies of mission. Instead of conducting theology from above, as the product of research and reflection by cloistered specialists, contextual theology is theology from below by the people of God—even the poor and culturally marginalized—engaged in action and reflection (praxis) *(TM, 423). Juan Luis Segundo of Uruguay describes the method as a "hermeneutical circle." It is for persons who are "more interested in* being liberative *than in* talking about liberation." *At the first ecumenical dialogue of EATWOT in 1976, Third World theologians called this* orthopraxis, *not* orthodoxy, *and admitted that they were making a radical break in epistemology. In his article "What Is Contextualization?" Justin Ukpong of Nigeria draws out the implications of the new perspective for mission. Aracely de Rocchietti of Uruguay develops implications for women as they struggle both for liberation and for full self-realization. Finally, Emefie Ikenga-Metuh of Nigeria contends that contextual theology is more missiological than conventional theology, as it aims primarily "to bring the Gospel as a truly Good News to the people in their concrete situations."*

THEOLOGY AS REFLECTION ON EXPERIENCE

"Doctrines are only expressions of inward experiences."

■ *Should Christian theology be based primarily on revelation, reason, or Christian experience? Influenced since the Early Church by the Greek belief that ideas and principles are primary and their application in experience only secondary, Christian theology developed an epistemology emphasizing deductive thought. Friedrich Schleiermacher (1768-1834), a Reformed German pastor, was one of the first theologians to question this approach. In his magnum opus entitled* The Christian Faith, *Schleiermacher pioneered the view that Christian faith begins with human experience of God-consciousness and redemption. He sought to make Christian experience intelligible and the theology reflection upon human perception of that work of God's grace.* The Christian Faith *was not only the most influential work of Protestant theology in the nineteenth century, but also a forerunner of the inductive approach to theology that would become ascendant in the late twentieth century.*

Doctrine from Religious Consciousness*

There is only one source from which all Christian doctrine is derived, namely, the self-proclamation of Christ; and there is only one type of doctrine, for whether more perfect or less perfect, it all arises out of the religious consciousness itself and its direct expression....

God-consciousness

The Redeemer assumes believers into the power of His God-consciousness, and this is His redemptive activity.

In virtue of the teleological character of Christian piety, both the imperfect stage of higher life, as also the challenge of it, appear in our self-consciousness as facts due to our own individual action—though we do not feel responsible for the latter in the same way as for the former. In virtue, however, of the peculiar character of Christianity this challenge is also apprehended in our self-consciousness as the act of the Redeemer. These two points of view can be reconciled only by supposing that this challenge is the act of the Redeemer become our own act....

This exposition is based entirely on the inner experience of the believer; its only purpose is to describe and elucidate that experience. Naturally, therefore, it can make no claim to be a proof that things must have been so; in the sphere of experience such proof is only possible where mathematics can be used, which is certainly not the case here. Our purpose is simply to show that the perfect satisfaction to which we aspire can only be truly contained in the Christian's consciousness of his [or her] relation to Christ in so far as that consciousness expresses the kind of relation which has been described here. If this content be lacking in the Christian consciousness, then either the perfect satisfaction must come from some other quarter, or it does not exist at all, and we must be content with an indefinite appeasement of conscience, such as may be found without any Redeemer; and in that case there would be no special possession of divine grace in Christianity at all. Now these negations cannot be logically refuted; they can only be removed by actual facts: we must seek to bring doubters to the same experience as we have had.

UNIVERSAL REVELATION AND INDIGENOUS FAITH

> "Incarnation is ...a necessary witness to the Incarnation of the Word of God."

■ *Before the term* contextualization *was coined, church leaders in Africa, Asia, Latin America, and Oceania were raising issues concerning the contextual*

---

*Excerpts from Friedrich Schleiermacher, *The Christian Faith*, Eng. trans. of the 1830 second German edition (Edinburgh: T. & T. Clark, 1928), 92, 425, 428; cf. Bosch, TM, 422-23.

particularity of Christian expression. Among them were student leaders active in the World Student Christian Federation, with the Student World *as the organ through which they explored new possibilities. Consider, for example, probes concerning "indigenization" in the following article by Joshua Russell Chandran (b. 1918) of India in 1958. He became a leading theological educator as principal and professor of theology and ethics at United Theological College, Bangalore (and later in retirement at the Pacific Theological College in Fiji and Gurukul Theological College in Madras, India). A founder of the Ecumenical Association of Third World Theologians, he served as its president from 1976 to 1981. A minister of the Church of South India, he has served as convenor of its Theological Commission, secretary of the Joint Council of the C.S.I., Church of North India, and Mar Thoma Church, and founder-president of the Christian Union of India. A world ecumenical leader, Dr. Chandran has been the vice-chairman of the Faith and Order Commission as well as of the WCC's Central Committee.*[3]

*What Is Indigenization?**

First it is important to clarify the meaning of indigenization. Often in India it is regarded as synonymous with Indianization or Hinduization. The word "indigenous" literally means born or produced naturally in a country. It is, however, rather difficult to see how any Christian theology can naturally belong to a country....

Indigenization is a principle and a process integral to the nature and role of Christian theology. Theology, as Professor Tillich rightly calls it, is a function of the Christian Church, and should fulfil two basic principles: first, the setting forth clearly of the Christian message, once for all revealed, and second, the interpretation of this message in a manner "challengingly relevant" for each generation. It is when a theology holds both these principles together that it is indigenous theology. Otherwise we may have something which is indigenous without being Christian theology, or something which is theology without being relevant. In fact, every Christian theology which has exercised transforming power in the Church and really called people to repentance has held the two principles together. Every Christian theology has taken categories of thought from the situation or the culture to which it addressed itself. Failure to recognize this truth has been largely responsible for the charge of irrelevance....

The Relevance of Indigenization

The need for indigenization may be demonstrated in various ways.

No particular formulation of the revelation is adequate for all times and situations. Nor can any one formulation exhaust the full meaning of revelation....The

---

*Excerpts from J. R. Chandran, "The Problem of Indigenization of Christian Theology in Asia," *Student World* 51 (1958): 334-35, 337-39, 341-42; cf. Bosch, TM, 427-28.

Christian revelation should, therefore, be reinterpreted and reformulated so as to call each generation to repentance and faith....

Only a theology that wrestles with the questions and problems of the age can effectively challenge the people and provide the principles and the power for the transformation of society.

Principles of Indigenization

Indigenization is not to be something peculiar to Asian Christianity. It is a process necessary for the Church's witness everywhere. Genuine indigenization takes place whenever and wherever the Church is alive to her mission of proclaiming the Gospel in the contemporary language of the people. It is not a technique for evangelism but a necessary witness to the Incarnation of the Word of God.

In order to be able to use a people's language with power, we should have a positive appraisal of their religion and culture. The way to look at non-Christian cultures is not as rigid, static structures or systems which can easily be compared to other cultures in terms of fixed norms. All great cultures have a dynamic dialectical relationship with the convictions of the people about things of ultimate concern. In order to penetrate such a culture with the claims of the Christian Gospel, we have to get into the dialogue that is implicit in it, and carry the dialogue forward to the dialectic of the question of Jesus Christ: "Whom do you say that I am?"...

It is, however, important to distinguish between the dialectics of indigenization and a kind of fancy-dressing of Christian theology with non-Christian terminology taken from classical forms of religions. A genuinely indigenous theology will address itself to the contemporary situation. In Asia, today, traditional religions are being reinterpreted in order to provide answers for the questions posed by the rapid social changes taking place in the region. The problems of nation building, the struggle for democracy, the fight against colonialism and communism call for a dynamic humanism. Undergirding the resources for humanism found in the modern reinterpretations of the Asian religions, in the Sarvodaya and Bhoodan movements and in secular humanism, as well as subjecting them to the judgment of Christian insights about man, society and the Church are necessary principles for the indigenization of theology. Indigenization so understood will remove the offensiveness belonging to the limitations of human language, but at the same time it will sharpen the offense which belongs to the Cross and the resurrection of Jesus Christ and his claims to Lordship over the Church and the world.

THEOLOGY UNMASKING "SITUATIONALITY"

> "Theology is not purely intellectual exercise but a stance of commitment."

■ *The watershed for Latin American theology occurred in 1968. The "Vatican II" of Latin America took place as the General Conference of the Latin American episcopacy (CELAM II) met in Medellín, Colombia. The Catholic bishops focused on the pervasive human injustice and oppression on their continent and asked, "What does God have to say and what ought the church as God's agent do about all this suffering?" In the years that followed, Catholic and Protestant theologians developed situational rather than propositional theologies. Representative of this shift is the following passage by Míguez Bonino, a Protestant theologian, from a 1971 presentation on theological perspectives derived from a social revolutionary situation. José Míguez Bonino was born in Argentina in 1924. An ordained Methodist minister, he pastored churches in Argentina and Bolivia and since 1954 has served as professor of systematic theology at the Higher Evangelical Institute for Theological Studies [ISADET] in Buenos Aires.*

*A New Way of Doing Theology**

A historical situation has been crystallizing which signifies the inexorable liquidation of the "modern world." To attempt to describe it without interpreting it is to blind oneself to the door to its meaning, since the new situation is, in one sense, a decision of conscience. We could characterize it from different angles, even though, in every case, we are referring ourselves to the same reality.

(1) We perceive that the reality is basically "conflictive and not developmental";

(2) The only meaningful analysis is the one that is made in structural terms;

(3) The privileged instruments of that analysis are necessarily the political-social sciences;

(4) The analysis begins and moves toward the adoption of an ideological position that, at the same time, determines and adapts its technological instruments;

(5) Consequently, there is no neutral science of [humanity] and society and we see ourselves obliged unceasingly to practice doubt as the critical instrument in our relationship with the different types of human thinking;

(6) Such a procedure permits us to see certain types of thinking as the interjection of structural relationship and, as a result, discussion as necessarily directed toward the change of these relationships to make possible the overcoming of the types of conscience that they create;

(7) Consequently, thinking generates itself and results in action, in a transforming *praxis,* considering the character of the reality, in a struggle which transforms.

This description, although rather formal, is clearly an extra-polarization of the concrete historical process that attains special clarity for us in Latin America. Its repercussion in theology has been brought about in our continent by crisis and by the renaissance of sociology....

The new Latin American theology legitimizes its option, first, in a critical manner, by means of an unmasking of the "situationality," the ideological option not confessed by the traditional theologies or by the so-called "scientific ones."...

---

*Excerpts from José Míguez Bonino, "New Theological Perspectives," *Religious Education* 66:6 (1971): 405, 406-7; cf. Bosch, TM, 425.

Recent Latin American theological documents that emphasize this affirmation: "theology is not purely intellectual exercise but a stance of commitment"; "it is pulled out from reality"; "it raises questions from the heart of reality"; "it lets itself be questioned by reality"; "I cannot do theology without having a living 'tuning-in,' without suffering, to a certain degree."[4]

How should we understand the raising up of the historic situation to the theological level? In what sense does theological reflection in the concrete *praxis* differ from sociological or political reflection in the same situation? What relationship is established in this reflection between the generating acts of the faith (concretely, the "history of salvation") and the historical *praxis?* What type and what form of social-political analysis decisively structures that theological reflection? ...the inflexible will to act from the historical situation, analysed by means of social-political instruments and adopted in a theological option, identifies ...the starting point of the theological task.

FROM INDIGENIZATION TO CONTEXTUALIZATION

"Contextualization of the Gospel is a missiological necessity."

■ *The term* contextualization *received its formal debut in a 1972 report issued by the Theological Education Fund of the World Council of Churches entitled* Ministry in Context. *It was a response to the growing ecumenical frustration with the term* indigenization. *Structured by mission theorists such as Henry Venn and Rufus Anderson in the nineteenth century, the "indigenous church" had been conceived to affirm the dignity of local churches as the people of God who could be self-supporting, self-governing, and self-propagating. The call for a fourth self principle of "self-theologizing," plus a renewed emphasis on God's continuing and dynamic mission* (Missio Dei), *were seedbeds for the new emphasis. Whereas indigenization referred often to relating the Gospel to traditional cultures, contextualization was used in relation to cultures undergoing rapid social change. It implied taking into account the processes of secularity, technology, and the struggles for human justice being experienced by peoples of the Third World.*

*Contextualization and the Church's Mission**

Contextualization should be the focal concern because through it alone will come reform and renewal. Contextualization of the Gospel is a missiological necessity. But there are dangers, one of which in the Third World is that such contextualization might not take place in response to the really urgent issues of its

*Excerpts from World Council of Churches, Theological Education Fund, *Ministry in Context: The Third Mandate Programme of the Theological Education Fund (1970-77)* (Bromley, England: TEF, 1972), 30-31; cf. Bosch, TM, 420-21.

own context, in its *own* time, and in its *own* place, but in those times and places which are out of date and out of place in the Third World, and so irrelevant.

All that is contextual may not be equally strategic for the mission of the Church, which is called to participate in the *Missio Dei.* This is the point where the Church, whether in the global or local sense, "walks on the water" in faith, heeding the signs which are God's way of talking to us in our time and context. Relevance takes contextuality seriously by discerning God's mission for [humanity] in history; it must also do so intelligently, understanding the contextual issues and their significance. Missiological orientation requires the incisive thrust, which is given three highlights in the mandate:

a) The widespread crisis of faith and search for meaning in life;

b) The urgent issues of human development and social justice;

c) The dialectic between a universal technological civilization and local cultural and religious situations.

The missiological imperative is not just for any contextualization, but for the contextualization *of the Gospel.* It is not just for any relevance, but for *theological relevance.*

THE HERMENEUTICAL CIRCLE

"*Being liberative* [rather] than *talking about liberation.*"

■ *Contextual theologies often can also be described as liberation theologies. The common threads binding them together are the process rather than the content of such theologies. A Uruguayan Jesuit, Juan Luis Segundo (b. 1925), defined this process clearly in his model of the "hermeneutical circle." It is an ongoing process in which persons must be willing to lay bare for continuous scrutiny their traditional interpretations of scripture. Scripture and society are to continually intersect and challenge each other. Believing that all theologies are culturally determined and that those of the West have been adapted to serve the interests of dominant social classes, Segundo calls for a hermeneutics of suspicion. His development of what might be called a process methodology reveals his close affinity with the views of Pierre Teilhard de Chardin.*

*Why the Hermeneutic Circle**

The fundamental difference between the traditional academic theologian and the liberation theologian is that the latter feels compelled at every step to combine the disciplines that open up the past with the disciplines that help to explain the present. [Such a theologian] feels this necessity precisely in the task of working

---

*Excerpts from Juan Segundo, *Liberation of Theology* (Maryknoll, NY: Orbis Books, 1976), 8-9; cf. Bosch, TM, 423.

out and elaborating theology, that is to say, in the task of interpreting the word of God as it is addressed to us here and now.

Without this connection between past and present there is no theology of liberation in the long run. You might get a theology which *deals with* liberation, but its methodological naiveté would prove to be fatal somewhere along the line. It would eventually be reabsorbed by the deeper mechanisms of oppression—one of these being the tendency to incorporate the idiom of liberation into the prevailing language of the status quo....

An approach which attempts to relate past and present in dealing with the word of God has to have its own special methodology....the *hermeneutic circle*...it is the continuing change in our interpretation of the Bible which is dictated by the continuing changes in our present-day reality, both individual and societal. "Hermeneutic" means "having to do with interpretation." And the circular nature of this interpretation stems from the fact that each new reality obliges us to interpret the word of God afresh, to change reality accordingly, and then to go back and reinterpret the word of God again, and so on.

Two Preconditions

Two preconditions must be met if we are to have a hermeneutic circle in theology. The first precondition is that the questions rising out of the present be rich enough, general enough, and basic enough to force us to change our customary conceptions of life, death, knowledge, society, politics, and the world in general. Only a change of this sort, or at the very least a pervasive suspicion about our ideas and value judgments concerning those things, will enable us to reach the theological level and force theology to come back down to reality and ask itself new and decisive questions.

The second precondition is intimately bound up with the first. If theology somehow assumes that it can respond to the new questions without changing its customary interpretation of the Scriptures, that immediately terminates the hermeneutic circle. Moreover, if our interpretation of Scripture does not change along with the problems, then the latter will go unanswered; or worse, they will receive old, conservative, unserviceable answers.

It is most important to realize that without a hermeneutic circle, in other words, in those instances where the two aforementioned preconditions are not accepted, theology is always a conservative way of thinking and acting. It is so not so much because of its content but because in such a case it lacks any *here-and-now* criteria for judging our real situation. It thus becomes a pretext for approving the existing situation or for disapproving of it because it does not dovetail with guidelines and canons that are even more ancient and outdated.

It is my feeling that the most progressive theology in Latin America is more interested in *being liberative* than in *talking about liberation.* In other words, liberation deals not so much with content as with the method used to theologize in the face of our real-life situation....

Four Decisive Factors

There must in turn be four decisive factors in our circle. *Firstly,* there is our way of experiencing reality, which leads us to ideological suspicion. *Secondly,* there is the application of our ideological suspicion to the whole ideological superstructure in general and to theology in particular. *Thirdly*, there comes a new way of experiencing theological reality that leads us to exegetical suspicion, that is, to the suspicion that the prevailing interpretation of the Bible has not taken important pieces of data into account. *Fourthly,* we have our new hermeneutic, that is, our new way of interpreting the fountainhead of our faith (i.e., Scripture) with the new elements at our disposal.

ORTHOPRAXIS NOT ORTHODOXY

"Commitment the first act of theology."

■ *Twenty-two theologians from Africa, Asia, and Latin America and a representative of black North America met in Dar es Salaam, Tanzania, in August 1976. Their aim was to reflect upon the significance of theology in the countries of the Third World. A common theme emerged: Third World Christians who looked at history from their perspective as citizens of poor and dominated countries had a quite different perspective than Christians in comparatively rich and powerful nations. They proposed to develop a theology that speaks with the voice of the poor and the marginated in history. Their commitment to continue their dialogue and common reflections resulted in the formation of the Ecumenical Association of Third World Theologians.*

*Toward a Theological Approach in the Third World**

(From "Final Statement")

We affirm our faith in Christ our Lord, whom we celebrate with joy, and without whose strength and wisdom our theology would be valueless and even destructive. In doing theology we are trying to make the gospel relevant to all people, and to rejoice in being his collaborators, unworthy as we are, in fulfilling God's plan for the world.

The theologies from Europe and North America are dominant today in our churches and represent one form of cultural domination. They must be understood to have arisen out of situations related to those countries, and therefore must not be uncritically adopted without our raising the question of their relevance in the context of our countries. Indeed, we must, in order to be faithful to the gospel and to our peoples, reflect on the realities of our own situations and interpret the word

---

*Excerpts from Ecumenical Dialogue of Third World Theologians (1st, Dar es Salaam, 1976), *The Emergent Gospel,* ed. S. Torres and V. Fabella (Maryknoll, NY: Orbis Books, 1978), 269; cf. Bosch, TM, 424.

of God in relation to these realities. We reject as irrelevant an academic type of theology that is divorced from action. We are prepared for a radical break in epistemology which makes commitment the first act of theology and engages in critical reflection on the praxis of the reality of the Third World.

CONTEXTUAL PARTICULARITY

"The contextual particularity of Christian expression."

■ *By 1987, the term* contextualization *had come into common usage among missiologists. Justin S. Ukpong, in his article "What is Contextualization?" provides an analysis of the origin and meaning of the term and its relation to similar terms. He introduced a typology of uses of the term: the indigenization type, including translation and inculturation models, and the socio-economic type, including evolutionary and revolutionary/liberation models. A biblical scholar and theological educator, Fr. Ukpong lectures at the Catholic Institute of West Africa in Port Harcourt, Nigeria. His ecumenical involvements include lecturing in the graduate studies program of the Ecumenical Institute in Bossey, Switzerland, and serving as the Africa representative on the executive of the International Association for Mission Studies.*

*All Christian Expression Is Contextual**

It is only in our century that we have become sufficiently aware that all forms of Christian expression[5] are tied up with the cultural context from which they originate. Religion, though having a finality that is both transcendent and eschatological, finds expression only in and through culture in so far as men and women are involved in it as actors. Thus all forms of Christian expression are tinted with the traits of the cultural context from which they originate even if we are unaware of this. As Robert Schreiter well puts it, "even the so-called 'perennial theologies' grow out of particular contexts and respond to specific needs in concrete believing communities...."[6] Claude Geffré also remarks that "dogmatic formulas themselves are inadequate human expressions within a determined cultural and religious context."[7]

One significant implication of this is that forms of Christian expression which were hitherto thought to be universal are being viewed differently today. Another important implication is the realization of the need to distinguish between Christianity which is an abstract concept, and the manifestation or expression of the Christian religion. A third important implication is that in the process of evangelization each new culture with which Christianity comes in contact should be respected and given the chance to give its own expression to the Christian message.

---

*Excerpts from Justin Ukpong, "What is Contextualization?" *Neue Zeitschrift für Missionswissenschaft* 43 (1987): 168; cf. Bosch, TM, 421-23.

Naturally this awareness of the contextual particularity of Christian expression has led to a critique of the traditional missionary and theological methods which regarded the forms of Christian expression belonging to the cultural contexts of the evangelizers as perennial and universal to be adopted by the new cultures into which Christianity was introduced. It has also opened up new vistas of missionary and theological methodologies in our age. In particular this has meant the search for new forms of Christian expression that will take the new cultural contexts seriously and be relevant to them.

WOMEN'S THEOLOGY FROM LATIN AMERICA

"Struggle for liberation ...on the road to full self-realization."

■ *The heightened awareness of Latin American liberation theology in North America was signaled by the publication of the fifteenth anniversary edition of Gustavo Gutiérrez's* A Theology of Liberation *(English edition) in 1988. Unfortunately the woman's voice and perspective is little known or appreciated. To fill that void, Elsa Tamez edited a landmark volume,* Through Her Eyes, *published by Orbis Books in 1989. In her essay in that volume on "Women and the People of God," Aracely de Rocchietti, a Methodist pastor in Uruguay, contrasts the non-institutional and liberative approach of Jesus to women with the marginalization of women in many historical and contemporary church structures. To follow the example of Jesus would be to reaffirm the creative roles of women in the people of God.*

*To Be the People of God**

This essay ...is an attempt to reinterpret our Church experience as the People of God in biblical and theological terms. This is a theme which we consider to be fundamental, realizing that *to be* the People of God in *current* Latin American history is what gives the Church of Christ both its mandate and its *raison d'être.*

Without the dynamic of a people living and on the move as the embodiment of our whole continent's struggle for liberation, the Church cannot be a sign and witness to the Kingdom inaugurated by Jesus; nor will it be on the road to full self-realization...

The Absence of Institutional Models

Another approach I should like to highlight is the resistance of Jesus to providing a model or paradigm for this new community and to institutionalizing it, partly because for him time was limited and pressing but fundamentally because of an

*Excerpts from Aracely de Rocchietti, "Women and the People of God," in *Through Her Eyes: Women's Theology from Latin America,* ed. Elsa Tamez (Maryknoll, NY: Orbis Books, 1989), 96-97, 103-05, 108-10, 116-17; cf. Bosch, TM, 425.

option for liberty and faithfulness which is a defense against temptations and worldly powers. This absence of models is compensated for by the diversity and wealth of images.

From the standpoint of the marginalized members of society, Jesus' steadfastness is seen in the clear indication that he rejected the creation of an exclusive and discriminatory community, and in his unquestionable solidarity and identification of himself with the marginalized, in his rehabilitation of the despised, his challenge to prejudice, and his confrontation with the institutionalized religion of the rich and powerful. The unmistakable universal nature in the changed composition of the New People is seen in the fact that access to them is by baptism and not by circumcision.

The life of Jesus itself manifests and fulfills the expectations of those poor members of society (Mary, Elizabeth, Zechariah, the shepherds) and at the same time is a threat to those who hold power and interpret the history of salvation in accordance with their own interests....

I think it is highly important to continue analysis of that initial urge of Jesus to open up a new scenario for the marginalized—women among them—because that urge has been repeatedly distorted and lost sight of in the life of the Church. We must not forget that the Word of God was spoken by the people but *interpreted, thought, put into writing, and transmitted* by the powerful of all ages: learned doctors, scribes, priests, kings, fathers of the Church; that the life of the Church necessarily had to develop within the prevailing structures in which Jesus was someone who belonged to the "counter culture"; that from its start, the Church trying to proclaim the Gospel of Christ was assimilating structures of power which it ultimately came to adopt for its own institutional structure as it grew. This has meant that successive reinterpretations reflect wholly biased aspects of Jesus' understanding of that New People which we have to incarnate and rediscover from the reality of our own situation in faithfulness to God.

Women's Responsibility

From the standpoint of faith, [women] feel that we are part of the People of God, of that people called to freedom and salvation—the People of God is at the same time the mystery of the presence of the risen Christ and the sociological expression of human activity at a particular juncture in history. We are part of that people and, as such, we are on the move, both in the historical process and transcendentally, toward a *kairos* that has been proclaimed: the time of the Kingdom which in part we know and toward which we are in part looking forward. As the People of God, we feel we are called to move forward toward the fulfillment of a divine covenant of salvation for all humanity and also to unite in a visible community which is the sign of the final fulfillment, and into which all those who accept the requirements of the covenant with God must be brought. As women, we feel our scope for movement reduced and constricted by the manifestations of human sin which, turning its back on God, has created structures of domination by some people over others. Our responsibility then is dual. We must go forward with the people in its struggle for liberation and for salvation which must be expressed in signs of life, love, and solidarity. But at the same time, we must reaffirm from God's revelation our own liberation as "created in the image and likeness (of God)," called to an equal status with men and united in the community of all who believe in Christ, as sensitive and thinking women who have received the message of salvation and can effectively proclaim that message to all humanity.

Taking on this dual responsibility will contribute to hastening the downfall of the obsolete structures which imprison the power of the Gospel and the potentialities of the People of God in a false interpretation of what it means for us to be the Church; and at the same time it will provide an opportunity for the emergence of new expressions of the Church which are more faithful to the demands of the Gospel.

CONTEXTUALIZATION AND INCARNATION

"God has always been incarnate in human cultures."

■ *What can we expect in mission as contextualization in the coming century? In the following article, Professor Emefie Ikenga-Metuh of Nigeria presents a creative projection out of the African context. In his judgment, existing socio-political and religious conditions will persist into the third millennium. Plagued by economic deprivation, hunger, and poverty, as well as with political instability in many countries, African liberation theologies will flourish. He calls also for a pursuit with greater vigor of the process of incarnating the Gospel in African culture.*

*God Incarnate in Cultures**

The call by the Report of the African Bishops to the 1974 Synod on Evangelization for the necessity "to foster the particular incarnation of Christianity in each country, in accordance with the genius and the talents of each culture," not only introduced a new terminology, but added a completely new dimension to the African theology of contextualization as well as to the theology of evangelization. African culture is no more seen as a product of demonic forces or even of neutral forces. They are produced by human genius alright, but under the guidance of God who "did not leave himself without witness" (Acts 14:17), God has always been incarnate in human cultures. For "at various times in the past, and in various different ways, God spoke to our ancestors through the prophets, but in our own time, the last days he has spoken to us through his son" (Heb. 1:1-2). Divine revelation reached its climax in Christ. Thus, historically, Christ the word of God incarnated in the Judeo-Hellenic culture, and he illuminated, judged and elevated

---

*Excerpts from Emefie Ikenga-Metuh, "Contextualization: A Missiological Imperative for the Church in Africa in the Third Millenium," *Mission Studies* 6:2 (1989), 5, 7, 11-12; cf. Bosch, TM, 427-28.

it. Hence, African incarnation theology seeks to incarnate the word of God into the African culture. When incarnation is fully and effectively accomplished the light of the gospel would radically transform different levels of African life, laws, customs, values and world-views.

By incarnation, the Bishops meant, "the movement by which what is considered essential in the message of Christ penetrates and takes flesh in a culture."[8] What is incarnated is not just exegeted teachings from the Bible, but also the teaching and believing traditions of the People of God....

Contextual Theology Is Missiological

Contextual theology is a theology which in clarifying faith is very sensitive to the situation of the people to whom the faith is addressed. It is not content with an abstract and intellectually satisfying systematic presentation of the faith. Rather its aims are primarily to bring the Gospel as a truly Good News to the people in their concrete situation. In a sense it is not a perennial theology addressed to all peoples, in all situations and for all time. Rather it is faith presented to a particular people, living in a concrete situation, at a particular time. This perhaps makes contextual theology more missiological than conventional theology....

We Need an African Theology

Much more than scientific biblical exegesis is needed to encounter the Christ who is now found wrapped in the swaddling clothes of Western European Christianity. There is need for African theology. The battle is not against the Word of God or its proclamation "Kerygma," rather it is against Western accretions which are now turned into dogma. For says the AACC Assembly at Lusaka: "If indeed Theology is reflection, in African Theology we attempt to break the seal of Western thought—forms and culture—so that we can come face to face with Christ and in Him see ourselves...and others."[9]

As we move into the third millennium and a new era of evangelization (intensive evangelization), there is need for an African theology, based on a scientific study of the Bible, to cope with the demand of a fast growing literate and educated African population to receive the Word of God in the concepts, language and symbols they can understand.

NOTES

1. Robert W. Pazmiño in Max L. Stackhouse, *Apologia: Contextualization, Globalization, and Mission in Theological Education* (Grand Rapids, MI: Eerdmans, 1988), p. 237.

2. Charles R. Taber, *The World Is Too Much with Us: "Culture" in Modern Protestant Missions* (Macon, GA: Mercer University Press, 1991), pp. 175-77.

3. Cf. "Chandran" in *DEM,* 143. For a collection of his major articles, see J. R. Chandran, *The Church in Mission* (Madras: Christian Literature Society, 1991).

4. Quotes in H. Assmann, "Theology of Liberation," in *Documentation Service* (Montevideo, MIEI-JECI, series 1, doc. 23-24), p. 12.

5. The expression "forms of Christian expression" designates elements or aspects of Christianity, whether tangible or intangible, through which we identify the Christian religion. Thus Christian theology is a form of Christian expression; so is liturgical rite, and so forth.

6. Robert Schreiter, "Issues Facing Contextual Theologies Today," *Verbum SVD* 21 (1980): 267. See also his *Constructing Local Theologies* (Maryknoll, NY: Orbis Books, 1985), pp. 24-36.

7. Claude Geffré, *A New Age in Theology* (New York: Paulist Press, 1972), p. 47.

8. Valentino Salvodi and Renato Sesana, *Africa, the Gospel Belongs to Us* (Ndola, Zambia: Mission Press, 1986).

9. Statement of the AACC Assembly at Lusaka 1973 (Nairobi: AACC, 1973).

11

Mission as Liberation

David Bosch developed his next paradigm of mission—as liberation—as a particular focus of mission as contextualization. He described it as "one of the most dramatic illustrations of the fundamental paradigm shift that is currently taking place in mission thinking and practice" (TM, 432).

The term liberation theology *was first coined in 1968, but received widespread usage following the 1973 publication in English of* A Theology of Liberation *by Gustavo Gutiérrez. The main themes were present more than a decade earlier. The liberationist concern for a theology relevant to social revolution was expressed by K. H. Ting of China as a Christian student leader in 1949. Latin American Catholic bishops, at their Second General Conference (CELAM II, Medellín, 1968), affirmed the biblical basis of that authentic liberation for which they prayed.*

Gustavo Gutiérrez is known as the father of liberation theology. Our all-too-brief selection from his magnum opus includes his vision of a theology from below, in which the oppressed can speak for themselves. His commitment to mission as liberation is symbolized in his closing words stating that "active participation to liberate humankind" is worth more than all written theologies.

The shift from development to liberation (Bosch, TM, 432-35) is highlighted in the next three selections. At its Fifth Assembly (Nairobi 1975), the WCC judged the goals of the UN's Decade for Development in the 1960s as inadequate and called upon the churches "to share with the oppressed their struggles for liberation." Third World theologians embraced the new paradigm in the EATWOT conference of 1976, calling upon theologians to be committed "to a lifestyle of solidarity with the poor and the oppressed and involvement in action with them." A key theme of liberation theology, the preferential option for the poor, was first articulated in the next selection from the 1975 conference of Latin American bishops (CELAM III) held in Puebla, Mexico.

Although liberation theologies originated in Latin America, they soon developed on other continents. Allan Boesak of South Africa, speaking to the AACC's General Assembly in Nairobi, Kenya, in 1981, affirmed his faith in God who demands love, justice, reconciliation, and shalom *for the world. Following Christ the liberator, Christian churches are called to join the struggle against all oppression and exploitation. No neutrality is possible. By 1985, 150 South African Christian leaders shared that same commitment in the Kairos Document and called upon the churches to end all collaboration with tyranny. They advocated a prophetic theology based on the conviction that God sides with the oppressed.*

Women theologians add their distinctive understandings to the paradigm of mission as liberation. Luz Beatriz Arellano, out of the Nicaraguan struggle, writes of a "new face of Jesus"—not the beneficent-robed Spanish Christ of the traditional processions, but the compañero (colleague, fellow revolutionary) in building the new society. Women are discovering God as the God of life who is close to them and journeys with them through history. Julia Esquivel of Guatemala describes the pilgrimage in mission of women. Many of the middle class formerly understood mission as charity for the poor. Through involvement in the struggle, they come to understand why there cannot be true peace without justice and they experience "conversion to the God of the poor." Finally, Chung Hyun Kyung of Korea relates how Asian women's theology was born "out of Asian women's tears and sighs and from their burning desire for liberation and wholeness."

HOW TO FACE REVOLUTION

"The Gospel itself is relevant to revolutionary China."

■ *In 1949, China was a nation in turmoil. The people were exhausted from twelve years of continuous warfare, first against the Japanese, and then the four-year civil war between Chiang Kai Shek's Nationalists and Mao Zedong's Communists. "How to face revolution?" was the question asked by Christians—both Chinese nationals and missionaries. In the following article, K. H. Ting (Ding Guangxun) gave his answer. Born in Shanghai in 1915, "K. H." was a secretary of the YMCA in China (1938-1946), secretary of the Student Christian Movement in Canada (1946-1947), and secretary of the World Student Christian Federation (1948-1951). In 1953, he became principal of Nanjing Theological Seminary, and in 1979, vice-president of Nanjing University. Ordained an Anglican priest while a student at Union Theological Seminary in New York in 1942, he became a bishop in 1955. Since 1981, he has been president of the China Christian Council and the National Three-Self Movement.*[1]

*How to Face Revolution**

The Asia which the Church finds itself in is today in a revolutionary upheaval. How is the Church to steer its course? If Nestorian Christianity could be uprooted after establishing itself in China for over two hundred years, how can we be sure that the Church is going to survive the present revolution?

We have no way to be sure of that and I do not think God wants to give us that assurance. This is perhaps His way to give us the discipline of obedience to the

---

*Excerpts from K. H. Ting, "The Task of the Church in Asia," *Student World* 42 (1949), 239-41, 242-43, 244-45; cf. Bosch, TM, 441.

Holy Spirit. Our survival and, indeed, our revival depends on the Church's striving to be true to its calling as the Church. As soon as we begin to be opportunist, we slip into being a mere human society. And we shall not be able to survive the changes of the world.

The first thing to be said about a revolution is that we should not be afraid of it or get too excited about it. We should understand it for what it is. A revolution is a fever in society. The revolution is not the disease itself but the result of the disease, just as the fever is not the disease itself, but an indication of the disease. No matter how we may dislike its terror we must learn to recognize it, once it happens, as an inevitable, passing phase. It happens only because of the decadence and evil of the status quo which lags way behind the changes which justice demands. While the Church cannot easily endorse the romance, the optimism, the method and the tendency to depreciate historic values and cultures in a revolution, the Church must resist the attempts of the status quo to make it a partner in its decadence and in its struggle to keep its clutch on the masses of the people....

Neither Optimism nor Pessimism

What is the Church to do in the revolutionary Asia or China? Basically it is just to do what it ought to do anywhere—to show forth the power of the Gospel through its words, deeds and the life of its community. A revolutionary situation brings with it an extreme optimism in what [humans] can do through their unity and gives fantastic promises to the people. It is like the Prodigal Son upon leaving his father's home with all his wonderful dreams of freedom and adventure. The Christian Gospel may look very pale in that situation and the non-Christian world, with its heart and soul overwhelmed by the revolutionary sentiment, tends to be skeptical of Christianity. Under that circumstance, Christians are tempted to revise their beliefs with the hope that they may conform to the optimism in fashion. But this revision is a fatal compromise and is utterly opportunistic. We should rather strengthen our evangelistic task so that, as soon as the post-revolutionary despair sets in, the Church will be ready to receive with open arms the many tired revolutionaries and worn-out optimists. Through his suffering the Prodigal Son is bound to come to himself and say, "I will arise and go to my Father." The Church can then offer him the hope and the task that are durable....

AUTHENTIC LIBERATION

> "For our authentic liberation, all of us need a profound conversion."

■ *The year 1968 was a year of failed hopes in many parts of the world. In Paris students rioted; in the United States Martin Luther King, Jr., and Robert Kennedy were assassinated and the cities erupted in violence. In Latin America hopes for the "Alliance for Progress" remained unfulfilled with military takeovers in several countries. Three years earlier, at Vatican II, the Catholic Church had been called to a ministry relevant to the needs of the modern world. The Latin American bishops took up the challenge at their Second General Conference held at Medellín, Colombia, in 1968. Their theme was "The Church in the Present-Day Transformation of Latin America in the Light of the Council." Although the bishops dealt with the traditional themes of evangelization and the church's order and structure, their primary focus was upon "human promotion." By beginning the call for church renewal with sensitivity to the cries of the poor and oppressed, Medellín represented a courageous breakthrough.*

*The Christian Quest for Justice**

The Latin American Church has a message for all [persons] on this continent who "hunger and thirst after justice." The very God who creates [us] in his image and likeness, creates the "earth and all that is in it for the use of all [persons] and all nations, in such a way that created goods can reach all in a more just manner,"[2] and gives them power to transform and perfect the world in solidarity.[3] It is the same God who, in the fullness of time, sends his Son in the flesh, so that He might come to liberate all...from the slavery to which sin has subjected them (Jn. 8:32-35): hunger, misery, oppression and ignorance, in a word, that injustice and hatred which have their origin in human selfishness.

Thus, for our authentic liberation, all of us need a profound conversion so that "the kingdom of justice, love and peace" might come to us. The origin of all disdain for [humankind], of all injustice, should be sought in the internal imbalance of human liberty, which will always need to be rectified in history. The uniqueness of the Christian message does not so much consist in the affirmation of the necessity for structural change, as it does in the insistence on the conversion of [persons] which will in turn bring about this change. We will not have a new continent without new and reformed structures, but, above all, there will be no new continent without new men [and women], who know how to be truly free and responsible according to light of the Gospel....

The Christian quest for justice is a demand arising from biblical teaching. All [persons] are merely humble stewards of material goods. In the search for salvation we must avoid the dualism which separates temporal tasks from the work of sanctification. Although we are encompassed with imperfections, we are [persons] of hope. We have faith that our love for Christ and our [brothers and sisters] will not only be the great force liberating us from injustice and oppression, but also the inspiration for social justice, understood as a whole of life and as an impulse toward the integral growth of our countries....

---

*Excerpts from CELAM II (Medellín, 1968), "The Medellín Conference Documents," in *Renewing the Earth: Catholic Documents on Peace, Justice and Liberation,* ed. D. J. O'Brien and T. A. Shannon (Garden City, NY: Image Books, 1976), 550, 551, 558; cf. Bosch, TM, 434.

Support to the Downtrodden

The Church—the People of God—will lend its support to the downtrodden of every social class so that they might come to know their rights and how to make use of them. To this end the Church will utilize its moral strength and will seek to collaborate with competent professionals and institutions.

LIBERATION THEOLOGY AND GENUINE SOLIDARITY

> "All theologies . . . of liberation. . . are not worth one act of genuine solidarity with exploited social classes."

■ *Gustavo Gutiérrez of Peru is recognized as the preeminent Third World liberation theologian. Born in Lima, Peru, in 1928, he experienced discrimination at an early age because of his mestizo blood and also knew poverty. Originally intending to become a doctor, he completed his studies of medicine at San Marcos University in Lima, meanwhile studying the writings of Karl Marx and engaging in student Christian movements protesting social and economic inequalities. Gradually his interests shifted—first to psychiatry, then philosophy, and finally theology, and he earned his Ph.D. in theology at the University of Lyon, France. Ordained a priest in 1959, he returned to Peru to pastor in a poor Lima parish, where he continues to minister. In heavy demand as an international spokesperson for liberation theology, he has limited his teaching at Lima's Catholic University to students not taking degrees in theology.* A Theology of Liberation, *published first in Spanish in 1971 and in English in 1973, was the premier work in the field.*[4]

The Problem*

To speak about a theology of liberation is to seek an answer to the following question: what relation is there between salvation and the historical process of human liberation? In other words, we must attempt to discern the interrelationship among the different meanings of the term *liberation*. . . .

If we look more deeply into the question of the value of salvation which emerges from our understanding of history—that is, a liberating praxis—we see that at issue is a question concerning *the very meaning of Christianity.* To be a Christian is to accept and to live—in solidarity, in faith, hope, and charity—the meaning that the Word of the Lord and our encounter with that Word give to the historical becoming of humankind on the way toward total communion. To regard the unique and absolute relationship with God as the horizon of every human action is to place oneself, from the outset, in a wider and more profound context. It is likewise more

---

*Excerpts from Gustavo Gutiérrez, *A Theology of Liberation* (Maryknoll, NY: Orbis Books, 1973, 1988), 29, 32, 174; cf. Bosch, TM, 443-47.

demanding. We are faced in our day with the bare, central theologico-pastoral question: *What does it mean to be a Christian? What does it mean to be Church in the unknown circumstances of the future?*[5] In the last instance, we must search the Gospel message for the answer to what according to Camus constitutes the most important question facing all persons: "To decide whether life deserves to be lived or not."[6]. . .

Conclusion

The theology of liberation attempts to reflect on the experience and meaning of the faith based on the commitment to abolish injustice and to build a new society; this theology must be verified by the practice of that commitment, by active, effective participation in the struggle which the exploited social classes have undertaken against their oppressors. Liberation from every form of exploitation, the possibility of a more human and dignified life, the creation of a new humankind—all pass through this struggle.

But in the last instance we will have an authentic theology of liberation only when the oppressed themselves can freely raise their voice and express themselves directly and creatively in society and in the heart of the People of God, when they themselves "account for the hope," which they bear, when they are the protagonists of their own liberation. For now we must limit ourselves to efforts which ought to deepen and support that process, which has barely begun. If theological reflection does not vitalize the action of the Christian community in the world by making its commitment to charity fuller and more radical, if—more concretely—in Latin America it does not lead the Church to be on the side of the oppressed classes and dominated peoples, clearly and without qualifications, then this theological reflection will have been of little value. Worse yet, it will have served only to justify half-measures and ineffective approaches and to rationalize a departure from the Gospel.

We must be careful not to fall into intellectual self-satisfaction, into a kind of triumphalism of erudite and advanced "new" visions of Christianity. The only thing that is really new is to accept day by day the gift of the Spirit, who makes us love—in our concrete options to build a true human fellowship, in our historical initiatives to subvert an order of injustice—with the fullness with which Christ loved us. To paraphrase a well-known text of Pascal, we can say that all the political theologies, the theologies of hope, of revolution, and of liberation, are not worth one act of genuine solidarity with exploited social classes. They are not worth one act of faith, love, and hope, committed—in one way or another—in active participation to liberate humankind from everything that dehumanizes it and prevents it from living according to the will of the Father.

FROM DEVELOPMENT TO LIBERATION

"Share with the oppressed their struggles for liberation."

■ *The 1960s had been declared by the United Nations as a decade of development. Rich nations were challenged to make basic changes that would enable the new and developing countries to improve dramatically the well-being of their peoples. In 1970, the World Council of Churches, in response to this priority, created its own Commission on the Churches' Participation in Development. Paradoxically, development, as the premier social goal, was already suspect. Instead of the economic gap between rich and poor nations and peoples narrowing, it was widening. Statistics in the 1970s gave evidence of a continuing marginalization of hundreds of millions of people. The resulting restiveness of the poor led many to seek violent means to secure justice. At the WCC's 1975 Fifth Assembly in Nairobi, Kenya, delegates reviewed the development debate, with liberation as an emerging theme. The report of Section 6 on "Human Development: Ambiguities of Power, Technology, and Quality of Life" contains a summary of the emerging new consensus.*

*Solidarity with the Poor**

(From Sec. 6, "Human Development: Ambiguities of Power, Technology, and Quality of Life")

The Church's concern for development has arisen primarily from the concern for the poor. But how does the Church express its solidarity with the poor and fight along with them for liberation and justice? In this quest we are led to new understandings of the problem and of our tasks. Poverty, we are learning, is caused primarily by unjust structures that leave resources and the power to make decisions about the utilization of resources in the hands of a few within nations and among nations, and that therefore one of the main tasks of the Church when it expresses its solidarity with the poor is to oppose these structures at all levels. Unjust structures are often the consequence of wrong or misdirected goals and values. This makes it necessary to examine critically the economic and social goals, the patterns of resource ownership and decision-making processes in the local and national situations, as also at the international context to reject all patterns that oppress the poor and to work for those which release the creative powers of people to satisfy their needs and decide their destiny....

Questioning Goals of Development

A new aspect in the development debate today is that not only the methods of development, but also the goals of development are being brought into question. Many factors have contributed to this mood of questioning. The growing weariness with consumerism in affluent societies, the warnings about the depletion of the natural resources and the dangers of the technological gap, the tensions between

---

*Excerpts from WCC (5th Assembly, Nairobi, 1975), *Breaking Barriers, Nairobi 1975: The Official Report*. . . , ed. David M. Paton (Grand Rapids, MI: Eerdmans, 1976), 121-23, 125, 129-30, 133; cf. Bosch, TM, 434.

economic and political aspirations and the new leads in theological thinking, have all forced on us questions about development as it is related to a meaningful life. In this search the churches have an opportunity to speak to [humankind] at large in their prophetic role supported by a "theology and spirituality for combat." In this sense the churches must favor an economy "as if people matter."

Toward Acknowledgment of Power

Since the Uppsala Assembly, the member churches of the WCC, through their commitment and action-research, have acknowledged the importance of power in decisions about development, understood as a liberating process geared towards social justice, self-reliance, and economic growth. This implies a sharp correction of the prevailing understanding of development as mere economic growth....

The Role of the Churches

It is impossible to ignore in this analysis the role and the power of churches. As social institutions they are engaged at all levels of social life. Some churches are landowners, related to feudal, capitalistic, and neo-capitalistic structures. Sometimes this alienates them from the poor and the oppressed. They are also involved in financial powers, i.e., shares, banks, investments, holdings. Equally various churches are influential elements of political power, either as active agents or as media of the establishment. Moreover, they are particularly influential at the ideological level in sharing and reinforcing dominant ideologies through religious teaching, shaping public opinion. Nevertheless, we cannot ignore through the whole history of the Church the existence of committed people and churches for whom to be faithful to Jesus Christ has implied and still implies to share with the oppressed their struggles for liberation. The participation of the Christian community in the struggle against poverty and oppression is a sign of the answer to the call of Jesus Christ to liberation. When this happens, the churches can no longer be considered as unconditional allies of the rich. On the contrary, they can be instruments of the renewing work of Christ whose strength is made known in weakness. The sufficiency of the Church to participate in tackling problems of such magnitude is based only on the sufficiency of the grace of the one who is the crucified and risen Lord.

COMMITMENT TO SOLIDARITY

> "Be with them [the poor and the oppressed] in their struggle for liberation."

■ *Third World theologians chose Dar es Salaam in Tanzania as the site for their 1976 dialogue, at which they agreed to form the Ecumenical Association of Third World Theologians (EATWOT). In Tanzania they witnessed the struggle of a poor Third World nation to achieve dignity and self-reliance in a world in which economic domination by multinational corporations, traders, and lending institutions mired the newly independent nations in continuing relationships of dependency. The theologians declared that a new focus upon mission as liberation would not only be true to the gospel message but also responsive to the cries of the poor and the oppressed.*

*Active Commitment with the Poor and Oppressed**

(From "Final Statement")

The church, the body of Christ, needs to become aware of its role in today's reality. Not only should it not remain insensitive to needs and aspirations, but also it must fearlessly announce the gospel of Jesus Christ, recognizing that God speaks in and through our human needs and aspirations. Jesus identified himself with the victims of oppression, thus exposing the reality of sin. Liberating them from the power of sin and reconciling them with God and with one another, he restored them to the fullness of their humanity. Therefore the church's mission is for the realization of the wholeness of the human person....

We call for an active commitment to the promotion of justice and the prevention of exploitation, the accumulation of wealth in the hands of a few, racism, sexism, and all other forms of oppression, discrimination, and dehumanization. Our conviction is that the theologian should have a fuller understanding of living in the Holy Spirit, for this also means being committed to a lifestyle of solidarity with the poor and the oppressed and involvement in action with them. Theology is not neutral. In a sense all theology is committed, conditioned notably by the socio-cultural context in which it is developed. The Christian theological task in our countries is to be self-critical of the theologians' conditioning by the value system of their environment. It has to be seen in relation to the need to live and work with those who cannot help themselves, and to be with them in their struggle for liberation.

A PREFERENTIAL OPTION FOR THE POOR

> "We affirm the need for conversion...to a preferential option for the poor."

■ *The Catholic Church in Latin America made a decisive turn in its history at the Medellín Conference (1968) as it responded more to the cries of the disadvantaged than to the concerns of the wealthy classes that had been the backbone of its leadership and financial support. In doing so, it drew upon the creative thought of liberation theologians (Gutiérrez, Assmann, Segundo, and so on), of religious educators (e.g., Paulo Freire's* Pedagogy of the Oppressed), *and the model of social involvement plus biblical reflection* (praxis) *of the base Christian*

---

*Excerpts from Ecumenical Dialogue of Third World Theologians (1st, Dar es Salaam, 1976) *The Emergent Gospel,* ed. S. Torres and V. Fabella (1978), 270; cf. Bosch, TM, 432.

communities. With great expectation, Catholics awaited the pronouncements of the third conference of Latin American bishops held October 12-28, 1978, in Puebla, Mexico. The report of Commission 18, showing traces of the fine hand of Gustavo Gutiérrez, introduced for the first time a call for "the preferential option for the poor." Rather than being simply "the church of the poor," the Catholic Church was called to become "the poor church." This would mean a radical break with the historic role of that church in Latin American culture, one of alliance with those in political and economic power.

*Commitment to the Poor**

(From Chap. 1, "A Preferential Option for the Poor")

With renewed hope in the vivifying power of the Spirit ... We affirm the need for conversion on the part of the whole Church to a preferential option for the poor, an option aimed at their integral liberation.

The vast majority of our fellow humans continue to live in a situation of poverty and even wretchedness that has grown more acute.[7] We wish to take note of all that the Church in Latin America has done, or has failed to do, for the poor since the Medellín Conference. This will serve as a starting point for seeking out effective channels to implement our option in our evangelizing work in Latin America's present and future.

We see that national episcopates and many segments of lay people, religious men and women, and priests have made their commitment to the poor a deeper and more realistic one. This witness, nascent but real, led the Latin American Church to denounce the grave injustices stemming from mechanisms of oppression.

Service to Our Poor Brothers and Sisters

When we draw near to the poor in order to accompany them and serve them, we are doing what Christ taught us to do when he became our brother, poor like us. Hence service to the poor is the privileged, though not the exclusive, gauge of our following of Christ. The best service to our fellows is evangelization, which disposes them to fulfill themselves as children of God, liberates them from injustices, and fosters their integral advancement.

Pastoral Guidelines

The objective of our preferential option for the poor is to proclaim Christ the Savior. This will enlighten them about their dignity, help them in their efforts to liberate themselves from all their wants, and lead them to communion with the Father and their fellow human beings through a life lived in evangelical poverty.

---

*Excerpts from CELAM III (Puebla 1979), *Puebla and Beyond,* ed. J. Eagleson and P. Scharper (Maryknoll, NY: Orbis Books, 1979), 264-65, 266-67; cf. Bosch, TM, 435.

"Jesus Christ came to share our human condition through his sufferings, difficulties, and death. Before transforming day-to-day life, he knew how to speak to the heart of the poor, liberate them from sin, open their eyes to a light on the horizon, and fill them with joy and hope. Jesus Christ does the same thing today. He is present in your Churches, your families, and your hearts."[8]

This option, demanded by the scandalous reality of economic imbalances in Latin America, should lead us to establish a dignified ...way of life together as human beings and to construct a just and free society.

The required change in unjust social, political and economic structures will not be authentic and complete if it is not accompanied by a change in our personal and collective outlook regarding the idea of a dignified, happy human life. This, in turn, disposes us to undergo conversion.[9]

The gospel demand for poverty, understood as solidarity with the poor and as a rejection of the situation in which most people on this continent live, frees the poor person from being individualistic in life, and from being attracted and seduced by the false ideals of a consumer society. In like manner the witness of a poor Church can evangelize the rich whose hearts are attached to wealth, thus converting and freeing them from this bondage and their own egotism.

To live out and proclaim the requirement of Christian poverty, the Church must re-examine its structures and the life of its members, particularly that of its pastoral agents, with the goal of effective conversion in mind.

Such conversion entails the demand for an austere lifestyle and a total confidence in the Lord, because in its evangelizing activity the Church will rely more on the being and power of God and his grace than on "having more" and secular authority. In this way it will present an image of being authentically poor, open to God and fellow human beings, ever at their disposal, and providing a place where the poor have a real chance for participation and where their worth is recognized.

"TO BREAK EVERY YOKE"

"Liberation involves joining the struggle."

■ *Allan Boesak is one of South Africa's best-known black theologians. Born in Somerset West, Cape Province, in 1946, he grew up amid the constant oppression of the apartheid system. From his strong Christian upbringing, he grew in conviction that a totally new social order could emerge, one based on the faith that "the gospel of Jesus Christ is the gospel of liberation."[10] After university and theological studies in South Africa, he studied at Union Theological Seminary in New York and Colgate-Rochester Seminary. Study of the writings of Martin Luther King, Jr., strengthened both his black pride and his advocacy of nonviolent resistance, a theme he developed in his Th.D. dissertation for the theological academy of Kampen in The Netherlands. In South Africa, he has served as a university chaplain, a leader in the Reformed Church, and a catalyst for black political unity. Through his writings and leadership as president of the World Alliance of Reformed Churches, he brought the struggle against apartheid to world attention. The following is an excerpt from an address delivered at the All Africa Conference of Churches' General Assembly (Nairobi, Kenya, August 2-12, 1981).*[11]

*A Wounded Continent**

This year, the churches of Africa will assemble under the theme: "Following the Light of Jesus Christ." For Africa, this theme cannot be a simplistic expression of joyful innocence or a triumphalistic war cry. Rather, let it reveal the pain, the sorrow, the suffering, and the fragile, hopeful faith of captive peoples. For Africa is a wounded continent, and the wounds have not yet healed....

Christ the Liberator

The God of the Bible is the God of Jesus Christ who took upon himself the condition of oppression and poverty. Jesus Christ sides with the poor and the weak. He speaks of himself as a "servant." Jesus becomes one of the *am ha-aretz,* the poor of the land. He is a man without majesty, a man of sorrows and familiar with suffering, whose life reflects so much of the life of oppressed peoples today.

But still his name is Yoshua: liberator. He brought the message and reality of hope and liberation....

This is the Christ whose light illuminates our darkness. His message of liberation is the message of the church in the world. This is the message the church in Africa must proclaim if it is to be authentic. It is the message of the God of the Bible: what God did for the people of Israel, God can do again today. It is a message that he who came to proclaim the acceptable year of the Lord is still the head of his church.

Total Liberation

The liberation the church proclaims is total. It is liberation from sin in all its manifestations of alienation from God and neighbor. It is liberation from economic exploitation, dehumanization, and oppression. It is liberation from meaninglessness and self-alienation, from poverty and suffering. It is liberation toward a meaningful human existence seeking freedom and human fulfillment. It is liberation for the service of the living God, so that God's people will no longer be subjected to the tyranny of false gods.

For the churches this liberation involves joining the struggle against political oppression and economic exploitation; against racism and all forms of human degradation; against the destruction of human-beingness wherever it may occur on the continent. Let me repeat here what I have said elsewhere: joining the struggle for human liberation in Africa does not mean christianizing the struggle, "taking

---

*Excerpts from Allan Boesak, *Black and Reformed: Apartheid, Liberation and the Calvinist Tradition* (Maryknoll, NY: Orbis Books, 1984), 70, 71-72, 73, 74-75; cf. Bosch, TM, 442-43.

over" as it were, what others have been doing long before. But it does mean taking responsibility for the historical reality into which the kingdom of God has entered. It does mean being a Christian presence in the midst of that struggle, keeping alive and witnessing to the goals of the kingdom of God for our world.

It means keeping alive, in the midst of the struggle, God's possibilities. It means being the embodiment of God's demands for love, justice, reconciliation, and shalom for the world that has been reconciled with God in Jesus Christ. In all this the church should be guided, not by fear, resignation, or any ideology, but by its desire to be true to the gospel of its Lord. The church should understand that it must take sides just as its Lord took sides with those "who had no helper." Neutrality is not possible.

PROPHETIC THEOLOGY AND VIOLENCE

"The Church cannot collaborate with tyranny."

■ *On September 13, 1985, over 150 Christians from more than twenty denominations in South Africa published their "Challenge to the Church: A Theological Comment on the Political Crisis in South Africa." It was truly theology from below, produced out of discussions—in dozens of local communities—of the crisis and possible Christian responses. These discussions began in Soweto with initiatives by staff members of the ICT (Institute of Contextual Theology). Since its release, thousands of South African Christians have added their signatures to this statement of theology that has become known as the Kairos Document. It contains a strong critique of both state theology, with its prevailing value of law and order, and church theology, which values reconciliation and nonviolence more than the ending of tyranny and oppression. Advocated is a prophetic theology based on the convictions that God sides with the oppressed, that systemic violence pervades situations of oppression, and that the church cannot collaborate with tyranny but must engage in civil disobedience.*

*Liberation and Hope in the Bible**

The Bible, of course, does not only *describe* oppression, tyranny and suffering. The message of the Bible is that oppression is sinful and wicked, an offence against God. The oppressors are godless sinners and the oppressed are suffering because of the sins of their oppressors. But there is *hope* because Yahweh, the God of the Bible, will *liberate* the oppressed from their suffering and misery. "He will redeem their lives from exploitation and outrage" (Ps. 74:14). "I have seen the miserable state of my people in Egypt. I have heard their appeal to be free of their slave-drivers. I mean to deliver them out of the hands of the Egyptians" (Ex. 3:7).

---

*Excerpts from *The Kairos Document: Challenge to the Church: A Theological Comment on the Political Crisis in South Africa,* rev. 2nd ed. (Braamfontein: Skotaville Publishers; Grand Rapids, MI: Eerdmans, 1986), 25-26, 29-30; cf. Bosch, TM, 444.

Throughout the Bible God appears as the liberator of the oppressed: "For the plundered poor, for the needy who groan, now I will act, says Yahweh" (Ps. 12:5). God is not neutral. He does not attempt to reconcile Moses and Pharaoh, to reconcile the Hebrew slaves with their Egyptian oppressors or to reconcile the Jewish people with any of their later oppressors....

There can be no doubt that Jesus, the Son of God, also takes up the cause of the poor and the oppressed and identifies himself with their interests....

At the very heart of the gospel of Jesus Christ and at the very centre of all true prophecy is a message of hope. Jesus has taught us to speak of this hope as the coming of God's kingdom. We believe that God is at work in our world turning hopeless and evil situations to good so that God's Kingdom may come and God's Will may be done on earth as it is in heaven. We believe that goodness and justice and love will triumph in the end and that tyranny and oppression cannot last forever. One day "all tears will be wiped away" (Rev. 7:17; 12:4) and "the lamb will lie down with the lion" (Isa. 11:6). True peace and reconciliation are not only desirable, they are assured and guaranteed. This is our faith and our hope. We believe in and hope for the resurrection....

Civil Disobedience

Once it is established that the present regime has no moral legitimacy and is in fact a tyrannical regime certain things follow for the Church and its activities. In the first place *the Church cannot collaborate with tyranny.* It cannot or should not do anything that appears to give legitimacy to a morally illegitimate regime. Secondly, the Church should not only pray for a change of government, it should also mobilize its members in every parish to begin to think and work and plan for a change of government in South Africa. We must begin to look ahead and begin working now with firm hope and faith for a better future. And finally the moral illegitimacy of the apartheid regime means that the Church will have to be involved at times in *civil disobedience.* A Church that takes its responsibilities seriously in these circumstances will sometimes have to confront and to disobey the State in order to obey God.

WOMEN, REVOLUTION AND SPIRITUALITY

> "The new spirituality ...of women means speaking of a faith incarnate in the revolutionary process."

■ *Authentic theology can never be divorced from practical life. Inasmuch as women (and girls) constitute more than half of the human family and churches of the Two-thirds World more than half of the world Christian family, the life experiences of Christian women of the Two-thirds World, and their reflection upon them, constitute one of the richest untapped veins for contemporary liberation theology. Building upon this premise, EATWOT encouraged its Women's Commission to convene an Intercontinental Women's Conference. This ground-breaking event took place in Oaxtepec, Mexico, December 1-6, 1986. The following selection is from a representative paper from that conference by Luz Beatriz Arellano. A Roman Catholic sister from Nicaragua, she was at the time a staff member of Centro Valdivieso in Managua, Nicaragua. Sister Arellano testified to the new spirituality of Nicaraguan women arising out of their living experience of God who they believe is intimately involved in the revolutionary process their nation is undergoing.*

*God Present in Faces of the Poor**

Our first experience of God was that of allowing ourselves to feel the impact of the situation of suffering and oppression that our people were undergoing. From that moment on, we began to discover God present in the suffering, oppressed, and outcast countenance of our poorest brothers and sisters....

The God of Life

Even in the 1960s many men and women did not see this situation of poverty as something natural, and they began to ask questions such as, "What is our role as Christian men and women in this subjugated, dependent, oppressed society where life is impossible?" In a very natural way, we began to search and we tried to uncover the roots of these problems. We began to confront this situation with the word of the Lord. This helped us to find specific approaches to solutions and changes. We were also discovering that God was different from what we had been taught. We were discovering God as the God of life, closer to us, as one who journeys with us through history.

I recall that it was women who most insisted on discovering God as God of life. I believe that women were better able to make this discovery and translate it into life more easily because of their calling to motherhood, among other reasons, since that is a calling to life and peace. Being essentially bearers and sustainers of life, women find a new meaning in the discovery of God as God of life, and they themselves become stronger and more conscious as defenders and bearers of life, not only in the biological sense but in all its dimensions, the fullness of life to which Jesus calls us as his followers: "I came so they might have life and have it in abundance" (Jn. 10:10). From this angle, Nicaraguan women walk beside their people in creating new life, in giving a meaning to life, taking part in and actively defending a project in history, one that is liberating and is generating new rights to justice....

---

*Excerpts from Luz Beatriz Arellano, "Women's Experience of God in Emerging Spirituality," in *With Passion and Compassion: Third World Women Doing Theology,* ed. Virginia Fabella, M.M., and Mercy Amba Oduyoye (Maryknoll, NY: Orbis Books, 1986), 135, 136-40, 145-46; cf. Bosch, TM, 442.

A New Image of Jesus

Out of their participation in the suffering of our people while also battling through their own struggle, women discover a new image of Jesus—a Jesus who is brother and sister, in solidarity on the journey toward liberation, the people's journey and their own journey; a Jesus who is a *compañero* in building the new society.

Jesus' face is present in all the men and women who endure weariness and give their life for others. Jesus is identified as God, man and woman, standing in firm solidarity with the struggle. This is a God who is sensitive to suffering, a God who goes along with the people incarnate in history. The discovery of, and faith in, a God who is in pilgrimage with the people, ...identified with the cause of justice, is a discovery that gives meaning to their struggle and makes everyday life bearable in the midst of oppression....

Crucifixion and Resurrection, Death and Life

Because of the war of aggression that our people are undergoing, crucifixion and death, resurrection and life are two realities present in all dimensions of life. In death, the mystery of life is already present: many die consciously surrendering their lives to defend an effort to build something within history, convinced of the new life gestating today in Nicaragua. Nicaraguan women feel the stimulus and strength of the Spirit, and out of their faith they actively accompany all those men and women who are defending life along the different warfronts. "God did not give us a Spirit of cowardice, but one of strength, of love, and good judgment" (2 Tim. 1:7).

The incarnation of this new spirituality transcends what is individual and commits us to struggle for the life of the whole body of the people and for all of life. Resurrection is already present in crucifixion. The road toward the building of the kingdom by way of the rise of the new society entails pain, death, and suffering, but it also means the hope of greater life, justice, peace, and love incarnate in history. Both aspects, crucifixion and resurrection, are part of the process of passing from death to life "through the body of Christ" (Rom. 7:4).

Joy Is Paschal

Out of the daily suffering of poor women and out of the lives surrendered in the struggle against the causes of this situation of death, people are living a renewed paschal experience. The experience of death, war, abduction, rape, and abandonment enables them to experience more profoundly the meaning of the Lord's resurrection. Joy is thus the result of the hope that the historic project of life will overcome the situation of death and war that the people are suffering. Hope in the resurrection in no way means escape from present reality but, rather, it means a deeper involvement in the struggle against death. Joy comes from faith, from the hope that death is not the last word. That is why we can already celebrate the joy of resurrection in the midst of war.

CONVERSION TO THE GOD OF THE POOR

> "Christian women who struggle for justice and real peace are true combatants—against death."

■ *Women, religion, and social change are three of the most important concerns in today's world. In June 1983, Harvard University convened an international interreligious conference to relate these concerns. Of the twenty-six women who made presentations from their own contexts and cultures, seventeen were from Asia, Africa, the Middle East, or Latin America, and nine from North America and Europe. They were not to give formal academic papers, but rather case studies illuminating the particular questions and ways of thinking specific to the experience of women as they work for social change in their own cultures and religious traditions. The following document is from the presentation made by Julia Esquivel, an exiled Guatemalan teacher and poet who lectures and works for human rights in Central America. She focused on the transformations which take place when women begin to understand why there cannot be true peace without justice. She called it "conversion to the God of the poor."*

*The Conversion**

Until very recently Christian women in Central America were still repeating religious formulas without questioning their true meaning. Middle-class women can see poverty, give alms to beggars, become involved in charitable projects and repeat the Our Father endlessly, and yet remain indifferent to the concrete problems and the profound structural causes of the miserable conditions in which most of our people live.

This is why conversion to the God of the poor is essential to begin to understand why there cannot be true peace without justice. It is not enough to be a woman, and as such oppressed and relegated to a secondary position. The real face of God is one of suffering, of a God who suffers when he hears the cry of the oppressed. Most women who call themselves Christians allow themselves to be imprisoned by the cultural, economic and traditional patterns that the consumer society imposes on them. They view themselves as Christian because they comply with certain Sunday religious practices.

Wealthy women believe they have the right to demand luxury, overabundance, even the superfluous—at the expense and exploitation of the poor in the Third

---

*Excerpts from Julia Esquivel, "Christian Women and the Struggle for Justice in Central America," in *Speaking of Faith: Global Perspectives on Women, Religion and Social Change*, ed. Diana L. Eck and Devaki Jain (Philadelphia: New Society Publishers, 1987), 22, 25-28, 29, 31-32; cf. Bosch, TM, 437-38.

World. Although it may be hard to believe, this type of woman exists even in our societies in Central America. There are women who torture other women, and who keep servants whom they treat like dogs.

Poor women, peasants, Indians, servants, and factory workers can also believe that their life is normal, and that it is God's will that they live, or rather survive, in the way they do. For centuries, most poor women with children have accepted the fact that their children die of malnutrition. To the question of how many children they have, peasant women might respond, "Five. Three dead and two living," or "Seven. Five dead and two living." These women also need to become acquainted with the face of a God for whom all people are equal, a face which is not visible in consumer societies and those called "developed."

For women, poor or not, the encounter with the real God is a realization that we are accepted by Him as daughters. It means encountering the God of the poor, and realizing that we are Jesus' sisters. It means remembering that He very clearly told the doctors and professors that all nations will be judged by the treatment they give their smaller brothers, the poor, and that He Himself is one of the poor. He demands of us pity, clemency, fraternity and service through each poor, weak or oppressed person we encounter (Mt. 25:31-46, Isa. 58).

When we women of faith begin to open our eyes to our human dignity, and to our brothers and sisters, the true meaning of Our Father, Our Daily Bread, and The Promised Land is revealed to us. We discover ourselves as destined to live a human life together, along with our brothers and sisters in Christ, the world over. We can no longer passively accept a life of enslavement, and even less the role of the oppressor or accomplice in a society which subverts God's will for all men and women.

But we women, liberated from our blindness, become dangerous. Many people would prefer to have a woman who is dependent, submissive and fearful, a complete follower of established traditions and cultural patterns....

Women Who Struggle for Justice

Christian women who struggle for justice and real peace are true combatants—against death. Death wears many faces in our countries. It appears as malnutrition, as abject poverty, as exploitation, repression, counter-insurgency and even as "development" and population control....

In Guatemala, I know of a 17-year-old Indian woman, the mother of a month-old baby. As do many Indian women, she cared for her plants, crops, and herbs which gave her and her people sustenance; she respected her elders. I have seen her contemplating her child with tenderness and grief, an orphan whose father was murdered by the army. She was a combatant who knew what it was to take up arms to defend her life. When her time came, Oshe left her companions and walked for six days through the mountains to give birth to her child, a preserver of her race.

This woman is a symbol of what we must be. We must combat the project of death which looms over humanity, disguised as development, consumerism, anti-communism. We must defend the life of the Creation, because all of humanity is waiting in anguish for the day in which all men and women can really live as brothers and sisters, and administer the resources of the world for the common good.

LIBERATION AND WHOLENESS

"Our struggle is a struggle for wholeness."

■ *When women start to consider their everyday, concrete life experiences as the most important source for theological reflection, they participate in a liberative process. They begin to free themselves from all imposed religious authority. In her introduction to Asian women's theology,* Struggle to be the Sun Again, *Chung Hyun Kyung begins by examining the historical and social contexts of Asian women's theology and their reflections on humanity. The excerpts below are from that chapter. Next, she explores specific manifestations of these theologies in christology, mariology, and spirituality. In her final chapter she analyzes the contributions of Asian women's theology to contemporary theology, and its future. Chung Hyun Kyung holds a doctorate from Union Theological Seminary in New York and teaches systematic theology at Ewha Women's University in Seoul, Korea.*

*The Burning Desire for Liberation and Wholeness**

Asian women's theology was born out of Asian women's tears and sighs and from their burning desire for liberation and wholeness. It is neither the logical consequence of academic debate of the university nor the pastoral conclusion of the institutional church. Asian women's theology has emerged from Asian women's cries and screams, from the extreme suffering in their everyday lives. They have shouted from pain when their own and their children's bodies collapsed from starvation, rape, and battering. Theological reflection has emerged as a response to women's suffering.

Throughout the long history of colonization, Asian women have cried out both openly and secretly as they confronted the injustices in their lives. Most of the time no one heard their cries. Seldom did Asian women hear words or experience deeds of comfort from male-dominated religions. Asian women's tears and sighs had been accumulated in their collective unconscious for thousands of years without many public channels for expression. As a consequence, today the pent-up anger is finally beginning to explode like a volcano with much fire and flame. They are challenging God, who Christians say loves everyone, about "his" silence. Asian women are asking, "*Where* were you when we were hungry? *Where* were you when we called your name as our bodies were raped, mutilated, and disfigured by our husbands,

---

*Excerpts from Chung Hyun Kyung, *Struggle to be the Sun Again: Introducing Asian Women's Theology* (Maryknoll, NY: Orbis Books, 1990), 22-24, 35; cf. Bosch, TM, 442-47.

policemen and the soldiers of colonizing countries? Have you heard our cries? Have you seen our bodies dragged like dead dogs and abandoned in the trash dump?" Faith for Asian women has been difficult, because their lives have been filled with so much agony....

Beyond Tokenism

Like black women, we are Asian women all the time. We cannot compartmentalize aspects of our struggle. Our struggle is a struggle for wholeness. What Asian women want from Asian men is not their "generous understanding" on the "women's problem" but their repentance, a genuine commitment to end their oppression over Asian women, a *metanoia* defined by concrete change. The male oppression of women is not a women's problem. It is a man's problem Asian men have to come to terms with. Only when Asian men in the liberation movement incorporate the liberation of women as an intrinsic ingredient for Asia's struggle for full humanity can their claim for people's liberation have integrity. This means Asian men's support for Asian women's liberation must go beyond tokenism. The Asian women's challenge also means Asian men must transform the way they relate to women, the way they produce and reproduce the world, and the content of their work and world view.

Asian women's theology is being made by women in Asian churches who realize that they cannot continue to accept the place for them defined by Asian men. With other religious and secular sisters, we are determined to create a theology, church, and society that are liberating for women.

NOTES

1. Cf. "Ting," in *DEM,* p. 1007.

2. Cf. Vatican Council II, pastoral constitution *Gaudium et Spes,* no. 69.

3. Ibid., no. 34.

4. Cf. "Gutiérrez," in *DEM,* p. 448; Deane William Ferm, *Profiles in Liberation,* pp. 154-58.

5. Many Christians have sought answers to these questions in relatively novel ways. This search has produced many experiences, sometimes confused. See in this connection René Laurentin's *Enjeu du IIe Synode et contestations dans l'Église* (Paris: Éditions du Seuil, 1969); see also *A la recherche d'une Église,* special issue of *Parole et Mission* 12, no. 46 (July 15, 1969); *Le due chiese* (Rome: IDOC, 1969); and the collection edited by Malcolm Boyd, *The Underground Church* (New York: Sheed and Ward, 1968).

6. In this context the starting point would be what P.-A. Liégé called some time ago "the human credibility of Christianity" ("Bulletin d'Apologétique," *Revue des Sciences Philosophiques et Théologiques* 33 [1949]: 67).

7. We referred to this in nos. 15ff. of this document. Here we would simply recall that the vast majority of our people lack the most elementary material goods. This is in contrast to the accumulation of wealth in the hands of a small minority, frequently the price being poverty for the majority. The poor do not lack simply material goods. They also miss, on the level of human dignity, full participation in sociopolitical life. Those found in this category

are principally our indigenous peoples, peasants, manual laborers, marginalized urban dwellers and, in particular, the women of these social groups. The women are doubly oppressed and marginalized.

8. John Paul II, Address to Workers in Monterey, January 31, 1979, p. 8.

9. "Justice," II: 39-51, in Second General Conference of Latin American Bishops (Medellín, Colombia, 1968), *The Church in the Present-Day Transformation of Latin America in the Light of the Council,* 2nd. ed. (Washington, DC: Latin America Division of the United States Catholic Conference, 1973); *Evangelii Nuntiandi,* Art. 30.

10. Allan Boesak, *Farewell to Innocence* (Maryknoll, NY: Orbis Books, 1976), p. 17.

11. Cf. Ferm, *Profiles in Liberation,* pp. 14-18.

12

Mission as Inculturation

For Bosch, a second variant of mission as contextualization is mission as inculturation. Predominately used by Roman Catholic missiologists, the term was first coined in 1962 by J. Masson (TM, 447). It has been defined by Robert Schreiter as a process which combines "the theological principle of incarnation with the social-science concept of acculturation (adapting oneself to a culture)."[1]

While the terminology is new, the issue for Christian missions of relating Gospel to culture is not. As missions accompanied western colonial expansion, missionaries increasingly sought cultural adaptations to expedite the conversion process. Catholics referred to this adjustment as accommodation. In the following selection from his dissertation, Johannes Thauren refers to the significant policy statement of the Propaganda Fide *in 1659 advising missionaries not to force people to change their customs, as long as these were not opposed to the Christian religion or morality. Protestants preferred the term* indigenization. *The classic statement of the three-self principles comes from Henry Venn, the outstanding nineteenth-century secretary of the Church Missionary Society, who believed that the goal in mission should be to form indigenous churches that will become self-supporting, self-governing, and self-extending.*

Nevertheless, a "kernel and husk" mentality prevailed. The depositum fidei *(the faith as understood and canonized by the western church) was believed to be an unchangeable core, while varying cultural forms of its expression could be permitted. Could a "fourth self" be added to the classical "three selfs"—self-theologizing? This was the central question behind the shift from mission as accommodation to mission as inculturation (Bosch, TM, 448-52).*

The remaining selections illustrate various aspects of the inculturation debate. As early as 1950, Daniel Johnson Fleming, professor of missions at Union Theological Seminary in New York, identified a prerequisite for the new approach—cross-cultural missionaries must begin as learners rather than teachers, as servants rather than masters, with the goal of empathy with those whom they wish to help. Laurenti Magesa of Tanzania would reverse the traditional mission approach to Africa. He advocates taking African culture, in the light of Christ, as the basis for inculturation. Charles Kraft, of the Fuller School of World Mission, contributes the concept of dynamic-equivalence theologizing. He argues that this was the process that Paul and other scriptural authors exemplified—the reproduction of Christian content in their contemporary cultural contexts. The most authentic biblical translation, he contends, is a dynamic-equivalence one in which the content is constant but the forms of expression vary from culture to culture. Aloysius Pieris of Sri Lanka adds social class analysis as an essential part of effective inculturation. Kwok Pui-lan of Hong Kong encourages Asian women to develop innovative styles of doing theology. She suggests that women's resources may include poems, songs, stories, dances, rituals, and even lullabies. The new theological style must reflect both male and female experiences. Pedro Casaldáliga of Brazil sees the church in mission as having a mediating role between people with their cultures and "the Spirit of Jesus." The resulting style is that "every mission should become dialogue and communion." In doing so, the church would encourage each group to "stand up and walk on their own cultural legs."

THREE-SELF PRINCIPLES

> "The Native Church ... independent of foreign aid or superintendence."

■ *Henry Venn (1796-1873) has been rated the outstanding European missionary leader, thinker, and administrator of the nineteenth century. In 1819, at the age of 23, be became a fellow of Queens' College, Cambridge. From 1841 to 1872, he served as chief secretary of the Church Missionary Society, which gained its major support from evangelical Anglicans in Great Britain. His vision, like that of his American counterpart Rufus Anderson, was of developing indigenous churches on the mission fields which would become self-supporting, self-governing, and self-extending. Far ahead of his time, he envisioned and worked for the "euthanasia of the mission." His deep commitment to the goal of a genuinely native church is evident in the following excerpts from an 1861 document—a position rejected by other Anglican mission societies that preferred continued control from a church center in Europe.[2]*

The Organization of Native Churches[3]*

The work of Modern Missionaries is of a two-fold character. The heathen are to be brought to the knowledge of Christ and the converts who embrace the truth are to be trained up in Christian habits, and to be formed into a native Christian Church. These two branches are essentially distinct; yet it is only of late years that the distinction has been recognized by appointing Missionaries to the purely Evangelistic branch under the designation of Itinerating Missionaries, in contradistinction from "Station" Missionaries.

The Missionary whose labours are blest to the gathering in of converts, naturally

---

*Excerpts from Henry Venn, "The Organization of Native Churches" (1861), in *To Apply the Gospel: Selections from the Writings of Henry Venn,* ed. Max Warren (Grand Rapids, MI: Eerdmans, 1971), 67, 68-69, 71; cf. Bosch, TM, 450.

desires to keep his converts under his own charge, to minister to them as a Pastor, and to rule them as a native congregation....

Under this system, the Missionary takes charge of classes of Candidates for Baptism, Classes of Candidates for the Lord's Supper, and Communicants-classes. The Missionary advances the converts from one class to another at his discretion. When the converts become too numerous or too scattered for the individual ministry of the Missionary, he appoints a Catechist or other Teacher, and the Society pays him. The Society establishes Schools and pays for the Teachers. As the Mission advances, the number of Readers, Catechists, and Ordained Pastors, of Schools and Schoolmasters, is increased. But all is dependent upon the Missionary: and all the agency is provided for at the cost of the Society....

This imperfection in Church Missions must be remedied by keeping in mind the distinction between evangelizing the heathen, and the ministering to the Native Church; and by introducing into the Native Church that elementary organisation which may give it "corporate life," and prepare it for its full development under a native ministry and an indigenous Episcopate.

For the introduction of such elementary organisation into the Native Church the following principles may be laid down:

Principles

It is expedient that native converts should be trained, at as early a stage as possible, upon a system of self-government, and of contributing to the support of their own native Teachers.

It is expedient that contributions should be made by the converts themselves for their own Christian instruction, and for schools for their children; and that for this purpose a Native Church Fund for an assigned Missionary District should be established, into which the contributions should be paid. The Fund must, at first, be mainly sustained by grants from the Missionary Society, these grants to be diminished as the native contributions spring up. Whilst the fund receives grants from the Society, the Parent Committee must direct the mode of its management.

It is expedient that the native Teachers should be divided into two classes, namely

(1) Those who are employed as assistants to the Missionary in his evangelistic work, and who are paid by the Society.

(2) Those who are employed in pastoral work amongst the native Christians, who are to be paid out of the Native Church Fund, whether Schoolmasters, Readers, Catechists, or Ordained Pastors, as the case may be; so that they be regarded as the ministerial agents of the Native Church, and not as the salaried agents of a Missionary Society.

It is expedient that the arrangements which may be made in the missions should from the first have reference to the ultimate settlement of the Native Church, upon the ecclesiastical basis of an *indigenous* Episcopate, independent of foreign aid or superintendence....

If the elementary principles of self-support and self-government and self-extension be thus sown with the seed of the Gospel, we may hope to see the healthy growth and expansion of the Native Church, when the Spirit is poured down from on high, as the flowers of a fertile field multiply under the showers and warmth of summer.

ADAPTATION OR ACCOMMODATION?

"The Church must adhere to the dogmatic and moral norms of the missionary countries."

■ *Johannes Thauren (1892-1954) devoted his life to the study of missiology. His doctoral dissertation, completed in 1926 in the Catholic theological faculty at the University of Münster, was on the history of accommodation in Catholic mission strategy. In the following excerpt, he recovered the remarkable 1659 policy statement of the* Propaganda Fide *advising missionaries not to force people to change their customs, as long as these were not opposed to religion or morality. Thauren taught missiology at the St. Gabriel seminary for mission priests in Mödling (1926-1932), and as professor of missiology at the University of Vienna (1932-1954).*[4]

*Boundaries and Perimeter**

The question needs to be raised to what perimeter accommodation in missions must be applied and in what boundaries it can move about. In order to determine what *manners* and customs may be chosen for accommodation, we distinguish these in a) such which stand in open opposition to belief and morals, such as idolatry, magic, human sacrifice; b) such which are good in themselves like honorable clothing, prudent division of the sexes; c) such which are of a civilian nature and thus do not touch upon belief and morals in any way, for example, lifestyle, etiquette, etc.; d) such which are or have been indifferent but were sanctioned by pagan religions or received superstitious character, such as caste system and Brahamanic braids; e) such which are indifferent in themselves, but that counteract our Church discipline, for example, the wearing of a head covering during the liturgy.[5]

What Is Morally Bad or Good

The question of what constitutes *morally bad or good* habits and customs can be answered briefly and plainly. The moral duty of missions is to promote and nurture the good and repress the bad. The morals of a civilian nature touch not upon the realm of mission activity, and therefore provide no justification for missions to

*Excerpts from J. Thauren, *Die Akkommodation im Katholischen Heidenapostolat* (Münster in Westfalen: Aschendorff, 1927); excerpts translated from the German by Daniel Hofmann; cf. Bosch, TM, 448.

work toward a change of the present situation. These principles have also been established by the Propaganda....[6] The battle against the depravity among the people[7] requires a great measure of wisdom and patience, without which any success must be questioned....

Questions of Traditional Religions

As easy as the answering of the principal questions of customs is, the more difficult it is to answer those which deal in any way with *pagan* religions or that are in contradiction to *ecclesiastical* morals and precepts. Considering the state of affairs in missions concerning schismatics and pagans, Thomas of Jesus [1564-1627] proposed the following guidelines: 1) a custom or rite is permissible if it is already customary within the nations and the churches that are connected with the Church; 2) when they are not in contradiction to natural reason and are not inhuman, dishonorable, and indecent, because all that violates human dignity and decency (*politia*) must be abolished; 3) any custom or rite which is against a dogma is to be completely destroyed; 4) all customs which are intended to uphold any of the mandates of the old Law abolished by Christ are to be removed (such as celebrating the Sabbath); 5) concerning the ceremonies in distributing the sacraments, the substance of the sacrament (matter, form, and celebrant) must conform to the regulations. However, under certain circumstances—and with the approval of the Church—such customs may be tolerated which are otherwise prohibited by regulations or sanctions of the positive and canonical law.[8]

No Double Standard

As far as the Church is concerned, her *decisions* are based upon the same *principles* as are our nations. As much as the Church cannot have a double standard concerning the social fabric of the people, so the Church must adhere to the dogmatic and moral norms of the missionary countries. Her position carries here the stamp of dogmatic "intolerance" in such a fashion that leaves no room for doubt that there exist immovable boundaries. Without exception, the Church claims even the most precise directives of a Tertullian.[9] The discourses of St. Augustine[10] validate the mandate for missions and is indebted to the clear definitions of St. Thomas[11] and of other great leaders of the Church.[12] She does not tolerate a superior demand for moral behavior in relation to the object of missions due to a moral obligation of all the peoples, but stresses an equal moral obligation for all.[13]

MISSIONARIES AS LEARNERS

> "Think oneself into the total mental and emotional attitude of the other."

■ *Daniel Johnson Fleming (1877-1969) was a graduate of Wooster College, Union Theological Seminary (New York), Columbia University, and the University of*

Chicago (M.Sc. and Ph.D.). Trained in both physics and theology, he served as director of Forman Christian College, taught physics (1904-1913), and developed a lifelong concern for village education and development. Returning to the United States in 1913, he became organizational director of the Presbyterian department of foreign service and then professor of missions at Union Theological Seminary (1918-1944). As teacher, lecturer, mentor, and author, he conveyed to new missionaries the importance of entering into cross-cultural ministries as learners seeking genuine community.

*Entering into Community**

One attainment that makes for community, whether in a neighborhood or in the world, is the capacity to enter understandingly and sympathetically into the lives of others. This involves acquiring such an intimate knowledge of [persons] and of their environment that there results a deep understanding of their systems of thought and reaction. There will be a mutual sharing of enjoyments, interests, and privileges resulting in such mutual sympathy that "we," "us," and "ours" are the spontaneous expressions for a sense of real community. One is no longer an outsider; one becomes an insider. The imagery of [others] is acquired; [their] point of view is appreciated so that mutual insight and the sharing of mental states becomes possible. Fellowship is experienced and a sense of belonging is developed....

From another viewpoint we may say that our ideal is to achieve what psychologists call "empathy" with the people whom we wish to help. Empathy is partial identification with the other in which you see and feel the other's point of view but at the same time retain your own identity.[14] Like an actor playing a part, you project your feelings into the experience of another and at the same time retain the consciousness of your own personality as cooperator or comrade. One part of your consciousness is devoted to feeling into the situation with the people to be reached, while the other part is maintaining the eager watchful attitude of the friendly or serving self. One enters into the life of the other and feels it as if it were one's own. Looking through the other's eyes with one's own mind, something refreshingly new will be the outcome.

Thus to gain a true and complete understanding essential to effective service, one must think oneself into the total mental and emotional attitude of the other....

Motivation for Closer Identification

Possibly on another level are those who, without any reflection on others, feel a definite sense of call to a life of identification. They conceive it to be their vocation to live out situations in immediate association with their [colleagues], if need be at grips with stark realities. Moral decisions are made in community with those they

---

*Excerpts from Daniel Fleming, *Living as Comrades* (New York: Agricultural Missions for the Foreign Missions Conference of North America, 1950), 6-7, 166-67; cf. Bosch, TM, 456.

wish to help and, therefore, in the adopted environment that they have made their own. Drawing on spiritual resources and on.... faithful friends, they are led to show by example what a difference Christianity may make in living under the stress and strain of practical life. They are possessed with the desire to translate their faith through daily living, overcoming all human barriers in commitment to Jesus Christ....

In these days solidarity of this kind has overtones relevant to interracial, international, and ecumenical relations little envisioned in the early period of missions. Spiritual community will hardly be achieved unless there are those who are willing to face hardship. But to *seek* adversity is to make into an end what should be accepted only as a possible corollary of a great obedience. Christ went to the Cross not that he might suffer but to do God's will.

In the background for such persons is the act of God in the Incarnation. If God took on human flesh to save [humanity], it is not too much for men [and women] to empty themselves and take on the form of servants. For them, when God speaks, he gives himself, and so they feel called to embody their message in a life of self-denial. Fortunate are those who, when the call comes, can without unjustifiable demands upon associates or dependents break away into a fundamentally different mode of life. Sometimes it is like being born again.

AUTHENTIC AFRICAN CHRISTIANITY

> "Inculturation would take African culture in the light of Christ, as its basis."

■ *Laurenti Magesa is a Roman Catholic diocesan priest from Musoma, Tanzania. He holds a doctorate in theology and is lecturer and head of the Religious Education Department at the Catholic Higher Institute of Eastern Africa, which is developing into a university. He is a frequent contributor of articles in* AFER, *the* African Ecclesial Review. *His 1973 article excerpted below was an early advocacy of African Christian theology.*

*Searching for Theological Accommodation**

Christianity is neither a culture nor a monolithic institution; but it is, rather, a personal message, which encounters persons, not superficially but concretely in life-situations. Thus, it must strive to reach people as they are, that is, in their cultural setting and, as it were, let Christ and his Spirit seize, capture, and possess them. The task of the Church, as "the salt of the earth," is to let Christ, the Word of God, assimilate a given people, as if by osmosis: by diffusing his Spirit into them

---

*Excerpts from Laurenti Magesa, "Authentic African Christianity," *African Ecclesial Review* 15:2 (April 1973): 110-17; *32 Articles Evaluating Inculturation of Christianity in Africa,* ed. Teresa Okure et al. (Spearhead Nos. 112-114; Eldoret, Kenya: AMECEA Gaba Publications, 1990), 115-17; cf. Bosch, TM, 454-55.

and transforming their thought, mentality and sensibility—their culture in its totality.

The main task of the Church is to manifest Christ to a people and let the people encounter him, dialogue with him, opt for him, and form a community with him in their midst, and establish a true *koinonia.* Thus, they would feel at home in their option....

However, "manifesting Christ" is easier said than done. The unfortunate consequences of political history (which things are better forgotten) still put the Church in Africa today in a difficult and awkward position, as far as sincere inculturation is concerned. These difficulties must, therefore, be recognized for what they are, and corresponding measures taken.

Authentic theological accommodation in Africa today can be no less than a radical revolution to new ways of interpreting and understanding the Word of God. Now this is dangerous, insofar as it involves the risk of mistakes. Yet, if we are not ready to risk these dangers, genuine accommodation and inculturation will never be effected, and we will only satisfy ourselves with a superficial theological syncretism, a syncretism which would only serve the undesirable purpose of forcing us to lead dualistic lives. Religiously, this would be disastrous. To avoid this, then, it appears, that for better or for worse, the leap into a theological "revolution" must be taken. This means that we must initiate drastic appropriate measures for broad programmes of experimentation in all ecclesiastical areas.

One may rightly ask at this point, whether in inculturation and formulation of a true African Christian theology, we must begin with a clean slate? Must African Christian theology shun all other theologies of the world in its attempt to be truly indigenous?...

The problem, simply put, is this: what is the difference, if any, between "beginning from the beginning" and "beginning from our cultural roots?" *Beginning from our cultural roots would mean that inculturation would take African culture in the light of Christ, as its basis.* This is clear. What may not be so clear is what would be the wisdom or otherwise of discarding all of Western Christian theology and beginning our theological investigation with reference to A.D. one. My own answer is, everything being equal, that this is not necessary. Properly studied, Western theological experience is a big asset in our favour, in the struggle for promoting theological inculturation in Africa. In actual fact, this is what theological inculturation or accommodation means.

There is in all people of all places a universal, univocal, constant element. Within this context of sameness and permanence in the human person, sincere dialogue between persons and encounter between the person and God is possible. Within this context, too, we can explain words which defy particular cultural conditionings, words such as life and death, love and hate, praise and trust—words which no one can fail to understand.

It is within this context that the religious experiences of the West transmit a thread of faithful continuity of the message of Christ. This must be identified and utilized in Africa: because here is one of those meeting places of the universal ecclesial community, providing that enrichment, that insight, that wisdom which no particular individual church can command, and without which it cannot but be so much the poorer.

The requirements of inculturational accommodation in present-day Africa are, in a word, a careful look into African culture as a whole; an intensive historical study of Western culture, in which the message of Christ was wrapped as it came to Africa; an honest separation of the divine message from those cultural wrappings; and a sincere incarnation of the message into the [cultural heritage and] contemporary African world-view.

DYNAMIC EQUIVALENCE THEOLOGIES AND CHURCHES

"Christians should feel that their church is an original work within their own culture."

■ *Charles H. Kraft and his family arrived in northeastern Nigeria in 1957 as pioneer Church of the Brethren missionaries among the Higi people. Trained as an anthropologist and linguist, with a Ph.D. from the Hartford Seminary Foundation and earlier studies at Wheaton College and Ashland Theological Seminary, Kraft sought to introduce mission as inculturation from the outset. On the one hand, he identified a cultural fit between Higi and western Christian worldviews. On the other hand, he found areas of conflict, most notably in the Higi requirement that their community leaders be polygamists. Later Kraft built on his field experience, and that of many others, in his teaching as professor of anthropology and intercultural communication at the School of World Mission, Fuller Theological Seminary. His concept of dynamic equivalence is now a widely accepted principle for indigenous Bible translation, as well as for the development of local theologies.*[15]

*Dynamic-Equivalence Theologizing**

Theologizing is a matter of dynamic-equivalence transculturation and of witness to Christianity in terms of culture. All theologizing is culture-bound interpretation and communication of God's revelation. Good theologizing is Spirit-led, even though culture-bound. In spite of the impression often given that theology is an absolute, once-for-all kind of thing, theologizing is a dynamic, continuous *process*. Static, once-for-all theologies are dead theologies. *Dynamic-equivalence theologizing is the reproducing in contemporary cultural contexts of the theologizing process that Paul and the other scriptural authors exemplify.* Any time that theologizing devolves into the mere "buying and selling" of past theological products (as it often does), it fails to serve its proper function....

---

*Excerpts from Charles Kraft, *Christianity in Culture* (Maryknoll, NY: Orbis Books, 1979), 291, 315, 318-19, 321; cf. Bosch, TM, 452.

Dynamic-Equivalence Churchness

The organism that we call "church" should also be dynamically equivalent to biblical models.... *It is crucial that each new generation and culture experience the process of producing in its own cultural forms an appropriate church vehicle for the transmission of God's meanings.* We may thus speak of and recommend "dynamically equivalent churchness." Such a new use of previously existing cultural forms plus the necessary borrowing and internal development of new forms bring about change in the culture....

Dynamic-Equivalence Transculturation

Contemporary churches should bear the same resemblance to the scriptural models (both Old Testament and New Testament) of God's interaction with humans in culture that a faithful dynamic-equivalence translation of the Scriptures bears to his interaction with humans in language. Such churches should not appear to be cultural "translationese." *A contemporary church, like a contemporary translation, should impress the uninitiated observer as an original production in the contemporary culture, not as a badly fitted import from somewhere else.*

Those planting and/or operating churches should work in accord with the seven basic propositions for Bible translators outlined in chapter 13. They should (1) recognize, (2) respect and work in terms of the unique genius of the receptor culture, knowing that (3) anything (such as the church) expressible in one culture is expressible in another. However, they should not hesitate (4) to alter the (Hebrew and Greco-Roman) forms in terms of which the original churches were expressed, for they should realize that *the content expressed, not the forms in terms of which that content was originally expressed, is sacred.* They should understand (5) that the biblical cultures were fully human cultures, dignified by the fact that God worked within them but not sanctified thereby; the Bible demonstrates God's willingness to work in terms of *any* culture rather than his desire to perfect and impose a single culture. They should further understand (6) that the church is meant to be intelligible to the world around it; that God expects to be made intelligible to humanity by means of the church. And faithful church people are (7) to work toward this end by consciously attempting to produce church structures within the receptor culture that are dynamically equivalent to those portrayed (though partially) in the pages of Scripture.

Applying this model to church planting would mean eschewing attempts to produce mere formal correspondence between churches in one culture and those in another. A church that is merely a "literal" rendering of the forms of one church—be it an American church or a first-century Greco-Roman church—is not according to the dynamic-equivalence model, for it is not structured in such a way that it can appropriately perform the functions and convey the meanings that should characterize a Christian church....

What is desired, then, is the kind of church that will take indigenous forms, possess them for Christ, adapt and employ them to serve Christian ends by fulfilling indigenous functions, and convey through them Christian meanings to the surrounding society....

Christians should feel that their church is an original work within their own culture.

INCULTURATION: INTO WHOSE CULTURE?

"Whose culture does the official church reflect?"

■ *Aloysius Pieris was born in Ampitiya, Ceylon (now Sri Lanka), in 1934. He entered the Society of Jesus at the age of nineteen and was ordained a priest in 1965. His university studies led to degrees in philosophy (India), South Asian languages (London), and theology (Naples). In 1972, he became the first Christian to earn a Ph.D. degree in Buddhist philosophy from the University of Sri Lanka. After teaching Buddhist philosophy at the Gregorian University in Rome, Pieris returned to Sri Lanka to establish the Tulana Research Center, which he directs. There dialogue between Buddhists and Christians is encouraged on the threefold basis of the experience of popular religion, textual study, and pastoral reflection in the context of social transformation. Pieris does not hesitate to use Marxist analysis as a tool for understanding cultural dynamics, as the following passage reveals.*[16]

*Inculturation, Indigenous Theology, and Oriental Spirituality**

Inculturation is something that happens naturally. It can never be artificially induced. A Christian community tends to appropriate the symbols and the mores of the people around it only to the degree it immerses itself in their lives and struggles. That is to say, inculturation is the by-product of an involvement with the people rather than the conscious target of a program of action. For it is the people who create a culture. It is therefore from people with whom one gets involved that one understands and acquires a culture.

The questions that are foremost in the minds of inculturationists are therefore totally irrelevant: namely, whether a particular church is inculturated or not, or why it is not inculturated and how it could be inculturated. Yet it is relevant to know why such irrelevant questions are asked so frequently in our local churches today. Our diagnosis is that the inculturationists are starting off from the observation, valid in itself, that the ecclesiastical culture of the ministerial church in Asia is elitist and stands aloof from the culture of the poor masses. This cultural gap is even more pronounced in former European colonies such as India, Malaysia, and Indochina, where the seminary training and all clerical communication is done in the language of former colonial masters. But what the inculturationists fail to perceive is that the

---

*Excerpts from Aloysius Pieris, "The Non-Semitic Religions of Asia," in *Mission in Dialogue*, ed. Mary Motte and Joseph R. Lang (Maryknoll, NY: Orbis Books, 1982), 429, 431; cf. Bosch, TM, 448.

aforesaid cultural gap has an economic base; that the church's twofold culture indicates a sociological process in which the class division of the wider society has been ecclesiologically registered in the life of the believing community—a sin against the body of the Lord, as Saint Paul would have put it; that the culture of the clerics represents the dominant sector of the believing community; and so on.

Moreover, the irrelevance of the above-mentioned questions, which is at the center of the inculturation debate, is rooted in the erroneous presupposition that churches in Asia are not inculturated. Every local church, being itself a people, is essentially an inculturated church. The relevant question to ask, therefore, is: Whose culture does the official Church reflect? Which is the same as asking: Which class of people is the church predominantly associated with? Do the poor—the principal addressees of the good news and the special invitees to Christian discipleship—constitute a culturally decisive factor in the local church? Thus the whole inculturation issue derives its significance from the local church's basic mission to bring—and become—the good news to the poor in Asia.

CONTINUE THE CULTURAL CRITIQUE

"Continue the cultural critique our foremothers have begun."

■ *Kwok Pui-lan of Hong Kong is part of two networks encouraging Christian women in Asia to do theology from their own particular perspective—the Women's Commission of EATWOT and the Asian Women's Resource Centre for Culture and Theology. She teaches theology at the Episcopal Divinity School and has engaged in doctoral studies at Harvard Divinity School with research on feminist theology in China. She believes that theological reflection on the dynamic relation between culture and theology is of critical importance for Asian women. The task is complex due to 1) religious pluralism; 2) Christianity's minority status in most Asian countries; and 3) the low degree of feminist consciousness. Her goal is both to reclaim the past and to chart a new future, as shown in the following passages.*

*Reclaiming the Past**

Contemporary Asian women theologians continue the cultural critique our foremothers have begun, pointing out that the patriarchal Asian traditions, such as Confucianism, Hinduism, and Buddhism still exert tremendous influences on women's lives. However, most of the criticism is based on the patriarchal teachings and motifs in the ancient Asian classic texts, without looking at how these traditions actually function to oppress women in the historical context....

---

*Excerpts from Kwok Pui-lan, "The Emergence of Asian Feminist Consciousness of Culture and Theology," in *We Dare to Dream: Doing Theology as Asian Women,* ed. Virginia Fabella, M.M., and Sun Ai Lee Park (Maryknoll, NY: Orbis Books, 1990), 96-99; cf. Bosch, TM, 453-54.

Besides criticizing patriarchal traditions, Asian women theologians also look into alternative resources to construct their theology, especially those repressed elements that have been labelled as "dangerous," or "unimportant." For example, Korean women are re-examining the songs and dances in shamanism, a popular religious tradition in which women often play significant symbolic and ritualistic roles. Indian women are looking at their invaluable treasures of folk-literature and the long tradition of goddess-worship to discern their significance for today.[17] Filipino women unravel layers of colonial traditions to examine the myths and legends before the Spanish conquest.[18]

Our serious digging into women's historical, cultural, and religious resources opens our eyes to the treasures that have hitherto been unexplored by Asian theologians....

Accommodation—A Limited Approach

In the sixties, Asian theologians used the paradigm of "inculturation," "indigenization," or "accommodation" to speak of the process of re-rooting Christianity into Asian soil.[19] Although these words might have slightly different meanings, they basically connote that there is a body of theological truths to be "adapted," or "accommodated" to the Asian context. Today, Asian women theologians must point out the limitations of such an approach. First, it takes the content of the Bible and the Gospel for granted, without seriously challenging the androcentric bias both in the biblical texts and in the core symbolism of Christianity. Secondly, it identifies with Asian culture too readily, often failing to see that many Asian traditions are overtly patriarchal.

In the past several years, a new paradigm has emerged as more Asian theologians are committed to do theology with Asian resources. It is more constructive and imaginative because this time we start not from Western theology and foreign concepts, but from local and indigenous resources, folk-literature, people's history, and religious texts. C. S. Song has said, "Doing theology in Asia today is exciting because it is no longer dictated by rules and norms established elsewhere outside our living space called Asia. Its contents are not determined any more by schools and systems of theology formed under the influence of cultural elements alien to cultural experiences of Asia. Its styles—yes, one must speak of styles of doing theology—do not have to be shaped by thought-forms and life-experiences remote from Asian humanity."[20]

Innovative Styles

This approach may be more promising for Asian women's theology since it encourages us to probe into a new arena and experiment with innovative styles of doing theology. For example, we must allow the possibility of doing theology in poems, songs, stories, dances, rituals, and even lullabies. But we must insist that women's resources must be treated with equal attention, and the new theological style must reflect both male and female experiences. Secondly, the feminist critique of culture and theology, which is an important legacy from our foremothers, must be one of the most significant norms in selecting and appropriating Asian resources. Thirdly, the challenge of Asian women's theology is nothing less than the reformulation of some basic elements of Christian theology and ethics such as the relations between divine and human, monotheism and plurality of religious symbolism, between cosmological vision and social action, and between male and female in the context of the international flesh trade and sex tourism.

Remembering the past, Asian Christian women gain fresh insight into the power of history in shaping hope. Encouraged by the daring examples of our foremothers, we are more committed to the struggle for justice and sexual equality of humankind. As we embark onto a journey full of risks and possibilities, we have to create our road along the way. Our hearts are warmed by the ecumenical fellowship of women and men who are also earnestly seeking God's Kingdom on earth. Together with Third World sisters, we are developing a new way of doing theology, which not only liberates us, but the generations to come.

WALKING ON YOUR OWN CULTURAL LEGS

"Help...a people to 'stand up and walk' on their own cultural legs."

■ *Mission as inculturation presupposes cultural conflict. Cultural values, institutions, rituals, and artifacts appear almost to take on a life of their own as their adherents resist innovations. Sometimes it is those very practices that once were considered foreign that are now defended because they provide distinctiveness to a religious group amid a pluralism of cultural options. At other times the resistance to change comes from those holding political and economic power. Bishop Pedro Casaldáliga of Brazil is remarkable as a Roman Catholic who, from a position of church authority, championed the dispossessed, thereby unleashing the wrath of both wealthy landowners and politicians. Born in Barcelona, Spain, in 1928, he was brought up in a cattle-raising family. Ordained a priest in 1952, he served his first fifteen years as a priest in Spain where, through the* cursillo *movement, he came to work with Latin Americans and Africans. Sent by his Claretian order to Brazil in 1968 and chosen bishop in 1971, he championed the indigenous peoples of the Amazon amid threats of violence and murders of his co-workers in the movement.*

*The Spirit Adopts and Adapts All Cultures**

Rather than seeing the church as established and particularized in a single culture or continent, today we regard it as in a state of mission; journeying and manifold;

---

*Excerpts from Pedro Casaldáliga, *In Pursuit of the Kingdom: Writings 1968-1988* (Maryknoll, NY: Orbis Books, 1990), 143-44, 145; cf. Bosch, TM, p. 453.

changing in its expression, "catholic" like the very Spirit of Pentecost speaking all tongues.

No continent has a corner on the church of Jesus. The cradle of Christendom may be the Mediterranean, but the cradle of Christianity is Jesus Christ's own heart.

No culture has more natural affinity with the church than any other. No cultures are either Christian or anti-Christian by nature. The Spirit of truth and of life, who is the soul of the church, adopts and adapts all cultures and all persons to the gift and the demands of the Reign of God.

The church's mission is thus to act in a mediating fashion, putting these cultures and these souls in contact with the Spirit of Jesus, which is poured out through the gospel. Or better: instead of speaking of cultures and souls, we should speak of *these peoples* (with their culture, their structures, and their present period in history) and *these persons* (who live their sufferings and their hopes historically and politically)....

Mission Becoming Dialogue and Communion

Engaging in mission cannot be—as it has been all too often—a matter of bringing in and implanting an alien and colonizing culture, but must mean bringing a message. Or drawing that message out of the culture and history of the "mission country," helping each people and each person to open up to the Spirit and the Reign. And if possible to open up into church—into the community of Christian faith called together.

Hence, every mission should become dialogue and communion. Missioners engage in mission to the extent they are also missionized. As Bishop Angelelli, the apostolic martyr of La Rioja, used to say: they should have one ear on the gospel and the other on the people to whom they are sent.

And this spirit of dialogue must be an essential attitude, not an opportunistic pose. Unfortunately the church, to take one example, begins to become African only after Africa succeeds in declaring itself Africa. And very seldom has the church in Africa, the Americas, or Asia, in its structures, known how to be "indigenous" in living communion with the natives and against the interests of the invaders and what they have imposed.

Hence, today less than ever can missioners be improvising with a paternalistic superiority. They must learn to be missioners, and ultimately that can be learned only in the mission land and under the roof of the people who receive them....

Service in Dialogue and Poverty

We should bear "neither gold nor silver," neither mathematics nor English, neither technology nor antibiotics, nor Western Christian culture. (At the right time and in the appropriate measure we can handle all that too, as long as it be in the manner of the poor and without any kind of colonialism so that the means of God's Reign may be poor and free.) What we must bear, as a gratuitous and liberating gift, is what we will be able to give in a gospel spirit: to help "in the name of the

Lord Jesus" a village, a tribe, a people, to "stand up and walk" on their own cultural legs, walking determinedly their own road, although in the direction of the Reign of God.

This missionary attitude that I have called essential obviously assumes a radical gospel poverty. Only the poor can engage in mission, without colonizing interference, without outside dependency, without cultural or ecclesiastical ethnocentrism. Only they can be sent, and the greater their abnegation, the more trustworthy they are. Completely at the disposal of the One who sends them and of the people to whom they are sent.

Mission is a service, in dialogue and poverty.

NOTES

1. Robert Schreiter, *Constructing Local Theologies* (Maryknoll, NY: Orbis Books, 1985), p. 5.

2. Cf. "Venn," in *CDCWM,* p. 636, and Wilbert R. Shenk, *Henry Venn—Missionary Statesman* (Maryknoll, NY: Orbis Books, 1983).

3. 10 G/AZI/1, no. 116, July 9, 1861. This Minute was submitted to the society's missionaries and managing committees—not by way of positive instructions, but to direct attention to a matter of great and increasing importance.

4. Horst Rzepkowski, *Lexikon der Mission* (1992), pp. 402-03.

5. Compare Grentrup, *Jus Missionarium* (Brussels: L'Edition Universelle, 1925), p. 17.

6. The sacred congregation of Cardinals *de propaganda fide,* commonly called the Propaganda, was established by Pope Gregory XV in 1622 to guard, direct, and promote foreign missions.

7. Concerning the struggle against unchastity on the mission field, compare *Düsseldorfer Kursus* (Aachen, 1920), pp. 60ff.; *Zeitschrift für Missionswissenschaft* (1914), 81; against superstition, *Düsseldorfer Kursus,* pp. 83ff.

8. *De procuranda salute omnium gentium* (Cologne, 1640), I, 7, ch. 7, 503.

9. Propaganda, *Instructiones Missionum,* Coll. I, 795.

10. Coll. II, 1465.

11. Coll. I, 425, 4ff.

12. Among others, Juan de Lugo (1583-1660), Charles Borromeo (1538-1584), Francis de Sales (1567-1622), and Francisco Suárez (1548-1617).

13. The Propaganda at this point prohibited the use of greater severity against the Chinese than that employed against other Christians, but also recommended to the missionaries "to give milk before solid food."

14. Cf. Josephine Strode and Pauline R. Strode, *Social Skills and Case Work* (New York: Harper and Brothers, 1942), pp. 21-28.

15. Cf. Charles H. Kraft, "Cultural Concomitants of Higi Conversion: Early Period," *Missiology* 4:2 (Oct. 1976): 431-42.

16. Cf. Ferm, *Profiles in Liberation,* pp. 96-101.

17. The Asian Women's Resource Centre for Culture and Theology convened a consultation on Goddesses and Asian women's theology in the fall of 1988. The papers will be published in a forthcoming issue of *In God's Image.* This quarterly journal is available by writing to the Asian Women's Resource Centre at 35 ChungChongno 2-Ga, Sodaemun-Ku, ChungChongno, P.O. Box 16, Seoul, 120-650, Korea.

18. Mary John Mananzan, "The Filipino Woman: Before and After the Spanish

Conquest of the Philippines," in *Essays on Women,* ed. Mary John Mananzan (Manila: St. Scholastica's College, 1987), pp. 7-36.

19. For example, Kosuke Koyama, *Theology in Contact* (Madras: Christian Literature Society, 1975), pp. 54-69; and Aloysius Chang, "The Inculturation of Theology in the Chinese Church," *Gregorianum* 63/1 (1982): 5-59.

20. C. S. Song, "Let Us Do Theology with Asian Resources!" *East Asia Journal of Theology* 3/2 (1985): 207-08.

13

Mission as Common Witness

What shall future historians find distinctive about the church of the twentieth century? Will they agree with William Temple who, at his enthronement as Archbishop of Canterbury in 1942, celebrated worldwide Christianity as "the great new fact of our time"? Will they label it the "ecumenical" century of the church? Christian mission has had a vital place in both of these transformations.

Our first five selections in this chapter represent important milestones in what David Bosch calls "the (re)birth of the ecumenical idea in mission" (TM, 457). The World Missionary Conference, held in 1910 at Edinburgh, Scotland, was the cradle of modern ecumenism. Out of it grew the movements for Faith and Order, and Life and Work, which were to merge to form the World Council of Churches in 1948, and the International Missionary Council (IMC), which became the mission and evangelism arm of the WCC in 1961. Convinced that God was calling them to world evangelization, the Edinburgh delegates saw church divisions as a mission weakness and unity in mission as a divine imperative. At the first World Conference on Faith and Order in 1927, V. S. Azariah of India was a prophetic voice, pointing out that church divisions thwart the witness to non-Christians and calling for one united church in India. The impact of Azariah's charge can be seen in the closing statement of the Lausanne 1927 conference, which acknowledged that the imperative for unity on the mission field had awakened the delegates to the scandal of Christian disunity. At the first meeting of the WCC's Central Committee in Rollé, Switzerland, in 1951, the term apostolicity *was introduced to express the biblical basis for the interrelationship between unity and mission. In a volume of his* Church Dogmatics *on reconciliation, Karl Barth gave an optimistic assessment of ecumenical initiatives by the churches.*

During the same period, Roman Catholics grew in ecumenical vision, with Vatican II as the catalyst. Nostra Aetate, *the Decree on Ecumenism, includes both a strong statement on the scandal of division "which contradicts the will of Christ" and a call "for the restoration of unity among all Christians." The WCC\Vatican joint working group on Common Witness, established at the close of Vatican II in 1965, shared findings concerning initiatives from around the world. They found that the impulse for common witness comes from awareness of our common communion with Christ and our openness to renewal in the power of the spirit. Mary Motte, a Catholic participant, goes further. She believes that common witness* *is "an essential element in the shaping of mission for the future" as Catholics and Protestants share human suffering in solidarity, and are renewed through common prayer and eucharist.*

As the selection from V. S. Azariah attests, the torch for Christian unity in mission, carried by missionaries in earlier years, has passed now to the people's leaders on every continent. The public image of Latin American Christianity has often been that of sectarian divisions, especially among Protestants. John Mackay of Princeton Theological Seminary, out of a lifetime of engagement in mission in Latin America, suggests building blocks for a distinctive Latin American ecumenism based on Hispanic spirit and tradition. Kosuke Koyama, one of Asia's most creative theologians, develops the household (oikos) *as both a biblical and contemporary Asian image for ecumenical openness. Gabriel Setiloane of South Africa likens African-style ecumenism to the extended family in which life together is acclaimed, revered, and celebrated despite doctrinal differences.*

CHRISTIAN UNITY IN MISSION

"The churches in the mission field may lead the way to unity."

■ *The 1910 World Missionary Conference at Edinburgh, Scotland, was a watershed event in ecumenical cooperation. Larger missionary conferences had been held earlier (e.g., London 1888 and New York 1900), but they were regional gatherings of interested individuals. Edinburgh was the first world missionary conference of delegates representing missionary societies. Thus it provided a new model for ecumenical conciliar cooperation that spawned three movements (Faith and Order, Life and Work, and the International Missionary Council) which were to come together in the World Council of Churches in 1948 and 1961. "Co-operation and the Promotion of Unity" was the theme of one of the preparatory commissions for Edinburgh. The following excerpts from its conclusions show that sense of concern by mission leaders that Christian divisions are a major mission weakness.*

*Divisions a Mission Weakness**

It is more than ever incumbent on the Christian Church to realise its responsibility to carry the Gospel to the lands which are now open to receive it, and to guide the awakening nations to God in Christ. For the accomplishment of this overwhelming task it seems essential that the Christian Church should present a united front. Its divisions are a source of weakness and impair the effectiveness of its testimony to the one Gospel of the Son of God which it professes. The issues are so great that

---

*Excerpts from *World Missionary Conference 1910* (Edinburgh and London: World Missionary Conference, 1910), 8: 132-39; cf. Bosch, TM, 458.

there can be no trifling in the matter. The evangelisation of nations, the Christianising of empires and kingdoms, is the object before us. The work has to be done now. It is urgent and must be pressed forward at once. The enterprise calls for the highest quality of statesmanship, and for the maximum efficiency in all departments of the work. It is not surprising that those who are in the front of this great conflict, and on whose minds and souls the gravity of the issues presses most immediately, should be the first to recognise the need for concerted action and closer fellowship....

Both Unity and Diversity?

How is it possible to attain that unity for which our Lord prayed, and yet to leave free play for the diversity which alone will give to the unity comprehension and life? How shall we at once give free recognition to our [brothers and sisters] who are with us in Christ, and yet refrain from compromising what we cannot surrender without disloyalty? How can we escape on the one hand the danger of insisting on some point with regard to which there should be liberty, and of thereby hindering the attainment of the unity that is so essential to the spread of the Gospel in the non-Christian world; or on the other hand the danger of failing to give to the Church in the mission field those views of truth which in the great strain that is coming upon it will enlarge and enrich and nourish its life? How can we help to lay the foundations of a Church that shall have its roots deeply planted in the national life, and which at the same time will not be so exclusively national in spirit as to forget its place and membership in the Church Universal? As a wise writer has said: "It is easy to be moderate and cool. It is easy to be ignorant and passionate. But to be wise and yet extravagant, to measure all and yet venture all, this is not easy."

Penitence and Prayer

It is evident that the growth of the Christian Church in Japan and China and India and Africa is producing a profound change in the religious situation, and is presenting problems of great complexity and gravity....The world has become a unity; and the nations once afar off have now, owing to improved communications, become our neighbours. The Churches in the mission field may lead the way to unity; but they cannot move far and move safely without the co-operation of the Church at home. The great issues which confront us in the modern situation are the concern of the whole Church of Christ; and the spiritual resources of the whole Church will be required to deal with them. The solution of problems so complex and difficult, and so vitally related to the advancement of the Kingdom of Christ, can be attempted only in a spirit of penitence and of prayer. Penitence is due for the arrogance of the past and for the lack of sympathy and of insight by which all of us have helped to create and perpetuate a situation that retards so seriously the advancement of Christ's Kingdom. Most of all do we need to lament that we carry about with us so small a sense of the harm that is wrought by our divisions, and so little pain for our lack of charity. Prayer is needed, because human wisdom can discern no remedy for the situation. Unity when it comes must be something richer, grander, more comprehensive than anything which we can see at present. It is something into which and up to which we must grow, something of which and for which we must become worthy. We need to have sufficient faith in God to believe that He can bring us to something higher and more Christlike than anything to which at present we see a way.

WE MUST HAVE ONE CHURCH!

"The divisions of Christendom ...are a sin and a scandal."

■ *The first World Conference on Faith and Order took place in Lausanne, Switzerland, in 1927. Over 400 participants, representing 127 Orthodox, Anglican, Reformation, and Free churches, assembled under the leadership of Episcopal Bishop Charles H. Brent of New York. Most participants came from Europe and North America. They accepted the long-standing viewpoint that denominational divisions are unchangeable historical realities. At Lausanne, however, a prophetic voice was heard out of Asia. Vedanayagam Samuel Azariah (1874-1945) had served as a YMCA secretary in India, and co-founded the Indian Missionary Society of Tinnevelly in 1903. At Edinburgh in 1910, he strongly criticized the unequal partnership between western missionaries and their indigenous colleagues. Consecrated bishop of Dornakal in 1912, the first native Anglican bishop in India, he became a champion of ecumenism and of that passion for organic union which resulted in the formation of the Church of South India in 1947. At Lausanne in 1927, he spoke eloquently of the scandal of Christian disunity in his sermon on "The Necessity of Christian Unity for the Missionary Enterprise of the Church."*

*The Necessity of Christian Unity**

Our Lord's prayer for unity was based on the one plea "that the world may believe that thou didst send me." The revelation of God in Christ, says our Lord, would only be recognised and acknowledged by the world when it sees visibly before it an exhibition of unity which will be after the pattern of the divine unity. In this world of strife and conflict, unity is so rare and so uncommon that when it is seen in the Church the world will recognise it as supernatural and coming from God Himself. We shall now consider some reasons why unity is necessary for the missionary enterprise of the world.

---

*Excerpts from Lausanne 1927, *Faith and Order: Proceedings of the World Conference...*, ed. H. N. Bate (Garden City, NY: Doubleday, Doran & Co., 1928), 492-95; cf. Bosch, TM, 461.

Unity Is Necessary in View of the World Opportunities Open before the Church Today

After nineteen centuries of Christianity, two-thirds of the world's population still remain outside the Church. In India alone we reckon that at least one hundred millions of the people, or a third of the population, are beyond the reach of existing missionary organisations. China with its four hundred millions has even a sadder story to tell. Africa with two hundred millions is not Christian yet. Moreover, the world is open today to the Gospel as it was in no previous generation.

And yet, with these world opportunities before it, the Church is feeble, its missionary work everywhere is under-manned, and its resources pitifully inadequate for this world-task. The Church is feeble because it is divided. It has been confidently asserted that if only the Church were one, at home and abroad, we have now at our disposal all the resources in [personnel] and money required to evangelise the whole world in our generation.

You know better than myself the wastage of Christian forces in the home lands. An Indian visitor is often saddened by seeing in some places churches built and ministers appointed, not to meet the needs of enlarged membership, but to have different denominations represented in the same locality. Such a multiplication of churches in the same area renders church discipline exceedingly difficult and ineffective. By our divisions, we not only waste our resources, but also diminish the Church's effectiveness for righteousness and purity in non-Christian lands. Unity, organic unity, is the only remedy.

A Common Witness before the Non-Christian World

Where the Gospel has entered in, the divisions in the Church cause the non-Christian to stumble. Thinking [persons] ask why, while claiming loyalty to the one Christ, we still worship separately, we still show exclusiveness in the most sacred acts of our religion. The divisions confuse the thoughtful enquirer. "Which church shall I join?" is often asked by such a convert. There have been many such "little ones of Christ" who have been caused to stumble by our divisions. Then again, hundreds of men [and women] in India today are hesitating to acknowledge Jesus as Lord and God because of the demands He is making upon them to break caste by entering into the fellowship of all believers for service in India. And the Church cannot speak with a united voice; its witness is confused by contrary voices; [persons] are not certain of their duty, and their consciences are not touched by the united authority of the One Church. We are unable in our divided state to give an authoritative call to repentance, faith and baptism. This confirms [others] in their doubt and hesitation, and weakens their will for the sacrifice which Christ demands. To present a common front and preach a common faith to the non-Christian world *we must be one.*

For the Life of the Church in Mission

The divisions of Christendom do not appeal to the Christians in these lands. Christians in India, for instance, did not have a share in creating them. They entered into this ready-made system, and it has not really taken hold of them....

We must have one Church. We want a Church of India, a Church which can be our spiritual home, a Church where the Indian religious genius can find natural expression, a living branch of the Holy, Catholic and Apostolic Church, a Church which, being a visible symbol in that divided land, will draw all [persons] to our blessed Lord....

Unity may be theoretically a desirable ideal in Europe and America, but it is vital to the life of the Church in the mission field. The divisions of Christendom may be a source of weakness in Christian countries, but in non-Christian lands they are a sin and a scandal.

GOD WILLS UNITY

"Labour, in penitence and faith, to build up our broken walls."

■ *Bishop Azariah's sermon at Lausanne did not fall on deaf ears. But what was the nature of Christian unity to be sought? Some North American delegates hoped that the conference would achieve a plan for a united church before it dispersed. In contrast, Orthodox delegates abstained from voting on most Lausanne reports because they contained references to reunion and a united church. Nevertheless, by unanimous vote, the conference was able to approve the following closing statement entitled "The Call to Unity" prepared by the officers of the conference and the chairpersons and secretaries of the six sections.*

*The Call to Unity**

God wills unity. Our presence in this Conference bears testimony to our desire to bend our wills to His. However we may justify the beginnings of disunion, we lament its continuance and henceforth must labour, in penitence and faith, to build up our broken walls.

God's Spirit has been in the midst of us. It was He who called us hither. His presence has been manifest in our worship, our deliberations and our whole fellowship. He has discovered us to one another. He has enlarged our horizons, quickened our understanding, and enlivened our hope. We have dared and God has justified our daring. We can never be the same again. Our deep thankfulness must

---

*Excerpts from Lausanne 1927, *Faith and Order: Proceedings of the World Conference....*, ed. H. N. Bate (Garden City, NY: Doubleday, Doran & Co., 1928), 460-61; cf. Bosch, TM, 461.

find expression in sustained endeavour to share the visions vouchsafed us here with those smaller home groups where our lot is cast.

More than half of the world is waiting for the Gospel. At home and abroad sad multitudes are turning away in bewilderment from the Church because of its corporate feebleness. Our missions count that as a necessity which we are inclined to look on as a luxury. Already the mission field is impatiently revolting from the divisions of the Western Church to make bold adventure for unity in its own right. We of the Churches represented in this Conference cannot allow our spiritual children to outpace us. We with them must gird ourselves to the task, the early beginnings of which God has so richly blessed, and labour side by side until our common goal is reached.

Some of us, pioneers in this undertaking, have grown old in our search for unity. It is to youth that we look to lift the torch on high. We men have carried it too much alone through many years. The women henceforth should be accorded their share of responsibility. And so the whole Church will be enabled to do that which no section can hope to perform.

It was God's clear call that gathered us. With faith stimulated by His guidance to us here, we move forward.

CHRIST ENJOINS BOTH UNITY AND MISSION

> "Every attempt to separate [mission and unity] violates the wholeness of Christ's ministry to the world."

■ *"Can we remain divided?" The World Council of Churches raised this question at its inaugural assembly (Amsterdam 1948). In its report on "The Church's Witness to God's Design," we find the statement: "If we take seriously our world-wide task, we are certain to be driven to think again of our divisions."*[1] *It was the WCC's Central Committee which issued a clarifying statement on "The calling of the Church to mission and to unity" at its 1951 meeting at Rolle. For the first time, it used the term* apostolicity *to express the biblical basis for the interrelationship between unity and mission. For the council, unity and mission both rest upon the completed work of Christ in Christ's cross, resurrection, and* parousia. *Every attempt to separate these two tasks violates a wholeness in ministry to the world that Christ initiated.*[2]

*The Biblical Basis for the Church's Unity and Apostolicity**

The division in our thought and practice between "Church" and "Mission" can be overcome only as we return to Christ Himself, in Whom the Church has its being and its task, and to a fresh understanding of what He has done, is doing, and will

---

*Excerpts from World Council of Churches, *The First Six Years, 1948-1954* (Geneva: WCC, 1954), 126-27; cf. Bosch, TM, 459.

do. God's eternal purpose is to "sum up all things in Christ." According to this purpose He has reconciled us to Himself and to one another through the Cross and has built us together to be a habitation of God in the Spirit. In reconciling us to Himself in Christ He has at the same time made us His ambassadors beseeching others to be reconciled to Him. He has made us members in the body of Christ, and that means that we are both members one of another and also committed thereby to partnership in His redeeming mission.

Christ's Redeeming Work

In more detail we may say that the Church's unity and apostolicity rests upon the whole redeeming work of Christ—past, present and future.

(a) It rests upon His finished work upon the Cross. He has wrought the atonement between [humanity] and God—an atonement for the whole human race. As we receive the reconciliation we are both reconciled to one another, and also constrained by His love to bring all men [and women] the good news of reconciliation.

(b) It rests upon His continuing work as the risen Lord Who, having conquered sin and death, sits at God's right hand, and by His spirit communicates to us His own fulness. By His spirit we are joined as members in His body, committed to His redemptive mission. We are enabled to abide in Him, and so to bear fruit. We are given power to be His witnesses to all the nations and to gather together peoples of all races and tongues.

(c) It rests upon His promise that He will come again. In His final victory the kingdoms of the world will be His, there will be one flock as there is one Shepherd, and all things will be summed up in Him. But first the Gospel of the Kingdom is to be preached throughout the whole world. In His mercy He gives us time and strength to fulfil this task.

Mission and Unity Are Indissolubly Connected

Thus the obligation to take the Gospel to the whole world, and the obligation to draw all Christ's people together, both rest upon Christ's whole work, and are indissolubly connected. Every attempt to separate these two tasks violates the wholeness of Christ's ministry to the world. Both of them are, in the strict sense of the word, essential to the being of the Church and the fulfillment of its function as the Body of Christ.

CHRISTIAN UNITY AND POLITICAL UNITY

"The Church ...is quite a few steps ahead of the world."

■ *Karl Barth (1886-1968), the noted Swiss Protestant theologian, was an active participant in the ecumenical movement and molder of ecumenical thought concerning mission and union. Barth hailed the movement that began at Edinburgh as a fundamental ecclesiological breakthrough. At Amsterdam, he inverted the theme to read, "God's Design and Man's Disorder," thereby giving it the characteristic Barthian emphasis on God's sovereignty. In the excerpt below from the volume of his* Church Dogmatics *on the doctrine of reconciliation, Barth gives an optimistic assessment of recent ecumenical initiatives by the churches. Later, at the time of the WCC's Fourth Assembly (Uppsala 1968), he addressed a local congregation in Basel and asserted: "Anyone who says 'Yes' to Christ must say 'No' to the division of the churches."*[3]

*Strivings for Unity**

The ecumenical conception, namely, the conception of the unity of the churches in the one Church of Jesus Christ, and the desire and striving for this unity, have not merely been latently present in the modern period from the very outset, but have visibly and palpably increased in strength....

Today, if not earlier, the meaning of the Church's strivings for unity has clearly come to be found in this turning of the Church to the world which has so remarkably accompanied the turning of the world from the Church, and which we have had occasion to notice from all the various aspects previously considered. In themselves and as such the Church's attempts at unity would not be a particularly interesting or relevant phenomenon. The practical or in the more general sense missionary teleology and dynamic with which they have been pressed forward so energetically during the last hundred years, and particularly in the last decades, force themselves upon our attention. It is no accident that what is denoted by the peculiar English word "evangelism" seems latterly to have become the focal point of ecumenical interest. Here, too, there is no cause for unrealistic optimism. We are only at the very beginnings, laboriously made and quickly passing. On the other hand, there is no cause for a skepticism which will not recognise these beginnings as such. Certainly, in relation to speech and action undertaken in common with a respect for that which is distinctive yet an avoidance of that which separates, we have no grounds whatever to say that the Church lags far behind advances long since made by the world. In this field it is obvious that it has seized the initiative, that it is quite a few steps ahead of the world and can be an example to it.

LATIN AMERICAN ECUMENISM

> "There is a native ecumenical quality in the Hispanic spirit and tradition."

■ *John Alexander Mackay (1889-1983), a contemporary of Barth, also spoke out of the Reformed wing of Protestantism in support of both mission and unity. Born in Inverness, Scotland, he ministered as a Presbyterian missionary in Peru, as*

---

*Excerpts from Karl Barth, *Church Dogmatics,* vol. IV, 3, 1, *The Doctrine of Reconciliation* (Edinburgh: T. & T. Clark, 1961), 35, 37-38; cf. Bosch, TM, 459.

a YMCA secretary in Uruguay and Mexico, and as secretary for Latin America and Africa of the Foreign Mission board of the Presbyterian Church in the USA. From 1932 to 1959, he served as professor of ecumenics and president of Princeton Theological Seminary. In ecumenical leadership, he chaired the IMC (1947-1957), the Amsterdam Assembly's Commission on "The Church's Witness to God's Design," served on the WCC's Central Committee, and chaired the joint committee of the IMC and WCC, as well as being President of the World Presbyterian Alliance (1954-59). In the passage below, Mackay contributes to the ecumenical vision a lost Hispanic tradition, thereby providing hope for ecumenism among Latin America's oft-divided Christians.

*A Great Lost Tradition in Hispanic Christianity**

It is profoundly significant that Protestant Christians in the Southern continent prefer to call themselves "Evangelicals," rather than "Protestants." It is not that they are unaware of the theological implications and historical witness of Protestantism, or that they are ashamed of being known as Protestants. Their preference, however, for being known as "Evangelicos" is twofold. In the first place, the associations which many years ago became attached to the term "Protestant" in religious and cultural circles in the Hispanic world, tended to be of a purely negative and derogatory character. In the second place, it was easier for Latin American Protestants to render positive and meaningful witness in their environment if the name they bore did not appear to suggest mere protest or dissent, but affirmed positively the truth for which they stood, a truth which constitutes the very core of the Christian religion. By adopting, therefore, the generic term "Evangelicos" to describe themselves, they were in fact quietly proclaiming that devotion to the Gospel, which centers in Christ and is the main theme of the Bible, is what makes people truly Christian across all denominational boundaries. They were in effect setting personal obedience to Christ and the Gospel over and above nominal unreflective membership in an institution called the Church.

Thus quietly, instinctively, and in no controversial spirit, Latin American Protestants, unknown to themselves, became heirs of a great lost tradition in Hispanic Christianity. That tradition was profoundly evangelical in character. It transformed the lives, and inspired the thinking, of many of the greatest men and women in Spain during the Sixteenth Century, which was Spain's Golden Age (*Siglo de Oro*). At the heart of this Hispanic evangelical tradition were Theresa of Avila, John of the Cross and Luis de Leon, the brothers Juan and Alfonso Valdes, Casiodoro de Reina and Cipriano de Valera. It is a fact of history that in the Iberian Peninsula in the Sixteenth Century there was a larger total of men and women, and among them a proportionally larger number of eminent figures, who were profoundly "Evangelical" in their theology and religious life, than there were at that time in any other

---

*Excerpt from John A. Mackay, *The Latin American Churches and the Ecumenical Movement* (New York: NCCUSA, 1963), 22-25; cf. Bosch, TM, 461.

country in Europe. Unhappily, however, the unfavorable political situation and the extreme violence of the Inquisition quenched the evangelical flame in that decisive period of Spanish history. Yet today in the American daughter lands of Spain and Portugal that flame is burning bright. In the mother lands themselves it is also still aglow, while the torch bearers wait the sunrise of their liberation which is coming fast.

In the meantime, Latin American Evangelicals become increasingly aware that they are not aliens or intruders in the Spanish religious tradition but rather heirs of a long lost and largely forgotten heritage....

Native Ecumenicalism

What could be more genuinely ecumenical than to set the Gospel, the "Evangel," in the forefront of thought and life? For let there be no mistake about this. In any movement worthy of the name ecumenical, what must come first, biblically and theologically, is the Gospel of Christ, which alone brings health in the deepest and widest sense. To be evangelical, to be centered in the Gospel, must always, therefore, have the primacy in responsible ecumenical circles, both in the Americas and in the world. For that reason, in everything pertaining to Christian unity, "evangelical" must ever be given the preeminence even over the classical designation "catholic." For unless Christian Churches are "evangelical" the fact that they claim to be "catholic" need have no more than empty institutional significance. First evangelical, then catholic. That is the divine order. It must also be the order in any movement that purports to be "ecumenical."

It is my profound conviction that, just as there is a native ecumenical quality in the Hispanic spirit and tradition, Latin American Protestantism, when left to develop freely, without the intrusion of sectarian influences from the outside, will show itself to be gloriously ecumenical. While it is true that there is a strong individualism in the Latin American soul, it is equally true that it possesses a marvelous sense of wholeness. This sense of wholeness has shown itself historically in the traditional Latin American attitude towards cultural universalism and political internationalism. In Latin America there is greater interest in what is world-wide than in what is purely hemispheric, more concern about Humanity than about Latinity.

RESTORING CHRISTIAN UNITY

> "Division openly contradicts the will of Christ, scandalizes the world."

■ *When Pope John XXIII announced on January 25, 1959, his intention to call an ecumenical council, he wanted it to be for the whole church. Vatican II's Decree on Ecumenism was close to his heart, and he lived to read the first draft and to commend it to council participants for further study. The final version retains his deep concern over the scandal of Christian disunity which openly contradicts the will of Christ and provides a stumbling block to those outside the community of faith.*

The Scandal of Division*

The restoration of unity among all Christians is one of the principal concerns of the Second Vatican Council. Christ the Lord founded one Church and one Church only. However, many Christian communions present themselves to [persons] as the true inheritors of Jesus Christ; all indeed profess to be followers of the Lord but they differ in mind and go their different ways, as if Christ himself were divided (cf. 1 Cor. 1:13). Certainly, such division openly contradicts the will of Christ, scandalizes the world, and damages that most holy cause, the preaching of the Gospel to every creature.

The Lord of Ages nevertheless wisely and patiently follows out the plan of his grace on our behalf, sinners that we are. In recent times he has begun to bestow more generously upon divided Christians remorse over their divisions and longing for unity.

A Movement to Restore Unity

Everywhere large numbers have felt the impulse of this grace, and among our separated [brothers and sisters] also there increases from day to day a movement, fostered by the grace of the Holy Spirit, for the restoration of unity among all Christians. Taking part in this movement, which is called ecumenical, are those who invoke the Triune God and confess Jesus as Lord and Saviour. They do this not merely as individuals but also as members of the corporate groups in which they have heard the Gospel, and which each regards as his Church and indeed, God's. And yet, almost everyone, though in different ways, longs for the one visible Church of God, a Church truly universal and sent forth to the whole world that the world may be converted to the Gospel and so be saved, to the glory of God.

COMMON WITNESS FOR RENEWAL AND MISSION

"Common witness is the essential calling of the Church."

■ *Among the windows opened by Vatican II was that of ecumenical dialogue. In 1965, a Joint Working Group was established between the WCC and the Roman Catholic Church. During the 1975-1983 period, it concentrated its work around three priority areas: "The Unity of the Church—the Goal and the Way," "Common Witness," and "Social Collaboration." After several years of collecting reports from churches around the world concerning new initiatives in common witness, it issued a 1980 study guide under that title. In it the JWG*

---

*Excerpts from "Unitatis Redintegratio" (1964), Art. 1, in *VC2,* 452; cf. Bosch, TM, 462.

affirmed that the impulse for common witness comes from awareness of our common communion with Christ and our openness to renewal in the power of the Spirit.

*New Initiatives**

All over the world Christians and churches have been increasingly able to give common witness. Formal theological dialogue about unity and the ways to overcome the existing divisions can record notable progress. At the same time the differences of many centuries are not quickly overcome and a good deal remains to be done before Christians reach the point where they are able to make a common confession of faith. Still it is already possible to point to many kinds of experience which have a positive potential for common witness in spite of ambiguities, difficulties, obstacles.

The impulse to a common witness comes not from any strategy but from the personal and community experience of Jesus Christ. Awareness of the communion with Christ and with each other generates the dynamism that impels Christians to give a visible witness together....

Renewal for Witness

The Holy Spirit constantly renews Christians and their communities in their relation to Christ. *This renewal centres in Christ and calls forth a new obedience and a new way of life which is itself a witnessing communion.* The Spirit invites each Christian community to conversion so that it may participate responsibly in the plan of salvation. It is a continuing conversion which renews the commitment of the individual and the community to Christ.[4] A common renewal requires openness to the Spirit who works in us teaching us in an evolving world to seek clear ways of expressing our faith, ways marked by our mutual love for each other (Jn. 15:17)....

Effects of Witness

Witness moves from one unity to another—from that of the members of the Body of Christ in the one Spirit to the greater unity in which all things in heaven and earth will come together under the one Head who is Christ (Eph. 1:10). Essentially it is a work of reconciliation, of people with God, and with one another. To take part in Christian witness also deepens the unity that already exists among Christians. *Witness tends always to extend the fellowship of the Spirit, creating new community.* At the same time it is an essential help for Christians themselves. It

---

*Excerpts from *Common Witness: a study document of the Joint Working Group of the Roman Catholic Church and the World Council of Churches* (Geneva: WCC, 1982), 1, 13, 28, 30; cf. Bosch, TM, 462.

promotes among them the conversion and renewal which they always need. It can strengthen their faith and open up new aspects of the truth of Christ. As such it is a fundamental part of the life of the community that is fully committed to Christ....

Common Witness

When he prayed that all be one so the world might believe (Jn. 17:21), Jesus made a clear connection between unity of the Church and the acceptance of the Gospel. Unhappily Christians are still divided in their churches and the testimony they give to the Gospel is thus weakened. There are, however, even now many signs of the initial unity that already exists among all followers of Christ and indications that it is developing in important ways. *What we have in common, and the hope that is in us, enable us to be bold in proclaiming the Gospel and trustful that the world will receive it.* Common witness is the essential calling of the Church and in an especial way it responds to the spirit of this ecumenical age in the Church's life. It expresses our actual unity and increases our service to God's Word, strengthening the churches both in proclaiming the Gospel and in seeking for the fulness of unity.

AN ECUMENICAL DIALOGUE OF CULTURES

> "Cultures ultimately meet in the light of Jesus Christ crucified and risen."

■ *Kosuke Koyama (b. 1929) is one of Asia's best-known and most creative theologians. Born in Tokyo, he received his theological education at Tokyo Union Theological Seminary and Drew and Princeton universities in the United States. A pioneer Third World missionary, he was ordained to the ministry of the United Church of Christ in Thailand in 1961. In* Waterbuffalo Theology *(1974),* No Handle on the Cross *(1977),* Three Mile an Hour God *(1980), and* Mount Fuji and Mount Sinai *(1985), Koyama developed understandings of God, humanity, the church, and mission out of the cultural realities of Asia. After fifteen years (1960-1974) as a theological educator in Southeast Asia, he taught theology in New Zealand (1974-1979) and, since 1980, as professor of ecumenics and world Christianity at Union Theological Seminary in New York City. In the following passage, Koyama develops the household (Greek* oikos) *imagery as important in the dialogue of cultures concerning ecumenism.*

*Cultures Meet in Christ**

Cultures, like languages, function in an amazing global network of interpenetration. Indeed, there is no such thing as an isolated culture. Japanese culture, for

---

*Excerpts from Kosuke Koyama, "The Ecumenical Movement as the Dialogue of Cultures," in *Faith and Faithfulness: Essays on Contemporary Ecumenical Themes,* ed. Pauline Webb (Geneva: WCC, 1984), 40, 40-42; cf. Bosch, TM, 463.

instance, is a complex mixture of a number of eastern and western cultures. In the ecumenical movement cultures ultimately meet in the light of Jesus Christ crucified and risen....

Ecumenical Openness

I remember a night I spent in a small hut in the hill country of Bali. The bamboo ceiling was in a form which suggested cosmic symmetry and balance. I remember another night I spent in a Maori meeting house (*marae*) in New Zealand. A Maori elder told us that we (some 70 of us) were going to have a good night's sleep together inside their ancestor. "Do you see that beam?" he said. "That is the backbone of our ancestor...." It is a good thing to sleep with the feeling of being embraced by the harmonious cosmos or protected by the strong backbone of the ancestors.

During the war our Japanese leaders told us that no American bombers could invade the Tokyo sky because here we had "the palace of the divine emperor, the palace of the divine emperor, the palace of the divine emperor"! The American B29s came in their thousands and utterly destroyed the city. Night after night I was awakened to flee to the bomb shelter. I prefer the cosmic culture of harmony and the company of ancestors to the contrived and forced ideological culture of "the palace of the divine emperor."

The word "oikoumene" is related to the word *oikos,* meaning house. The theology of oikoumene challenges us to see the whole world as the house of God. In the words of Philip Potter, the ecumenical movement is "the means by which the churches which form the house, the *oikos* of God, are seeking so to live and witness before all peoples that the whole oikoumene may become the oikos of God through the crucified and risen Christ in the power of the life-giving Spirit."[5]

This house is different from a comforting cosmological or ancestral house. It is also different from the house of the destructive ideology of the emperor worship. It is different from all the various manifestations of the house of bondage (Ex. 20:2). The house of God is different from all these, but that does not mean it is unrelated to these other houses.

T. V. Philip speaks about "our first-hand experience of Jesus in Asia" and writes: "I remember going to the famous Kali temple once. A great crowd was there seeking *darsan* (sight) of the deity, weighed down with their burden of sin and guilt. Next to the Kali temple is Mother Teresa's home where people who are old and sick and dying are looked after and cared for. Close by is the Hare Krishna centre where people chant and sing with abandon."[6] Mother Teresa's home is not isolated from other houses. It does not stand alone. The most fundamental thing which can be said about her house is that it is built "through the crucified and risen Christ," and that it stands between the temples of Kali and Krishna. The ecumenical movement (good-house-keeping movement) finds its theological basis for the programmes to combat racism, militarism and economic exploitation in the crucified and risen Christ.

A "house" is a space we make for ourselves to create and to express our human sense of purpose and meaning. It expresses human meaning through architectural design (our image of the cosmos), by the way we arrange various items of furniture (our cultural life), and by the kind of spirituality with which we live (our religious life) in this arranged space. In the house (in this inhabited world) we eat, reproduce, impart and acquire education, communicate and debate politics and "gods." "Oikos," then, represents a rich and busy cultural space, though it could be the house of freedom (creation) or the house of bondage (destruction). The ecumenical movement is called to witness to the crucified and risen Lord within this human house and to proclaim the coming of redemption to this human house (Mk. 1:15; Lk. 11:20).

The house of God is not a finished and closed house. It is being built upon the corner-stone which is Christ. "...like living stones be yourselves constantly built into a spiritual house..." (1 Pet. 2:5)—this concept of the house of God suggests that the creative act of God continues from the beginning to the end of time. If the work of creation continues, then there must be a creative openness in history. The great population centres of Sodom and Nineveh (Tokyo, Sydney, London, Moscow, New York, Shanghai...) are called upon to repent before the coming of the judgment of God. The grace of an open future touches them and their cultures (Gen. 18:22-33; Jon. 3:6-9). This sincere openness derives from the dependability of the corner-stone of the house (1 Pet. 2:6). Into this house peoples of all languages and cultures are invited to come. Without that invitation what is the meaning of the continuous creation of God? No ecumenical movement can come from a closed God. There is no grace in a closed God.

ECUMENISM, AFRICAN STYLE

> "Other forces at work in the African soul...reduce the dividedness of the church."

■ *"I am essentially African," wrote Gabriel Setiloane of South Africa. "My ethnic roots are in Tswanaland. That is where my life is.... I have Methodist roots that go back longer than 167 years. Fully African, fully Methodist; that is who I am."*[7] *An ordained Methodist minister, Dr. Setiloane received his university education in three countries (South Africa, the United States, and Great Britain) on three continents. His dissertation,* Image of God Among the Sotho-Tswana *(1976), is a movement from the basically religious life of his own people to a reassessment of their Christian beliefs and practices in faith, rather than an indigenization of "western" Christianity for Africa. After leadership as youth secretary of the All Africa Conference of Churches, he moved into theological education, first at the University of Botswana, Lesotho & Swaziland, and currently at the University of Cape Town. In the following passage he advocates a distinctively African style of ecumenism.*

*Ecumenism, African Style**

For many the most important goal of the ecumenical movement is the attainment of unity despite doctrinal differences. For this reason the few achievements of unity are acclaimed and revered. In the minds of many forward-looking missionary planners the Church of South India was the norm, surpassing even the United Church of Canada. Throughout Africa, talks were held by the missionaries seeking church unity. Except for Zambia where in 1964 unity of sorts was attained between Methodists, the Paris Evangelical missionaries, the Baptists, and the United Church of Canada Mission to the Copperbelt, church unity on the continent seems to have proved unsuccessful. Here and there some small struggling missions have rationalised their work and come together out of financial considerations. In some cases it has happened because of non-theological pressures. In all cases where church unions have been achieved on the continent, the initiators have been white and often missionaries. Why does it seem as if the fervour for "organic" unity of the church does not burn in the African bosom with the same intensity as it does among some whites? Furthermore it seems that since the "younger churches" of Africa joined the WCC, the emphasis in the ecumenical movement has moved from the concerns of the Faith and Order Commission to those of practical human predicaments: Church and Society, Development Aid, the Programme to Combat Racism, and Dialogue with Other Faiths.

It may well be that Africa, having inherited the divided church from abroad, has not felt the pangs of this division as deeply as have European Christians: "The sin of our divisions" is not felt as Africa's sin, and therefore there is no inner compulsion to repent of it. Yet tolerance, mutual acceptance and co-operation between the churches are more evident on the African continent than elsewhere, and denominational barriers are criss-crossed with amazing ease, especially at the congregational level.

A feature that has developed over the years in many African towns and cities is the fraternal organisation of ministers and pastors....

Symbolic Acts of Unity

African ecumenism is also present at a more obvious grassroots level. Donald M'Timkulu describes it adequately:

> The social ties binding the African Christian to his extended family and clan have always been stronger than the forces of separation that arise from membership in different denominations. The important family occasions like births, marriages, funerals and clan festivals bring together in one place of

---

*Excerpts from Gabriel Setiloane, "The Ecumenical Movement in Africa: From Mission Church to Moratorium," in *Resistance and Hope: South African Essays in Honour of Beyers Naudé*, ed. Charles Villa-Vicencio and John W. de Gruchy (Grand Rapids, MI: Eerdmans, 1985), 146-47; cf. Bosch, TM, 464-65.

worship relatives with different confessional backgrounds. On these occasions they not only share in common acts of worship with gay disregard of denominational differences, but they also take part in symbolic acts of family and clan unity that have their roots in the traditional past.[8]

Perhaps this is the reason for the lack of fervour for so-called "organic unity." There are other forces at work in the African soul that continue to reduce the dividedness of the church as planted in Africa from abroad.

PARTICIPATION AND COMMON WITNESS

"Solidarity [is] needed if the gospel is to be proclaimed with credibility."

■ *As we contemplate the future of world Christian mission, participation and common witness are significant issues. Their importance derives both from the experience which they create and from the larger questions they raise about the issues of ecclesiology and ecumenism. Sr. Mary Motte, F.M.M., director of mission education for the Franciscan Missionaries of Mary, chose these as her themes in the following essay. Her missionary service included almost ten years in Rome. She co-edited* Mission in Dialogue, *the papers from the important Roman Catholic SEDOS Research Seminar on the Future of Mission (Rome 1981).*

*Roots of Ecumenism**

Two areas of experience...are in fact undergirding much of the present transition in mission and...even now shape the way we will go about mission in the years ahead. Both participation and common witness are issues found at the roots of ecclesiology and ecumenism respectively, and to some extent they overlap....

Participation

A *Pro Mundi Vita* study five years ago defined participation as "the association of leaders and ordinary members in the making of decisions" (1981). While this study was particularly directed to the question of participation in the Roman Catholic Church, it nevertheless pointed to a concern prevalent in the world today, namely to be involved and engaged in decision-making in a meaningful way. Increasingly, decisions made by groups of persons who come together around common concerns are impacting gradually the institutional structures of church

---

*Excerpts from Mary Motte, "Participation and Common Witness: Creating a Future in Mission," *Missiology 15* (1987), 25-26, 26-29; cf. Bosch, TM, 463.

and society. The process by which these groups arrive at convictions and decisions is basically a process of participation...

What are the characteristics of this participation? First of all, the persons who are present must be taken into consideration. In almost all of the [global mission conferences] persons have represented a *diversity* of nationality, of culture, and/or of Christian confession. These diversities in turn implied a diversity of historical experience and awareness.

This multifaceted diversity became effective because of a quality *listening* which has led to genuine *dialogue,* allowing the *articulation of concerns,* spoken with varying accents and nuances of meaning, to be heard effectively. This effective hearing, has in turn, brought about a growing sense of *community,* of *sharing,* and a *new awareness and appreciation for other ways of perceiving reality and of doing theology*....

Bringing together, in effective participation, Orthodox Christians, ecumenical Protestants, evangelical Protestants, and Roman Catholics continues to be a limited reality. Unfortunately, it is not given appropriate priority by all groups. There is an urgency to "display to the world our unity in proclaiming the mystery of Christ," but before that can happen, we have to find participatory models in the search for unity, which presupposes "getting to know each other and removing the obstacles blocking the way to perfect unity" (John Paul II, 1979). What happens when persons gather and participate becomes then a fundamental contribution to shaping the missionary task in the future. From this kind of activity, new models of working together will become possible, and these models will be the basis for new ways of understanding the task of mission in relation to the church and the world.

Common Witness

The above instances of gatherings around the themes of mission have also been instances of common witness, to the extent that there has been a diversity of Christians present and participating in the event. The *focus on the concerns of mission* is an important element in the developing of common witness, and reciprocally, this common witness is an essential element in the shaping of mission for the future. In this reciprocal process, there has been a growing discovery from different gatherings and experiences of common ground from which Christians proclaim the good news of Jesus Christ to the world.

This common ground is found in the *growing consensus* around the evangelical values which determine the relation between church and world, and which question the predominant values defining the way economic, political, and sociological factors operate in society today. Related to this area of consensus is the *willingness to confront* cultural, historical values with the gospel values, and the awareness of *bringing about the fullness of God's reign* through missionary commitment.

An awareness has also grown of the *need to further the exploration of what each understands about the kingdom or reign of God,* since we write our objectives for mission in light of what we understand by the kingdom. An increasing concern has developed about the presence of suffering and what this means both traditionally and for the future in the carrying out of the missionary task. The present situation in world mission is seeded with a variety of martyrs, and this gift that has traditionally been associated with the missionary task since the early church has been given without respect for confessional differences.

The moments of *worship* are the privileged times at these gatherings when the common ground discovered is celebrated, and the barriers to growth are challenged most deeply. The dynamic sharing of God's Word often experienced at these times of prayer, is painfully evocative of the division which keeps us from a common eucharist....

Conclusion

Participation and common witness are related issues which provide, through the experiences they engender, an important basis for considering the larger questions of ecclesiology and ecumenism. The experience of both, as these have been developed through various gatherings of Christians concerned about mission, point toward growing convictions about commitment to the missionary task for the future, and the solidarity needed if the gospel is to be proclaimed with credibility. The question remains whether the experience of both participation and common witness will be sufficiently strong to move us beyond the limitations and barriers, traditional and new, and allow us to find a way of commitment to the proclamation of the good news that evokes with clarity the comment of those who observed the early Christians, "See how they love one another!"

NOTES

1. World Council of Churches, Assembly (1st., Amsterdam 1948), *The First Assembly of the World Council of Churches,* ed. W. A. Visser 't Hooft (New York: Harper & Brothers, 1949), p. 69.

2. Cf. Willem Saayman, *Unity and Mission* (Pretoria: UNISA, 1984), pp. 14-15.

3. *Dictionary of the Ecumenical Movement,* ed. N. Lossky, et al. (Geneva: WCC, 1991), p. 90.

4. Vid. *Evangelii Nuntiandi* nos. 15 & 36.

5. *Gathered for Life,* Report of the Sixth Assembly of the WCC, Vancouver, 1983, ed. David Gill (Geneva: WCC, 1983), p. 197.

6. *Occasional Bulletin of the Commission on Theological Concerns,* Christian Conference of Asia, May 1981, p. 10.

7. "The Church in Africa: Growth, Movement and Theology," in *Pangs of Growth: A Dialogue on Church Growth in Southern Africa,* ed. Gabriel M. Setiloane and Ivan H. M. Peden (Braamfontein, South Africa: Skotaville Publishers, 1988), p. 11.

8. D. G. S. M'Timkulu, *Beyond Independence: The Face of New Africa* (New York: Friendship Press, 1971), p. 22.

14

Mission as Ministry by the Whole People of God

"The movement away from ministry as the monopoly of ordained men to ministry as the responsibility of the whole people of God, ordained as well as non-ordained, is one of the most dramatic shifts taking place in the church today" (Bosch, TM, 467). With these words, David Bosch introduces the church's recovery of mission as ministry by the whole people of God. This was the secret of the phenomenal growth of the early Church—that witness and ministry were the prerogative and duty of every church member.[1]

The selections below go beyond Bosch's analysis as contributions to a theology of the laity. M. M. Thomas of India is representative of those Christian leaders who advocated a radical laicism following World War II. In contrast to those who would build the community of faith as a haven in the midst of a secular society, Thomas encourages laypersons to understand that theirs is a Christian vocation and ministry in every sphere of society. Rajaiah D. Paul of India concurs. To encourage laymen and laywomen to conceive of their ministries primarily as supplemental to overburdened clergy is a travesty, he argues. Nor can the peoples of Asia ever be won to Christ by that strategy! Instead, he favors laypersons in ministry in secular situations permeating society with Christian ideas supported by Christian living. In his important work, A Theology of the Laity, Hendrik Kraemer of The Netherlands judges missions since the eighteenth century to have been crippled, amputated missions due to their preoccupation with missionary specialists. For Kraemer, if the church is to be true to its calling to be diakonia, the entire membership must have a missionary or apostolic stamp, with the laity manifesting their ministries in all spheres of secular life. D. T. Niles of Sri Lanka concurs, adding the probing question to every Christian, "why not be a missionary?" He argues that to be a Christian is to be a member of a missionary community obedient to a missionary God.

For Roman Catholics, the theme of the apostolate of the laity has been a rallying cry for renewal. Selections from two Vatican II documents illustrate this understanding. Lumen Gentium (The Dogmatic Constitution of the Church), in its section on "The Laity," states that "the apostolate of the laity is a sharing in the salvific mission of the Church." Every layperson, therefore, is to be "the living instrument *of the mission of the church" in the world.* Apostolicam Actuositatem *(Apostolate of the Laity) elaborates on the Catholic theology of the laity. The apostolate is defined in terms of evangelization, sanctification, and the renewal of the temporal order.*

How shall the laity be equipped for their distinctive missional callings? Jürgen Moltmann of Germany believes that all Christians need to understand how God is at work in a world come of age and their own vocations within it. He proposes that theologians provide that equipping both in university settings and in other centers for the education of the laity.

The issue of women in mission and ministry, scarcely mentioned by Bosch, deserves major development. Elizabeth Behr-Sigel challenges leaders of Orthodox churches to take the women's movement seriously. She contrasts the pyramid of authority (male-dominated) of the church with the example of Christ, finding the church's true koinonia *to be that of "fellowship with Jesus Christ through the spirit, as a community of prayer and love." If through baptism all are in communion with Christ, and if the Creator has called women to fulfillment as persons, can not women aspire "to the charism of the priesthood?" she asks.*

Virginia Fabella of the Philippines seeks to recapture the early egalitarian model of the ecclesia. *The true disciple of Jesus was a person who heard the word of God and acted upon it. For St. Luke, Mary, the mother of Jesus, was the exemplary disciple and the model for both men and women in ministry.*

What new models do we have of ministry by the whole people of God? Leonardo Boff of Brazil believes that the base church communities are salvific events, liberating the church from the hierarchical dominance of clergy and freeing the people of God for their ministries in the world. Finally, John de Gruchy of South Africa adds examples from the charismatic movement and the African independent churches of recapturing the New Testament vision of ministry "given to the whole church and to a variety of people within it."

LAY LIFE AS VOCATION AND MINISTRY

"Lay life as 'vocation and ministry' ...in the secular world."

■ *World War II proved a watershed in Christian thought concerning the ministries of the church. Established patterns of church leadership were disrupted. Where clergypersons were absent, lay women and men assumed new leadership roles. Conversely, some clergy assumed "secular" roles, as with the Catholic worker-priests in France. Following the war, the World Student Christian Federation resumed its avant-garde function in espousing the importance of the ministry and mission of the laity. In 1950, M. M. Thomas of India was its vice-chairman, as well as youth secretary of the Mar Thoma Church in India. The following article, based on a speech that "M.M." gave at the Federation Theological Students' Conference at Stein, Germany, contains his advocacy of a radical laicism.*

*The Significance of the Secular**

The more one considers the relevance of the professional ministry in relation to the wholeness of the Church, the more one is led to think of the meaning of the lay and the secular world. I am not unaware of the present tendency in the ecumenical world to emphasize the place of the laity in the Church; but I have a strong suspicion that much of it is not within the perspective of *the significance of the secular to the wholeness of the Church.* The question we have to ask is, What is the meaning of the lay and secular to the life of the Church?...

There is no religion which is secure into which those who feel the insecurity of the secular life may run and be safe, or whose domination will save the secular world. The Church and the world stand together in sin, and therefore together under judgment. Any attempt of the Church to point to itself as the saviour is pure idolatry.

A Radical Laicism

What then is the Church and the nature of its relation to the secular world? "The Church is not a sphere of existence distinct and separate from the natural world and from history," says J. H. Oldham. "It is *a new dimension* of reality permeating these realms and transforming them. The *world* contains the elements which find their renewal in the Church."...The Church is therefore not something other than the secular, but the secular which knows its own true reality in the new age inaugurated in Christ; it is the world which knows itself to be "in Christ" under the judgment and grace of the Crucified and Risen One....

Christian religion, therefore, is "a radical laicism," and the Church consists *primarily* of [laypersons] doing their secular jobs and witnessing to the true life of the secular "hid with Christ in God." This was the insight of the Reformation in its conception of the Call and Vocation of the [layperson]; "but the attempt of the Reformation to fill secular activities with Christian meaning was not carried to a successful conclusion." And even today when we think of the Church, we are not primarily thinking of the [laity] and their witness to Christ in and through their Christian participation in the world, but of the bishops, the clergy, and perhaps also [laity] who are doing full time "religious" work. And when we speak about the Church acting in the world, again our thoughts are about the sometimes relevant and more often irrelevant declarations of the ecclesiastics. And here, perhaps more than anywhere else, there ought to occur a real revolution in thought regarding the nature and witness of the Church, if we are to regain the *wholeness* of the Church. The famous Anglican Collect for Good Friday bids us to pray "for all estates of men [and women] in Christ that every member of the same in his [or her] vocation and ministry" may "truly and godly serve" Him; herein is a vision of the Church

---

*Excerpts from M. M. Thomas, "An Irrelevant Profession," *Student World* 43 (1950): 319, 320-21; cf. Bosch, TM, 473.

fulfilling its ministry in the world through [laypersons] who consider their lay life as "vocation and ministry," seeking to serve Him in the day-to-day decisions they make in the secular world. This is the vision we have to recapture about the Church in the world today.

THE ONLY EFFECTIVE ASIAN MISSION STRATEGY

"'Ministry' in secular occupations."

■ *The Christian churches of India live amid a dominant Hindu culture. Swimming in that pond, they are in constant danger of becoming incapsulated caste-like communities, receiving new members only by birth, with young people rarely marrying outsiders. How can the church be the "salt of the earth" and the "light of the world" in such a cultural context? In 1956, Rajaiah D. Paul of India placed his hope in the witness of laypersons in their secular occupations. A retired civil servant, he served also as general secretary of the Synod of the Church of South India and as chairman of the Working Committee of the WCC's Department of the Laity.*

*The Spearhead of the Christian Enterprise**

It cannot be said that in India and other countries of east Asia there are what may be called [laity] movements, in the technical sense in which this term is used in some countries of Europe and in America. But the churches in the East are just beginning to understand that, in the new and changing situation in which they find themselves, the laity can no longer be kept in the background. They are coming to realize that "only by the witness of a spiritually intelligent and active laity can the Church meet the modern world in its actual perplexities and life situations." It is gradually being comprehended that the laity are not there to be used, if at all, to supplement or relieve an over-burdened and under-staffed ordained ministry, but that in the Christian effort to establish the rule of God in the world, [laypersons] in their secular callings form the most important, and can be the most effective, agency to be employed.

It is now widely recognized that in the present situation the message of the Gospel can be most effectively spread by the unobtrusive spiritual activity and imperceptible religious influence exercised by Christian [laypersons] in their daily life and work, rather than by paid preachers and elaborate evangelistic organizations. In the light of this, much thinking is being done in all Asian churches on the vocation, function and responsibility of [the laity], in order that they may be used more effectively in the Church's strategy....

---

*Excerpts from Rajaiah D. Paul, "Towards a New Strategy in Asia: The Layman as the Spearhead of the Christian Enterprise," *Student World* 49 (1956): 271-73, 275-76; cf. Bosch, TM, 473.

"Ministry of the Laity"

The churches are anxious that the laity be helped to perform their "ministry"—but only within the Church. They have not yet planned for the "ministry of the laity" outside the Church in the secular callings. They still need to learn, what Evanston so emphatically asserted, that "all Christians must become ministers of Christ's saving purpose and messengers of the hope revealed in Him," and that "in daily living and work the laity are not mere fragments of the Church who are scattered about the world but are the Church's representatives"—Christ's own ambassadors—"no matter where they are. It is they who manifest in word and action the Lordship of Christ over that world which claims so much of their time, energy and labour. This is the ministry of the laity."[2]

"Ministry" in Secular Occupations

What has been left out is that very large body of lay people who work full time in the secular world and who have no time, inclination or intellectual competence to help in the administration or day-to-day running of the Church and its organizations. These people are the majority. They are in the very heart of the secular world and are open to all its corrupting influences. If they could be helped to use their very occupations as the means by which they serve the Church in her mission to the world, they would then perform the real ministry of the laity—the most effective of all....

The time has come, especially in the countries of the East, to emphasize the essential unity of the laity and the clergy as ministers of God and together making up the *laos*, the people of God. The view of the laity as a non-essential portion of the Church which exists merely to enable the clergy to exercise their ministry, or at best so that some of the good ones among them may be used for reading lessons in church, for teaching Sunday school, or as secretaries of committees and members of synods, must all be changed. For their part, the laity must rid themselves of the pernicious idea that their Christianity involves no further responsibilities than living "goody-goody," socially respectable lives, committing no overt sin, and providing no occasion for scandal, and that their relation to the Church need only be one of benevolent passivity, nominal adherence and conventional submission to her regulations.

Evangelism from Within

It is fast becoming clear that the only way in which the lives of these Eastern nations can be Christianized—if they are to be Christianized at all, and if that is what the Church is trying to do—is through a process of leavening, of fermentation from within, a process which has already begun and which has now become sufficiently evident to cause alarm. If the social, political, economic and administrative systems of these Eastern nations are to be brought under the sway of Christ, if this is what we Christians are after, it can only be done by Christians who have been placed by God within those very systems and who have been called by Him to exercise their Christian ministry as the *laos* in their own secular situations, by intense devotion to their Lord in the power of His redemption. The people of these countries can no longer be preached to in the old way. They can only be reached from within. The whole system must be permeated with Christian ideas and ideals which must be supported by Christian living. The only effective evangelistic method for the future in this part of the world is the promulgation of the gospel by consecrated Christian laymen [and laywomen] in their secular occupations.

THE MISSIONARY CALLING OF THE LAITY

"The laity as the proper missionary body of the Church."

■ *Fundamental to the rethinking of the church's mission is a recovery of the apostolic understanding that all Christians are called to witness and service. The noted Dutch theologian and missiologist Hendrik Kraemer, in* A Theology of the Laity *(1958) provides one of the clearest statements. Kraemer judges missions since the eighteenth century as "crippled, amputated missions" in their preoccupation with missionary specialists.* Diakonia *(service) has its root in the being and work of Jesus Christ. We are called to join Christ in that ministry in the world—a ministry which laity far more than clergy can carry out.*

*A Theology of the Laity**

The only *fully* legitimate Mission is the Mission of the one Church. Missions as they have been happening since the 18th century up to now, grateful as we must be for them, are crippled, amputated Missions. The Unity or Oneness of the Church is the legitimation of Christ's and the Church's apostolate. The missionary or apostolic aspect expresses as well the being as the calling of the Church. This applies to the whole Church, to *all* its members. All members have this basic stamp and should acknowledge it with heart and mind. This has to stand as a basic affirmation and basic orientation of the Church. "All the members" for whom this is indicative as well as imperative, means to say that "ministry" or "clergy" and laity are equally implied. The particular emphasis upon the laity as the proper missionary body of the Church, which in all present writing on the laity is customary, is understandable and justified from the angle of the history of the Church, in which the laity has been so perseveringly ignored. It is understandable too in our present situation, because it is not exaggeration to say that in the last decades the laity as an essential part of the Church, especially also in the discharge of its task, is a new discovery. This explains why the missionary calling of the laity is figuring so largely in the ever-increasing literature on the laity. From the

---

*Excerpts from Hendrik Kraemer, *A Theology of the Laity* (Philadelphia: Westminster Press, 1958), 135, 147, 149, 154; cf. Bosch, TM, 470.

standpoint of thinking on the meaning of the Church, however, it should be kept in mind that this missionary or apostolic stamp regards the total membership of the Church, and consequently the laity.

Diakonia—Rooted in the Person of Christ

Our conclusion is therefore that diakonia as the true spirit and pattern of the Church has its root in the being and the work of Jesus Christ her Lord Himself....

The laity, living in the world as an integral part of it, is the primary body through which the reality of the phrase: the Church *is* diakonia, *is* Ministry, has to be manifested in all spheres of secular life.

The Church then as a whole being ministry or diakonia, it follows that, theologically speaking, the ministry of the laity is as constituent for the true being and calling of the Church as the ministry of the "ministry" (the office-bearers or clergy). Both, the ministry of the clergy and the ministry of the laity, are *facts* inherent in the Church's being, are divine data. Only from this angle has the present much-used expression "the ministry of the laity" real content, and is not a mere pious phrase.

WHY NOT BE A MISSIONARY?

"All Christians share in the Church's missionary task."

■ *Who is a missionary? Just as the entire church of Jesus Christ is weakened whenever the ministry is narrowed to the set-apart ordained clergy, so also the church's mission is stunted when only those in missionary orders or commissioned are affirmed as missionaries. The noted Sri Lankan ecumenical church leader D. T. Niles brought a radically different understanding out of Asia. God's nature is to reach out for the lost. The church, the living body of Christ, exists to be in mission. Therefore, every Christian is called to be a missionary.*

*All Are Missionaries**

The ordinary Christian and every Christian has so to face the missionary implications of his faith as to recognize that a description of the mission of the Church is, in a true sense, but a description of the Church's day-to-day life.

All Christians must face the question "Why not be a missionary?" because to be a Christian is to be a member of a missionary community and to become a participant in the activity of a missionary God. The apostolic privilege belongs to all who are Christ's, and each has to decide in what form and what measure to share in the Church's missionary task and destiny. So that no responsible answer to the question "Why not be a missionary?" is possible except as it is rooted in an obedient

---

*Excerpts from Daniel T. Niles, *Upon the Earth* (New York: McGraw-Hill, 1962), 10-11; cf. Bosch, TM, 472.

answer to the more primary question "Why not be a Christian?" If the missionary is a symbol of the Christian faith it is because all Christians share in the Church's missionary task and the missionary enterprise belongs to the very nature of the Gospel.

LAITY'S COMMISSION TO WITNESS AND MISSION

> "Every lay person...the living instrument of the mission of the Church."

■ *Vatican II gave a new and creative approach to the role of the laity in the church. In the Dogmatic Constitution of the Church* (Lumen Gentium), *the church is understood first and foremost not as an institution but as a people to whom God communicates in love. The result is a new people* (laos) *of God called to be witnesses and prophets for their Lord. Their baptism and their confirmation is their commissioning for this missionary apostolate.*

*The People of God**

(From Chapter 2, "The People of God")

12. The holy People of God shares also in Christ's prophetic office: it spreads abroad a living witness to him, especially by a life of faith and love and by offering to God a sacrifice of praise, the fruit of lips praising his name (cf. Heb. 13:15).

Vocation of the Laity

(From Chapter 4, "The Laity")

33. Gathered together in the People of God and established in the one Body of Christ under one head, the laity—no matter who they are—have, as living members, the vocation of applying to the building up of the Church and to its continual sanctification all the powers which they have received from the goodness of the Creator and from the grace of the Redeemer.

The apostolate of the laity is a sharing in the salvific mission of the Church. Through Baptism and Confirmation all are appointed to this apostolate by the Lord himself. Moreover, by the sacraments, and especially by the Eucharist, that love of God and man which is the soul of the apostolate is communicated and nourished. The laity, however, are given this special vocation: to make the Church present and fruitful in those places and circumstances where it is only through them that she can become the salt of the earth.[3] Thus, every lay person, through those gifts given to him, is at once the witness and the living instrument of the mission of the Church itself "according to the measure of Christ's bestowal" (Eph. 4:7).

---

*Excerpts from "Lumen Gentium" (1964), Art. 12, 33, in *VC2,* 363, 390-91; cf. Bosch, TM, 471.

Besides this apostolate which belongs to absolutely every Christian, the laity can be called in different ways to more immediate cooperation in the apostolate of the hierarchy,[4] like those men and women who helped the apostle Paul in the Gospel, laboring much in the Lord (cf. Phil. 4:3; Rom. 16:3ff.). They have, moreover, the capacity of being appointed by the hierarchy to some ecclesiastical offices with a view to a spiritual end.

All the laity, then, have the exalted duty of working for the ever greater spread of the divine plan of salvation to all [persons], of every epoch and all over the earth. Therefore may the way be clear for them to share diligently in the salvific work of the Church according to their ability and the needs of the times.

THE APOSTOLATE OF LAY PEOPLE

"Bearing clear witness to Christ ...in the midst of the world."

■ *Although the lay apostolic had existed in the church since the time of Christ, no official Catholic Church document set forth the theology of the laity until the Second Vatican Council. For five years, a Preparatory Commission worked on drafts of the Decree on the Apostolate of the Laity* (Apostolicam Actuositatem). *Adopted by the council in 1965, it sets forth an understanding of the laity as co-responsible for the mission of Christ, both in the gathered community of faith and in the world.*

*Participation of the Laity in the Church's Mission**

(From Chapter 1, "The Vocation of Lay People to the Apostolate")

2. In the Church there is diversity of ministry but unity of mission. To the apostles and their successors Christ has entrusted the office of teaching, sanctifying, and governing in his name and by his power. But the laity are made to share in the priestly, prophetical and kingly office of Christ; they have therefore, in the Church and in the world, their own assignment in the mission of the whole People of God.[5] In the concrete, their apostolate is exercised when they work at the evangelization and sanctification of [persons]; it is exercised too when they endeavor to have the Gospel spirit permeate and improve the temporal order, going about it in a way that bears clear witness to Christ and helps forward the salvation of men [and women]. The characteristic of the lay state being a life led in the midst of the world and of secular affairs, laymen are called by God to make of their apostolate, through the vigor of their Christian spirit, a leaven in the world.

---

*Excerpts from "Apostolicam Actuositatem" (1965), Art. 2, 6, 7, in *VC2,* 768, 773-75; cf. Bosch, TM, 471.

The Apostolate of Evangelization and Sanctification

(From Chapter 2, "Objectives")

6. [Laypersons] have countless opportunities for exercising the apostolate of evangelization and sanctification. The very witness of a Christian life, and good works done in a supernatural spirit, are effective in drawing men [and women] to the faith and to God; and that is what the Lord has said: "Your light must shine so brightly before men that they can see your good works and glorify your Father who is in heaven" (Mt. 5:16).

This witness of life, however, is not the sole element in the apostolate; the true apostle is on the lookout for occasions of announcing Christ by word, either to unbelievers to draw them towards the faith, or to the faithful to instruct them, strengthen them, incite them to a more fervent life; "for Christ's love urges us on" (2 Cor. 5:14), and in the hearts of all should the apostle's words find echo: "Woe to me if I do not preach the Gospel" (1 Cor. 9:16).[6]

The Renewal of the Temporal Order

7. That men [and women], working in harmony, should renew the temporal order and make it increasingly more perfect: such is God's design for the world.

All that goes to make up the temporal order: personal and family values, culture, economic interests, the trades and professions, institutions of the political community, international relations, and so on, as well as their gradual development—all these are not merely helps to [humanity's] last end; they possess a value of their own, placed in them by God, whether considered individually or as parts of the integral temporal structure: "And God saw all that he had made and found it very good" (Gen. 1:31)....

It is the work of the entire Church to fashion men [and women] able to establish the proper scale of values on the temporal order and direct it towards God through Christ....

[Laypersons] ought to take on themselves as their distinctive task this renewal of the temporal order. Guided by the light of the Gospel and the mind of the Church, prompted by Christian love, they should act in this domain in a direct way and in their own specific manner. As citizens among citizens they must bring to their cooperation with others their own special competence, and act on their own responsibility; everywhere and always they have to seek the justice of the kingdom of God. The temporal order is to be renewed in such a way that, while its own principles are fully respected, it is harmonized with the principles of the Christian life and adapted to the various conditions of times, places and peoples. Among the tasks of this apostolate Christian social action is preeminent. The Council desires to see it extended today to every sector of life, not forgetting the cultural sphere.[7]

A THEOLOGY FOR CHRISTIANITY "COME OF AGE"

"A theology for the laity in their callings in the world."

■ *Should seminaries monopolize the future development of theology? No! answers the noted German Lutheran theologian Jürgen Moltmann. He believes that in the future Christian theology will become more practical and political. All Christians need to understand how God is at work in a world come of age and their own callings (vocations) in the world. Both university departments of religion and Christian centers for the education of the laity will be lively places for theology to develop in future.*

A Theology for Christianity "Come of Age"*

Christian theology will in the future become more and more a practical and political theology. It will no longer be simply a theology for priests and pastors, but also a theology for the laity in their callings in the world. It will be directed not only toward divine service in the church, but also toward divine service in the everyday life of the world. Its practical implementation will include preaching and worship, pastoral duties, and Christian community, but also socialization, democratization, education toward self-reliance and political life.

Until now, most churches have developed theology in their seminaries. Theology was studied in a professional school for preachers. But theologians were thereby separated from the members of their communities—the educated from the uneducated as Greeks from Barbarians (cf. Rom. 1:14). The more people begin to "grow up" in our communities today, the more we shall need a theology for the [layperson] who has "come of age," and for the theologians who can answer his critical questions as well as listen to the [laity's] answers. In many Western countries today, seminaries are becoming empty, wherever they are not integrated into universities. Courses in departments of religion in the universities are surprisingly well attended, and indeed by students who are interested in theology and religion but do not want to become clergymen. I believe this is a good development. First of all, it removes the distinction between clergy and laity; and secondly, the church must finally accept the fact that its theologians do not have to be sent into the world before anything can happen: its laity are already in the world.

Pastoral-theology remains a part of theological formation, but it must be integrated into the wider horizon of the theological formation of the whole of Christianity, which is at work in very different practical spheres of society. This theology for the whole of Christianity "come of age" is only in its initial phases. Lay persons should not be trained to become "mini-pastors" who can relieve the pastor of his work. They should rather be trained to become men and women who can think independently and act in a Christian way in their own vocations in the world. It seems to me, therefore, meaningful to choose the expression *political theology* for this wider theology of Christianity in the world, for the *res publica* is of concern to all citizens. Man is a *zoon politikon* (political animal). The kingdom

---

*Excerpts from Jürgen Moltmann, *The Experiment Hope* (Philadelphia: Fortress Press, 1975), 11-12; cf. Bosch, TM, 467, 473.

of God is to be anticipated in politics, not in a separate sphere, called religion. This new form of theology, namely, the political, will, in my opinion, enable us to bridge two gaps—the one inside the church which divides the clergy from the laity and the one outside which divides the church from the world. In the practical order, this means: first, the integration of church seminaries into universities, wherever this is possible; secondly, the building of our own Christian or free universities, wherever the first practice is not possible; and thirdly, the gathering of theologians in Christian centers for the education of the laity.

THE CHARISM OF WOMEN FOR MINISTRY

> "The present women's movement is challenging the Church today."

■ *Some of the most vigorous debate concerning the place of the laity in ministry and mission has taken place in those historic churches with long-standing traditions confining ministerial roles exclusively to men. In 1976, women of both the Eastern and Oriental Orthodox traditions met for the first time at the women's monastery of Agapia in Greece. Their consultation on "The Role of Orthodox Women in the Church and in Society" was initiated by the WCC's Unit on Education and Renewal. The lay president of the French Orthodox Community of the Holy Trinity in Paris presented the keynote address on "The Meaning of the Participation of Women in the Orthodox Church." Dr. Elizabeth Behr-Sigel was at that time professor of philosophy at the Graduate Institute of Ecumenical Studies in Paris and co-editor of* Contacts, *the French review of Orthodoxy.*

*Women Challenging the Church**

We are living in an age of violence, in many cases violence of the most atrocious kind. The proud, though fragile, facade of our old western humanism has finally crumbled. Paradoxically, however, the violence has brought with it an immense longing for human liberation, respect for human dignity and the right to be different whether in terms of ethnic group, culture, or sex. The movement, or more correctly, the various movements for the liberation of women share both in this violence and in these noble aspirations which have their roots in the Gospel.

There is a tendency among the Orthodox to think that the women's movement concerns only secular society, "the changing face of this passing world," and not the Church. There is an element of truth in this attitude of detachment. Yet while

---

*Excerpts from Elizabeth Behr-Sigel, "The Meaning of the Participation of Women in the Life of the Church," in *Orthodox Women: Their Role and Participation in the Orthodox Church* (Geneva, Switzerland: World Council of Churches, 1977), 18, 21-22, 26-28; cf. Bosch, TM, 472.

our hope of salvation is rooted in the *eschaton* and our eyes are turned towards the eternal divine mystery, we cannot and must not forget that the Church is also the pilgrim people of God moving towards the Kingdom *through history,* in solidarity with all humanity and bearer of its hopes of fulfillment. The Church is not "an enclave of the Kingdom of God in this world" separated from the world by high protective walls. It is the sacrament of the Kingdom mysteriously present in us and among us. Irritating as it sometimes is, and for all its unattractive, even ridiculous, aspects, the present women's movement is challenging the Church today....

An Orthodox Perspective

Like any form of growth, the growth of the Kingdom of Heaven in us is irregular, sometimes sudden, sometimes very gradual. This is particularly true as far as recognition of the moral and existential implications of the Gospel as dogmas of the Church is concerned. Though it is latent in the Church's consciousness, the clear recognition that men and women are equal before God is only just beginning to pierce the thick layer of prejudice and cultural conditioning....

Questions concerning the cooperation of men and women in the Church and the better utilization of women's energies and gifts to serve the growth of the Kingdom of God are very much in the minds of many Orthodox women and they must, nonetheless, define them clearly. We shall do so with the boldness of sons and daughters of God, but we shall do it, happily, in an atmosphere of calmness and serenity which sometimes seems to be lacking elsewhere. This serenity seems to be connected with the way in which we Orthodox women feel and experience our membership of the Church. In spite of its hierarchical structure, which we do not call into question, we do not experience the Church as a pyramid of authority; we experience it at the deepest level, linking us in fellowship with Jesus Christ through the spirit, as a community of prayer and love. The mysterious presence of a woman, the Mother of God, shines through the Church's whole life....

Ministry and the Priesthood

Surely the fundamental ontological unity through communion in the crucified and risen Christ as created by baptism is the foundation of the royal priesthood of all the baptized in which the ministry has its origins as a special, personal vocation, according to the sovereign liberty of God. Moreover, the Church is a body made up of many limbs, with a hierarchy of functions to which corresponds the diversity of the gifts of the Spirit granted to each person (1 Cor. 12: Eph. 4:1-7). So the question that arises is this: as a human being called by the Creator to fulfill herself according to the particular modes of her feminine being, can a woman not, therefore, aspire to the charism of the priesthood? In giving a negative answer to this, are we not in fact subordinating grace to a biological determinism, to nature which it can and will transform as the fire blazes in the burning bush yet does not consume it?

WOMEN'S DISCIPLESHIP

"Recapture the early egalitarian model of *ecclesia*."

■ *Doing theology from the perspective of Asian women is a relatively new phenomenon. Following a series of regional consultations in Africa, Asia, and Latin America, EATWOT—under the leadership of Sergio Torres and Virginia Fabella—held its Fifth International Conference in New Delhi, India, in 1981. There EATWOT agreed for the first time to examine "the feminist claim that 'the male-dominated patterns of culture and social organization' oppress women in society and manifest themselves in the life and theology of the church."[8] Furthermore, EATWOT created a Women's Commission as "a sisterhood of resistance to all forms of oppression, seeking creative partnership with men of the Association."[9] From her bases as Asia coordinator for EATWOT and academic dean of the Sister Formation Institute in Manila, Fabella became the spokesperson for many as she redefined the mission of women in the church in Asia.*

*Our Common Mission as Disciples**

I believe that all Christians have the same basic mission, whether they be lay, cleric or religious, whether they be male or female—and that is to continue the mission of Jesus Christ on earth. The mission of Jesus is summarized succinctly in John 10:10: "I have come that all may have life and have it to the full." This is God's plan for all humanity, which St. Irenaeus expressed in his famous phrase: "The glory of God is the human being fully alive." . . .

Mary, the Exemplary Disciple

The gospel writers are in agreement that a true disciple of Jesus is one who hears the word of God and acts upon it. For St. Luke, the first and exemplary disciple is Mary, the mother of Jesus. Luke portrays Mary as a young maiden who accepts the challenge of the Holy Spirit at the Annunciation, as one who ponders God's word in her heart and responds with courage and determination, as one who is ever ready to be of service to her neighbour, as one who, while persevering in prayer, is filled with the Spirit of prophecy and justice together with the other disciples at Pentecost.

For too long, Mary has been depicted for us principally as "virgin" and "mother"—rarely as "disciple." Yet for Jesus himself, physical motherhood, important as it is, is not the basis of his own mother's greatness. For Jesus, discipleship

---

*Excerpts from Virginia Fabella, M.M., "Mission of Women in the Church in Asia: Role and Position," in *New Eyes for Reading: Biblical and Theological Reflections by Women from the Third World,* ed. John S. Pobee and Barbel von Wartenberg-Potter (Geneva: World Council of Churches, 1986), 82-84, 89; cf. Bosch, TM, 472-73.

has priority over family ties. Pointing to his disciples, he said: "Here are my mother and my brothers. For whoever does the will of my Father in heaven is my brother and sister and mother" (Mt. 12:49-50). Mary's special claim is not her having given birth to Jesus, but that she qualified and formed part of Jesus' family of disciples through her obedient response to God's word. Mary then remains a model for all Christians, not so much of motherhood as of faith and discipleship.

The community of disciples Jesus brought into existence definitely included a number of women. We gather this even from the sparse references to women in the New Testament. Given the male-oriented and androcentric bias of the New Testament authors, we can deduce that what is available to us in scriptures is only a fraction of the information which was available to the writers then. What was de-emphasized by the writers is the fact that women were part of the discipleship of equals that existed for a period in early Christianity. A non-androcentric reconstruction of early church history reveals that during the early church, women were full-fledged disciples, and equally missionaries, prophets, church leaders, and apostles in the broad sense of the term....

Recapture the Egalitarian Church

How can we as disciples who seek a full life for all be content with a relationship of inequality and dominance within the very church committed to God's kingdom and God's justice? Clearly there must be a concerted effort to recapture the early egalitarian model of *ecclesia,* which was based on the equality of all Christians, male and female alike.

The recent phenomenon of basic ecclesial communities or BECs is closer to this egalitarian model of *ecclesia* than the hierarchical model still persisting in the universal church today; therefore BECs should be encouraged especially in rural and depressed areas and become the locus of new and creative ministries for both men and women in the church today.

The Aim of Women's Liberation

The aim of women's liberation and struggle for equality in the church and in society is not to get even with men or to replace them as oppressors. The true end of our struggles is a more just and human society for all, a society that reflects God's kingdom of love, truth, justice and peace. But liberation will come only if we first admit we need it, only if we truly want it, only if we are willing to struggle for it with all the other women—together.

> Once again I am looking at an Asian woman:
> She has a round face, a small nose.
> She has short legs.
> She is short in height.
> She is elegant and graceful.

She hears a voice assuring her: Woman, you are set free from your infirmities (Lk. 13:12). And immediately she stands up and praises God.

A NEW EXPERIENCE OF CHURCH

"The base church communities...as salvific events."

■ *Leonardo Boff was born in Concórdia, Canta Catarina, Brazil, in 1938. His father was a schoolteacher who identified himself with the cause of the poor, including the blacks in Concórdia. From his youth, Leonardo was helped to see the world from the perspective of the poor and oppressed. Ordained a Franciscan priest, he discovered while working in a Petrópolis slum that Christian base communities, as they enable persons to find hope and a sense of self-worth, can be for them the real church of Jesus Christ. Following graduate studies in Brazil and Germany in philosophy and theology, he became professor of systematic theology in Petrópolis (since 1970) and an advisor both to the Brazilian Conference of Bishops and the Latin American Confederation of Religious.*[10]

*The Basic Church Community**

Through the latter centuries, the church has acquired an organizational form with a heavily hierarchical framework and a juridical understanding of relationships among Christians, thus producing mechanical, reified inequalities and inequities. As Yves Congar has written: "Think of the church as a huge organization, controlled by a hierarchy, with subordinates whose only task it is to keep the rules and follow the practices. Would this be a caricature? Scarcely!"[11]

In reaction, the basic church communities have sprung up. They represent a new experience of church, of community, of communion of persons within the more legitimate (in the strict sense of the word) ancient tradition. It would be simplistic and would betray the lack of a sense of history to conceive of the basic church communities as a purely contingent, transitory phenomenon. They represent "a specific response to a prevailing historical conjuncture."[12] Theologically they signify a new ecclesiological experience, a renaissance of very church, and hence an action of the Spirit on the horizon of the matters urgent for our time.[13] Seen in this way, the basic church communities deserve to be contemplated, welcomed, and respected as salvific events....

A Leaven of Renewal

The basic church communities are helping the whole church in the process of declericalization, by restoring to the People of God, the faithful, the rights of which

---

*Excerpts from Leonardo Boff, *Ecclesiogenesis: The Base Communities Reinvent the Church* (Maryknoll, NY: Orbis Books, 1986), 1, 32-33; cf. Bosch, TM, 473.

they have been deprived in the linear structure. On the level of theory, theology itself has already gone beyond the old pyramid. *But it is not enough to know. A new praxis must be implemented.* This is what the basic communities are saying. They are helping the whole church to "reinvent itself," right in its foundations. Experiment is gradually confirming theory, and inspiring in the church-as-institution a confidence in the viability of a new way of being church in the world today.

MINISTRY OF THE CHURCH AS A WHOLE

> "The ministry of the church as a whole...helps to equip it for mission in the world."

■ *Professor John de Gruchy, a South African by birth, was ordained a Congregational minister in 1961. A graduate of Rhodes University in South Africa, Chicago Theological Seminary, and the University of South Africa, he is known in southern Africa as a prophetic church leader and scholar. From 1968 to 1973, he was director of studies and communications for the South African Council of Churches. Author of many books, including* The Church Struggle in South Africa *and* Bonhoeffer and South Africa, *he is also founder and editor of the* Journal of Theology for Southern Africa. *Since 1973, he has taught theology at the University of Cape Town and is currently its professor of Christian studies. In the following selection from* Theology and Ministry in Context and Crisis, *de Gruchy calls for the church to recapture the New Testament vision of participation in ministry by the whole people of God.*

*Ministry within the Community of Faith**

There are traditions within the Christian church which reject the need for an ordained ministry. This protest by communities stemming from the Radical Reformation, such as the Quakers, is a salutary warning against a narrow and false understanding of the Christian ministry....

The ordained ministry, or, ministry of the Word and Sacraments, is only one form of ministry within the community of faith. Schillebeeckx, in reflecting on the ministry in the early Christian communities, reminds us that this diversity of ministry was, however, soon lost in the process of institutionalisation. He writes:

> The development of ministry in the early Christian churches was not so much, as is sometimes claimed, a historical shift from charisma to institution but a shift from the charisma of many to a specialized charisma of just a few.[14]

---

*Excerpts from John de Gruchy, *Theology and Ministry in Context and Crisis: A South African Perspective* (Grand Rapids, MI: Wm. B. Eerdmans, 1987), 25-28, 29-30; cf. Bosch, TM, 468, 474.

Thus, for example, the diaconate, instead of being a ministry in its own right, became a stepping-stone to the priesthood and remained such within the Catholic tradition until Vatican II.

In seeking the reformation of the church in the sixteenth century, some of the Protestant Reformers, especially Calvin, recognized the need for such diversity and restructured the church accordingly. Lay people, for example, were brought into the centre of the ministry of the church in the office of elder and deacon. Distinctions were also made in some Reformed churches between teaching elders and ruling elders, so that the work of preaching and teaching was separated from that of governing the church. In the Second Helvetic Confession (1566), which has been formative for the Reformed tradition, we are told that the ordained ministry "is not to be despised" (chapter 18). But in the very next paragraph we are warned not to "attribute too much to ministers and the ministry." Yet the diversity of ministry often became more a matter of form and order rather than a dynamic ministry in its own right, and the caution of the Second Helvetic Confession was not always borne in mind. Protestant pastors became *the* ministry in the church, princes of the pulpit, managers of the congregation and executives of the denomination, even if not Cardinals within a medieval Curia.

Recapture the New Testament Vision

The ministry of the church is that of Jesus Christ through the Spirit. This ministry is given to the whole church and to a variety of people within it. The need to recapture this New Testament vision and practice of ministry has been strongly emphasized in our century by the independent churches in Africa, the Charismatic renewal movement within the mainline churches, the base communities within Latin America, some Vatican II decrees, World Council of Churches studies on ministry and the laity, and is affirmed by theologians of many different traditions in their studies on ministry. Any other view is contrary to the New Testament and the best in Christian tradition; it results in a truncated, inadequate and impoverished ministry. The ministry of the church as a whole builds up the church in faith and love, and helps to equip it for mission in the world.

NOTES

1. Michael Green, *Evangelism in the Early Church* (Grand Rapids, MI: Eerdmans, 1970), p. 274.

2. Report of Sect. 6, "The Laity: The Christian in His Vocation," in *The Evanston Report: The Second Assembly of the World Council of Churches, 1954* (New York: Harper and Bros., 1955), pp. 160-70.

3. Cf. Pius XI, encyclical "Quadragesimo anno," May 15, 1931, *AAS* 23 (1931), pp. 221f.; and the allocution of Pius XII, "De quelle consolation," October 14, 1951, *AAS* 43 (1951), pp. 790f.

4. Cf. Pius XII, allocution "Six ans se sont écoulés," October 5, 1957, *AAS* 49 (1957), p. 927.

5. Cf. Second Vatican Council, *Dogmatic Constitution on the Church,* Art. 31; *AAS* 57 (1965), p. 37.

6. Cf. Pius XI, encyclical "Ubi Arcano," December 23, 1922, *AAS* 14 (1922), p. 659; Pius XII, encyclical "Summi Pontificatus," October 20, 1939, *AAS* 31 (1939), pp. 442-443.

7. Cf. Leo XIII, Encyclical Letter *Rerum Novarum: AAS.* 23 (1890-1891), p. 647; Pius XI, Encyclical Letter *Quadragesimo Anno: AAS* 23 (1931), p. 190; Pius XII, *Nuntius Radiophonicus,* June 1, 1941: *AAS* 33 (1941), p. 207.

8. *Irruption of the Third World: Challenge to Theology,* ed. Virginia Fabella and Sergio Torres (Maryknoll, NY: Orbis Books, 1981), p. 250.

9. Virginia Fabella and Mercy Amba Oduyoye, "Introduction," in *With Passion and Compassion: Third World Women Doing Theology,* ed. Fabella and Oduyoye (Maryknoll, NY: Orbis Books, 1986), p. x.

10. Cf. Ferm, *Profiles in Liberation,* p. 124-28.

11. Yves M.-J. Congar, "Os Grupos informais na Igreja," in Alfonso Gregory, ed., *Comunidades eclesiais de base: utopia ou realidade?* (Petrópolis, Brazil: Vozes, 1973), pp. 144-45.

12. Pedro Demo and Elizeu F. Calsing, "Relatório da pesquisa sobre as comunidades eclesiais de base," in Conferência Nacional dos Bispos do Brasil (CNBB), *Comunidades: Igreja na base* (São Paulo: Edições Paulinas, 1977), pp. 18-19.

13. Pope Paul VI, in statement appearing in *Revista Eclesiástica Brasileira* 34 (1974): 945.

14. Edward Schillebeeckx, *The Church with a Human Face* (London: SCM Press, 1985), p. 121.

15

Mission as Interfaith Witness

The encounter of Christianity with other faiths is as old as Jesus' dialogue with the Samaritan woman (John 4) or Paul's testimony for an unknown God in Athens (Acts 17). Motifs from earlier mission eras persist. Some Christians in mission search for points of affinity, as Hellenistic Christians did with Greek philosophy. Others continue to favor conquest and displacement (the medieval motif), understanding Christianity to be unique, exclusive, and superior. Still others seek an alliance with other faiths to combat the Enlightenment view that all religions would disappear with the rise of scientific thinking.

The fact is that all the world's religions, instead of withering away as Karl Marx and other secularists predicted, have experienced renewal and revival. In addition, many who formerly were agnostics or nominal believers have been attracted to new religious movements. Bosch contends that the two largest unsolved problems for Christian churches are their relationship to worldviews offering this-worldly salvation, and to other faiths (TM, 476-77).

Bosch goes on to identify three contemporary positions held by Christians: exclusivism, fulfillment, and relativism. Each carries with it elements of both the modern and postmodern paradigms.

Exclusivism is advocated by persons having either premodern or modern rationales for their positions. Bosch considers Karl Barth postmodern in his perspective. Reacting against Enlightenment confidence in the autonomous human being, Barth declares all religion to be unbelief, because all is "a human attempt to anticipate what God in His revelation wills to do and does do." He believes that the Christian stands under as much judgment for idolatry and self-righteousness as the Hindu, Jew, or Muslim. Only God's revelation is true. Hendrik Kraemer, in his influential 1938 book on The Christian Message in a Non-Christian World, *presented a Barthian theology of biblical realism that all religions, including Christianity, are to be judged by Christ as the ultimate standard of reference.*

Fulfillment found early advocacy in 1913 by John Nicol Farquhar in his magnum opus, The Crown of Hinduism. *He deemphasized institutional Christianity, preferring to offer to other faiths the person and spirituality of Jesus as what can provide fulfillment of their religious desires. D. T. Niles of Sri Lanka had faith that God is at work among persons of other faiths—therefore, those faiths can become the soil in which Christian faith can blossom and grow. Bosch places Vatican II in this category. Reject nothing true and holy in other religions, the bishops declared in* Nostra Aetate. *They wished to acknowledge, preserve, and encourage all spiritual and moral truths. Others focus on divesting Christianity of its western garb. Aloysius Pieris of Sri Lanka builds on this motif in seeking a Hindu Christianity.*

Relativism, the belief that all religions are different human responses to the one divine Reality, was the thesis of Ernst Troeltsch and is the present position of John Hick, Paul Knitter, and others (TM, 478-83).

Next, Bosch turns to the interrelationship between dialogue and mission, giving seven perspectives illustrated in the selections below. From a major WCC consultation on dialogue (Chiang Mai 1977) came guidelines including a plea that "conviction and openness be held in balance." Raimundo Panikkar, a person of two cultures (Hindu and Christian, Indian and Spanish) advocates an ecumenical ecumenism in which participants of various faiths would engage in a common search for truth with openness to new possibilities for immanence and transcendence. Marjorie H. Suchocki of the Claremont School of Theology prefers to focus dialogue upon issues of justice. She believes that this shifts the conversation from a metaphysical debate to concrete human problems that persons of different faiths share. Lamin Sanneh, a native of the Gambia teaching at Yale University, finds a model for dialogue in the translation process in which vernacular particularity is encouraged. He believes that application of this principle to dialogue could lead to "cultural maturity and openmindedness on a staggering scale." SEDOS, a Catholic mission study center, identifies fourteen aspects of dialogue today, including a commitment to "seek to find Christ already present in the other person." Finally, Emilio Castro of Uruguay, general secretary of the WCC, eschews value-free dialogue in favor of honest and open sharing of faith perspectives.

CHRIST, THE FULFILLMENT OF RELIGIONS

"Christianity is the Crown of Hinduism."

■ *At the end of the nineteenth century, depreciation of other faiths by Christians was deeply entrenched. At best, other forms of religious belief and practice were judged to be broken lights; at worst, they were called deceptions of the devil. One of the pioneers of a more open-minded approach was John Nicol Farquhar (1861-1929). Born in Aberdeen, Scotland, he entered the service of the London Missionary Society in 1891, teaching for eleven years at a school in Calcutta. Between 1902 and 1923, he held various posts in the Indian YMCA. In 1923 he left India to become professor of comparative religion at the University of Manchester in England. His magnum opus,* The Crown of Hinduism, *was first published in 1913 and reprinted in India as recently as 1971. In it he deemphasized institutional Christianity. Instead he argued that in the figure of the historical Jesus we have a purely spiritual and ethical religion that can provide fulfillment and bring to completion the various desires and quests found in the religious histories of nations and peoples.*[1]

*Christ's System Is Truly Universal**

When we say that Christianity is the Crown of Hinduism, we do not mean Christianity as it is lived in any nation, nor Christianity as it is defined and elaborated in detail in the creed, preaching, ritual, liturgy, and discipline of any single church, but Christianity as it springs living and creative from Christ Himself. Christ is the head of the whole Church, not of any one denomination. Christ is human, not Western. Far less is He English, Scottish, American, or German.

Only in this way can we be true to Christ. For He set forth no detailed laws for the Church, for the moral life, or for the State. While Hinduism, Muhammadanism, and other religions have laid down detailed rules for human conduct in the matter of the family and other institutions, Christ deliberately refused to do so. In all these things He taught merely the spiritual principles which are necessary for our human life and left us to apply them in detail ourselves. The contrast between the Old and New Testaments in this regard is so striking as to leave no room for doubt. The Law of Moses differs very seriously in many ways from the Law of Manu; yet both bring every aspect of human life under religious law; both mix up religious, political, moral, and sanitary regulations in a way that is most disconcerting to a modern mind; and both contain numerous rules for [our] guidance in social matters. Thus, in their general form, the Hindu Law and the Jewish Law stand on a par. But there is no law in the New Testament. Jesus left no detailed social and religious regulations for His followers. Instead of a multitude of commands and prohibitions, He left them His own principles and the divine freedom of sons [and daughters] of God. In this way He gained two most valuable ends.

First of all, His system is truly universal, applicable to all races...to all countries, and to all times; while every detailed system of laws, however wisely drawn up, necessarily becomes obsolete as civilization advances....

Secondly, the method of Christ gives each people freedom, allows them to build up the fabric of their social life according to their national genius. The systems remain Christian, so long as they are guided in every detail by the spiritual principles of Jesus. But that is not all. The complement to the freedom of the Church is the constant presence and activity of the Holy Spirit:

"He will guide you into all truth" (Jn. 16:13).

The Divine Social Order

In Christ even the more detailed ideals of caste find fulfilment. The Brahman is the [person] of prayer and sacrifice, the [one] who has direct access to God: in Christ Jesus this is every [person's] birthright. Every man and every woman is fit to be a priest of God, to offer spiritual sacrifice, to have unceasing, personal

---

*Excerpts from J. N. Farquhar, *The Crown of Hinduism* (London: Oxford University Press, 1913), 58-60, 64, 209-10; cf. Bosch, TM, 479.

intercourse with the heavenly Father. The Sudra was bid serve the three castes: Christ, who came not to be served but to be a servant (Mt. 20:28), shows us that the true [person] is a servant of [others]. The Sudra ideal, as well as the Brahman ideal, is universalized in Him.

The Hindu holds that even [those] who are by birth spiritually fit for the highest privileges, viz. the Brahman, the Kshatriya, and the Vaisya, cannot enter upon these privileges until they have passed through a second birth. Originally, this sacred birth consisted in a long course of religious training and discipline; and an infinitesimal minority still take the course; but for the vast majority it has shrunk to the ceremony of initiation. That which was originally so great has become an empty bubble shaming its high name.

But turn to Christ. Here the second birth is conversion, a revolution within the soul, a spiritual transformation of the [person]. Only [the one] who undergoes the overturning change of repentance, forgiveness and union with Christ, enters upon the privileges of the kingdom of heaven. But the change is open to every one. Any child of God may yield to the influences of the Holy Spirit, repent of his [or her] past life, surrender to Christ, and through Him enter by the portal of the second birth into the new life. That which in Hinduism has become a formal ceremony is in Christ a spiritual reality.

WITNESS TO OTHER FAITHS

> "Christ, as the ultimate standard of reference, is the crisis of all religions."

■ *Protestant debate in the 1920s and 1930s concerning Christianity and other faiths crystalized at two missionary conferences (Jerusalem 1928 and Tambaram 1938) sponsored by the IMC, with Hendrik Kraemer (1888-1965) as a key participant. After studying Javanese at the University of Leiden and Islam at El Azhar University in Cairo, Kraemer worked for the Dutch Bible Society in Indonesia from 1922 to 1937. At the Jerusalem conference he argued that all faiths contained spiritual values but needed conversion in the light of God's revelation in Christ. His book,* The Christian Message in a Non-Christian World, *was the preparatory volume for the Tambaram conference. In it he advocated a biblical realism, arguing that the biblical revelation of the living, holy, righteous God of love provides the standard by which to evaluate all religious truth-claims, including those of Christians.*[2]

*The Attitude toward the Non-Christian Religions**

The argument of value does not coincide in any way whatever with that of truth.

---

*Excerpts from Hendrik Kraemer, *The Christian Message in a Non-Christian World* (New York: International Missionary Council, 1938), 106-10, 113-14, 128-29; cf. Bosch, TM, 478-79.

The non-Christian religions can just as well as Christianity show up an impressive record of psychological, cultural and other values, and it is wholly dependent on one's fundamental axioms of life whether one considers these non-Christian achievements of higher value for [humankind] than the Christian....The subjectively motivated superiority of religious truths, experiences and values can never substantiate the claim for truth or justify and keep alive a missionary movement. The only possible basis is the faith that God has revealed *the* Way and *the* Life and *the* Truth in Jesus Christ and wills this to be known through all the world. A missionary movement and obligation so founded is alone able to remain unshaken and undiscouraged, even when it is without visible result as, for example, is so largely true in the case of Islam....

Christianity as an historical religious body is thoroughly human, that is, a combination of sublime and abject and tolerable elements ...there are many traits in which Christianity in its historical manifestation is superior to other religions; but of other traits the same can be said in regard to the non-Christian religions. The truly remarkable thing about Christianity as an historic and empirical reality, which differentiates it from all other religions, is rather that radical self-criticism is one of its chief characteristics, because the revelation in Christ to which it testifies erects the absolute superiority of God's holy Will and judgment over *all* life, historical Christianity included....

Christ, the Crisis of All Religions

Christ, as the ultimate standard of reference, is the crisis of all religions, of the non-Christian religions and of empirical Christianity too. This implies that the most fruitful and legitimate way to analyse and evaluate all religions is to investigate them in the light of the revelation of Christ....

The Christian revelation places itself over against the many efforts to apprehend the totality of existence. It asserts itself as the record of God's self-disclosing and re-creating revelation in Jesus Christ, as an apprehension of existence that revolves around the poles of divine judgment and divine salvation, giving the divine answer to this demonic and guilty disharmony of [humanity] and the world....

Radical Humility

Inspired by this biblical realism, the attitude towards the non-Christian religions is a remarkable combination of down-right intrepidity and of radical humility....

If revelation in Christ is well understood, the eye is opened for the depravity and the perversion of human religious life which occur in the non-Christian religions and in empirical Christianity, and no weak or meek judgment will be pronounced. The eye is also opened for the deep aspirations and longings and magnificent embodiments of these longings and aspirations. Nevertheless, in the light of this revelation in Christ and of what *God* has wrought through it, all things necessarily undergo a drastic re-evaluation and re-creation. One will often meet representatives of the non-Christian religions who justly fill one with deep reverence, because they represent in their whole life an extraordinary degree of devotion to the reality of the world of the spiritual and eternal. Nevertheless, in the light of Christ's revelation it is a disturbing thing that such highly developed spiritual personalities often do not show the least comprehension of the greatest gift of Christ—forgiveness of sins.

RELIGION IS UNBELIEF

> "Religion is unbelief...a human attempt to anticipate what God in His revelation wills to do and does do."

■ *Of all theological interpretations of the religions in Protestantism in the twentieth century, that of Karl Barth (1886-1968), the Reformed Swiss theologian, has probably been the most influential. In reaction to the plethora of new liberal ideas about religion of his day, with their confidence in the power of human reason to know ultimate reality, Barth renewed his faith in God's power to save. His fundamental premise was that only God can make God known. Therefore, Barth called all human striving to know God "unbelief." In doing so, he played no favorites. Christianity, as a human striving to know God, came under the same judgment as other faiths, as shown in the following passage from his* Church Dogmatics.[3]

*Religion a Human Manufacture**

We begin by stating that religion is unbelief. It is a concern, indeed, we must say that it is the one great concern, of godless [humanity]....

From the standpoint of revelation religion is clearly seen to be a human attempt to anticipate what God in His revelation wills to do and does do. It is the attempted replacement of the divine work by a human manufacture. The divine reality offered and manifested to us in revelation is replaced by a concept of God arbitrarily and wilfully evolved by [humans].

"Arbitrarily and wilfully" means here by [our] own means, by [our] own human insight and constructiveness and energy. Many different images of God can be formed once we have engaged in this undertaking, but their significance is always the same....

True Religion

Religion is never true in itself and as such. The revelation of God denies that any religion is true, i.e., that it is in truth the knowledge and worship of God and

---

*Excerpts from Karl Barth, *Church Dogmatics,* vol. I, 2, *The Doctrine of the Word of God* (New York: Charles Scribners, 1956), 299, 302, 325-27; cf. Bosch, TM, 478-79.

the reconciliation of [humanity] with God. For as the self-offering and self-manifestation of God, as the work of peace which God Himself has concluded between Himself and [humanity], revelation is the truth beside which there is no other truth, over against which there is only lying and wrong. If by the concept of a "true religion" we mean truth which belongs to religion in itself and as such, it is just as unattainable as a "good [person]," if by goodness we mean something which [persons] can achieve on [their] own initiative. No religion is true. It can only become true, i.e., according to that which it purports to be and for which it is upheld. And it can become true only in the way in which [a person] is justified, from without; i.e., not of its own nature and being, but only in virtue of a reckoning and adopting and separating which are foreign to its own nature and being, which are quite inconceivable from its own standpoint, which come to it quite apart from any qualifications or merits. Like justified [persons], religion is a creature of grace. But grace is the revelation of God. No religion can stand before it as a true religion....

All Religions Are under Judgment

In our discussion of "religion as unbelief" we did not consider the distinction between Christian and non-Christian religion. Our intention was that whatever we said about the other religions affected the Christian similarly. In the framework of that discussion we could not speak in any special way about Christianity. We could not give it any special or assured place in face of that judgment. Therefore the discussion cannot be understood as a preliminary polemic against the non-Christian religions, with a view to the ultimate assertion that the Christian religion is the true religion. If this were the case, our task now would be to prove that, as distinct from the non-Christian religions, the Christian is not guilty of idolatry and self-righteousness, that it is not therefore unbelief but faith, and therefore true religion; or, which comes to the same thing, that it is no religion at all, but as against all religions, including their mystical and atheistical self-criticism, it is in itself the true and holy and as such the unspotted and uncontestable form of fellowship between God and [humanity]. To enter on this path would be to deny the very thing we have to affirm.

If the statement is to have any content, we can dare to state that the Christian religion is the true one only as we listen to the divine revelation. But a statement which we dare to make as we listen to the divine revelation can only be a statement of faith. And a statement of faith is necessarily a statement which is thought and expressed in faith and from faith, i.e., in recognition and respect of what we are told by revelation. Its explicit and implicit content is unreservedly conditioned by what we are told. But that is certainly not the case if we try to reach the statement that the Christian religion is the true religion by a road which begins by leaving behind the judgment of revelation, that religion is unbelief, as a matter which does not apply to us Christians, but only to others, the non-Christians, thus enabling us to separate and differentiate ourselves from them with the help of this judgment.

On the contrary, it is our business as Christians to apply this judgment first and most acutely to ourselves....

We must insist, therefore, that at the beginning of a knowledge of the truth of the Christian religion, there stands the recognition that this religion, too, stands under the judgment that religion is unbelief, and that it is not acquitted by any inward worthiness, but only by the grace of God, proclaimed and effectual in His revelation.

GOD'S BUSY-NESS WITH ALL PERSONS

> "In flight from God or search for God or acceptance of God...[persons are] reacting to the action of God upon them in His work of salvation."

■ *D. T. Niles was born in Ceylon in 1908, the son of a distinguished lawyer and the grandson of a much-loved Tamil pastor and poet. After school and college in his native Jaffna, he studied theology in Bangalore, India, from 1929 to 1933. After serving as an SCM secretary in Ceylon and a WSCF secretary in Geneva, he returned to Ceylon, was ordained to the ministry of the Methodist Church, and served as a district evangelist. He was also involved in interfaith dialogue. At the IMC conference in India (Tambaram 1938), he was much influenced by Hendrik Kraemer's Christocentric theology of the religions, yet moved beyond Kraemer in the interreligious world of Asia to greater openness to the "busy-ness of God" among persons of all faiths.*[4]

*The Religious Frontier**

There is a natural home to which each [person] belongs. Indeed, [one] may belong to many such homes—a home being defined in terms of neighbourhood or family, of occupation or social class, of culture or religion, of race, tribe or nation. The Gospel must become present in each home, and everywhere also make its pressure felt against the boundaries which separate home from home, for there is but one household of faith.

The world of religions and the world of nations are two of the insistent realities which condition the homes in which [humans] live. Into these two worlds, interpenetrating one another, the missionary must enter with the Gospel....

When the Gospel Is Proclaimed

The story of the Old Testament is abundant proof that God was busy all the time not only with Israel but with all peoples. When the Gospel declares that God loved

*Excerpts from Daniel T. Niles, *Upon the Earth: The Mission of God and the Missionary Enterprise of the Churches* (New York: McGraw-Hill Book Co., 1962), 227, 236, 237-39; cf. Bosch, TM, 484.

the world, it is this truth that it is declaring. The Gospel is for all [persons] with each of whom and all of whom God is still busy. Christ is seeking them to bring them into His fold (Lk. 15:4). The Christian witness does not grasp the true inwardness of [that] work where [the witness] does not see that God is [previously at work] in the life of the person whom [the witness] is seeking to win for the Gospel, and also previous to [that person] in whatever area of life he [or she] is seeking to make the Gospel effective....

The activity of God in the world, His busy-ness, can be set out within four different frames of thought. 1) There is God in His activity to win [persons] to live in fellowship with Him. 2) There is God in His activity to reveal to [humanity] His true nature and purpose. 3) There is God in His activity to create for Himself a people who will be His instrument in the world. 4) And there is God in His activity to bring to pass His Kingdom into which will be gathered all the treasures of the nations.

It is on this fourfold activity of God that the Church's commission to proclaim the Gospel depends....

God in His Activity of Salvation

God is always busy with every [person], because each [of us] is made in God's image. While it is true that [some] call themselves Hindus or Muslims or Buddhists or Christians and that each of these religions has identifiable and defined beliefs, it is nevertheless also true that the religion of one [person] is not exactly like the religion of another [person]. There is a true sense in which each [one's] religion can be more or can be less than his [or her] religious system. Whether [they] are engaged in flight from God or search for God or acceptance of God (and all [persons] are involved in all these three attitudes at the same time), they are, in all these things, reacting to the action of God upon them in His work of salvation. No [one's] religion and no religious system is purely a [human] product. To say that they are, is to deny that [we are] made in God's image....

The relation between Christian faith and non-Christian faith (both words being used in the singular) is not a relation that can be systematized. The work of the Holy Spirit in each soul cannot be described in the same way. There are those who, because of their previous faith, find themselves prepared to accept the Lordship of Jesus Christ. They also find that, once they have accepted His Lordship, their previous faith undergoes a radical transformation. There are others who, because of their faith, find themselves hindered from accepting the Lordship of Jesus Christ, but who find that, once the Holy Spirit has led them to accept Christ's Lordship, then their original faith is not something they need to throw away. It becomes part of the soil in which their faith in Christ grows and blossoms.

REJECT NOTHING TRUE AND HOLY

> "Acknowledge, preserve and encourage the spiritual and moral truths."

■ *Of all Vatican II documents, the Declaration on the Relationship of the Church to Non-Christian Religions* (Nostra Aetate) *had the most turbulent history. Originally the draft Decree on Ecumenism contained a section on Catholic-Jewish relations. Unable to agree on the text, in part due to fears of Eastern patriarchs, the bishops broadened their horizon. The historic document is an affirmation of the oneness of the human family and that the church respects the spiritual, moral, and cultural values of Hinduism, Buddhism, and Islam.*

*Awareness of a Hidden Power**

2. Throughout history even to the present day, there is found among different peoples a certain awareness of a hidden power, which lies behind the course of nature and the events of human life. At times there is present even a recognition of a supreme being, or still more of a Father. This awareness and recognition results in a way of life that is imbued with a deep religious sense. The religions which are found in more advanced civilizations endeavor by way of well-defined concepts and exact language to answer these questions. Thus, in Hinduism [persons] explore the divine mystery and express it both in the limitless riches of myth and the accurately defined insights of philosophy. They seek release from the trials of the present life by ascetical practices, profound meditation and recourse to God in confidence and love. Buddhism in its various forms testifies to the essential inadequacy of this changing world. It proposes a way of life by which men [and women] can, with confidence and trust, attain a state of perfect liberation and reach supreme illumination either through their own efforts or by the aid of divine help. So, too, other religions which are found throughout the world attempt in their own ways to calm the hearts of [all] by outlining a program of life covering doctrine, moral precepts and sacred rites.

The Catholic Church rejects nothing of what is true and holy in these religions. She has a high regard for the manner of life and conduct, the precepts and doctrines which, although differing in many ways from her own teaching, nevertheless often reflect a ray of that truth which enlightens all. Yet she proclaims and is in duty bound to proclaim without fail, Christ who is the way, the truth and the life (Jn. 14:6). In him, in whom God reconciled all things to himself (2 Cor. 5:18-19), [persons] find the fullness of their religious life.

The Church, therefore, urges her sons [and daughters] to enter with prudence and charity into discussion and collaboration with members of other religions. Let Christians, while witnessing to their own faith and way of life, acknowledge, preserve and encourage the spiritual and moral truths found among non-Christians, also their social life and culture.

---

*Excerpts from "Declaration on the Relation of the Church to Non-Christian Religions" (*Nostra Aetate,* 1965), Art. 2, in *VC2,* 738-39; cf. Bosch, TM, 480.

DIALOGUE IN COMMUNITY

"In dialogue conviction and openness are held in balance."

■ *What are the characteristics of effective interreligious dialogue? In 1971, the Central Committee of the World Council of Churches adopted "interim" guidelines for the ecumenical movement. Major progress in their revision took place at the consultation held in Chiang Mai, Thailand, in 1977 on the theme "Dialogue in Community." The Central Committee received it that year, "welcoming the degree of agreement and mutual understanding represented by it among those who held different theological views." This statement, revised in the light of responses received from the churches, became the WCC's theological basis for its dialogue program.*

*The Theological Significance of People of Other Faiths and Ideologies**

(From Part II, "On Dialogue")

20. Christians engaged in faithful "dialogue in community" with people of other faiths and ideologies cannot avoid asking themselves penetrating questions about the place of these people in the activity of God in history. They ask these questions not in theory, but in terms of what God may be doing in the lives of hundreds of millions of men and women who live in and seek community together with Christians, but along different ways. So dialogue should proceed in terms of people of other faiths and ideologies rather than of theoretical, impersonal systems. This is not to deny the importance of religious traditions and their inter-relationships but it is vital to examine how faiths and ideologies have given direction to the daily living of individuals and groups and actually affect dialogue on both sides.

21. Approaching the theological questions in this spirit Christians should proceed...with repentance, because they know how easily they misconstrue God's revelation in Jesus Christ, betraying it in their actions and posturing as the owners of God's truth rather than, as in fact they are, the undeserving recipients of grace; with humility, because they so often perceive in people of other faiths and ideologies a spirituality, dedication, compassion and a wisdom which should forbid them making judgements about others as though from a position of superiority; in particular they should avoid using ideas such as "anonymous Christians," "the Christian presence," "the unknown Christ," in ways not intended by those who proposed them for theological purposes or in ways prejudicial to the self-understanding of Christians and others; with joy, because it is not themselves they preach; it is Jesus Christ, perceived by many people of living faiths and ideologies as

---

*Excerpts from World Council of Churches, *Guidelines on Dialogue with People of Living Faiths and Ideologies* (Geneva: WCC, 1979), 11-13, 16; cf. Bosch, TM, 484, 487.

prophet, holy one, teacher, example; but confessed by Christians as Lord and Saviour, Himself the faithful witness and the coming one (Rev. 1:5-7); with integrity, because they do not enter into dialogue with others except in this penitent and humble joyfulness in the Lord Jesus Christ, making clear to others their own experience and witness, even as they seek to hear from others their expressions of deepest conviction and insight. All these would mean an openness and exposure, the capacity to be wounded which we see in the example of our Lord Jesus Christ and which we sum up in the word vulnerability.

22. Only in this spirit can Christians hope to address themselves creatively to the theological questions posed by other faiths and by ideologies. Christians from different backgrounds are growing in understanding in the following areas in particular: that renewed attention must be given to the doctrine of creation, particularly as they see it illuminated by the Christian understanding of God as one Holy Trinity and by the resurrection and glorification of Christ; that the aim of dialogue is not reduction of living faiths and ideologies to a lowest common denominator, not only a comparison and discussion of symbols and concepts, but the enabling of a true encounter between those spiritual insights and experiences which are only found at the deepest levels of human life.

Guidelines Recommended to the Churches for Study and Action

(From Part III, "Guidelines...")

It is Christian faith in the Triune God—Creator of all humankind, Redeemer in Jesus Christ, revealing and renewing Spirit—which calls us Christians to human relationship with our many neighbours. Such relationship includes dialogue: witnessing to our deepest convictions and listening to those of our neighbours. It is Christian faith which sets us free to be open to the faith of others, to risk, to trust and to be vulnerable. In dialogue, conviction and openness are held in balance.

TOWARD AN ECUMENICAL ECUMENISM

> "Ecumenical ecumenism would be the way for the religions of the world to enter into a multivoiced dialogue."

■ *Raimundo Panikkar (b. 1918) has lived within two cultures: Hindu and Christian, eastern and western. With earned doctorates in chemistry, philosophy, and theology, he has served as professor at the universities of Madrid, Rome, Harvard, and California. His thirty books have appeared in several languages since he first published* The Unknown Christ of Hinduism *in 1968. He has written more than 300 articles dealing with the philosophy of science, metaphysics, comparative religions, theology, and ideology. A Roman Catholic priest (of the Diocese of Varanasi, India), Panikkar's theology of the religions is theocentric, with Christ understood as authentically universal—as both the symbol and substance of a nondualistic unity between God, humanity, and the world. Since the 1960s, he has called for what he terms an "ecumenical ecumenism"—a striving for "unity without harming diversity" of the world faiths.*[5]

*Unity without Stifling Diversity**

Any serious theological reflection today confronts us with ecumenical problems. We can no longer do theology in isolation or only within our "own" group. Ecumenism is said to be in crisis nowadays. Perhaps it has lost its novelty, but it could also be that it requires a more catholic perspective. The human predicament today requires an extension and transformation of the meaning of the word "ecumenism." Twenty-five years ago I proposed the term "ecumenical ecumenism" to describe the genuine and sincere encounter of religions, following certain tendencies in Christian ecumenism.

Christian ecumenism tries to reach a unity among Christians without stifling their diversity. It does not wish to be a contest which tallies winners and losers. The goal is always a new point of agreement, in deeper loyalty to a principle both transcendent and immanent to the various Christian confessions. And because of the recognition of this transcendence-immanence, agreement does not entail uniformity of opinions; it means harmony of enlightened hearts.

Ecumenical ecumenism attempts to extend this new openness to the entire [human] family. The goal is better understanding, corrective criticism, and eventually mutual fecundation among the religious traditions of the world, without diluting their respective heritages or prejudging their possible harmony or eventual irreducible differences. The task is still ahead of us, but already some fruits can be seen ripening.

Ecumenical ecumenism has a twofold meaning, both Christian and ecumenical:

(a) Christian ecumenism, if it is really to be ecumenical, cannot be reduced to settling Christian family feuds, as it were, or healing old wounds. It has also to take into account the entire world situation and try to find the place of the religions of the world in the "Christian Economy of Salvation," without any *a priori* subordination of other religions to the Christian self-understanding. And this cannot be done without watering down this latter Christian sense of identity.

(b) Ecumenical ecumenism would be the way for the religions of the world to enter into a multivoiced dialogue. I would call it *dharma-samanvaya* or harmonization (convergence, coming together) of all dharmas or religions, i.e., of all traditions dealing with human ultimacy. I repeat that *samanvaya* does not have to mean sameness, but it conveys the hope that today's cacophony may be converted into a symphony tomorrow.

Christians should not shun participating in this ecumenical round table. They have been pioneers in modern ecumenism, as they have also distinguished themselves in intolerance and exclusivism. Both the positive and the negative experi-

---

*Excerpts from Raimundo Panikkar, "Editorial: Toward an Ecumenical Ecumenism," *Journal of Ecumenical Studies* 19, no. 4 (Fall 1982): 781-82, 782-83; cf. Bosch, TM, 477-78.

ences are an invaluable contribution. Ecumenical ecumenism represents the common search for truth in a genuine dialogical (not just dialectical) attitude which is open not only to one another but also to any other possible dimension of immanence and/or transcendence.

The basic premise of ecumenical ecumenism is that no one individual or collectivity has universal awareness. Awareness dawns with the discovery of the other: no other, no awareness. Whether the other encountered is the physical environment (science), the metaphysical realm (religion), or other people and their works (humanities), human awareness can only be stillborn unless and until it begins to assimilate this fundamental polarity. Yet we have a tendency to construct for ourselves an increasingly uninhabitable world broken into combat zones between "us" and "them." The very word *ecumene* should be redeemed from its ethnocentric connotations.

This either/or mentality seems to be at the root of the current human malaise. And obviously religions, which deal with ultimate problems, are especially sensitive to this kind of exclusivism which condemns the other. We should distinguish here between "relativism" which is agnostic and untenable and "relativity" which is realistic and takes into account that truth itself is relational. On the existential level it is the question of how people and peoples are to relate constructively to one another. It is the most pressing, and often the most studiously avoided, human question of our day. It should not be necessary to evoke the specter of world famine and nuclear weapons to make this point clear. It is obvious that we need to draw upon the strengths of all the traditions of humankind in order to surmount this impasse.

A HINDU CHRISTIANITY

> "Asian theology is...a baptism in the Jordan of our Precursor's religiosity."

■ *Had St. Paul founded a church in Benares, Bangkok, or Beijing and written a letter to the Christians there, we would possess some scriptural norm or apostolic tradition to follow in contextualizing Christianity in non-Semitic cultures. Aloysius Pieris, a Sri Lankan Jesuit theologian, wrestles with the reality that the doctrinal traditions of the early church were born almost exclusively out of encounters with the Semitic and Greco-Roman worlds. Although Christianity reached India and Central Asia during the first five centuries, we lack written sources concerning those missionary efforts. Although early medieval missions to northern Europe provide models for the encounter of Christianity with local cosmic (folk) religions, Pieris finds them of limited value in relating to the metacosmic high religions (Hinduism and Buddhism). He advocates an Asian theology "baptised in the waters of Asian religiosity."*

*Inculturation in Non-Semitic Asia**

Had St. Paul founded a Church in Benares, Bangkok or Beijing and had he written an epistle to the Christians there, we would have had some scriptural norm or some kind of Apostolic tradition to follow in forging our ecclesial identity in the non-Semitic cultures of Asia. Granted that the early Church might have had some such experience in the case of the "St. Thomas" Christians in Kerala or the Nestorians in Central Asia, the fact remains that the doctrines and opinions articulated as the authoritative tradition of the early church were almost exclusively born of her encounter with the Semitic and the Graeco-Roman worlds, and not with the Sino-Indian religiosity. Most Asian churches have no precedent to follow. They are called upon to create something new, the orthodoxy of which cannot be gauged from the available models....

Greco-Roman Models Not Applicable in Asia

The separation of religion from culture (as in Latin Christianity) and religion from philosophy (as in Hellenic Christianity) makes little sense in an Asian society. For instance, in the South Asian context, culture and religion are overlapping facets of one indivisible soteriology which is at once a view of life and a path of deliverance; it is both a philosophy which is basically a religious vision, and a religion which is a philosophy of life.[6]

The very word *inculturation* which is of Roman Catholic origin and inspiration is based on this culture-religion dichotomy of the Latins, in that it could, and often does, mean the insertion of "the Christian religion minus European culture" into an "Asian culture minus non-Christian religion." This is inconceivable in the South Asian context just alluded to; what seems possible and even necessary, there, is not just in*cultur*ation but "in*religion*isation" of the Church....

Baptized in the Waters of Asian Religiosity

Whoever...thinks of inculturation not as an ecclesiastical expansion into non-Christian cultures but as the forging of an indigenous ecclesial identity from within the *soteriological* perspectives of Asian religions, has begun moving along the right direction. Let me then indicate three road signs which have already helped us move further along this new path.

Firstly, the bidimensional soteriology of the non-Christian religions wherein our cosmic involvement with the Present is tempered by a metacosmic orientation towards a Future which constantly relativises the Here and Now, offers us a ready-made frame of reference for our spirituality, liturgy, ecclesial witness, social engagement and theological formulations. Secondly, Asian theology is not the fruit

---

*Excerpts from Aloysius Pieris, "Inculturation in Non-Semitic Asia," *The Month,* no. 1420 (1986) 83-85; cf. Bosch, TM, 477-78.

of excogitation but a process of explicitation, or more specifically a Christic apocalypse of the non-Christian struggle for Liberation. Thirdly, since we only explicitate a pre-existent theology implicitly contained in the non-Christian soteriologies, the procedure adopted is not one of "Instrumentalising" the non-Christian schemas, but one of assimilation through participation in the non-Christian ethos, a baptism in the Jordan of our Precursor's religiosity, a sort of *communicatio in sacris* which allows the "little flock of Christ" to feed freely on Asian pastures which it has been trampling for centuries. There is no danger of theological vandalism here.

Here I think it quite appropriate to cite the example of the Benedictine monk, Swami Abhishiktananda (Henri le Saux) whose fair complexion and French accent were about the only things left of his European past after his baptismal immersion in the waters of Hinduism. He has so well absorbed the Hindu spirituality (i.e., theology in the primordial sense of God-experience) that his many utterances on the Christ-Mystery (theology in the secondary sense of God-Talk) have become indispensable guide posts in the Church's search for the Asian Face of Christ.

DIALOGUE AS A SEARCH FOR JUSTICE

> "In the process of dialogue, justice is not only affirmed, but also created."

■ *In her teaching and writing, Marjorie Hewitt Suchocki combines concerns for process theology, feminism, and dialogue with world religions. From a feminist perspective, she affirms the struggles of all women throughout the world for selfhood, well-being, and justice. From this perspective, she contends, one must radically affirm religious pluralism. Dr. Suchocki is presently vice-president for academic affairs and dean at Claremont School of Theology in California. Formerly dean at Wesley Theological Seminary in Washington, D.C., she also taught and directed the Doctor of Ministry program at Pittsburgh Theological Seminary.*

*Justice a Focus of Dialogue**

Liberation theology has pointed to the invidious effects that follow when one mode of humanity is made normative for others. Such normativeness, combined with power, allows and invites exploitation of all those falling outside the norm. Furthermore, it distorts the perspective of those counted as falling within the norm, leading to problems in adequately knowing either self or others. As liberation

---

*Excerpts from Marjorie Hewitt Suchocki, "In Search of Justice: Religious Pluralism from a Feminist Perspective," in *The Myth of Christian Uniqueness: Toward a Pluralistic Theology of Religions,* ed. John Hick and Paul F. Knitter (Maryknoll, NY: Orbis Books, 1987), 149, 159, 160; cf. Bosch, TM, 489.

theologians—whether feminist, black, or Third World—have dealt with this theme, they have focused on universalized norms in the realm of social, political, and personal structures of existence. The thesis of this essay is that the principle holds for religion as well: universalizing one religion such that it is taken as the norm whereby all other religions are judged and valued leads to oppression, and hence falls short of the norm that liberationists consider ultimate—the normative justice that creates well-being in the world community.

A feminist perspective, therefore, suggests that one must radically affirm religious pluralism, but not without bringing a critical consciousness of well-being in human community to interreligious and intrareligious discussion. Justice is thus to be the fundamental criterion of value and the focus of dialogue and action among religions....

Justice as Norm

We must look to the heart of justice in each religion as that which renders life meaningful in light of a vision of what existence should be. Using justice as a norm means that the primary visions within each religion of what societal life should be in a "perfect" world is a source of judgment that can be used internally within each religion to judge its present societal forms of justice. Dialogue among the religions can likewise proceed from the development of mutual concerns for justice that can lead to concerted actions for justice in the world. Justice is a dynamic and transformative notion, capable of being used even to judge itself....

Interreligious dialogue at the societal/personal levels of justice will discover that what constitutes dignity will be defined differently in various cultures. There may be no single standard. The situation may be even more culturally specific at the third level—that is, openness to self-development and self-determination within the context of community. Even to name this as an aspect of justice may be to witness to Western culture, with its emphasis on the individual. However, the phrase "within the context of community" should mitigate even Western individualism, for it indicates that what constitutes self-development is relative to the community in which it takes place. Divergences of communities on these issues are not antithetical to justice, but in fact become the test of justice.

Affirming religious pluralism within the context of justice shifts the focus of dialogue to the concreteness of human well-being. The very exploration of human well-being, however, inevitably directs our attention to questions concerning how we determine what constitutes well-being, or into the heart of the ideological nature of the religions. Interreligious dialogue focused on justice promotes intrareligious dialogue concerning ultimate and penultimate values. The pluralism among religions then finds itself calling attention to the pluralism within each religion; dialogue engenders dialogues. Affirming one another's diversity may grant us the privilege of "listening in" to the internal dialogues, in the hope of understanding and mutual transformations. One vision of justice can temper, criticize, and deepen another, and through dialogue each vision might grow richer in understanding and implementation.

In any case, a norm of justice used in the valuation of religions allows the affirmation of religious pluralism without plunging us into religious relativism, wherein we have no rational ground for distinguishing between a "Jonestown" religion and an Amish village. The norm, however, must be used self-consciously and dialogically in recognition of the fact that the norm is hardly culture-free. In the process of dialogue, justice is not only affirmed, but also created.

THE OPENMINDED TRANSLATOR

> "Translation...is cultural maturity and openmindedness on a staggering scale."

■ *Lamin Sanneh, a native of Gambia, is professor of missions and world Christianity at Yale Divinity School, Yale University. Formerly he taught at the Center for the Study of World Religions, Harvard University, and at the University of Aberdeen in Scotland. In* Translating the Message: The Missionary Impact on Culture *(1988), he developed further the thesis presented in the following essay that Christian missionaries who promoted the translation of the Bible into vernacular languages thereby affirmed both a pluralism of cultures and of religious perspectives.*

*Pluralism and Commitment Can Go Together**

In much of the literature on religious pluralism, Christians are presented with a stark, uncompromising choice: *either* they accept pluralism as the way of being religious and so cast doubt on the uniqueness of Christianity, *or* they reject pluralism as the price for continuing to hold to some form of Christian orthodoxy. The choice, thus framed, suggests a relentless conflict between Christian commitment and the wider demands of pluralism.

The issue of pluralism, however, may be approached from a different position in which Christian commitment is seen as compatible with genuine pluralism, at least in such a way that it is not necessary or even helpful to bargain away Christian commitment lest there result a diminution of the full potential of pluralism....

The Vernacular Principle

Christian missionaries assumed that since all cultures and languages are lawful in God's eyes, the rendering of God's word into those languages and cultures is valid and necessary. Even if in practice Christians wished to stop the translation

---

*Excerpts from Lamin Sanneh, "Pluralism and Christian Commitment," *Theology Today* 45:1 (April 1988): 21, 27, 33; cf. Bosch, TM, 484.

process, claiming their own form of it as final and exclusive, they have not been able to suppress it. At any rate, Christian mission became the most explicit machinery for the cultivation of vernacular particularity as a condition of universal faithfulness to the gospel. In centering on the primacy of God's word, Christian translators invested the vernacular with consecrated power, lifting obscure tribes to the level of scriptural heritage and into the stream of universal world history. Almost everywhere vernacular participation in the Christian movement led to internal religious and cultural renewal, often with immediate consequences for political nationalism. The Christian view that culture may serve God's purpose stripped culture of idolatrous liability, emancipating it with the force of translation and usage....

Much of the heat with which mission has been attacked as Western cultural imperialism begins to dissipate when we apply the vernacular principle, for that principle soon brings us upon the safety plank of indigenous appropriation as the fulfilling mode of mission. Those missionaries who were uncompromisingly committed to the gospel, whether Catholic or Protestant, could scarcely fall back on Western caricatures of others after they had conceded through translation the autonomy of indigenous arrangements for conveying God's word. In fact, the logic of such translation work was to make missionaries and their complex bundle of motives peripheral, with serious-minded ones among them willing to see God's will done, however surprising the results.

This is cultural maturity and openmindedness on a staggering scale....

Conclusion

Christian pluralism in its uncompromising, rigorous form is not only a committed state of mind with respect to God's undivided sovereignty but a committed style of living with respect to culture's pluralist and accountable status, and in that convergence we may find remedy for the conflict in our time between religion and contending cultural ideologies.

AUTHENTIC DIALOGUE

"Seek to find Christ already present in the other person."

■ *In 1991, SEDOS, a study and documentation center at the service of seventy-two Catholic missionary societies, convened an important seminar in Rome on the occasion of its Silver Jubilee. "Dialogue" was one of the ten subthemes in the report entitled* Trends in Mission: Toward the Third Millenium. *Participants identified two forms of Christian proclamation. The first, with a "centripetal" purpose, is concerned with leading people directly into the church, with conversion as its chief aim. The second, more "centrifugal" in nature, seeks to recognize and further the values of the Kingdom, with dialogue, inculturation, and liberation as its chief concerns. Next, they identified the following fourteen aspects of dialogue today.*

Aspects of Dialogue Today*

1) Dialogue presupposes a strong faith in God, a deep hope in the continuing action of the Holy Spirit in all men and women, and a fidelity to prayer. It is often exercised in a dynamic of "faith supporting faith."

2) It is a fruitful "locus" of theology. The reflection of the church on situations of dialogue and the practice of dialogue is itself a valuable source of theology. Theology should not only underpin dialogue but should arise from it.

3) A dialogical attitude is an absolute necessity for all engaged in mission today. There is a sense in which dialogue can be described as constitutive of mission, as an integral part of proclaiming the gospel. Nevertheless it is not an end in itself. The coming of God's Reign is the goal of dialogue.

4) The love of Christ leaves us no option but to dialogue. Questions like "How? With whom? Where?" call for practical approaches as a consequence of this love.

5) Unless one goes to meet the other in life situations, one may never become involved with him or her in dialogue. It is necessary to risk taking the first step in breaking what is often a vicious circle of misunderstanding.

6) Dialogue is multifaceted: there is interreligious dialogue with people of other faiths, as for example the great religions of Asia; dialogue with people of ancestral religions in Africa, Asia, and Latin America; dialogue with "post-Christians"; with non-believers; with followers of secular ideologies; and there is dialogue between the followers of the great Asian religions themselves which Christians can only observe and accompany sympathetically.

7) Recognition and acceptance of legitimate pluralism in interpreting the Christian message is essential for Christians entering into dialogue. So also is the self-understanding of other faiths—how they themselves understand their religious beliefs.

8) Discerning the values of God's Reign is of paramount importance in dialogue which often begins in a common search for these values in particular contexts. The pursuit of these values can bring about solidarity, understanding, confidence and trust, mutual enrichment, communion, and participation. These values transcend the confines of different religions; it could be said that the soul of dialogue is "disinterested" communion.

9) Dialogue has an ecclesial dimension for Christians. This implies communion with, support of, and encouragement by the appropriate church institutions. Members of Mission Societies have an analogous relationship with the appropriate authorities of their Societies to whom they look for understanding and encouragement.

10) The quality of dialogue within the church itself affects the wider dialogue.

---

*Excerpt from "Authentic Dialogue Today: Reflections of Participants at the SEDOS Conference," in *Trends in Mission: Toward the Third Millenium; Essays in Celebration of Twenty-five Years of SEDOS,* ed. William Jenkinson, CSSp, and Helene O'Sullivan, MM (Maryknoll, NY: Orbis Books, 1991), 288-89; cf. Bosch, TM, 483-85.

It is difficult to participate in dialogue and to emphasize the need for and values of dialogue, if within the institutional church itself there is lack of dialogue at appropriate levels and in appropriate situations.

11) In dialogue with ancestral religions, the church is called to be a real and significant protector of these religions and of the values of God's Reign found in them.

12) The experience of dialogue can be one of great joy, but when dialogue is rejected or made seemingly impossible by one party, the experience is closer to that of the "suffering servant." One must be able to absorb criticism and suffer pain in dialogue.

13) Christians in dialogue seek to find Jesus Christ already present in the other person, in other institutionalized religions, and even in ideologies or secular realities. This search, in honest and respectful dialogue, involves risks on both sides.

14) Any kind of dialogue is rooted in a "dialogue of life" which supports more formal exchanges and brings about a growing together in closer communion. This often effects a kind of conversion in both parties by a deeper submissiveness to the truth.

Some Criteria for Identifying Authentic Dialogue

The following emerged as criteria for an authentic dialogue.

1) Dialogue cannot take place from a position of power. There is "powerlessness" that is empowering, the powerlessness manifested in the life of Jesus. Dialogue requires this powerlessness. It is not contrived. It does not seek to dominate or to pressurize.

2) Dialogue is not a technique or a process necessarily bringing about results. When there is an impasse it may continue only as a dialogue of life or a dialogue of prayer, but these are not alternative or further steps undertaken because dialogue at the level of mutual conversation has ceased.

3) Basic to dialogue is an understanding of oneself, of one's values, attitudes, and prejudices. Without this inner or intradialogue and centeredness, dialogue with others is extremely difficult. Growth in self-knowledge is not only a prerequisite but also a consequence of dialogue. It is part of the wider requirement needed in order to understand the other and to understand the situation in which dialogue is taking place.

4) Dialogue of life frequently involves sharing poverty and insecurity, and being involved in a search for justice and integral liberation. In many of the situations of dialogue "the option for the poor" is crucial. Such an option frequently brings its own rewards: a deeper awareness of the bonds of humanness which unite all women and men, a deepening of one's own faith, and liberation from a ghetto mentality.

5) Without a certain simplicity of lifestyle dialogue is difficult, often meaningless.

Questions That Emerged for Further Discussion

1) "God wanted all perfection to be found in him and all things to be reconciled through him and for him" (Col. 1:19-20). On the basis of this and similar texts the "fulfillment" theory has been developed: the Good News of the gospel is to subsume the values, fill the lacunae, and overcome the negative or evil dimensions of the culture it encounters. This theory is intolerably patronizing for many, not least many Hindus. It does not recognize that the Good News is necessarily conveyed through a cultural medium, a contextual situation. Is the church not always a searching church, always seeking to reform itself regardless of the culture in which it is incarnated, even Western culture? Does the "fulfillment" theory effectively block dialogue?

2) When one partner is clearly unwilling to remain open, dialogue cannot lead to mutual enrichment. How can dialogue continue in the face of such an impasse? By praying? Living in hope? Learning to ask the right questions? Hearing the answers and simply trying to understand the significance of the answers?

3) The difficulty of dialogue from a position of power raises questions for professional experts in mission. The exercise of a profession in mission even in a spirit of service can place one in a position of quasi-dominative power. What is the effect of this on dialogue?

4) Does the possibility of conversion militate against sincere dialogue? What are the criteria for sincere conversion?

5) Dialogue leads to an even more fundamental question: what is the nature of the Christian presence in the world today? How can we distinguish the essential from the nonessential elements in the church? The Christian was "the soul of the world" for some of the Fathers of the church. What relevance has this in the dialogical approach of today?

6) Is aptitude for interreligious dialogue a special charism which should be given consideration in formation programs and in assignments?

DIALOGUE AS MISSION

> "A dialogical situation allows for the affirmation of our respective identities."

■ *In 1992, Emilio Castro, general secretary of the WCC, published a collection of essays on the occasion of his retirement. Entitled* A Passion for Unity, *they represented the mature reflections of the distinguished Uruguayan Methodist on key issues of ecumenism and mission. In his chapter on "Missionary Identity and Interfaith Dialogue," Dr. Castro sought to rescue interreligious dialogue from the rarified atmosphere of the academic debate. Instead, he prefers dialogue to be the joyful encounter of persons eager to share their deepest faith convictions and receive those of others.*

*Missionary Identity**

It is my contention that in the encounter with people of other religious persuasions or no religious persuasion, Christians should confess openly their missionary identity. It belongs to the centre of our faith, to our understanding of God. It is basic to our Christology and to our anthropology. God is love, consuming love for creation and creature; and the whole of creation should be conceived as the visible manifestation of that love of God which communicates existence and life. The Spirit of God is affirmed as the sustaining life-giving reality. We recognize God's communicative, sustaining nature in all the stories of the Bible, but fully in Jesus Christ—the redeeming, reconciling, suffering, liberating God calling all human beings to partnership and communion. This awareness of God's own nature, which is the secret source of all human creativity, is for Christians the foundation of their testimony....

The Elements of Dialogue

But this of course gives importance to the discussion of the "rules of the game." How do we relate to each other? How do we encounter each other? What factors need to be taken into consideration in our interreligious encounters in the light of our experience and the diversity of situations in the world?

1. First, in every dialogical situation the relations of power between the participants should be taken into consideration. Dialogue does not happen in a void; it is not an intellectual exercise behind the protected walls of a Western university. Dialogue is very often a matter of life and death. It is carried on in the middle of tensions that divide human communities, at both the level of options to be considered and of emotions that are being raised....

While the ideal situation for a dialogue is that in which neither partner is afraid of the other, this ideal does not always prevail. Yet because dialogue is absolutely necessary, risks should be taken to promote it. Why? This leads us to our second consideration.

2. Much present-day religious dialogue seems to originate in the affirmation of rational discourse and a tolerant attitude towards others that is accompanied by a certain relativism of convictions. If we do not believe that anybody can come to final philosophical truth, we can invite everyone to express his or her own convictions in the hope that all will learn in the process without having to pass judgement and without being threatened....

My contention is that the dialogical attitude should not be bound to a specific philosophical presupposition, least of all to a relativist one. Dialogue should be an encounter of loyalties, in which the question of reciprocal identity is fundamental. Dialogue, respect and openness to the other should be so anchored in our own

---

*Excerpts from Emilio Castro, *A Passion for Unity: Essays on Ecumenical Hopes and Challenges* (Geneva: WCC Publications, 1992), 44-45, 46, 47, 48, 49-50, 51, 52; cf. Bosch, TM, 487-88.

religious conviction as to be an integral part of the central core of our confession.... Only as we anchor the value of dialogue in the central convictions of our faith are we able to eliminate the elitist character of our dialogue and multiply the normal and joyful encounter of all members of all religious communities....

Multilateral Dialogues

3. While the normal dialogical situation is bilateral, involving people of two different religious persuasions living side by side and coming together to share experiences and concerns, multi-religious dialogue is growing. Though multilateral dialogues may have a certain artificiality because the problems remain so general, they do fulfill several important roles....

4. Interreligious dialogue is a value in itself and should be recognized as a vocation within our different religious communities, just as in the Christian community we recognize certain persons whose main vocation is diaconal service and others who have a particular gift of rendering testimony of their faith. Interreligious encounter does not need to be justified in terms of other values but has a validity in itself. At least two components of dialogue should be highlighted within that specific vocation:

Reciprocal testimony to the basic convictions of each of the partners....

Care for the building up of the total society...."It is in the search for a just community of humankind that Christians and their neighbours will be able to help each other break out of cultural, educational, political and social isolation in order to realize a more participatory society."

Religious Syncretism

5. It is necessary to speak very briefly on the question of religious syncretism. Many are afraid of entering into dialogue because they think that behind it lies a hidden or open attempt to produce one "world religion" by mixing different components of our respective traditions. As far as I know, no religion is interested in a kind of basic world religion and even less in a religion whose identity lies in its pretension to express the future world religion. Syncretism as a project is totally artificial. Religions respond to historical developments and have created different cultures, different perspectives. They have a life and value of their own, and no one can bring them together into a single pattern.

Of course, in a dialogical situation we live side by side, and thus there are many opportunities for encounter and recognition of the best of our respective traditions. It is unavoidable that some reciprocal penetration takes place. We might talk of cultural syncretism. Christians hope that this will be a Christ-centred syncretism. Others will look at it from a different perspective. But we will not be closed to the possibilities of reciprocal influence that exist in our dialogical encounter, even to the risk of conversion....

Syncretism is not a goal; it is not something to be sought. On the contrary, a dialogical situation allows for the affirmation of our respective identities. At the same time, only God is in control of the future, and only the Spirit knows the dimension of truth that God will open in front of us.

NOTES

1. Cf. Eric J. Sharpe, *Faith Meets Faith: Some Christian Attitudes to Hinduism in the Nineteenth & Twentieth Centuries* (London: SCM Press, 1977), pp. 19-32.

2. Cf. "Kraemer," in *DEM,* pp. 574-75, and Carl F. Hallencreutz, *New Approaches to Men of Other Faiths* (Geneva: WCC, 1969), pp. 21-39.

3. Cf. Paul F. Knitter, *No Other Name?* (Maryknoll, NY: Orbis Books, 1985), pp. 80-87.

4. Cf. "Niles," in *DEM,* p. 729-30.

5. Cf. Knitter, *No Other Name?* pp. 152-57.

6. [For] a theological reflection on this, see A. Pieris, S.J., "Towards an Asian Theology of Liberation: Some Religio-Cultural Guidelines," in *Asia's Struggle for Full Humanity,* ed. V. Fabella (Maryknoll, NY: Orbis Books, 1980), p. 91.

16

Mission as Theology

In 1956, members of the North American Association of the Professors of Mission heard Creighton Lacy's somber assessment of the place of the study of Christian mission (missiology) in the theological curriculum:

> *We in the field of missions are lost sheep, scattered among folds of history, theology, comparative religions, and education, wandering from theological to practical fields and back again. We are so busy looking at the world revolution and the fresh strategies of the mission field that we have failed to analyze the changes required in our own teaching. We have barely nibbled at the ecumenical movement and missionary education and theology. We proclaim in our lectures and sermons that the World Mission is the central task of the Church, yet we have all too often allowed it to become peripheral in our curricula.*[1]

In the same year, a blue-ribbon commission headed by H. Richard Niebuhr of Yale University included non-Christian religions, but not missiology, in the recommended fields of study for Christian ministry.[2]

From this nadir, missiology has risen to become an important interdisciplinary field of theological study.[3] *Bosch traces the earlier history, from mission as the "mother of theology" in the first century to the loss of theology's missionary dimension as Christianity became the established religion of Europe. The Protestant Reformation, on the whole, did not change this reality; mission remained on the periphery of the church and did not evoke any theological interest (Bosch, TM, 489-90).*

The selections below cover varied contemporary understandings of mission as theology. In Chapter 5 we traced the recovery of mission for the church. Fearful that this recovery may result in the exporting of cultural brands of Christianity, Visser 't Hooft, the WCC's first general secretary, called for a renewed grounding of mission in the apostolic kerygma.

"The church exists for mission as a fire exists for burning," wrote Emil Brunner, the noted Swiss theologian. If the church recovers this understanding of its purpose,

what will be missiology's place in the theological curriculum? Is it to be a theological discipline in its own right, alongside church history, theology, ethics, and so on? Or is it to be more of a catalyst, enabling theology to recover its essential missionary dimension (Bosch, TM, 494)? Wilhelm Andersen, the noted German missiologist, argues that theology ceases to be theology if it loses its missionary character. Winburn Thomas concurs that "to teach theology is to affirm the missionary imperative" and suggests implications of this understanding for teaching in various theological disciplines. Out of a lifetime of teaching missiology in Germany, Hans-Werner Gensichen warns his colleagues to "fight all temptation to isolation from within and without." From Canada, Virginia Peacock would refocus the goal of all theological education. Instead of a focus on acquiring religious knowledge, she would prepare persons "for mission in and to a world in need," with missiology as the essential catalyst in that transformation.

All these are contributions from the North. Turning to the South—to Latin America, Asia, and Africa—the basic understandings of mission as theology change. Instead of knowing God through abstract thought, the emphasis is on knowing God in action. Theology—whether biblical, historical, or ecclesiological—must be reflection on the church's action, and that action must be missional. Orlando Costas of Puerto Rico, when dean of the Andover Newton Theological Seminary (USA), called the theological schools both to "a deeper understanding of the human mosaic" and to a spirituality of missional engagement. J. Paul Rajashekar, out of the Indian cultural reality, would make interreligious encounter an essential component of equipping for mission and evangelization. Jean-Marc Éla of Cameroon believes that theology is learned only in the act of liberating the poor. In each of these approaches, mission as theology finds its enabling role in both action and reflection.

THE MISSIONARY ENTERPRISE AND THEOLOGY

"The missionary enterprise...provides theology with its themes, its problems, and the correct presuppositions for their solution."

■ *In the 1950s, theological education in Europe and North America was in danger of divorcing theology from the missionary enterprise. Concerned about this trend, the International Missionary Council engaged Wilhelm Andersen to write a research pamphlet on* Towards a Theology of Mission: A Study of the Encounter between the Missionary Enterprise and the Church and its Theology. *In it, the noted German missiologist demonstrated how each of the theological disciplines (biblical, historical, theological, practical) was obliged to pay attention to the problem of the missionary enterprise if it were to be true to itself.*

*The Mutual Relationship between the Missionary Enterprise and Theology**

The relationship between theology and the missionary enterprise cannot, if it is genuine, remain one-sided. Just as the critical theological reflection of the missionary enterprise has demonstrated its character as a spiritual necessity to the Church, if the Church is to remain a living body, so conversely for the theological work of the Church, it is a question of life or death whether or no it remains in contact with the missionary enterprise.

To make such contact a reality, it is not enough that, now and then and in one fashion or another, the missionary enterprise should be referred to or glanced at within the framework of the conventional programme of theological studies. There is hardly one of the major theological disciplines in which the very nature of the subject itself does not make it obligatory to pay some attention to the problem of the missionary enterprise. It is hardly evidence of intellectual and spiritual vitality in theology, when missions are treated only under the heading "practical theology" and in connection with the Church's works of charity. In reality, the missionary enterprise should find its place first and foremost in the development of the programme of biblical exegesis; for the material with the interpretation of which the exegete is concerned is the Word of God spoken to, and sent forth into, the world. [Exegetes], who [have] not understood that [their] exegetical labours have to do with those acts of God Himself which are the source and origin of all missionary effort, [have] not found the right presuppositions with which to approach [their] work. Exactly the same is true of the Church historian, that is, of the [person] who has undertaken the responsibility of tracing out the path of the Church among the nations and through the successive epochs of history. For the Church, in regard to its history, can in the last resort be understood only from the standpoint of the missionary enterprise....

Mission Provides Theology's Themes

The Church has a history only because God has given to it the privilege of participating in His own mission. It is only from this point of view that its history can be seen to have a meaning and a purpose. Finally, a true dogmatic theology, which poses the problem of the content of the Church's witness to the world and tests the proclamation of the Church's message in the light of the revealed Word of God, cannot be imagined as subsisting without innumerable points of contact with the missionary enterprise.

Nevertheless, when we have said all this, the problem of the establishment of a fruitful relationship between theology and the missionary enterprise has not yet been solved. It is not a case of theology occupying itself with the missionary enterprise as and when it seems to it appropriate to do so; it is rather a case of the

---

*Excerpts from Wilhelm Andersen, *Towards a Theology of Mission* (London: SCM Press, 1955), 59-60; cf. Bosch, TM, 494-96.

missionary enterprise being that subject with which theology is to deal. This is meant in the most literal sense of the words. The missionary enterprise in the strict sense of the term, that is to say the self-revelation of the triune God in the Son and in the Holy Spirit, provides theology with its themes, its problems, and the correct presuppositions for their solution. The Lord of the Church is also the Lord of theology. It is only in this relationship of service that theology can find its true freedom.

MISSIONS THROUGHOUT THE CURRICULUM

> "Missions ...must be taught by every conscientious professor of Theology."

■ *Dr. Winburn T. Thomas arrived in Japan in 1933 as a Presbyterian missionary. Repatriated on the eve of World War II, he engaged in doctoral studies at Yale University, writing his dissertation, which was finally published in 1959, on* Protestant Beginnings in Japan. *In that same year, his "Notes on Missions in the Curriculum" was published in a* festschrift *honoring the distinguished German missiologist Walter Freytag. At a time when many North American theological schools dismissed the study of missions as anachronistic and unessential, Thomas countered that missions has a central place in every discipline of theology. At the time of writing this essay, Thomas was the Chicago representative of the Commission on Ecumenical Mission and Relations of the United Presbyterian Church in the U.S.A. and guest professor of missions at McCormick Theological Seminary.*

*Concentric Circles**

Thirty years ago, in accepting the call to be professor of Homiletics in an Eastern theological seminary, [a scholar]...insisted that his subject be made the hub of the curriculum. As he outlined the seminary courses, each of the theological disciplines was related to preaching, like the spokes in a wheel which focus on the center.

A better figure to describe the field of theological disciplines is that of a series of concentric circles. The nucleus or central hub is not equidistant from every other; rather the separate disciplines vary considerably in the extent of their mutual relations. Biblical studies and dogmatics, for instance, are more closely related than is Hebrew to Pastoral Theology. But at some point in the field, one of the circles of each discipline intersects one of the orbit circles of every other subject....

---

*Excerpts from Winburn T. Thomas, "Notes on Missions in the Curriculum," in *Basileia: Walter Freytag zum 60. Geburtstag,* ed. von Jan Hermelink and Hans Jochen Margull (Stuttgart, Germany: Evang. Missionsverlag, 1959), 326, 327-29; cf. Bosch, TM, 498.

Missions in the Curriculum

Departments of missions or ecumenics in American seminaries tend to stress the classic disciplines more than the practical approach. Then missionary history may be taught as Church History, for it is the story of the expansion of the world Christian community. The studies of non-Christian religions may be considered as a branch of ethics or anthropology. The theology of missions may be subsumed under the department of theology, or of dogma. The biblical basis of missions may be studied in the department of the Old and New Testaments. Methods of mission work, however, is taught in only a few institutions, and primarily for professional missionaries or national Christians from abroad.

The emergence of national churches in most lands where missions have gone must inevitably affect the curricular approach. The indigenous ecclesiastical institutions are replacing those operated by missions. The missionary is quantitatively unimportant compared with the workers in the national and local churches. The relation of western church bodies to the younger churches has changed from parental to fraternal. These changes in the life and work of the younger churches must be reflected in the courses being taught in seminaries.

Too many missionary sermons are based on "The Great Commission." But the entire Bible is saturated with missionary motivation and purpose. The Indonesian language does not distinguish between the terms "evangelism" and "missions." The *apostles* of the Book of the Acts would have been *missionaries* had the language in which the original was written been Latin instead of Greek. To be a Christian is to proclaim the Word of God in Christ reconciling the world to Himself; to make such a witness is to be a missionary. This fact is writ large throughout the Bible. The division of labor whereby some believers have been set aside as professional "missionaries" has diluted the biblical concept. God's revelation of Himself through the Word, Christ, is recorded in the Bible, and through study and meditation upon it, God can and does reveal Himself to each of us anew. Missions is the believer's proper response to the God who acts, an action set forth in the Old and New Testaments, and incarnate anew in the faithful of every age.

Missions, therefore, must be taught by every conscientious professor of Theology. There is no separate "Theology of Missions," for to place our power of thought in the service of faith—which is the function and activity of the theologian—is to deal with God's supreme revelation through Christ. God has spoken this Word for all...if in [its] conquest of space human beings who are guilty of self-will are discovered, then they too are objects of God's love, to whom His message of reconciliation and redemption should be preached....To teach *Theology* is to affirm the *missionary imperative.*

The History of the Christian Church is both an account of its missionary expansion, and the development of the clue to world history. Church History can be and is taught from other perspectives, e.g., the History of Dogma, or the History of Christian Social Teachings. Too frequently, Seminary courses taper off after the Protestant Reformation, as though little of import had been said since Luther and Calvin. Each of the younger churches has been so absorbed in the making of ecclesiastical history that its leaders have to develop a historical sense. Yet when they do, indigenous church history will trace the coming of the missionaries, the origin and establishment of the church, the development of national church institutions, the emergence of indigenous Christian thought, and the impact of the younger life upon the world church. With the exception of the Japanese, no self-conscious attempt has been made to analyze and record the history of the younger churches. When these studies finally are undertaken, they will enrich the thought and life of the entire Ecumenical Movement....

Homiletics is the study of preaching: how to communicate the Word. God reveals Himself to those whom He will, yet how can the ignorant learn unless there be preachers, and how can preachers go unless they be sent? We therefore are chosen to be instruments of the revelation of the holiness and mercy of God, and of his divine plan of salvation....

To have this passion for communication, that [persons] might comprehend God and be saved through His Word, is to be an evangelist, a missionary. Homiletics then is closely tied to missions, and cannot be taught in isolation.

The curriculum of the theological seminary then is a *unit*. Each of the disciplines is closely related to all the others. The division of studies is in part arbitrary in order to facilitate the comprehension of the whole.

Each of the subjects in the theological curriculum is a portion of the whole. It should be so interpreted as to relate to each of the other disciplines. Even in those specialized departments which prepare students for church professions other than that of minister and pastor, the required courses should and must treat the overarching revelation of God, and the concern of the Christian for the whole of history. The world mission of the church is the outworking of God's will, finding expression wherever men [and women] live. The frontier may be in one of the underdeveloped countries of the globe, or among one of the forgotten minority groups in a nation, or among the masses whether they be proletariat or bourgeois.

MISSION AS A TEST OF FAITH

> "The missionary witness is at all times a test of the faith of the Church."

■ *The meeting of the WCC's Commission on World Mission and Evangelism held in Mexico City in December 1963 was the first full meeting of the commission following the integration of the IMC and the WCC at New Delhi in 1961. Dr. Visser 't Hooft gave the keynote address on "Missions as the Test of Faith" in a meeting focused on recovering the biblical bases for mission. The WCC's general secretary began by recalling Søren Kierkegaard's admonition that to live in this world means to be tested. "Faith is tested in various ways," he continued, "but there is no more decisive test than the one concerning the translation of faith into missionary witness."*[4]

Translating Faith into Christian Witness*

Faith is tested in various ways, but there is no more decisive test than the one concerning the translation of faith into missionary witness. A central question in the great examination is: are you ready in all circumstances to proclaim that Christ is the Lord? It is with specific reference to the divine judgment that Jesus says: "Whoever therefore shall confess me before men, him I confess also before my Father which is in heaven. But whosoever shall deny me before men, him will I also deny before my Father which is in heaven" (Mt. 10:32-33)....

It is in that witness that the Church proves or disproves whether its faith is the real article, that is whether it is wholly and exclusively rooted in the apostolic *kerygma.* It seems to me that this comes out most clearly in the following three questions:

1. It is in the missionary situation that the Church has to give a clear answer to the question: whether it believes in the "happenedness" of the great deeds of God in Christ. The word "happenedness" has, I believe, been introduced into the English language by von Hügel. He uses it to make the following decisively important point:

> Christianity...is not simply a doctrine of certain laws and principles of the spiritual life...the central conviction and doctrine of Christianity is the real prevenience and condescension of the real God...it is not a simple idea, but a solid fact; not something that so universally *ought* to happen, that in fact it never happens at all...Christianity cannot really do without this most humble seeming assurance of sheer happenedness.[5]

Now whether the Church believes fully in this happenedness will become manifest in its missionary witness. A Church which is not deeply penetrated by the faith that the crucial centre of all human history is what God has done, in and through Christ, will hardly undertake a sustained missionary effort and its witness will never have the toughness and resiliency, the patience and endurance without which missions cannot accomplish their task. It is only those who offer real news about divine deeds who will stand the test in the day of trouble.

2. In the second place it is in the missionary situation that the Church has to give a clear answer to the question whether it really believes in the universality of the Gospel. It is so easy to pay lip service to the truth that Christ is the Lord of [humanity] and that Christ died for all [persons], but to live in fact as if Christ were a local saviour and the inventor of values for one of the many possible cultures or civilizations. By becoming missionary the Church confesses that Christ is the Saviour of all. The report on the main theme of the Evanston Assembly says:

---

*Excerpts from Willem A. Visser 't Hooft, "Missions as the Test of Faith," in *Witness in Six Continents: Records of the Meeting of the Commission on World Mission and Evangelism of the World Council of Churches held in Mexico City, December 8th to 19th, 1963,* ed. Ronald K. Orchard (London: Edinburgh House Press, 1964), 21-22, 24; cf. Bosch, TM, 493.

It is of special significance when the Gospel crosses geographical frontiers, for it is when a Church takes the Gospel to another people and another land that it bears its witness to the fact that the new age has dawned for all the world.[6]

3. In the third place it is in the missionary situation that the Church has to give a clear answer to the question whether it really believes that the Word of God is not bound. A Church may have great missionary fervour and yet fail to be truly apostolic, because its missionary work consists in the exporting of its own culturally conditioned brand of Christianity and in the imposing of that brand on another people. If so, it has not grasped that the Word of God cannot and must not be imprisoned in any human form of expression but claims the sovereign right to make its own impact upon every people and to create its own forms of expression.

The missionary witness is at all times a test of the faith of the Church.

MISSIOLOGY AS CATALYST

"Fight all temptation to isolation from within and without."

■ *Hans-Werner Gensichen (b. 1915) is one of Germany's most prominent missiologists. After theological studies at the University of Leipzig, with a brief exposure at Princeton Theological Seminary to North American thought, he began teaching at the University of Hamburg with his mentor, Walter Freytag. Exposure to the global church in mission came initially through service in India (1952-1957) as a teacher in Tranquebar and Madras, and later as assistant director of the WCC's Theological Education Fund. For thirty years, beginning in 1957, Gensichen taught as professor of the history of religions and missiology at the University of Heidelberg, Germany. A prolific writer, he was one of the founders of the International Association for Mission Studies and its first president.*[7]

*Crossing Cultural Borders**

According to the New Testament, what gives mission its special acuity and direction is not *only* the reaching out to the geographic "end of the world" but rather the commission to witnessing to a world which is entirely [Christ's] area of lordship....In carrying out the commission, it might be more urgent today to cross over cultural borders instead of geographical ones. It might be that the encounter with a secularized world may not become less important than the confrontation with the claims of religions. It might be that the advance into the fields of social structures is as indispensable as the gathering of the "world-diaspora." Mission

---

*Excerpts from Hans-Werner Gensichen, *Glaube für die Welt: Theologische Aspekte der Mission* (Gütersloh: Gerd Mohn, 1971), 92-93, 252-53; excerpts translated from the German by Domenico Nigrelli; cf. Bosch, TM, 494.

stands or falls whether or not it holds on to the intention "to cross the borderline between faith in Christ as the Lord and unbelief."[8] That is the concreteness of the "must" of mission, as it stays even today bindingly valid: "The original connection of Christendom to the world is the command and will to the proclamation of Christ. 'All people' shall experience what God has done for the world....'Mission' in that sense is first the only, and therefore, also the proper bridge from Church to world."[9]

The World—Theology's Common Field

In its dimensional aspect, missiology must, in free partnership with other theological disciplines, fight all temptation to isolation from within and without. In the conventional operation in theological institutions it is customary that missiology accept a modest position (if it has its own representation at all), and that it relieves all other fields of their relation to Christian world mission, by building its own field somewhere in the outskirts. But this field is none other than the world itself, the world concretely understood as two-thirds of all humanity, which theology so far has been scarcely concerned with, which now, however, at the doorsteps of the third Christian millennium, can no longer be ignored with good conscience. The dogmatician, for example, today can no longer write on the "Christian faith in God in a changed world" without earnestly engaging in a dialogue of Christianity with non-Christian religions,[10] not to mention the attempts to make theological statements on the horizon of non-Western cultures and non-Western modes of thinking. Church history today can no longer be practiced without being at the same time mission-history—and that not only merely by means of conspicuous considerations of organized Christian mission arrangements; rather under the encompassing view of God's history with his people for a world and in a world which breaks all regional and confessional limitations. It is superfluous to outline the missionary intention of biblical interpretation or of practical theology. Also, for these departments, mission is obviously not only accidental; rather it is a constitutive element of their execution, an integrative part of their foundation out of which they grow and out of which their permanent support-strength is to prove itself today: "The more the church becomes a minority in all nations, and the more religious and secular salvation expectation are forming themselves as counter-forces, the more important becomes the insight that all theology can be practiced meaningfully only missionally and ecumenically."[11]

Here again everything comes to its proper place: what was said in a different context about the fundamental meaning of *Missio Dei* as the "decisive life-dimension" of the Church,[12] now as a critical demand to a theology which had to grasp that the loss of its missionary dimension not only affected its well being, but also its very being—a critique that naturally should no less target a "theology-less" mission and missiology.

MISSIOLOGY AS ENGAGEMENT

"We need a spirituality of missional engagement."

■ *"Passion for Christian mission, seriousness about its study, and creativity in the means to accomplish it were the notes that characterized the ministry of Orlando E. Costas." With these words, Samuel Escobar eulogized his recently departed friend. Founder of the Latin American Center for Pastoral Studies, active promoter of the Latin American Theological Fraternity, founder of Hispanic Ministries at Eastern Baptist Theological Seminary, and dean at Andover Newton Theological Seminary, Orlando Costas (1942-1987) had a lifelong commitment to developing a relevant theology of mission. In the following excerpt from* Christ Outside the Gate *(1982), his major work on mission in North America, Costas wrote out of a liberationist perspective concerning mission and theology. Deep understanding of the human mosaic and of social structures which dominate and oppress is one goal. Equally important for Costas is faith commitment and a spirituality honed during involvement in human suffering and struggle.*

*The Human Mosaic**

If Christian theological schools today want to be dedicated not only in word but also in deed to the communication of the whole gospel in the whole world, they shall have to develop at all levels a deeper understanding of...the human mosaic. This demands more than a theoretical awareness of the role of institutions in North American and other societies. It demands a firsthand encounter with them at the point of their most negative manifestations, namely, in cross-cultural, oppressive situations. Students and faculty will need to experience the world of institutions from the side of those who suffer its impact the most, whether it be the religious experience of the poor masses of the third world, the educational deformation that takes place in the urban ghettos, the mechanisms of economic exploitation that are usually present among poverty-stricken masses, or the gloomy and depressed atmosphere that one finds in politically repressive contexts. The sinful character, the human limitations, and the transcendent possibilities of social institutions will become so much clearer and deeper if they are seen from the side of the disfranchised and outcast. This in turn will help teachers and students to focus their teaching and learning more realistically and penetratingly, enabling them further to develop more effective missional responses to the challenge of institutions. This is another way of stating what Ronald J. Sider has said in another context, namely, "if it is true that God is on the side of the poor and oppressed and therefore that God's people must also be on the side of the little ones, then visible, tangible identification with the oppressed and weak is a *sine qua non* of seminary education."[13]

---

*Excerpts from Orlando E. Costas, *Christ Outside the Gate: Mission beyond Christendom* (Maryknoll, NY: Orbis Books, 1982), 169, 171-72; cf. Bosch, TM, 496-97.

A World of Structures

Institutions are interconnected by networks of global relations. These networks determine the life and function of institutions. Therefore they are denominated "structures" and constitute a...dimension of our contemporary world....

Any church, mission agency, or theological institution that claims the whole world as its mission field and wants to proclaim faithfully the whole gospel must make the kerygmatic encounter with the structures that dominate and oppress human life a fundamental component of its agenda. We must avoid deluding ourselves, however. This is not an easy task. Because churches, mission agencies, and schools are assailed by the same invisible forces that dominate and control the institutions of society, especially in a consumer society, the powers that be have a way of creeping in and permeating all institutions, *including those that are committed to Christ.* The temptation to accommodate to the "spirit of the age" rather than to the spirit of Christ, to compromise Christian convictions rather than to stand firm on the Lord's calling, to be more loyal to public-relations techniques than to the values of God's kingdom is ever before us. Subtle and overt pressures are brought to bear upon institutions that are committed to God's liberating mission, that are actively unmasking the principalities and powers and proclaiming Christ's triumph and authority over them....

A Mission Spirituality

To take head-on oppressive structures like consumerism, technology, militarism, multinational capitalism, international communism, racism, and sexism, we need a spirituality of missional engagement: a devotional attitude, a personal ethic, a continuous liturgical experience that flows out of and expresses itself in apostolic obedience.[14] Prayer, Bible study, personal ethics, and worship will not mean withdrawal from the world but an immersion in its sufferings and struggles. Likewise participation in the struggles of history will not mean an abandonment of piety and contemplation, but an experience of God from the depths of human suffering.

Mission without spirituality cannot survive any more than combustion without oxygen. The nature of the world in which we live and the gospel that we have been committed to communicate therein demand, however, that it be a spirituality of engagement and not of withdrawal. Such a spirituality can only be cultivated in obedience and discipleship, and not in the isolated comfort of one's inner self. By the same token, it can only be verified in the liberating struggles against the principalities and powers that hold so many millions in bondage.

THE MISSIONAL TASK OF THEOLOGY

> "Seeing the goal of theological education as preparing for mission."

■ *Like Orlando Costas, Virginia Peacock of Toronto is concerned that the curriculum of theological education include adequate analysis and understanding of the world in which the church ministers. She would include the analysis of sociology, economics, and anthropology, with special attention to minority, feminist, and Third World critiques. She would refocus the goal of theological education from acquiring knowledge to "preparing for mission in and to a world in need." Ms. Peacock wrote her essay while serving as a priest at St. Michael and All Angels Anglican Church in Toronto, Canada, and a doctoral candidate in theology and ethics at St. Michael's College, Toronto School of Theology.*

*Mission Is Action in Response to Need**

Jesus' followers were commissioned. They were sent on a mission.[15] The mission was defined on the basis of what they were to *do*. Mission was to be defined in terms of *action,* in terms of *doing.* What they were to do was to be determined by the need they found—just as it was for Jesus himself. Jesus' own action was in response to human need. What the mission of Jesus' followers ought to "look like" is to be determined by the need in the world found by the would-be follower.

Theology as Reflection on God's Action

Now, what does all this mean for the task of theology? First, theology retains the task of having to say what it has to say in different cultural settings, in various places and times. It will continue to have to articulate who God is and who Jesus is by being able to say what they do and how that action is to be seen and even how that action is to be "understood" as delivering, redeeming, serving....

Second, theology has gained a new task of fundamental importance, subordinate only to the first, which remains talk about God and about Christ. That new task involves defining the need of the world in which the action of discipleship—the act of the church as church—is to take place. A new emphasis for theology upon the world in which mission takes place, or the world in which the church ministers comes to the fore here. Understanding the world in which the church ministers and its need, which the church as church is obligated to view with compassion and toward which it is to be drawn into serving action—even healing action, because reconciliation is, after all, healing—becomes, in this view of theology, a major task of theology....

Refocus the Goal of Theological Education

Seeing the goal of theological education as preparing for mission in and to a world in need of being served, both by ordained and lay members of the *laos* (people

---

*Excerpts from Virginia Peacock, "Theological Education and the Mission of the Church," in *Justice as Mission: An Agenda for the Church,* ed. Terry Brown and Christopher Lind (Burlington, Ontario: Trinity Press, 1985), 81-83; cf. Bosch, TM, 494.

of God), might serve to help integrate all the pieces which contribute to theological education in a way in which they have not been integrated before. Finally, ethics, through this approach which envisions a foundational emphasis upon *action,* might achieve the prominence which, in my view, the Gospel intends....

THEOLOGY AMID POVERTY AND OTHER FAITHS

> "The theology of religion and the theology of dialogue are the central theological questions today."

■ *In 1985, according to Dr. David Barrett, the premier statistician of world Christianity, the fulcrum of world Christianity shifted to the South. For the first time, a majority of professing Christians were to be found in the churches of Africa, Asia, Latin America, and Oceania. At the same time, he reminded his readers that Christianity remains a minority world faith, claiming as adherents only one-third of the world's population.*[16] *Reflecting on these realities, Dr. J. Paul Rajashekar of India calls for a reassessment of theological education in the North. To what extent does it take seriously the new pluralistic context in which increasingly Christians engage in ministry and mission? At the time of writing, Dr. Rajashekar was director of the Church and People of Other Faiths' program of the Lutheran World Federation based in Geneva, Switzerland.*

*Theological Education and Religious Pluralism**

The situation of material poverty and underdevelopment on the one hand and the situation of religious pluralism on the other provide the general matrix within which theological reflections in Asia ought to take place. But in actual fact, very minimal attention is paid to questions posed by Asian religious sensitivities and spiritual traditions....

The tradition of negative approach to other faiths is dominant in all of Asia. Maintaining a Christian distinctiveness in the sea of diverse Asian spirituality has been the major concern for most Asian Christians.

Irrespective of the specific situations within which Christians find themselves within Asia, most Asian churches—Protestant and Catholic—subscribe to an ecclesio-centred understanding of mission and ministry. In other words a quantitative understanding of mission and a maintenance model of ministry ("word-sacrament-pastoral care") are the legacy of Asian churches. Given this fact, theological education in Asia is faced with the enormously difficult task of attempting to broaden the church's conception of ministry and mission, moving from its narrow exclusivist emphasis towards a broader, inclusive and community-centred under-

---

*Excerpts from J. Paul Rajashekar, "Theological Education in a Pluralistic Context: An Overall Assessment," in *Ministerial Formation in a Multi-faith Milieu: Implications of Interfaith Dialogue for Theological Education,* ed. Sam Amirtham and S. Wesley Ariarajah (Geneva: WCC, 1986), 107, 109, 111, 112-13, 114; cf. Bosch, TM, 497.

standing. It is here that the nature, structure and vision of theological education needs to be closely scrutinized....

Part of a Wider Religious Experience

Christians need to cultivate the habit of seeing their religious experience as part of a wider religious experience rather than something apart. Recognizing this fact, we will be led to reconsider the practice of assigning the study of other faiths as a distinct discipline, to see it as something peripheral to theological studies with little relevance to, say, biblical studies, systematics, church history and practical theology. It has become increasingly evident that the theology of religion and the theology of dialogue are the central theological questions today, with enormous implications for every theological discipline....

An appreciative encounter with people of other faiths enables us to better grasp the mission of God in our world. Mission is not an enlargement of the domain of the church at the expense of the world. For the church, mission is basically a "test of faith" in the world. Similarly, evangelism is not a mere public statement of certain beliefs; it is also a quality of living and sharing in the midst of people that draws attention to the uniqueness of God's love. It is in the context of people, especially people of other faiths, in their suffering, hopes and aspirations, that we discover the meaning of mission and evangelism. Mission and evangelism cannot therefore be anything but dialogical. The aim of teaching mission and evangelism in theological training is not to win people for Christianity but to think theologically and respond appropriately in different situations of mission and ministry....

The Wider Context

Incorporating the perspectives of religions and religious pluralism along with issues of socio-economic liberation will perhaps force theological education to develop an inter-disciplinary approach which in turn will enable us to contextualize the gospel and our theology in Asia.

THEOLOGY UNDER THE TREE

> "Theology in our time can be learned only in the act of liberating the poor."

■ *To all who seek a living theology in the university or seminary, Jean-Marc Éla of Cameroon issues a probing challenge. Can a living theology today develop apart from the struggles of people? Éla approaches theological reflection from a base of ten years of pastoral activity among the Kirdi of northern Cameroon, where he was apprentice and then successor to "Baba Simon," a truly great modern indigenous apostle. The result is a liberation theology with an African face. His faith in God, the Gospel, and especially the people themselves is eloquent. Out of their struggle—out of hunger, marginalization, impoverish-*

ment, "modernization," alienation, uprooting, flight, fear, and so on—emerges a profound theology. He shares with us his conviction that every authentic inculturation of the Christian faith is conditioned on the liberation of the oppressed.

A Theology Emerging out of Struggle*

It is very clear to me that it is becoming more and more dangerous to speak about God if nothing concrete can verify the statements that conform to Christian dogma. We glimpse the dangers of blasphemy and of betrayal to which churches open themselves when human distress and situations of death provide more evidence each day for the trial of the God whom they announce. The plan of God the Creator and Savior is endangered and blocked by the failure of our systems and the deadlock brought about by structures that unceasingly burden us.

Today, considering all of this, what story can we tell about God as we recall Jesus Christ? Evidently we must return to the tree of the cross to remake theology, starting with the struggles of black people to prevent their world from being plunged back into the chaos that reigned before creation. In that sense, doing theology is no longer an academic exercise, but a spiritual adventure. That is why what is happening today in the villages and slums of Africa prevents theologians from shutting their eyes and drifting off to sleep with the purring of a clear conscience—created by producing the type of discourse that, up until now, has been oriented around demands for indigenization and acculturation….

The explosive force of people and groups in villages and shanty-towns, working to get themselves out of dependency and injustice, is the place where a theology will emerge that renounces talk about God and faith on the basis of a ready-made "revelation." If God speaks through history, theology can no longer be learned through the words of manuals that simply perpetuate from one generation to another a faith that has been defined once and for all. Theology in our time can be learned only in the act of liberating the poor.

I dream of a "theology under the tree," which would be worked out as brothers and sisters sit side by side wherever Christians share the lot of peasant people who seek to take responsibility for their own future and for transforming their living conditions. In order for that to happen, people must leave the libraries and give up the comfort of air-conditioned offices; they must accept the conditions of life in the insecurity of study in poor areas where the people have their feet in water or in mud and can neither read nor write.

Oral Theology

Perhaps this theology will not use the vocabulary of scholars and philosophers. But didn't God also speak the language of peasants and shepherds in order to be

---

*Excerpt from Jean-Marc Éla, *My Faith as an African* (Maryknoll, NY: Orbis Books, 1988), 179-82; cf. Bosch, TM, p. 498.

revealed to humanity? We must rediscover the oral dimension of theology, which is no less important than the *summae* and the great treatises. Christian theology must be liberated from a cultural system that sometimes conveys the false impression that the Word has been made text. Why can't the language of faith also be poetry, song, game, art, dance, and above all the gesture of humanity standing up and marching wherever the gospel elicits and nourishes a liberating effort? To create a poetics of faith, we must rediscover the African soul, or *anima,* where symbol appeals through metaphor and helps us speak of that God who raises up the meek and feeds the hungry.

Such a step cannot come about in isolation. A theology in context must also be a theology in dialogue, open to exchange and confrontation. African theology requires a deepening of the methods involved in working out any theology; it also needs to let itself be questioned by all the theologies based on the solidarity of peoples, continents, or groups struggling for the coming of a new world. Certainly that will not happen without free and responsible theological work.

No Longer Spectators or Hermits

We must give each local church responsibility for its own theological thinking. We must bring about the decentralization of producing "official" theological meaning, and we must end the seclusion of theological discourse in the West.

One thing is certain. Christian theology has entered a new era. The task at hand is to pass from a conflict of cultures to a culture of confrontation. At a time when the unbridled expansion of the affluent is constantly tightening the noose that strangles Africa, we must return to our people, become their companions in life and their travelling partners. Even though it may be suicidal, that is the only possible outcome for theologians who no longer want to live as spectators or hermits.

Hence, the great challenge to faith and to theology in Africa is our historical situation that snatches Christianity out of meaninglessness, and restores its relevance in the places of tension where the midwives of the future and the witnesses of freedom are to be found. We live in a continent marked by supposedly inescapable unhappiness, a continent where poverty alone seems to have a prosperous future. Where are the men and women who have made up their minds to sow life, so that hope may germinate? How can the Easter message once again become a well where Christians and churches can draw strength to march ahead? "O Death, where is thy victory?" That is the question I ask myself, in my faith as an African, as the third millenium draws near.

NOTES

1. Creighton Lacy, "Missions in the Curriculum," in *APM Proceedings,* Third Biennial Meeting (Naperville 1956), pp. 115-16.

2. Norman E. Thomas, "From Missions to Globalization: Teaching Missiology in North American Seminaries," *IBMR* 13:3 (July 1989): 104-05.

3. See James A. Scherer, "Missiology as a Discipline and What It Includes," *Missiology* 15:4 (October 1987): 507-22.

4. *Witness in Six Continents,* ed. Ronald K. Orchard (London: Edinburgh Press for the Division of World Mission and Evangelism of the WCC, 1964), pp. 21-22.

5. F. von Hügel, *Essays and Addresses on the Philosophy of Religion,* Second Series (London & Toronto: J. M. Dent; New York: E. P. Dutton, 1926), pp. 107-08.

6. "Report of the Advisory Commission on the Main Theme of the Second Assembly of the World Council of Churches," in WCC, *The Christian Hope and the Task of the Church* (New York: Harper & Brothers, 1954), p. 18.

7. See Hans-Werner Gensichen, "My Pilgrimage in Mission," *IBMR* 13 (1989): 167-69.

8. Lesslie Newbigin, *Die Eine Kirche—das Eine Evangelium—die Eine Welt* (Stuttgart: Evang. Missions-verlag, 1959), p. 26.

9. Hans von Campenhausen, "Die Christen und das bürgerliche Leben," in *Tradition und Leben* (Tübingen: Mohr, 1960), p. 200.

10. Bengt Sundkler, "Ort und Aufgabe der Missiologie in der Gegenwart," *Evangelische Missionszeitschrift* 25 (1968), 114f.

11. M. Linz, "Missionswissenschaft und Ökumenik," in *Einführung in das Studium der evangelischen Theologie,* ed. R. Bohren (Munich: C. Kaiser, 1964), p. 37.

12. K. Rahner, "Grundprinzipien zur heutigin Mission der Kirche," in *Handbuch der Pastoraltheologie II/2,* ed. F. X. Arnold, et al. (Freiburg: Herder, 1966), p. 48.

13. Ronald J. Sider, "The Christian Seminary: Bulwark of the Status Quo or Beachhead of the Coming Kingdom?" Inaugural lecture, Eastern Baptist Theological Seminary (Oct. 31, 1978), p. 22.

14. For a recent systematic treatment of missional spirituality, see the excellent work of Michael Collins Reilly, S.J., *Spirituality for Mission* (Maryknoll, NY: Orbis Books, 1978).

15. I am using *commissioned* here in the sense of "charged" and "given authority." I am using *mission* in the sense of "task."

16. David B. Barrett, "Annual Statistical Table on Global Mission: 1985," *IBMR* 9:1 (Jan. 1985): 30.

17

Mission as Action in Hope

What is the source of one's hope? An important characteristic of Enlightenment thought, according to David Bosch, was "the elimination of purpose from science and the introduction of direct causality as the clue to the understanding of reality." In the Newtonian worldview, with its deterministic philosophy of cause and effect relationships, human planning took the place of trust in God (TM, 265, 271). Teleological thinking and eschatology had no place.

Twentieth-century physics, however, as symbolized in Einstein's formula $E=mc^2$*, suggests a radically new way of post-Enlightenment thought. Subsequent empirical study verified that matter is being transformed into energy all the time, and energy into matter. In the quantum physics of Werner Heisenberg and others, physics, which previously supported a deterministic philosophy of nature, shifted to view the universe as inherently indeterminate. Meanwhile post-Darwinian biology discovered that organisms can evolve through purposive responses to their environments. Consistent with these new perspectives, the world can now be seen as radically self-creative, once again the place of God's creative and providential power.*[1]

A theologian or missiologist's view of history is also influenced by the times in which they live. Those who shared the late Victorian optimism concerning human progress often expressed confidence in human efforts to build the kingdom of God on earth. By contrast, those who wrote against the immediate background of the catastrophes of World Wars I and II conveyed a different source of hope.

The following selections support Bosch's argument that the paradigm of mission as action in hope is based on a new teleology and eschatology. "What is the significance of eschatology for the Church's mission?" was one of the central questions discussed at the IMC's Willingen Conference in 1952. Oscar Cullmann, the noted French biblical theologian, found New Testament support for the understanding that God's action in history is continuous. Knowing that we live in Christ's age between his resurrection and the end time, mission is living in tune with God's action. German missiologist Walter Freytag adds the understanding that biblical sending is linked inextricably with eschatological hope. He chides Christian missionaries for not preaching with urgency, as Muslim clerics do in Java. Hans Margull, writing as head of the WCC's Department of Evangelism, argued that evangelism is more than proclamation—it is eschatological ministry as we partici-

pate in Christ's ministry. Jürgen Moltmann of Germany, in his Theology of Hope, *refers to the indeterminacy principle of modern physics. Consistent with this new worldview is the Christians' conviction that we live with freedom in history and with new "possibility thinking."*

Selections from the Two-thirds World illustrate what Bosch calls eschatology and mission in creative tension (TM, 507). C. René Padilla of Ecuador builds on the realized eschatology of C. H. Dodd. God's reign is already present in the cross and resurrection, yet still to come in its fullness. We live between the times. Rose Fernando of Sri Lanka draws upon her Franciscan heritage in advocating a theology of presence by which we live as persons of hope in a troubled world. Jean-Marc Éla, building upon Orlando Costas's concept of "Christ outside the gate," asks: can we be signs of hope in a world of hunger, poverty, and exploitation? Following the apostle Paul (Phil. 2:5-11), he prefers mission as kenosis*—joining Christ in suffering in "the awesome birthpangs of God's new creation" (Bosch, TM, 510). Michael Amaladoss of India envisions that the Church's mission in its third millennium will be future oriented. He believes that God is calling persons to be co-creators "of a new humanity in a new world."*

MISSION AND GOD'S SOVEREIGNTY

"God's rule has come upon us."

■ *In 1952, the world missionary movement faced a crisis of confidence. All missionaries had been expelled from that "jewel" of missions—China. Facing squarely "the contagion and the power of rival and revolutionary faiths," the delegates to the Willingen Conference of the International Missionary Council renewed their confidence in the providence of God. They also identified as issues for further study the relation of the church and the significance of eschatology for mission, and the relation of the church's mission to the Kingdom of God.*

*The Basis of Our Hope**

The compelling fact is that the missionary movement of the Church is confronted by the contagion and the power of rival and revolutionary faiths. Not since the seventh century, when the missionary expansion of the Church stood before the ominous threat of Islam, have the message and the strategy of the Christian mission been so searchingly tested and tried. It will not do to say the same old things in the same old way. Nor are we called upon to supply the missionary movement with a fully elaborated missionary theology. Willingen has only to say what it must say to

---

*Excerpts from International Missionary Council (Willingen 1952), *Missions Under the Cross: Addresses delivered at the enlarged meeting at... Willingen*, ed. N. Goodall (London: Edinburgh House Press for the IMC, 1953), 238-39, 244-45; cf. Bosch, TM, 502.

the Church and to the world about the missionary responsibility of the Church in this convulsive time.

Our word is not one of retreat but of advance; not one of discouragement but of confidence. Our God is the Lord, let the people rejoice; the Lord is King, be the people never so impatient. It is open to us to do again what our [brothers and sisters] thirteen centuries before us set their hearts and hands to. We must take up the cutting edge of our confidence and our commitment and, with urgency, and intensity, seek to bring the world to acknowledge and serve the Kingship under which we stand. The conflict is on between Him whom God in His almighty purpose has raised up and made both Lord and Christ and the rival loyalties and commitments which govern the hearts and the minds of [persons] in our time. The missionary task of the Church is to make its obedience to the Lordship of Jesus Christ plain and persuasive wherever this Lordship is still unknown and still unacknowledged. In the providence of our God who is King, the present paradoxical situation of the missionary movement is this: That at the very moment when dark and forbidding curtains have abruptly altered missionary manoeuvreability and advance, the mission field is unmistakably as wide as the world. In this situation, the missionary movement is being judged for its failures and called to repent. At the same time, the opportunities which open out before the Christian mission are gifts of God which call for fresh obedience.

By faith in Christ crucified, by love which begins at the Cross, and by hope fixed on Him who triumphed there, the Church has to proclaim by word and deed that God in Christ is ruling this world. With the coming of Christ, God's rule has come upon us, and we look forward to Christ's coming again. Living between Christ's coming and His coming again, we see by faith the signs of the Kingdom. But to every appearance and human insight God is not ruling this world.

Problems for Further Study

Nevertheless, in our discussions some problems have emerged to which we desire to draw attention....

1. Is the missionary obligation of the Church to be understood primarily as derived from the redemptive purpose and acts of God or as derived from the nature of God Himself?...

2. What is the precise relation of the Church to its mission?...

3. What is the relation of the Church's mission to the Kingdom of God?...

4. What is the significance of eschatology for the Church's mission? Some would stress the eschatological significance of Christ's present activity in the Church. Others, while not denying this, would add that an eschatology of the Church is an important element in the missionary message. There was agreement that the missionary drive in Marxism which derives from its secularized eschatology of the classless society, is a judgment on us for neglecting the eschatological element in our missionary message.

MISSION IN GOD'S ESCHATOLOGY

"'Missions' are an essential element in the eschatological divine plan of salvation."

■ *Oscar Cullmann was born in Strasbourg, France, in 1902 and baptized in the Lutheran Church of Alsace. Educated at his home University of Strasbourg, Cullmann served professorships in New Testament Studies at the University of Basel, the University of Strasbourg, and the École des Hautes-Études of the Sorbonne in Paris. A biblical theologian, he has made his major contribution in interpreting the biblical view of time. For Cullmann, all history at its deepest level is the history of salvation* (Heilsgeschichte). *The period of the church is that between Christ's resurrection and his return. The meaning of its existence, its faith and life, and its mission, can be properly understood only in terms of this position in the history of salvation.*[2]

*True and False Eschatology**

Does the expectation of the end paralyze the missionary impulse? Does it divert our attention from the task of preaching the Gospel here and now? It is sometimes said that this "hope" has an inhibiting influence upon Christian action; is this true? To give an affirmative answer to these questions would mean that "missions"—on the grand scale—would have been possible only because the eschatological hope had gradually faded. In point of fact, the missionary enterprise of the Church is often represented as a kind of "second best"—something which has been substituted for the unrealized hope of the kingdom of God. If this were true, then the Church has carried on its mission because it has been obliged to renounce eschatology.

Such ideas are due to a mistaken conception of early Christian eschatology. It is of course true that in the early Church there was a tendency to distort the Christian hope, which diverted the attention of Christian people from the sphere of present duty, as for instance at Thessalonica, in the time of Paul, and one hundred years later, in Asia Minor, in Montanism. But in the New Testament itself this tendency was explicitly rejected and condemned as heretical. The genuine primitive Christian hope does not paralyze Christian action in the world. On the contrary, the proclamation of the Christian Gospel in the missionary enterprise is a characteristic form of such action, since it expresses the belief that "missions" are an essential element in the eschatological divine plan of salvation. The missionary work of the Church is the eschatological foretaste of the kingdom of God, and the biblical hope of the "end" constitutes the keenest incentive to action....

---

*Excerpts from Oscar Cullmann, "Eschatology and Missions in the New Testament," in *The Theology of the Christian Mission,* ed. Gerald H. Anderson (New York: McGraw-Hill Book Co., 1961), 42-45, 46; cf. Bosch, TM, 502-04.

The close relation between Christian action and the expectation of the end comes out in two prominent characteristics of New Testament eschatology: (a) we do not know when the end will come; (b) although the end lies in the future, the present is already part of the period which begins with the death and resurrection of Christ....

Confidence in God

We cannot achieve the coming of the kingdom of God by our own action: *we* cannot "bring in" the kingdom of God. The whole witness of the New Testament is so clear on this point that no further proof is needed. Then does this mean that all that is required from us, in response to the eschatological hope, is a passive attitude and not a stimulus to action? By no means! For it is only those who are firmly convinced that the kingdom comes from God who are given the courage to work here and now, whether success or failure be their portion. If we believed that the coming of the kingdom depended on us, when confronted by failure we would inevitably despair. But we can work joyfully and courageously, not in order to "hasten" the coming of the kingdom, but because we know that the kingdom comes from God....

Living in Christ's Age

This brings us to the second characteristic of New Testament eschatology, which is indeed the basis of Christian action. The end is not yet, it is true, but since the Resurrection has taken place we know that the decisive event leading to the end has already happened. The end may seem to be delayed, but this should cause no disappointment, doubt, or despondency. When faith in the Resurrection is strong, it breeds a firm conviction that the royal sovereignty of Christ has already begun, and that it will be exercised for a period of unknown length until Christ "delivers the kingdom to God the Father after destroying every rule and every authority and power" (1 Cor. 15:24). Thus it is a mistake to think that eschatology has nothing to do with the present day, and, therefore, that it has a paralyzing effect upon Christian action. Indeed, it is rather the other way round, because the kingdom of God has actually come nearer, with Christ, than would have been the case if all had been left to the usual course of events. From the chronological point of view, something has happened: the present "age" has taken a great leap forward. We are reminded that God is Lord of time. We have entered the final phase of this "age," which will end with the return of Christ....

Eschatology and Mission

It is the presence of the Holy Spirit which makes the action of the Church, as such, eschatological. The Church itself is an eschatological phenomenon. It is in the center of the present lordship of Christ. It was constituted by the Holy Spirit at

Pentecost. That is why the task of the Church consists in the proclamation of the Gospel to the whole world. This is the very essence of the Holy Spirit's work, and the meaning of the miracle of Pentecost, when, quite suddenly, all present understood one another. Precisely in the period to which we belong—between the Resurrection and the return of Christ—it is the duty of the Church to go out "into all the world, and preach the Gospel to every creature," looking toward the end. That is why the disciples' question to the risen Lord: "Will you at this time restore the kingdom to Israel?" receives this answer: "It is not for you to know times or seasons which the Father has fixed by his own authority. But you shall receive power when the Holy Spirit has come upon you; and you shall be my witnesses in Jerusalem and in all Judea and Samaria and to the end of the earth" (Acts 1:7-8).

The Holy Spirit, and the world mission: these are the "signs" of the final phase, determined by the future, in which we stand. Does this mean, however, that the kingdom of God will come only when all [people] have been converted? If that were so, then its coming would depend on [us], and the divine omnipotence would be ignored. On the other hand, the conviction that evil will be intensified during the last days is part of Christian eschatology. All that matters, however, is the fact that the Gospel should be preached to all nations. Evidently, God means that everyone should have an opportunity of hearing the Christian message; therefore the call to repentance must be made to all. But the coming of the kingdom does not depend upon [human] acceptance of the call. This view contains the strongest incentive for human decision, and yet the divine sovereignty is not in the least impaired. The proclamation of the Gospel to all nations itself becomes a "sign" of the end, an integral element in the eschatological divine plan of salvation.

MISSION IN VIEW OF THE END

"Mission is part of God's end-time working."

■ *Walter Freytag (1899-1959) began his mission service in 1928 as director of the German Evangelical Missions Aid Society. For thirty years he was known best as a missiologist, teaching as professor of missions and ecumenical relations in the University of Hamburg. Freytag saw it as his task both to lead the church back to its mission and the missions back to the church. Writing in the immediate background of the catastrophe of World War II, Freytag was critical of major prevailing understandings of mission and God's reign. Pietists, with their concern for saving souls, spiritualized and individualized the mission. Church growth enthusiasts equated the kingdom with the institutional expansion of the church. Social activists appealed to persons of good will to promote kingdom goals. In contrast, Freytag viewed progress in human history as a series of catastrophes. He placed hope in God's end-time working and believed authentic mission to be a sign of God's action to bring in God's reign.*[3]

*Salvation-Time and End-Time**

1. In the New Testament missionary instruction and missionary proclamation are set firmly in time definitions. "First" must the Gospel be proclaimed; "then" the end will come. Between this "first" and "then" the course of the word of God is completed among the world peoples as a "now" running from place to place. "That which is *now* preached before you," says Peter in Acts 3:20. "*Now*, therefore, calls God everyone to repentance," proclaims Paul in Athens. As it is not day simultaneously everywhere on our earth, but rather the sunrise repeats itself hour after hour, so rises the time of salvation from people to people and it separates that which was unfruitful from that which *now* breaks out and will then be completed. The ambassador in Christ's place leads on toward the commencement of salvation-time and end-time from people to people by means of delivering his message. The knowledge of this "first" and this "then" and of the eschatological "now," in which it occurs, gives mission an incomparable weight. In it is accomplished the meaning of history and the line of salvation in history. From the viewpoint of the New Testament all human history stands under the sign of the maturation of the demons of this world. But here in mission God's goal for humanity is accomplished, in the midst and among and despite these demons, namely, the gathering of the congregation. That makes mission, in its innermost, independent of time and non-time; indeed Jesus puts mission in the middle of "war and rumors of wars" (Matt. 24). For Jesus mission is the proper occurrence on which everything else depends.

Mission Is God's End-Time Working

2. Mission is part of *God's end-time working*....Mission is the sign of the end time set up by God. It has its dignity not in the good will of humans; still less is a human act the sufficient reason for the coming end. But where mission occurs, God shows that his hour is coming closer, because "now is our salvation nearer, than when we first believed. The night is advanced, and the day is at hand" (Rom. 13:11-12). Because it is a piece of God's end-time working, it has in it God's assurance. It is the unfailing sign of the end-time. *It* will be preached; it occurs. Although thousands of witnesses become mute, and entire Christendoms be extinguished, it is occurring. Indeed, especially such necessity and such indignation against the word of God is the surest sign that the Lord is on his way.

Mission—The Act of Hope

3. At the same time, however, the accomplishment of mission is *Jesus' end-time commission to his disciples.* They ask the Risen One (Acts 1) whether he will set up the kingdom now, and they receive as an answer the promise of the Spirit and

---

*Excerpts from Walter Freytag, *Reden und Aufsätze* (Munich: Chr. Kaiser, 1961), 2: 188-92; excerpts translated from the German by Domenico Nigrelli; cf. Bosch, TM, 502, 506-07.

the commission of witnessing to the ends of the world. Also the mission-command, whose relationship with Daniel 7:13-14 can not be overlooked, is closely connected with a view to the end, as is clear to us in many ways. As the passage in Daniel is based on the three-step oriental accession of the throne—namely elevation, declaration and transference of lordship—so follow in Matt. 28:18-20 sequentially the word of authority, the proclamation of Christ's Lordship among the people, and the promise of the completion of the end.

Mission is the positioning of Christ's lordship toward the end.[4] It is the central commission of the Church. The Church does not stand still. She is not condemned to endure under fire-attacks. She may and must go forward....Mission is the act of hope, which soberly holds the view to the end. It lives from the hidden glory of Jesus, in its entire fullness. This sending is not only the salvation of souls, but it also sees the coming world of God. Neither does it occur solely because of obedience, as we have made it clear to ourselves again and again over against other mission-motives in the last decade. Rather, it stretches out towards the promise. It is the work of the Church, which witnesses nothing else but the fact that "every knee in heaven, on earth, and under the earth" will bow and every tongue confess "that Jesus Christ is Lord, to the glory of God the Father" (Phil. 2:10 ff). Nowhere else like this, from the view toward the end, does mission become clearly an essential characteristic of the existence of the Church of Jesus Christ.

Preach about the End

At first that seems to us an obvious thing because that is the case in the mission proclamation of the New Testament; if one only thinks about the aforementioned texts of Acts, and of 1 Thess. 1:9ff; 4:15ff; 1 Cor. 15:51; 2 Cor. 5:10, and whatever else one can add.

However, how is it today? In contemporary mission proclamation—we are speaking now of the opening preaching in the encounter with the pagan world—is for the most part speaking of Jesus' resurrection, but far less of his second coming, the resurrection of the dead, the judgment and the end-time.

What are the reasons? I have spoken on different mission fields with missionaries concerning this. Most clear in my memory is a discussion with Professor Dr. [Hendrik] Kraemer, who was then still a missionary on Java. He answered me that the same question moves him very strongly. Recently, he was invited to speak on a Friday-sermon in the well-known Moslem speaker pulpit in Batavia. He was allowed, though he was an "unbeliever," to sit in the front next to the pulpit before more or less 2,500 members. The sermon portrayed the horrors of judgment in a manner that tears were running down hundreds of men's cheeks. In view of this shock the missionary involuntarily asked himself, "can we not also do this?" Of course he did not mean by that producing cheap effects; rather the possibility that we also speak of judgment....There is no authentic mission-preaching without a foundational eschatological position.

EVANGELISM AS ESCHATOLOGICAL MINISTRY

"Evangelism is hope in action."

■ *How does the human initiative in mission and* evangelism *relate to God's action? In* Hope in Action, *Hans Jochen Margull argued that the concept of the missionary "is abused and depleted" when it is not regarded as "an eschatological ministry." Evangelism is perverted if understood as the churches' attempts to reproduce and propagate themselves instead of proclaiming the Gospel. Evangelism for Margull is "participation in Christ's mission to the world." Margull, the head of the department of evangelism of the World Council of Churches, formerly professor of theology at the University of Hamburg, called for the church to go forward into the secular world and witness, because there Christians will meet the living Lord.*

*Missionary Proclamation**

The term "evangelism" is always used in such a way as to imply both "to move forward" and "to be sent forth." It is impossible to be missionary within an established congregation. The missionary enterprise is possible only where no congregation exists. The concept of evangelism [missionary proclamation] in the West, then, depends on the designation of evangelism as the churches' proclamation in those very places into which the Word has not yet penetrated and in which even the presuppositions for the appearance and acceptance of the Word are not given.

In evangelism it is a matter of overcoming the boundary and gap, which are mostly sociological, between the churches and the new element of confrontation. The nature of evangelism is defined by its aim, i.e., to break in wherever a milieu has been formed which is alien to the churches or is pitted against them and which lacks even the slightest connection with the churches. A classical expression of this sort of milieu and a classical, new element of confrontation for evangelism is provided by the socialistic community of the East European countries, by the class-conscious groups of the proletariat (especially in France), and by the associations of a definite intelligentsia in Western cities. Through these elements the new frontiers of faith become manifest which exist more or less throughout the undulatory terrain of modern society. Evangelism addresses itself to these elements and, in doing so, is genuinely missionary.

An Eschatological Understanding of Evangelism

The association of evangelism with foreign missions insures an eschatological

---

*Excerpts from Hans J. Margull, *Hope in Action* (Philadelphia: Muhlenberg Press, 1962), 277-80; cf. Bosch, TM, 510.

understanding of evangelism. Evangelism stands with this, and without it, fails as missionary proclamation.

If evangelism does not regard itself as an eschatological ministry, it will not, in the last analysis, gather on the strength of Jesus Christ and his coming, even though this be its intention. It will gather instead for the churches and their increase. If that happens, the concept of the missionary is abused and depleted. Of itself evangelism has no power.

If evangelism is not understood eschatologically, it will, in the last analysis, be merely an effort to shape attitudes and an attempt to establish contact, but nothing more. Such has been the death of many a worthy beginning in church work. Invitations and conversations are then regarded as missionary activities; behind them lies hazily, if at all, the goal of a change in authority for the elements confronting the gospel. The evangelistic undertaking remains a matter of approaches (important as these are initially).

If gathering with a view to the end is at stake, though, the message in evangelism will be concentrated on "regard for the end" and will always be a direct call to Christ and to obedience, which must be decided upon through the "Yes" to Christ as the sole hope. Inasmuch as evangelism betokens com-passion with Christ, it must simultaneously express a com-passion with the one to whom the message is addressed. And evangelism must act this way in patient solidarity with the addressees in their distress, distant though it be from Christ. For evangelism is *participation* in Christ's mission to the world! This applies universally. It means, in terms of the eschatological context of evangelism: *kerygma* and *diakonia* in *koinonia.*

Definition

In view of the preceding elaborations, a definition[5] of evangelism would have to read as follows: Evangelism is the churches' participation in the messianic work of Jesus Christ. It is eschatological ministry to all [persons] who have not as yet heard the gospel's call to repentance. In evangelism the churches live out their hope that Jesus Christ, with a view to his future, gathers men [and women] throughout the whole world for his congregation. More briefly: *Evangelism is hope in action.*

MISSION AND A THEOLOGY OF HOPE

> "The call and mission of the 'God of hope'...requires responsibility and decision for the world of history."

■ *The 1960s were a time of vigorous debate in European continental theology concerning eschatology. C. H. Dodd, Rudolf Bultmann, and others considered biblical eschatology to be unacceptable to the modern mind. A young German theologian, Jürgen Moltmann, took an alternate position. Professor of systematic theology at Tübingen since 1967, Moltmann argued that eschatology was important in making the Christian faith credible and relevant in the modern world. He found it determinative for understanding the biblical faith. In his*

Theology of Hope, *Moltmann identified the ideas of future and hope in the Bible. God's promise in salvation history is of new creation in the risen Christ. The resurrection set in motion that historical process of promise that is the church's mission. The hope is to transform the world in anticipation of its promised eschatological transformation by God.*[6]

*Eschatology and History**

The real point of reference for the exposition and appropriation of the historic Bible witness, and the one that is their motive and driving force, lies in the mission of present Christianity, and in the universal future of God for the world and for all [humanity], towards which this mission takes place....

The point of reference and the aim in the exposition of the biblical witness is not something universal which lies at the bottom of history or at the bottom of existence and keeps everything moving, but the concrete, present mission of Christianity towards the future of Christ for the world....The missionary direction is the only constant in history. For in the front-line of present mission new possibilities for history are grasped and inadequate realities in history left behind. Eschatological hope and mission thus make [human] reality "historic." The revelation of God in the event of promise reveals, effects and provokes that open history which is grasped in the mission of hope....

Open to the Future

The eschatological hope shows that which is possible and transformable in the world to be meaningful, and the practical mission embraces that which is now within the bounds of possibility in the world. The theory of world-transforming, future-seeking missionary practice does not search for eternal orders in the existing reality of the world, but for possibilities that exist in the world in the direction of the promised future. The call to obedient moulding of the world would have no object, if this world were immutable. The God who calls and promises would not be God, if he were not the God and Lord of that reality into which his mission leads, and if he could not create real, objective possibilities for his mission. Thus the transforming mission requires in practice a certain *Weltanschauung,* a confidence in the world and a hope for the world. It seeks for that which is really, objectively possible in this world, in order to grasp it and realize it in the direction of the promised future of the righteousness, the life and the kingdom of God. Hence it regards the world as an open process in which the salvation and destruction, the righteousness and annihilation of the world are at stake. To the eye of mission, not only [humanity] is open to the future, full of all kinds of possibilities, but the world, too, is a vast container full of future and of boundless possibilities for good and for

---

*Excerpts from Jürgen Moltmann, *Theology of Hope* (London: SCM Press, 1967), 283-84, 288-89; cf. Bosch, TM, 508.

evil. Thus it will continually strive to understand world reality in terms of history on the basis of the future that is in prospect. It will therefore not search, like the Greeks, for the nature of history and for the enduring in the midst of change, but on the contrary for the history of nature and for the possibilities of changing the enduring. It does not ask about the hidden wholeness by which this world, as it is, is intrinsically held together, but about the future *totum* in which everything that is here in flux and threatened by annihilation will be complete and whole. The totality of the world is not here seen as a self-dependent cosmos of nature, but as the goal of a world history which can be understood only in dynamic terms. The world thus appears as a correlate of hope. Hope alone really takes into account the "earnest expectation of the creature" for its freedom and truth. The obedience that comes of hope and mission forms the bridge between that which is promised and hoped for and the real possibilities of the reality of the world. The call and mission of the "God of hope" suffer [women and men] no longer to live amid surrounding nature, and no longer in the world as [their] home, but compel [them] to exist within the horizon of history. This horizon fills [them] with hopeful expectation, and at the same time requires of [them] responsibility and decision for the world of history.

MISSION BETWEEN THE TIMES

"Called to manifest the Kingdom of God here and now."

■ *C. René Padilla, a native of Ecuador, is today recognized as one of Latin America's leading evangelical theologians. In 1970, he joined with a small group of evangelicals, including Orlando E. Costas, Samuel Escobar, and Andrew Kirk, to form the Latin American Theological Fraternity (LATF), of which he was later to become general secretary. Together they presented at Lausanne I in 1974 their conviction that evangelism and social concern are inextricably linked, and succeeded in having this affirmation included in the Lausanne Covenant. Pastor of a Baptist church in Buenos Aires, Argentina, Padilla continues to develop his theology with the reign of God as its central theme. In* Mission Between the Times *(1985), a collection of his essays, he develops a realized eschatology which he believes should motivate the church to mission.*

*God's Reign Is Both Present and Future**

Although the midpoint of the timeline has appeared, the consummation of the new age still remains in the future. The same God who has intervened in history to initiate the drama is still acting and will continue to act in order to bring the drama to its conclusion. The Kingdom of God is, therefore, both a present reality and a

---

*Excerpts from C. René Padilla, *Mission between the Times: Essays on the Kingdom* (Grand Rapids, MI: Eerdmans, 1985), 187-88, 198-99; cf. Bosch, TM, 508-09.

promise to be fulfilled in the future: it has come (and is thus present among us), and it is to come (and thus we wait for its advent). This simultaneous affirmation of the present and the future gives rise to the eschatological tension that permeates the entire New Testament and undoubtedly represents a rediscovery of the Old Testament "prophetic-apocalyptic" eschatology that Judaism had lost.[7]

Between the Times

According to God's will, the church is called to manifest the Kingdom of God here and now in what it is as well as in what it proclaims. Because the Kingdom of God has already come and is yet to come, "between the times" the church is both an eschatological and a historical reality. If it does not fully manifest the Kingdom, that is not because God's dynamic reign has invaded the present age "without the authority or the power of transforming it into the age to come"[8] but because the consummation has not yet arrived. The power that is active in the church, however, is like the working of God's mighty strength, "which he exerted in Christ when he raised him from the dead and seated him at his right hand in the heavenly realms, far above all rule and authority, power and dominion, and every title that can be given, not only in the present age but also in the one to come" (Eph. 1:20-21). The mission of the church is the historical manifestation of that power through word and deed, in the power of the Holy Spirit.

Because of his death and resurrection, Jesus Christ has been enthroned as Lord of the universe. The whole world, therefore, has been placed under his Lordship. The church anticipates the destiny of all [humankind]. Between the times, therefore, the church—the community that confesses Jesus Christ as Lord and through him acknowledges God as "both the Creator and the Judge of all men"—is called to "share his concern for justice and reconciliation throughout human society and for the liberation of men from every kind of oppression."[9] Commitment to Jesus Christ is commitment to him as the Lord of the universe, the King before whom every knee will bow, the final destiny of human history. But the consummation of God's Kingdom is God's work.

TO BE PERSONS OF HOPE

> "That God is active in the process of transforming this world . . . is the hope that sustains us."

■ *Rose Fernando, F.M.M., developed her theology of hope in the multi-faith and multi-cultural society of Sri Lanka. Since childhood, Buddhism, Hinduism, Islam, as well as Christianity, have been part of the fabric of her life. In a nation torn by ethnic strife, Sister Fernando asks, "What is the Christian mission?" First, we are called to be artisans of peace and reconciliation. Like Francis of Assisi, wherever there is hatred and discord, we are called to sow love and forgiveness. Second, we are called to be persons of dialogue. Listening, receiving and giving—this can become our way of life. Finally, we are called to be persons of hope, rekindling the embers of love which others try to extinguish. At the time of writing the following essay, Sister Fernando was a general counselor at the Franciscan Missionaries of Mary headquarters in Rome.*

Called to Be Persons of Hope*

When we look around and see what is happening, *humanly* speaking, we see void—that is, a world that can be completely destroyed by the constantly threatened nuclear world war. But this is not the only world vision we possess. As Christians, we visualize a world where there will be a "new heaven and a new earth" (Rev. 21:1), because we believe that God is active in the process of transforming this world. This is the hope that sustains us and makes us ever more creative to bring out what is best in human beings. In Lebanon, plagued by a politico-religious war during the past ten years, in the Philippines where rival factions have been fighting each other, in Sri Lanka where certain groups have been the cause of outbursts of violence and bloodshed during the past three decades and in so many other countries where violence is escalating, Christians continue to hope. They rebuild and begin anew, because deep within them, they hope that the situation will improve. They hope that hearts will be softened and lives transformed; they hope for a better future. Among non-Christians too, there are signs of hope; it is in the midst of such growing violence that religious leaders are working together for peace and harmony; at the grassroots level, neighbours have become closer to each other, loving and supporting each other, organized and unorganized neighbourhood groups have brought new hope to peoples.

Hope has taken on a new meaning because of Jesus Christ, and therefore hope is the hallmark of Christians. It is because we are convinced that God's love is active in the world that fear and discouragement do not cripple us. It is because we continue to hope that we continue to participate actively with God in God's creation and redemption. By vocation we are called to be persons of hope, so that we can rekindle the embers of love that are being extinguished through violence....

Mission in Christ's Love

What greater challenge is there for Christians today than to be another Christ? God revealed God's very being in the person of Jesus Christ so that the world may understand what it means to be a perfect human being. All humanity has been glorified by Christ and through Christ, who personified love in his whole being. What he preached about love, he lived, especially during the love-meal, from which the word *agape* has taken its name.

Our mission as Christians is to live the faith experience in Jesus Christ, so that we are credible, and our credibility can be evangelizing.

---

*Excerpts from Rose Fernando, F.M.M., "God's Love Cuts Across History," *IRM* 74 (1985), 498-99, 500-501; cf. Bosch, TM, 510.

FAITHFULNESS TO THE GOD OF HOPE

"As black Africa becomes increasingly impoverished, must we close the door on hope?"

■ *Half of the world's twelve million refugees are in Africa! Uprooted, forced to flee, strangers in their own continent, they wander—homeless and often forgotten—seeking food, friends, and a future. In the essay below, Jean-Marc Éla of the Cameroon grapples with the forces which cause such dehumanization. His hope is less with international aid agencies and the charity of the "haves" of this world, and more with the people themselves. He writes of that caring and sharing which takes place in the base Christian communities among Christians who, like Mary, sing the Magnificat because they have hope in the God who lifted up the poor and fed the hungry.*

*The Granary Is Empty**

The reality of Africa—after it has been stripped of its folklore—demands attention. Twenty years of independence have not brought development, but rather developed underdevelopment. The situation becomes more serious when the state itself is the instrument of repression. It is important to understand the relationship in Africa between the government and the people. There is little effective participation of the people in public affairs, and the masses have practically no way of controlling government power, but only of applauding its use. Did God really plan that our continent be a land of oppression, poverty, and injustice? As black Africa becomes increasingly impoverished, must we close the door on hope?

The Irruption of the Poor

But there is a sign of hope in the ferment of small communities committed to the poor and the downtrodden....The work of our faith must be understood in reference to the overall situation in Africa today. We must deal with down-to-earth questions, and get back to ground level where the Kingdom of God is built day by day. For the hope for a new world that is built in the framework of justice, peace, and freedom is the heart of the Christian message. We must get involved in this experience and use it as our starting-point for a radical critique of all that is happening before our eyes. This is the only source of energy that will impel us to interpret Christian responsibilities in the current context of black Africa.

The irruption of the poor throughout the countries of the Third World is radically changing the mission of the church. Religious communities, pastoral workers, and

---

*Excerpts from Jean-Marc Éla, *My Faith as an African* (Maryknoll, NY: Orbis Books, 1988), 90, 91, 99, 100, 101; cf. Bosch, TM, p. 510.

lay movements are shifting their focus. New questions are being asked of theological reflection, pastoral practice, and spiritual life in many different places where the church is getting out of its traditional rut, and being born again from the dominated and exploited people. The poor and oppressed are reclaiming the Word of God and changing the structures of a world that is incompatible with God's plan. Working through historical dynamics, the poor are called by the gospel to ask hard questions and to become participants with the power to change their own living conditions....

The Cross of the Third World

If we view the cross of Jesus Christ as the cross of the Third World, the very existence of the Third World shows us what sin is and how it is structured in history. The Third World carries within itself the hidden Christ. It is the historic body of Jesus Christ today.

We must go and rediscover Christ in the slums, in places of misery and domination, among the majority of the poor and the oppressed people. It is the Third World that allows the church to make salvation in Jesus Christ visible. How do we say "I believe in God" in a community where Christians are organizing to resist a society structured in injustice and corruption? And this is the question asked of our faith today in most of the countries of our continent. Our choice is simple: either we choose to work with the agents of change to create a world habitable for all, or we choose not to work with them. If we choose to be agents of liberation, how do we talk about God?...

Sing the Magnificat In Deeds

In the painful march of the peoples of the Third World toward the victory of life, perhaps Christians should remember that the God of Life has lifted up the poor and fed the hungry. Today that God calls us to struggle for justice and right. Then we shall be able to sing the Magnificat, not in Latin, but in deeds, wherever faith is lived among the poor. We shall be able to sing the Magnificat in the slums, in the villages, in the streets—wherever we are—because the truth of God is fully engaged both in the countries of hunger and in the dominating societies....

To believe today is a matter of faithfulness to the God of hope, who went out from himself to place himself at the side of human beings as they struggle to stand up erect in the image of the Risen One. Such a faith requires a fresh re-reading of revelation.

MISSION AS NEW CREATION

"Mission as new creation is ...oriented ...to its transformation."

■ *In 1992, the International Association for Mission Studies chose as the theme of its Eighth Congress "New World, New Creation—Mission in Power and*

Faith." While reflecting backward on 500 years of colonialism and mission in the Americas and 200 years of Protestant worldwide missions since William Carey's famous Enquiry *motivated thousands to respond to Christ's Great Commission, the Congress looked forward toward the coming third millennium of Christian missions. The association's president-elect, Michael Amaladoss, S.J., set the tone in a preparatory article excerpted below. Mission, he said, is oriented toward the future, looking forward to "the new creation of a new humanity in a new world." Our response in faith is to a God who is "calling us to be co-creators with God's self of a new heaven and a new earth." An Indian Jesuit, noted theologian and liturgist, Father Amaladoss has served in the General Secretariat of the Jesuit order in Rome, with special responsibilities in the fields of evangelization, ecumenism, inculturation, and dialogue with other religions.*

*Mission as New Creation**

Mission does not focus on the past, but is oriented to the future. It is not the restoration of a primordial unity in the world and in creation that existed before sin; it is the new creation of a new humanity in a new world. It is historical, but it also transcends history. It is our hope, but it is also a divine gift that is a realization of God's promise. It is our task, but it is also the work of the Spirit. It is a call to conversion, but also to commitment. It is prophecy that directs our attention to a creative future, guaranteed by God's gracious action in the past.[10]

The future with which the newness is concerned is an eschatological future. It is actually the ongoing present, but not as an aimless, chaotic movement, but as a clear, goal-directed process. It offers a vision, but it calls for discernment and concrete, historical options and action plans. Mission as new creation is in continuity with creation, but oriented not to its preservation, but to its transformation.[11]

Co-Creators with God in Faith

The new world and the new creation we are working for are not the goals pointed to by futurology, but are perspectives of the faith. Faith offers us a way of looking at reality and at our experience. It also points to a goal that is at once historical and transcends history at the same time. The light of faith helps us to judge history and to discern the movements of the Spirit in history. It leads us to prayer because the new world and the new creation are gifts of God.

Faith is also a response to God calling us to be co-creators with God's self of a new heaven and a new earth. It is a commitment to action. It is a call to obedience. It is a challenge to engage ourselves concretely in the ongoing reality of life and

---

*Excerpts from Michael Amaladoss, S.J., "New World, New Creation—Mission in Power and Faith," *Mission Studies* 8:2 (1991), 140-41, 143-44; cf. Bosch, TM, 508-10.

of the world. It is an invitation to keep on listening, everywhere and at all moments, to the Word that may come to us from any source.

Perhaps the role and importance of the faith in mission will become clear if we compare it with the attitudes of people who either believe too little or too much. There are people who seek to build a new world, but without God. They have no use for moral or spiritual principles. They may still speak of human rights, but more as expressions of individualism and selfishness than as commitment to community. Efficiency, utility, convenience, profit, pleasure, absolute freedom, etc. are the kind of values that guide their choices in life. Everything and everyone is instrumentalized in some way. What concerns them is their immediate, personal future and advantage. These people have little or no faith.

Others, on the contrary, believe too much. Their faith is either fundamentalistic or evasive. It ceases to be a personal historical challenge. They believe that God will fulfill God's promises without their having to do anything. Some would ascribe the fulfillment of these promises to the next world so that it absolves them of all involvement in this one. Their dreams of a new world are empty utopias, psychologically satisfying, but not a challenge to action. Their mission focus is alienating. Their God is a "Deus ex machina."

In comparison with these two extremes, one can see that authentic faith involves not only obedience to the mystery, but also a commitment to creative involvement....The new world is really a new human world and the new creation is a new human community living in both inner and outer harmony: with oneself, with the community, with the world and with God.

NOTES

1. See David Ray Griffin, *God & Religion in the Postmodern World* (Albany, NY: State University of New York Press, 1989), pp. 51-81, for a succinct summary of these scientific changes and their implications for theology.

2. Cf. Martin E. Marty and Dean G. Peerman, eds., *A Handbook of Christian Theologians,* enlarged edition (Nashville, TN: Abingdon, 1985), pp. 338-54.

3. Horst Rzepkowski, *Lexikon der Mission* (1992), pp. 167-68; Hans-Werner Gensichen, "The Legacy of Walter Freytag," *IBMR* 5:1 (Jan. 1981): 13-18; *Basileia: Tribute to Walter Freytag,* Jan Hermelink and Hans Jochen Margull, eds. (Stuttgart: Evang. Missionsverlag, 1959).

4. See Otto Michel, in *Evangelische Missionszeitschrift* 2 (1941): 257ff.

5. Cf. J. R. Mott, ed., *Evangelism for the World Today* (New York: Harper, 1938). *Towards the Conversion of England,* Being the Report of a Commission on Evangelism appointed by the Archbishops of Canterbury and York, Westminster, p. 1, offers the following definition: "To evangelise is so to present Christ Jesus in the power of the Holy Spirit, that [persons] shall come to put their trust in God through Him, to accept Him as their Saviour, and serve Him as their King in the fellowship of His Church." This definition has been adopted by the Madras Foreign Missions Council, the National Council of the Churches of Christ, and, among others, the Commission on Evangelism of the Presbyterian Church, U.S.A.

6. Cf. Marty and Peerman, eds., *A Handbook of Christian Theologians,* pp. 660-76.

7. Eldon Ladd, *The Presence of the Future: The Eschatology of Biblical Realism* (Grand Rapids, MI: William B. Eerdmans, 1974), pp. 318ff.

8. Arthur P. Johnston, "The Kingdom in Relation to the Church and the World" (paper presented at the Consultation on the Relationship between Evangelism and Social Responsibility, Grand Rapids, MI, June 19-26, 1982), p. 23.

9. "Lausanne Covenant," Par. 5 in *Let the Earth Hear His Voice,* ed. J. D. Douglas (Minneapolis: World Wide Publications, 1975), p. 4.

10. Cf. Walter Brueggemann, *Hopeful Imagination: Prophetic Voices in Exile* (Philadelphia: Fortress, 1986); Rosemary Haughton, "Prophecy in Exile," in *Cross Currents* 39 (1989): 420-30.

11. For an excellent summary of contemporary reflection on mission, see Bosch, *Transforming Mission* (1991).

Permissions

The following excerpts are used as permitted by making this acknowledgement of source: World Council of Churches, Theological Education Fund, *Ministry in Context: The Third Mandate Programme of the Theological Education Fund (1970-77)* (Bromley, England: TEF, 1972).

The following excerpts are used with permission of **American Society of Missiology**: Mary Motte, "Participation and Common Witness: Creating a Future in Mission," *Missiology* 15 (1987).

The following excerpts are used with permission of **Gerald H. Anderson**: Oscar Cullmann, "Eschatology and Missions in the New Testament," in *The Theology of the Christian Mission,* ed. Gerald H. Anderson (New York: McGraw-Hill Book Co., 1961).

The following excerpts are used with permission of **Aschendorffsche Verlagsbuchhandlung**: J. Thauren, *Die Akkommodation im Katholischen Heidenapostolat* (Münster in Westfalen: Aschendorff, 1927).

The following excerpts are used with permission of **Augsburg Fortress Publications**: Hans J. Margull, *Hope in Action,* © by Muhlenberg Press (Philadelphia: Muhlenberg Press, 1962); Jürgen Moltmann, *The Experiment Hope,* © by Fortress Press (Philadelphia: Fortress Press, 1975); and Martin Luther, "Large Catechism: Third Part, The Lord's Prayer," Par. 41-54, in *The Book of Concord,* ed. Theodore G. Tappert (Philadelphia, PA: Fortress Press, 1959).

The following excerpts are used with permission of **Ayer Co. Publishers, Inc.**: Samuel Hopkins, *A Treatise on the Millennium* (Boston: Isaiah Thomas and Ebenezer T. Andrews, 1793; reprint ed., New York: Arno Press, 1972).

The following excerpts are used with permission of **Herbert W. Bainton**, deceased author's son: "The Conversion of Clovis; Translated from Gregory of Tours," *Historia Francorum,* in *Patrologia Latina* 71: 225, section xxx; translation by Roland Bainton in Roland Bainton, *The Medieval Church,* © by Ronald H. Bainton (Huntington, N.Y.: Robert E. Krieger, 1979), 99-100; 193-94

The following excerpts are used with permission of **Banner of Truth Trust**: John Calvin, Sermon on "David's Dealings with the Jebusites and Hiram" (1562), in *Sermons on 2 Samuel, Chapters 1-13* (Edinburgh, Scotland: Banner of Truth Trust, 1992).

The following excerpts are used with permission of **Cambridge University Press**: Augustine of Hippo, "Letter 199" (c.419), in *Documents in Early Christian Thought,* ed.

Maurice Wiles and Mark Santer, © by Cambridge University Press (Cambridge, U.K.: Cambridge University Press, 1975); and Thomas Aquinas, *Summa Theologica* (New York: McGraw-Hill; London: Eyre & Spottiswoode, 1964). [Reprinted with permission of Cambridge University Press].

The following excerpts are used with permission of **Chr. Kaiser Verlag**: Johannes Christian Hoekendijk, *Kirche und Volk in der deutschen Missionwissenschaft* (Munich: Chr. Kaiser, 1967); and Walter Freytag, *Reden und Aufsätze,* © by Chr. Kaiser Verlag (Munich: Chr. Kaiser, 1961).

The following excerpts are used with permission of **Christian Literature Society**: Bartolomäus Ziegenbalg, "Letter to Christopher Wendt, 15th August 1718," in E. Arno Lehmann, *It Began at Tranquebar* (Madras: Christian Literature Society, 1956).

The following excerpts are used with permission of **Christliches Verlagshaus**: Winburn T. Thomas, "Notes on Missions in the Curriculum," in *Basileia: Walter Freytag zum 60. Geburtstag,* ed. von Jan Hermelink and Hans Jochen Margull (Stuttgart, Germany: Evangelisches Missionswerk in Deutschland, 1959).

The following excerpts are used with permission of **T. & T. Clark**: Friedrich Schleiermacher, *The Christian Faith,* Eng. trans. of the 1830 second German edition (Edinburgh: T. & T. Clark, 1928); and Karl Barth, *Church Dogmatics,* vol. IV, 3, 1, *The Doctrine of Reconciliation* (Edinburgh: T. & T. Clark, 1961).

The following excerpts are used with permission of **Costello Publishing Company**: *"Ad Gentes"* (1965), *"Lumen Gentium"* (1964), *"Gaudium et Spes"* (1965), *"Nostra Aetate"* (1964), *"Apostolicam Actuositatem"* (1965), *"Evangelii Nuntiandi"* (1975), in *Documents of Vatican II,* ed. Austin P. Flannery, © by Costello Publishing and Rev. Austin Flannery, O.P. (Grand Rapids: Wm. B. Eerdmans, 1975). [No part of these excerpts may be reproduced, stored in a retrieval system, or transmitted in any form or by any means—electronic, mechanical, photo-copying, recording or otherwise, without express permission of Costello Publishing Company.]

The following excerpts were used with permission of **John De Gruchy**: John de Gruchy, *Theology and Ministry in Context and Crisis: A South African Perspective,* © John W. de Gruchy (Grand Rapids: Wm. B. Eerdmans, 1987).

The following excerpts are used with permission of **Discipleship Resources**: Emilio Castro, "Salvation Today—An Evangelistic Approach," in *Beginning in Jerusalem,* ed. Rueben P. Job (Nashville: Tidings, 1974).

The following excerpts are used with permission of **Division of Order of St. Benedict, Inc.**: Pope Paul III, *Sublimis Deus* (1537), in *Documents of American Catholic History,* edited by John Tracy Ellis, © by John Tracy Ellis (Wilmington, DE: Michael Glazier, 1987).

The following excerpts are used with permission of **Duke University Press**: *Sainted Women of the Dark Ages,* edited and translated by Jo Ann McNamara and John E. Halborg with E. Gordon Whatley (Durham and London: Duke University Press, 1992).

The following excerpts are used with permission of **Les Éditions du Cerf**: Yves Congar, *Chrétiens Déunis: Principes d'un "Oecuménisme" Catholique* (Paris: Les Éditions du Cerf, 1937).

The following excerpts are used with permission of **Wm. B. Eerdmans Co.**: John Calvin, *Institutes of the Christian Religion* (1559), ed. Warfield (Grand Rapids: Wm. B. Eerdmans, 1949); Orlando E. Costas, *Liberating News: A Theology of Contextual Evangelization*

(Grand Rapids: Eerdmans, 1989); *Evangelical Witness in South Africa: A Critique of Evangelical Theology and Practice by South African Evangelicals* (Grand Rapids: Wm. B. Eerdmans, 1986); Henry Venn, " The Organization of Native Churches" (1861), in *To Apply the Gospel: Selections from the Writings of Henry Venn,* ed. Max Warren, © by Wm. B. Eerdmans Publishing (Grand Rapids: Eerdmans, 1971); and C. René Padilla, *Mission between the Times: Essays on the Kingdom* (Grand Rapids: Wm. B. Eerdmans, 1985).

The following excerpts are used with permission of **Evangelischer Verlag**: Karl Barth, *Theologische Fragen und Antworten* (Zollikon: Evangelischer Verlag, 1957).

The following excerpts are used with permission of **Fathers of the Church**: Eusebius of Caesarea, *Ecclesiastical History* 3:37, *The Fathers of the Church* (New York: Fathers of The Church, 1953).

The following excerpts are used with permission of **GABA Publications**: Laurenti Magesa, "Authentic African Christianity," *African Ecclesial Review [AFER]* 15:2 (April 1973); *32 Articles Evaluating Inculturation of Christianity in Africa*, ed. Teresa Okure et. al. (Spearhead Nos. 112-114; Eldoret, Kenya: AMECEA Gaba Publications, 1990).

The following excerpts are used with permission of **Hans-Werner Gensichen**: Hans-Werner Gensichen, *Glaube für die Welt: Theologische Aspekte der Mission*, © by Gütersloher Verlagshaus Gerd Mohn (Gütersloh: Gerd Mohn, 1971).

The following excerpts are used with permission of **Lord Griffiths of Fforestfach**: Samuel Escobar, "Evangelism and Man's Search for Freedom, Justice and Fulfillment," in *Is Revolution Change?,* ed. Brian Griffiths (Downers Grove, IL: InterVarsity Press, 1974).

The following excerpts are used with permission of **HarperCollins Publishers, Inc.**: Jürgen Moltmann, *The Church in the Power of the Spirit,* © by SCM Press, Ltd. (New York: Harper & Row, 1977); World Council of Churches (1st Assembly, 1948), *Man's Disorder and God's Design* (New York: Harper & Brothers, 1949); Daniel T. Niles, *That They May Have Life,* © by The Student Vounteer Movement for Christian Missions (New York: Harper & Brothers, 1951); the Nestorian Monument (781), text in Samuel Hugh Moffett, *A History of Christianity in Asia* (San Francisco: Harper San Francisco, 1991); and Dietrich Bonhoeffer, *Letters and Papers from Prison: The Enlarged Edition,* ed. Eberhard Bethge, © by William Collins Sons & Co., Ltd and Harper & Row (New York: Macmillan, 1971).

The following excerpts are used with permission of **C. Hurst & Co. Ltd.**: Sabelo Ntwasa and Basil Moore, "The Concept of God in Black Theology," in *Black Theology: The South African Voice,* ed. Basil Moore, © by C. Hurst & Co. Ltd. (London: C. Hurst & Co., 1973).

The following excerpts are used with permission of **Image Books**: CELAM II (Medellín, 1968), " The Medellín Conference Documents," in *Renewing the Earth: Catholic Documents on Peace, Justice and Liberation,* ed. D. J. O'Brien and T. A. Shannon, © by David J. O'Brien and Thomas Shannon (Garden City, NY: Image Books, 1976).

The following excerpts are used with permission of **International Association for Mission Studies**: Emefie Ikenga-Metuh, "Contextualization: A Missiological Imperative for the Church in Africa in the Third Millennium," *Mission Studies* 6:2 (1989); and Michael Amaladoss, S.J., "New World, New Creation—Mission in Power and Faith," *Mission Studies* 8:2 (1991).

The following excerpts are used with permission of ***International Bulletin of Missionary Research***: Emilio Castro, "Liberation, Development, and Evangelism: Must We Choose in Mission?", *Occasional Bulletin of Missionary Research* 2 (1978).

The following excerpts are used with permission of ***Journal of Ecumenical Studies:*** Raimundo Panikkar, "Editorial: Toward an Ecumenical Ecumenism," *Journal of Ecumenical Studies* 19, no.4 (Fall 1982).

The following excerpts are used with permission of **Alfred A. Knopf**: Bartolomé de Las Casas, "The Only Method of Attracting All People to the True Faith" (1530s) in *Bartolomé de Las Casas: A Selection of His Writings* by Bartolomé de Las Casas, edited and translated by George Sanderlin (New York: Alfred A. Knopf Inc., 1971), reprinted in *Witness: Writings of Bartolomé de Las Casas* (Maryknoll, N.Y.: Orbis Books, 1992).

The following excerpts are used with permission of **Liturgical Press**: *St. Benedict's Rule for Monestaries* (Collegeville, MN: St. John Abbey Press, 1948).

The following excerpts are used with permission of **Lutterworth Press**: Harry Sawyerr, *Creative Evangelism: Towards a New Christian Encounter with Africa* (London: Lutterworth Press, 1968); and Hendrik Kraemer, *A Theology of the Laity,* © by Hendrik Kraemer (Philadelphia: Westminster Press, 1958).

The following excerpts are used with permission of **Macmillan Publishing, Co**.: Karl Barth, *Church Dogmatics,* vol. I, 2, *The Doctrine of the Word of God* (New York: Charles Scribners, 1956).

The following excerpts are used with permission of **Mambo Press**: Canaan Banana, *The Gospel According to the Ghetto* (Gwelo, Zimbabwe: Mambo Press, 1980).

The following excerpts are used with permission of the **Donald A. McGavran Trust Fund**: Donald McGavran, "Will Uppsala Betray the Two Billion?", WCC (4th Assembly, Uppsala 1968), "Renewal in Mission," and Eugene Smith, "Renewal in Mission," in *The Conciliar-Evangelical Debate,* ed. Glasser & McGavran, © by Word Books (Waco, TX: Word Books, 1972).

The following excerpts are used with permission of **McGraw-Hill**: Daniel T. Niles, *Upon the Earth: The Mission of God and the Missionary Enterprise of the Churches,* © by D.T. Niles (New York: McGraw-Hill Book Co., 1962).

The following excerpts are used with permission of **Mennonite Publishing House**: Balthasar Hubmaier, "On the Christian Baptism of Believers" (1525), in *Balthasar Hubmaier: Theologian of Anabaptism,* ed. H. Wayne Pipkin and John H. Yoder (Scottdale, PA: Herald Press, 1989).

The following excerpts are used with permission of ***The Month:*** Aloysius Pieris, "Inculturation in Non-Semitic Asia," *The Month,* no 1420 (1986).

The following excerpts are used with permission of **National Council of Churches of Christ in the U.S.A.**: John A. Mackay, *The Latin American Churches and the Ecumenical Movement* (New York: N.C.C.U.S.A., 1963); and Daniel Fleming, *Living as Comrades,* © by Foreign Missions Conference of North America (New York: Agricultural Missions for the Foreign Missions Conference of North America, 1950).

The following excerpts are used with permission of **National Christian Council of India**: Mathai Zachariah, "Introduction," in *The Church: A Peoples' Movement* (Nagpur, India: National Christian Council of India, 1975).

The following excerpts are used with permission of ***Neue Zeitschrift für Missionswissenschaft:*** Justin Ukpong, "What is Contextualization?", *Neue Zeitschrift für Missionswissenschaft* 43 (1987).

The following excerpts are used with permission of **New Society Publishers**: Julia Esquivel, "Christian Women and the Struggle for Justice in Central America," in *Speaking of Faith: Global Perspectives on Women, Religion and Social Change,* ed. Diana L. Eck and Devaki Jain (Philadelphia: New Society Publishers, 1987).

The following excerpts are used with permission of **Northwestern University Press**: "A Brief Account of Saints Cyril and Methodius and the Baptism of the Moravian and Bohemian Lands" in Marvin Kantor, *The Origins of Christianity in Bohemia: Sources and Commentary* (Evanston: Northwestern University Press, 1990).

The following excerpts are used with permission of **Orbis Books**: Pablo Richard, *Death of Christendoms: Birth of the Church* (Maryknoll, N.Y.: Orbis Books, 1987); C. S. Song, *Theology from the Womb of Asia* (Maryknoll, NY: Orbis Books, 1985); John Mbiti, "Some Reflections on African Experience of Salvation Today," in *Living Faiths and Ultimate Goals: Salvation and World Religions,* ed. S. J. Samartha (Maryknoll, NY: Orbis Books, 1974); Ecumenical Association of Third World Theologians, Assembly (2nd., Oaxtepec, Mexico, December 1986), *Third World Theologies: Commonalities and Divergences,* ed. K. C. Abraham (Maryknoll, NY: Orbis Books, 1990); Juan Segundo, *Liberation of Theology,* © by Orbis Books (Maryknoll, NY: Orbis Books, 1976); Ecumenical Dialogue of Third World Theologians (1st, Dar es Salaam, 1976), *The Emergent Gospel,* ed. S. Torres and V. Fabella (Maryknoll, NY: Orbis Books, 1978); Aracely de Rocchietti, "Women and the People of God," in *Through Her Eyes: Women's Theology from Latin America,* ed. Elsa Tamez (Maryknoll, NY: Orbis Books, 1989); Gustavo Gutiérrez, *A Theology of Liberation,* © by Orbis Books (Maryknoll, NY: Orbis Books, 1973, 1988); CELAM III (Puebla 1979). *Puebla and Beyond,* ed. J. Eagleson and P. Scharper (Maryknoll, NY: Orbis Books, 1979); Allan Boesak, *Black and Reformed: Apartheid, Liberation and the Calvinist Tradition* (Maryknoll, NY: Orbis Books, 1984); Luz Beatriz Arellano, "Women's Experience of God in Emerging Spirituality," in *With Passion and Compassion: Third World Women Doing Theology,* ed. Virginia Fabella, M.M. and Mercy Amba Oduyoye (Maryknoll, NY: Orbis Books, 1986); Chung Hyun Kyung, *Struggle to be the Sun Again: Introducing Asian Women's Theology,* © by Orbis Books (Maryknoll, NY: Orbis Books, 1990); Charles Kraft, *Christianity in Culture,* © by Charles H. Kraft (Maryknoll, NY: Orbis Books, 1979); Aloysius Pieris, " The Non-Semitic Religions of Asia," in *Mission in Dialogue,* ed. Mary Motte and Joseph R. Lang (Maryknoll, NY: Orbis Books, 1982); Pedro Casaldáliga, *In Pursuit of the Kingdom: Writings 1968-1988* (Maryknoll, NY: Orbis Books, 1990); Marjorie Hewitt Suchocki, "In Search of Justice: Religious Pluralism from a Feminist Perspective," in *The Myth of Christian Uniqueness: Toward a Pluralistic Theology of Religions,* ed. John Hick and Paul F. Knitter (Maryknoll, N.Y.: Orbis Books, 1987); "Authentic Dialogue Today: Reflections of Participants at the SEDOS Conference," in *Trends in Mission: Toward the Third Millennium; Essays in Celebration of Twenty-five Years of SEDOS,* ed. William Jenkinson, CSSp and Helene O'Sullivan, MM (Maryknoll, NY: Orbis Books, 1991); Orlando E. Costas, *Christ Outside the Gate: Mission beyond Christendom,* © by Raúl Fernández Calienes (Maryknoll, N.Y.: Orbis Books, 1982); Jean-Marc Éla, *My Faith as an African* (Maryknoll, N.Y., Orbis Books, 1988); Leonardo Boff, *Ecclesiogenesis: The Base Communities Reinvent the Church* (Maryknoll, NY: Orbis Books, 1986); Virginia Fabella, "Christology from an Asian Woman's Perspective," and Kwok Pui-lan, " The Emergence of Asian Feminist Consciousness of Culture and Theology," in *We Dare to Dream: Doing Theology as Asian Women*, ed. Virginia Fabella, M.M. and Sun Ai Lee Park (Kowloon, Hong Kong: Asian Women's Resource Centre for Culture and Theology; Manila, Philippines: EATWOT Women's Commission in Asia, 1989; Maryknoll, NY: Orbis Books, 1990); and James H. Cone, *A Black Theology of*

Liberation, Twentieth Anniversary Edition, Copyright © 1986, 1990 by James H. Cone (Maryknoll, NY: Orbis Books, 1990).

The following excerpts are used with permission of **Overseas Missionary Fellowship, U.S.A. Headquarters**: J. Hudson Taylor, *A Retrospect* (London: China Inland Mission, 1875, 1954).

The following excerpts are used with permission of **Paulist Press**: St. Athanasius, " The Life of Antony," in *Athanasius: The Life of Antony and the Letter to Marcellinus,* trans. Robert C. Gregg, *The Classics of Western Spirituality,* © by The Missionary Society of St. Paul (New York: Paulist Press, 1980).

The following excerpts are used with permission of **David Philip Publishers**: Gabriel Setiloane, " The Ecumenical Movement in Africa: From Mission Church to Moratorium," in *Resistance and Hope: South African Essays in Honour of Beyers Naudé,* ed. Charles Villa-Vicencio and John W. de Gruchy (Grand Rapids: Wm. B. Eerdmans, 1985).

The following excerpts are used with permission of **Princeton University Press**: Raymond Lull, *The Book of the Gentile and the Three Wise Men* (1275?), in *Selected Works of Ramon Llull,* edited and translated by Anthony Bonner, © by Princeton University Press (Princeton: Princeton University Press, 1985).

The following excerpts are used with permission of ***Religious Education:*** José Miguez-Bonino, "New Theological Perspectives," *Religious Education* 66 (1971). [Reprinted from the journal, RELIGIOUS EDUCATION, Volume 66, Number 6, by permission from the publisher, The Religious Education Association, 409 Prospect Street, New Haven, CT 06511-2177. Membership information available upon request.]

The following excerpts are used with permission of **SCM Press**: Wilhelm Andersen, *Towards a Theology of Mission* (London: SCM Press, 1955); and Jürgen Moltmann, *Theology of Hope* (London: SCM Press, 1967).

The following excerpts are used with permission of **Senate of Serampore College**: Francis Xavier, "Letter of January 1545," in *History of Christianity in India: Source Materials,* compiled by M. K. Kuriakose (Madras, India: Senate of Serampore College, 1982).

The following excerpts are used with permission of **Servant Publications**: Mother Teresa, *Total Surrender,* revised edition © 1995 by Missionaries of Charity; selections and arrangement of material copyright © 1995 by Brother Angelo Devanada Scolozzi.

The following excerpts are used with permission of ***Theology Today:*** Lamin Sanneh, "Pluralism and Christian Commitment," *Theology Today* 45:1 (April 1988).

The following excerpts are used with permission of **Trinity Press**: Virginia Peacock, " Theological Education and the Mission of the Church," in *Justice as Mission: An Agenda for the Church,* ed. Terry Brown and Christopher Lind (Burlington, Ontario: Trinity Press, 1985).

The following excerpts are used with permission of **The United Church of Christ**: Samuel Worcester, "1816 Report," in *First Ten Annual Reports of the American Board of Commissioners for Foreign Missions with Other Documents of the Board* (Boston: ABCFM, 1834).

The following excerpts are used with permission of **University of Iowa Press**: Nicholaus Ludwig Count von Zinzendorf, *Nine Public Lectures on Important Subjects in Religion . . . 1746,* translated and edited by George W. Forell (Iowa City: University of Iowa Press, 1973).

The following excerpts are used with permission of **Verlag der Liebenzeller Mission**: Philipp Nicolai, *Kommentar zu den Weissagungen der Propheten und Apostel über das Reich Gottes,* in *Mission in Quellentexten,* comp. Werner Raupp (Bad Liebenzell, Germany: Verlag der Liebenzeller Mission, 1990).

The following excerpts are used with permission of **Westminster/John Knox Press**: "Letter to Diognetus," in *Early Christian Fathers,* ed. Cyril C. Richardson, *The Library of Christian Classics* (Philadelphia: Westminster Press, 1953); and Letty Russell, *Human Liberation in a Feminist Perspective—A Theology* (Philadelphia: Westminster Press, 1974).

The following excerpts are used with permission of the **William Carey Library**: Donald McGavran, "Salvation Today," in *The Evangelical Response to Bangkok,* ed. Ralph Winter, © by The William Carey Library (South Pasadena: Wm. Carey Library, 1973).

The following excerpts are used with permission of **Word, Inc.**: "Wheaton Declaration", in *The Church's Worldwide Mission,* ed. Harold Lindsell, © by Word Books (Waco: Word Books, 1966).

The following excerpts are used with permission of the **World Council of Churches' Commission on World Mission and Evangelism**: Anastasios of Androussa, "Orthodox Mission—Past, Present, Future," in *Your Will Be Done: Orthodoxy in Mission,* ed. George Lemopoulos (Geneva: WCC Publications, 1988); World Council of Churches, *The Church for Others and the Church for the World: A Quest for Structures for Missionary Congregations,* © by World Council of Churches (Geneva: WCC, 1967); WCC/CWME, *Bangkok Assembly 1973: Minutes and Report of the Assembly . . .* (Geneva: WCC, 1973); Willem A. Visser't Hooft, " The Mandate of the Ecumenical Movement," in WCC, *The Uppsala Report,* ed. Norman Goodall (Geneva: WCC, 1968); WCC (4th Assembly, Uppsala, 1968), *The Uppsala Report: Official Report of the Fourth Assembly . . .,* ed. Norman Goodall, © by World Council of Churches (Geneva: WCC, 1968); World Council of Churches, *Minutes and Reports of the 4th Meeting of the Central Committee of the World Council of Churches . . . Rolle, 1951* (Geneva: WCC, 1951); World Council of Churches, *The First Six Years, 1948-1954* (Geneva: WCC, 1954); *Common Witness: a study document of the Joint Working Group of the Roman Catholic Church and the World Council of Churches* (Geneva: WCC, 1982); World Council of Churches, *Guidelines on Dialogue with People of Living Faiths and Ideologies,* © by World Council of Churches (Geneva: WCC, 1979); Mercy Oduyoye, "Churchwomen and the Church's Mission," and Virginia Fabella, M.M., "Mission of Women in the Church in Asia: Role and Position," in *New Eyes for Reading: Biblical and Theological Reflections by Women from the Third World,* ed. John S. Pobee and Barbel von Wartenberg-Potter (Geneva: World Council of Churches, 1986); Julia Esquivel, "The Crucified Lord: A Latin American Perspective," and Raymond Fung, "Good News to the Poor—A Case for a Missionary Movement," in World Council of Churches, *Your Kingdom Come: Report on the World Conference on Mission and Evangelism, Melbourne, Australia, 12-25 May 1980,* © by World Council of Churches (Geneva: W.C.C., 1980); Elizabeth Behr-Sigel, " The Meaning of the Participation of Women in the Life of the Church," in *Orthodox Women: Their Role and Participation in the Orthodox Church* (Geneva, Switzerland: World Council of Churches, 1977); Emilio Castro, *A Passion for Unity: Essays on Ecumenical Hopes and Challenges,* © by World Council of Churches (Geneva, Switzerland: W.C.C. Publications, 1992); Philip Potter, *Life in all its Fullness* (Geneva: W.C.C., 1981); J. Paul Rajashekar, " Theological Education in a Pluralistic Context: An Overall Assessment," in *Ministerial Formation in a Multi-faith Milieu: Implications of Interfaith Dialogue for Theological Education,* ed. Sam Amirtham and S. Wesley Ariarajah (Geneva, W.C.C., 1986); M. M. Thomas, " The Meaning of Salvation Today—A Personal Statement," *IRM* 62 (1973); J. N.

Zvomunondita Kurewa, "Conversion in the African Context," *IRM* 68 (1979); Rose Fernando, F.M.M., "God's Love Cuts Across History," *IRM* 74 (1985); "A Bolivian Manifesto on Evangelism in Latin America Today," *A Monthly Letter About Evangelism,* no. 2 (Feb. 1975); Kosuke Koyama, " The Ecumenical Movement as the Dialogue of Cultures," in *Faith and Faithfulness: Essays on Contemporary Ecumenical Themes* (Geneva, Switzerland: WCC, 1984); International Missionary Council (Tambaram, Madras, India, 12-29 December 1938), *The World Mission of the Church: Findings and Recommendations...,* © by International Missionary Council (London: I.M.C., 1939); International Missionary Council (Ghana, 28 December 1957 to 7 January 1958), *Minutes of the Assembly...* (London and New York: I.M.C., 1958); Hendrik Kraemer, *The Christian Message in a Non-Christian World* (New York: International Missionary Council, 1938); Visser 't Hooft, "Missions as the Test of Faith," in *Witness in Six Continents: Records of the Meeting of the Commission on World Mission and Evangelism of the World Council of Churches held in Mexico City, December 8th to 19th, 1963,* ed. Ronald K. Orchard, © by Edinburgh House Press (London: Edinburgh House Press, 1964); International Missionary Council (Willingen, 1952), *Missions Under the Cross: Addresses delivered at the enlarged meeting at...Willingen,* ed. N. Goodall (London: Edinburgh House Press for the IMC, 1953); and WCC (5th Assembly, Nairobi, 1975), *Breaking Barriers, Nairobi 1975: The Official Report . . .,* ed. David M. Paton, © by World Council of Churches (Grand Rapids: Eerdmans, 1976).

The following excerpts are used with permission of **World Student Christian Federation**: J. R. Chandran, " The Problem of Indigenization of Christian Theology in Asia," *Student World* 51 (1958); K. H. Ting, " The Task of the Church in Asia," *Student World* 42 (1949); M. M. Thomas, "An Irrelevant Profession," *Student World* 43 (1950); and Rajaiah D. Paul, "Towards a New Strategy in Asia: The Layman as the Spearhead of the Christian Enterprise," *Student World* 49 (1956).

The following excerpts are used with permission of **World Wide Publications**: Samuel Escobar, "Evangelism and Man's Search for Freedom, Justice and Fulfilment," in International Congress on World Evangelization, Lausanne, Switzerland, *Let the Earth Hear His Voice: Official Reference Volume,* ed. J. D. Douglas (Minneapolis: World Wide Publications, 1975).

The following excerpts are used with permission of **Yale University Press**: Jonathan Edwards, *The Life of David Brainerd* (1749), ed. Norman Pettit, vol. 7 in *The Works of Jonathan Edwards,* © by Yale University (New Haven & London: Yale University Press, 1985).

Every attempt was made to locate those who held permissions for the works in this book.

Index of Scriptural References

Index of Subjects

Index of Names